AMERICAN HIGHER EDUCATION
SINCE WORLD WAR II

AMERICAN HIGHER EDUCATION

★ SINCE ★

WORLD WAR II

A HISTORY

ROGER L. GEIGER

PRINCETON UNIVERSITY PRESS

Princeton & Oxford

Copyright © 2019 by Princeton University Press

Published by Princeton University Press
41 William Street, Princeton, New Jersey 08540
6 Oxford Street, Woodstock, Oxfordshire OX20 1TR

press.princeton.edu

All Rights Reserved

Library of Congress Control Number 2019933035
ISBN 978-0-691-17972-8

British Library Cataloging-in-Publication Data is available

Editorial: Peter Dougherty & Jessica Yao
Production Editorial: Ali Parrington
Production: Erin Suydam
Publicity: Tayler Lord, Julia Hall, and Nathalie Levine
Copyeditor: Gail K. Schmitt

This book has been composed in Garamond Premier Pro,
Avenir LT Std, and Alternate Gothic

Printed on acid-free paper. ∞

Printed in the United States of America

1 3 5 7 9 10 8 6 4 2

★ CONTENTS ★

6

SURVIVING THE SEVENTIES
217

★ PART IV ★
THE CURRENT ERA IN AMERICAN HIGHER EDUCATION

7

THE DAWN OF THE CURRENT ERA, 1980–2000
269

8

AMERICAN HIGHER EDUCATION IN
THE TWENTY-FIRST CENTURY
313

INDEX

PREFACE

OST RESPONDENTS TO A 2018 PEW RESEARCH CENTER survey felt that American higher education was "headed in the wrong direction." Not for the first time, substantial numbers of Americans were critical of the country's colleges and universities, although not all for the same reasons. Some objected to the high cost of attendance; others were concerned that graduates were not prepared for the workforce; and a substantial number disapproved of the politicization of campuses. These reactions may have been shaped and exaggerated by the media, but they reflected actual conditions involving the most basic functions of higher education: namely, providing a large subset of American youth with opportunities for social advancement; supplying expertise and skills for the economy; and generating a significant portion of the intellectual content of our culture. Higher education occupies a strategic position in American civilization. For more than two-thirds of teenagers, an institution of higher education is the gateway to life's possibilities. Initial and recurrent acquisitions of knowledge and expertise are strong determinants of productivity and rewards in the economy. And universities not only dominate the discovery of basic knowledge, they also supply intellectual frameworks for understanding everyday ideas and events. Higher education does not determine social status, economic productivity, or intellectual culture. It plays a unique and indispensable role chiefly in the early stages of all these social processes: intellectual foundations that will grow over time, skills that will be honed through experience, and understanding that will deepen over lifetimes. In that sense, it is a central institution of society and a legitimate concern of its citizens.

This has not always been the case. Prior to World War II, higher education played an important role in defining high culture, professional careers, and academic knowledge, but its incidence was limited to a circumscribed population, and its limited currency was considered by many intrinsic to its value. After 1945, higher education served an ever-growing portion of the population. Academic knowledge underwent even greater growth, as did its assimilation into American society. As the impact on American life and culture became more apparent, so did the salience of colleges and universities for American society.

This history describes and analyzes these transformations—in institutions, students, faculty, and the subjects they teach; in the advancement of knowledge; and in the impact of that knowledge on American society. As higher education expanded, institutions were redefined. Over these decades, the relative vitality of the public and private sectors oscillated. The growth of student enrollments occurred in successive waves, as social participation included additional groups from wider social strata. Institutions differentiated their roles and clienteles to serve these expanding populations. The cultural significance of college, which is enshrined in the notion of a liberal education, was continually debated and reformulated. Conflict between academic culture and the prevailing social consensus at times transcended campuses—in the era of McCarthyism, the protests of the late 1960s, the culture wars of the 1980s, and again after 2010. The growth of research and the ascendancy of the research university model add a further dimension to this history. In addition to the amazing achievements in science and technology, academic knowledge inexorably enlarged its social imprint, as did the role of academic credentials. This history of higher education thus depicts the transformation of a social institution.

Yet, higher education is also embedded in society. The enterprise ultimately has depended upon American society for students, for resources, and for the prevailing culture that framed its purposes and legitimacy. This history places the evolution of American higher education since 1945 in the context of its changing relationships with American society. Conditions in American culture and society have allowed or precluded certain possibilities, encouraging and supporting some courses of development and discouraging others. Higher education's enduring functions of instruction, advancement of knowledge, and cultural formation have thus been affected by the political, social, and intellectual currents that formed the history of the United States in these years. This study explicates the history of higher education across four successive eras in which institutions, attitudes, patterns of attendance, and means of support were shaped by the evolution of American society.

Following World War II, a powerful consensus formed that venerated the "American way of life." It included an aversion to communism, domestic and Soviet, but chiefly stressed an idealization of family, church, and nation. It reflected growing American prosperity and a rising standard of living, but it also fostered complacency and blindness toward those not sharing those benefits. An expanding middle class sent increasing numbers of students to college. Growing affluence facilitated the modernization of colleges and universities, and federal support for academic research enhanced the scientific productivity of major universities.

Chapter 1 examines the principal issues facing higher education in the decade following the war. Hectic measures to accommodate the GI-Bill students dominated the first five years but left little lasting legacy in the colleges. The nature and purpose of higher education were debated on a national stage when the President's Commission on Higher Education projected a vision of unprecedented expansion, federal guidance if not control, and a curriculum designed to inculcate democratic citizenship. Instead, the vision favored by the private sector prevailed. Harvard articulated a widely accepted ideal for liberal education, and a blue-ribbon commission of private universities defended institutional autonomy and the private sector. McCarthyism, the most vicious phase of a postwar anticommunist purge, cast a pall over the early 1950s and largely silenced liberal and internationalist views in universities.

Chapter 2 describes the consolidation of the American system of higher education during the conservative 1950s. Traditional patterns of college-going prevailed, but a growing proportion of students enrolled in public institutions. Colleges became increasingly standardized around a core of liberal arts and sciences. The California Master Plan embodied the emergence of a dominant institutional paradigm of flagship universities, regional colleges, and local community colleges. Federal support enabled American research universities to form "the most powerful system for advancing knowledge the world had ever seen" (Chapter 2).

From the late 1950s, a more critical spirit emerged. Growing liberal sentiments advocated government initiatives to address civil rights, poverty, cities, the environment, and education. Dubbed the Liberal Hour, it culminated in a blizzard of social legislation in the mid-sixties. For higher education, the Soviet launch of Sputnik in 1957 was a catalyst for major commitments of state and federal funds to build and enlarge colleges and universities and to multiply scientific research. From 1958 to 1968, the American public looked more favorably on higher education than at any time before or since, facilitating an "academic revolution" in research and graduate education and accommodation of the Tidal Wave of baby-boom cohorts now reaching higher education.

The ramifications of the academic revolution are analyzed in Chapter 3. Federal and foundation support for advancing academic knowledge energized faculty, disciplines, graduate education, and universities. This quantum expansion of knowledge and expertise prompted commentators to recognize their central role in the American economy and culture. Chapter 4 is focused on the other transformative development of the 1960s. The Tidal Wave expansion of enrollment resulted from an increasing supply of accessible institutions and widening social participation. The desegregation of higher education in the South was an important chapter in the civil rights movement, and it was followed by dedicated efforts to remedy underrepresentation of African Americans in the North. These years brought both the zenith of the liberal arts and the beginning of their fragmentation.

The student protests at the end of the 1960s signaled the end of an era, but they scarcely foreshadowed the no less monumental changes of the 1970s, especially an expanded federal role in higher education and a revolutionary transformation in the status of women. Public commitments shifted from academic to demographic expansion, including nontraditional students. Institutions were hard-pressed to adapt to the economic uncertainty of the period.

Chapters 5 and 6 depict the unraveling of what appeared, retrospectively, to have been a golden age. The New Left evolved from challenging the status quo to delusional visions of revolution. It was largely responsible for the traumatic confrontations of the 1968 Era. Student protesters altered campus life, but the major changes that followed came from other sources. Attitudes of the public and the higher education establishment now placed greater emphasis on making the opportunity for higher education available to all. Congress bolstered this effort by enacting financial aid for lower-income students, and federal regulations mandated greater social inclusion in all aspects of higher education. Perhaps most far-reaching was the rise of women in higher education, resulting in large measure from the grassroots efforts of the women's movement on campuses. With broadened career possibilities, female enrollments rose to compose a majority of students by 1980. The 1970s marked the end of the postwar economic expansion, and the decade's financial turbulence undermined the aspirations of the previous decade. Student idealism, on balance, was displaced by concern for careers, and the academic ambitions of many universities were curtailed or abandoned.

The current era of higher education that began around 1980 has been characterized by an overriding trend toward privatization. The major trends of the 1980s, which are the focus of Chapter 7, reversed the preoccupations of the previous decade and persisted into the twenty-first century. Financial privatization resulted from a relative decline in state funding for higher education and a greater financial burden imposed on students and their families. Steadily rising tuition in both public and private sectors was made possible by differential pricing and student financial aid. As the cost of attendance exceeded affordability, the difference was supplied by federal student loans. The achievement of high participation, or universal higher education, was accompanied by differentiation of institutional roles and student clienteles—an implicit bifurcation into selective and open sectors. Given the consumer-driven nature of the American system and the exaggerated impact of donative funds, this development favored wealthy private colleges and universities. The attraction of high-cost, high-quality education soared in the 1980s, and the advantages of the wealthiest institutions became magnified. A new appreciation of research universities emerged in the 1980s, based on their contributions to innovation and economic growth. State and federal policies encouraged cooperation with industry and commercialization of intellectual property, but most significant was a steady expansion of support for research and scientific advancement. Finally, the resentments of an academic Left, which had been brewing since the 1960s, burst into public attention in the

1980s. Critics protested that leftist views were distorting university practices, but they had little effect on campuses. Conflict in the higher education theater of the culture wars nonetheless persisted, with varying intensity, and reflected the growing political polarization of American society.

Chapter 8 extends the historical perspective of this study to the evolving realities of American higher education in the twenty-first century. Drawing upon empirical data and social science studies, it explicates changes in participation and affordability, the growing differentiation of elite and open sectors, differential economic returns to higher education, the uncertain state of undergraduate learning, the persistence of the culture wars, and the enduring scientific eminence of American universities.

This history encompasses the seventy-three years from the end of World War II to the date of this writing. It is unusual for a historian to have been present in some form for the period under study. Of course, I was growing up during the 1950s, but I vividly recall the atmosphere of the American way of life. By the end of that decade, I became involved with higher education, and ever more deeply ever since. For most of these years I have been both a participant and a professional observer. As one or the other, I can attest to personal reactions, sometimes visceral, to many of the broad developments related in this study. Researching and writing about them for this study has meant revisiting and reevaluating this past. I have attempted to maintain historical discipline by focusing strictly on what happened, sticking as much as possible to verifiable or plausible sources and basing interpretations as closely as possible on such evidence. The result has been both an intellectual journey and a personal experience. I learned a great deal that I had not known or had known incompletely, and I had to qualify and contextualize former convictions—intellectual gains as well as a measure of self-discovery. Readers will bring to this study their own trove of experiences with higher education. I hope this work will also provide them greater understanding of the developments that have informed the unfolding of American higher education, and an appreciation of the forces that may have influenced their own lives.

ACKNOWLEDGMENTS

THE GENESIS OF THIS VOLUME OCCURRED IN TWO PHASES: the years 2014–2018, when I spent a good part of my time composing it, and the three previous decades, in which I was immersed in studying and writing about the history and current state of American higher education. Accordingly, I have somewhat different intellectual debts to acknowledge for each phase.

I have described the circumstances that brought me to write the history of American higher education in a contribution to *Leaders in the Historical Study of American Education* (2011), edited by Wayne Urban. In addition, three other opportunities have provided the foundations for this volume. In 1992 I was persuaded to assume the editorship of the *History of Higher Education Annual* by Les Goodchild and Harold Wechsler, both learned and talented historians now sadly deceased. Editing the *Annual* (later, *Perspectives on the History of Higher Education*) until 2018 immersed me in a meaningful way with all facets of the history of American higher education, as well as acquainting me with the established and neophyte historians who created that history. From 1987 until my retirement in 2016, I taught a survey history of American higher education to successions of cohorts in the Higher Education Program of Pennsylvania State University. These courses and, when feasible, more focused historical seminars were a continuous learning experience. They provided the map for both *The History of American Higher Education: Culture and Learning from the Founding to World War II* and the current volume, although I scarcely appreciated how much more I would have to learn to complete the map. My other activities as a scholar of higher education contributed as well. Beginning with my studies of research universities, I have investigated aspects of science policy, finance, commercialization, selective admissions, and university development. For several decades I analyzed such topics as current policy issues confronting colleges and universities; in this volume I have reexamined this same ground as history.

I would like to thank the many individuals who have helped me with *American Higher Education since World War II: A History*. Portions of the drafts received helpful comments from Nancy Diamond, Julianna Chaszar, Roger Williams, and Steve Brint. My debt to the extensive sociological studies of Steve Brint and associates is evident in the references to Chapter 8. Conversations with colleagues at Penn State, especially Paul Hallacher, David Baker, and David Post, helped to clarify issues. David Jones has given invaluable advice on both the prose and the logic of this manuscript. Doctoral students whose work has enlightened my own include Christian Anderson, Susan Richardson Barnes, Julianna Chaszar, Jordan

ACKNOWLEDGMENTS

Humphrey, Creso Sá, and Nathan Sorber. I am deeply grateful for the dedication and competence of the staff at Princeton University Press, who greatly facilitated the publishing process. Special thanks to Peter Dougherty, whose phone call was the spark that ignited this whole process and whose judgment and encouragement have guided it to fruition. Finally, special appreciation for Julianna for encouraging the nonacademic side of life over these years.

Portions of Chapter 5 are reproduced by permission of Taylor and Francis Group, LLC, a division of Informa PLC, from work previously published in *American Higher Education in the Postwar Era, 1945–1970* edited by Roger L. Geiger, Nathan M. Sorber, and Christian K. Anderson (copyright 2017).

PROLOGUE:
AMERICAN HIGHER EDUCATION
AND WORLD WAR II

ECEMBER 7, 1941: WAR CAME LIKE A THUNDERCLAP TO THE
United States and to its colleges and universities. The next four years
would be a hiatus in the normal course of affairs—for the nation and for
higher education. Although no one could foretell it at that moment, neither would ever be the same again.

Within a month, the higher education community gathered under the auspices of the American Council on Education (ACE) to pledge to the war effort
"the total strength of our colleges and universities ... our faculties, our students,
our administrative organizations, and our physical facilities."[1] A similar commitment had been made when the U.S. entered World War I, but now scarcely a
quarter century later that service would be far more extensive and strategic. In
1918, rather than tapping the resources of institutions and the talents of college
students, the Army had turned college campuses into infantry training camps—
with lamentable results for all concerned.[2] For the enormous challenges of mobilizing for World War II, the federal government would tap the physical and intellectual assets existing on the nation's campuses. Of the 15 million men and
women mobilized into the armed forces for the war, campus training programs
prepared well over one million for leadership as junior officers and as noncom-
batant specialists for the myriad tasks required to operate the gargantuan war machine.[3] Universities also sponsored programs to educate civilians in war-related
skills. On average, 20–25 percent of faculty took leave to join the war effort,
some in uniform but many to staff the 150 federal offices and agencies established
to prosecute the war. The Office of Strategic Services largely chose academics for
intelligence work, where they revealed unsuspected talents for spying. Of crucial
importance—for winning the war and shaping the future—university scientists

---

1   V. R. Cardozier, *Colleges and Universities in World War II* (Westport, CT: Praeger, 1993), quote
p. 6.

2   Roger L. Geiger, *The History of American Higher Education: Learning and Culture from the
Founding to World War II* (Princeton: Princeton University Press, 2015), 423–28; Carol S. Gruber, *Mars
and Minerva: World War I and the Uses of Higher Learning in America* (Baton Rouge: Louisiana State
University, 1975), 213–48.

3   Army and Navy campus training programs (below) enrolled more than one-half million, in addition to the Reserve Officers' Training Corps (ROTC) and Enlisted Reserves, plus large numbers in technical training courses.

formed the core of the mobilization of expertise that produced momentous war-time technological advancements. And all this happened quite fast. Three years after Pearl Harbor, American universities were already beginning to contemplate how they would adapt to new conditions emerging in the postwar world.

When the European war began in August 1939, the myopic isolationism that plagued the country was particularly evident on American campuses. A year later this sentiment waned appreciably with the fall of France and the ongoing Battle of Britain. Responsible leaders, from President Roosevelt to university presidents, perceived the inevitability of American involvement, but few could foresee the magnitude of the commitment or the decisive role that the United States would have to play. Roosevelt had authorized the organization of American science under the National Research Defense Committee in June 1940, and Congress passed the Selective Service Act (for one year) in August. The same month, ACE president George Zook spearheaded the coordination of higher education by organizing the National Committee on Education and Defense. By the next March, after Roosevelt had proclaimed the U.S. to be the Arsenal of Democracy and the Lend-Lease Act committed the U.S. to the defense of Great Britain, public opinion had largely swung to support some degree of involvement. However, the United States was unprepared psychologically or militarily for total war. Pearl Harbor triggered a psychological mobilization, but militarily the U.S. had far to go.

The war experience on college and university campuses passed through four phases. For the first year, institutions and their students largely waited in grim but resigned anticipation; the next year was the high point of war-related activities on campuses as government programs kicked in and civilian students were called away; wartime programs were then abruptly curtailed as trainees were mobilized for combat; and institutions hung on during the final year, enduring growing hardships but looking forward to a happier postwar world.

Institutions reacted to the outbreak of war by making what adaptations they could. Nearly all instituted year-round calendars to speed students toward graduation. Many students volunteered following Pearl Harbor, despite pleas from presidents and the Selective Service to maximize their education before entering the service. Enrollments had already shrunk in 1941 as students also departed for well-paying jobs in the burgeoning defense economy. Later, as manpower shortages developed, many women also chose employment, motivated by patriotism, unprecedented new opportunities, and high wages. The gradual attrition of civilian students was compensated in part by government contracts for a variety of programs providing short-term, technical instruction, particularly at the larger universities. These trainees took over dormitories and fraternity houses, and the income helped to keep institutions solvent. In addition, institutions retained students in ROTC and the Enlisted Reserves. This interlude, however, was superseded at the end of 1942.

In November the draft age was lowered to eighteen. At the same time, the armed services, at Roosevelt's behest, responded to repeated pleas from ACE to utilize the instructional potential of colleges and universities. The Army, Navy, and Army Air Forces each formulated programs to prepare inductees for technical specialties or officer candidacy.[4] Thus, institutions were certain to lose what remained of able-bodied males but sure to gain a body of uniformed soldiers for at least some academic instruction. These programs brought badly needed students and income, and they employed the faculty in teaching mostly science and engineering, but also some English and history. For the sponsors, each service pursued its own purposes.

The Navy's V-12 Program was the most compatible with academic culture and most beneficial for the 131 institutions that hosted these units. The Navy sought to recruit and train officer candidates for the armada of new ships being built. They rigorously selected qualified candidates and started them on an academic curriculum. V-12 students took some classes with civilians and were allowed to participate in extracurricular activities, including athletics. This mission was compatible with liberal arts colleges, and 100 of the V-12 programs were intentionally placed at small institutions.[5] Since the program was coordinated with the production of ships, it persisted for the duration of hostilities—unlike the Army programs. The Army Specialized Training Program, as the name indicated, was intended to prepare technical specialists in a variety of areas, including languages, medicine, dentistry, and especially engineering. Originally presented as a possible route to Officers Candidate School, in practice few program students became officers. The Army contracted with 227 institutions and assigned approximately 200,000 students. The Army Air Forces had its own program for the preparation of air crews. Although it contracted with 153 colleges and yielded 223,000 "graduates," the course lasted just twenty-one weeks. It was intended to serve as a holding pen for volunteers to be trained later at flight schools as space became available. The course was consequently neither rigorous nor focused. Launched in the spring and summer of 1943, these programs, in addition to all the others, filled many campuses with badly needed paying students. All told, government programs provided 36 percent of institutional income in 1943–1944. Civilian enrollments in 1943 were only 60 percent those of 1940, and mostly

---

4 These numerous programs are described in Cardozier, *Colleges and Universities*, chaps. 2–4. See also Hugh Hawkins, *Banding Together: The Rise of National Associations in American Higher Education, 1887–1950* (Baltimore: Johns Hopkins University Press, 1992), 146–56.

5 Jordan R. Humphrey, "Liberal Arts Colleges in the Tumultuous 1940s: Institutional Identity and the Challenges of War and Peace," PhD diss., Pennsylvania State University, 2010.

female. At many smaller schools, military personnel outnumbered civilians, and even large universities resembled military camps. But this situation also quickly changed.

In early 1944, the Army's need for combat troops caused an abrupt termination of the college training programs. By June, 100,000 trainees were transferred to active duty, largely in the infantry. Only students in advanced technical training—medicine, engineering, and languages—remained on campuses. The Air Force training program was dismantled at the same time. The Army was never enthusiastic about these programs, considering them failures and complaining that they were intended more to benefit the colleges than the military. The colleges received a small compensation from another program that enrolled seventeen-year-old high school graduates, who attended as members of the Enlisted Reserve until they turned eighteen. Termination of the Army programs dealt a financial blow to some of the smaller schools that had depended on them.

For higher education the final phase of the war spanned the summers from 1944 to 1945. Civilian male students were reduced to just 27 percent of prewar numbers, and budgetary strains were now most pressing. Yet, this was a time of growing optimism. The successful conclusion of the war was increasingly likely, if not yet in sight. Institutions tended to look beyond the current privations and makeshift arrangements. Congress too looked ahead and in June 1944 passed the Serviceman's Readjustment Act, which promised to boost future enrollments.

Overall, the impact of the war on institutions of higher education was uneven. Civilian enrollments declined by 46 percent by 1943, 69 percent for men. Units in business, law, and agriculture were depleted by more than 80 percent; these were fields in which faculty most often took wartime assignments. From the outset, demand for instruction in math, science, and engineering boomed, even as instructors in these subjects were also needed elsewhere. Liberal arts courses languished as instructors helped with training programs or offered war-issues courses. Institutions juggled their faculties, using retirees and adjuncts when feasible and reassigning or retooling professors as necessary.

The nation's 550 liberal arts colleges, with more than a quarter of prewar collegiate enrollments, were particularly challenged. Almost 200 of them obtained a military training program, but they lacked the personnel for the more lucrative technical programs. The 70 men's liberal arts colleges were most severely affected, in some case reduced to fewer than 100 civilian students. Teachers colleges and junior colleges, with poorly paid instructors, lost a quarter of their faculty to the military or higher paying civilian employment and received few federal contracts. Civilian enrollments became increasingly female, and many college women volunteered to assist the war effort. They harvested crops on labor-short farms, spent summers in war-related work, and organized activities to boost the morale of

GIs. Women altered their studies to more war-relevant subjects, deserting education and home economics for engineering, nursing, and business. The services created women's units in 1942, and by the next year Army WACs were training at 28 colleges. The Navy utilized colleges even more extensively, to train WAVES to become officers and specialists.

In retrospect, the wartime activities reveal the enormous scale and variety of resources that by 1940 had been concentrated in major universities and could be tapped for national needs. The University of Wisconsin exemplified this situation. In 1942 the campus accepted a number of short-term technical programs to train radio operators, diesel-engine specialists, and pilots, as well as a Navy school for cooks and bakers. As the radio school grew in size, President Clarence Dykstra wondered if the services were using the university as a "hotel" for technical trainees—a role it was soon happy to fulfill as regular students were called away. By mid-1943, 4,500 civilian students represented just 40 percent of prewar enrollments, but the campus now housed 1,200 men and 500 WAVES in the radio school, 110 student pilots, 500 meteorology students, and 3,000 Army and Navy trainees in extended programs. The last were college students, enlisted but taking regular classes. The medical school was also engaged in numerous programs throughout the war. University faculty showed an unsuspected flexibility in altering the curriculum toward wartime needs. The introductory physics class was three times its normal size; science and mathematics classes were given an applied emphasis; underused faculty taught high-demand classes outside their normal fields; and forty-five specially designed wartime courses were created. In addition, university faculty engaged in research and service for the war effort in Madison and elsewhere.[6]

The war experience of colleges and universities was hectic, exhilarating, trying at times, and, above all, temporary. As the conflicts drew to a close in 1945, institutions looked ahead to the resumption of something like normality. Two paramount issues loomed on the horizon, one pointing toward tradition and the other toward possible change. After the turmoil of the war years, institutions felt a powerful impulse not just to return to their previous tasks but also to define themselves and their essential mission. Above all, this meant identifying and articulating the essence of a liberal education. And, after willingly and enthusiastically doing the government's bidding for four years, the question now became one of the future relationship between the federal government and higher education. Institutions were inclined to look inward to their own affairs, but American higher education was fated to be drawn into the national arena.

6   E. David Cronin and John W. Jenkins, *The University of Wisconsin: A History. Vol. 3, Politics, Depression, and War, 1925–1945* (Madison: University of Wisconsin Press, 1994), 416–41.

PART I

AMERICAN HIGHER EDUCATION

1945–1957

★ 1 ★

THE GI BILL AND BEYOND:
HIGHER EDUCATION, 1945–1955

F OR THE UNITED STATES, THE YEARS AFTER WORLD WAR II
were anything but a return to "normalcy." Politically, Congress and the
president faced an enormous workload in legislating the transition from a
war economy and the foundations of a new peacetime order. Liberals envisioned building on the legacy of the New Deal to advance the social and
economic commitments of the federal government and to promote world peace
through American-led internationalism. But such expectations were frustrated
in the postwar years by an increasingly conservative mood in the country, by
labor unrest, and by the onset of the Cold War. Political life was soon dominated
by an escalating confrontation with the Soviet Union, an anti-communist crusade at home, and the Korean War. Not until 1955 did the rhetoric and passions
generated by these developments begin to diminish, allowing the country to
dwell on more mundane domestic affairs.

Conditions in American higher education traced a similar path. The Harvard
report *General Education in a Free Society* (aka the Redbook) and the President's
Commission on Higher Education were the most publicized manifestations of
an intellectual ferment over the structure, purpose, and curricula of collegiate
education. Postwar institutions struggled to accommodate the flood of veteran
students enrolling under the GI Bill. Universities were next drawn into the trauma
of the anti-communist witch hunt. The Korean War then cast a pall of uncertainty over government policies affecting students. For colleges and universities
too, the armistice in Korea and the attenuation of McCarthyism finally offered
the relative tranquility to focus on institutional development. However, for
Americans inside or outside of the higher education system, the dominant influence during the postwar decade was what the historian James Patterson called the
"Booms": "Economic growth was indeed the most decisive force in the shaping
of attitudes and expectations in the postwar era."[1]

---

1   James T. Patterson, *Grand Expectations: The United States, 1945–1974* (New York: Oxford University Press, 1996), 61: the following draws from pp. 61–81; and John Patrick Diggins, *The Proud Decades:
America in War and Peace, 1941–1960* (New York: Norton, 1988), 177–88.

3

In the twenty five years following the war, the United States experienced one of the longest periods of sustained economic growth the world had seen. Consumer spending and the standard of living began rising almost immediately, and by the late 1940s this growth affected a broad swath of the population. By the end of the decade, Americans on average were nearly twice as affluent as the next wealthiest countries, and the rapid rate of economic growth continued with scarcely a pause. Moreover, this prosperity was widely shared. Poverty, which may have affected 30 percent of Americans, slowly declined. For the majority of Americans, life was materially improved by a cornucopia of consumer goods—household appliances, automobiles, and televisions, among others. Fifteen million new homes were constructed from 1945 to 1955, mostly in Levittowns and their like, which gave new homeowners their own turf in burgeoning suburbs. American consumers by no means lived lavishly; the original Levittown house consisted of a living room, kitchen, two bedrooms and a bathroom. America's emerging middle class advanced from a constrained to a comfortable life style. In the process, middle-class families sought more education for their children, which first buoyed high school graduation rates and then affected colleges.

But first, higher education faced a series of postwar challenges, which are considered in this chapter: accommodating a surge of veteran students; responding to the radical recommendations from a presidential commission; and reacting to the threat of McCarthyism. Chapter 2 then details the elaboration of a postwar system of American higher education.

THE GI BILL

The Serviceman's Readjustment Act that Roosevelt signed on June 22, 1944—the GI Bill—had its origins in conventional thinking about the place of higher education in American society, but its eventual impact altered higher education's status and conventional thinking too. The 1942 election returned the most conservative Congress that Roosevelt would face in his presidency. Republicans and conservative Southern Democrats quickly eviscerated New Deal activism by terminating the National Resource Planning Board—the locus of New Deal visions for social reconstruction. Roosevelt kept the ghost of the New Deal alive in 1944 with a speech outlining an "economic bill of rights" for Americans, with the last being "the right to a good education."[2] More pressing, and overhanging the vast mobilization then underway, was the issue of how to treat the veterans; specifically, how to prevent social disruption following demobilization and how to re-

2 Diggins, *Proud Decades*, 21–22; Cass Sunstein, *The Second Bill of Rights: FDR's Unfinished Revolution and Why We Need It More Than Ever* (New York: Basic Books, 2004).

integrate servicemen into American society while avoiding the neglect and subsequent resentment experienced by World War I veterans. Multiple bills were introduced dealing with one or more aspects of this challenge. Roosevelt then proposed a comprehensive plan that, among other things, would provide one year of educational or vocational training for all veterans and possible additional years for those "with exceptional ability and skills." Thus, the first iteration of veteran's benefits assumed that a full college education should be reserved for a small minority of ex-servicemen who were exceptionally smart.[3]

At this point the issue was joined by the American Legion, whose chief goal was to maximize veteran benefits and who possessed the means to promote their cause. The legion rewrote the original proposal, extending educational benefits to four years for all who had served. It then used its grassroots network to garner support across the country—and in Congress—for what it dubbed the GI Bill of Rights. The conservative legion allied with anti–New Deal members of Congress, who above all wished to prevent New Deal federal agencies from transforming GI benefits into wider social programs. To exclude these agencies, administration of the GI Bill was entrusted to the Veteran's Administration and its implementation to the states. In addition, Congress was assured that few ex-servicemen and women would want or need the generous provisions for attending college. At first this seemed to be the case, as few of the soldiers demobilized in 1944 and 1945 used their educational benefits—or the other benefits of the bill for that matter. In December 1945, Congress responded by increasing students' monthly stipend, removing eligibility restrictions on older students, and including correspondence courses. An unanticipated boom in veteran enrollments soon followed, with an impact on the colleges and universities that will be described below. For the next five years, colleges and universities would be linked with the federal treasury through the Veterans Administration.

Although the GI Bill would bolster the finances of American colleges and universities, the immediate postwar years were dominated by the strains of accommodating the deluge of veterans. Some 2,232,000 veterans attended college under Title II of the GI Bill from 1945 to 1954, or less than 15 percent of eligible servicemen.[4] Another 36 percent received on-the-job training or vocational education under the educational provisions of the act, programs that were riddled with fraud and waste. However, the GI Bill has always been identified chiefly

3   Suzanne Mettler, *Soldiers to Citizens: The G.I. Bill and the Making of the Greatest Generation* (New York: Oxford, 2005), quote p. 20; Glenn C. Altschuler and Stuart M. Blumin, *The GI Bill: A New Deal for Veterans* (New York: Oxford, 2009); Kathleen J. Frydl, *The GI Bill* (New York: Cambridge University Press, 2009).

4   Keith W. Olson, *The G.I. Bill, the Veterans, and the Colleges* (Lexington: University Press of Kentucky, 1974), 41–56, 76.

with those veterans who went to college, how this opportunity transformed their lives, and how this most enlightened of public investments enlarged the nation's intellectual capital.[5]

For the 1946–1949 academic years, an average of 1 million veterans enrolled, compared with a total prewar enrollment of 1.4 million. For the first two of these years the veterans comprised almost half of all students, 70 percent of males. The $500 they were allowed for expenses covered tuition at private or public schools, and a slight majority enrolled in the private sector. Unconstrained by costs, veterans preferred the best known and academically strongest institutions. Still, the largest number enrolled in convenient, local urban universities (mostly private), followed by state flagship universities and prominent liberal arts colleges. These institutions were deluged with applications and typically expanded by 50–100 percent while still rejecting many applicants. Teachers colleges, junior colleges, and the smaller private colleges, on the other hand, had room to spare. At the favored schools, the tide of veterans created acute crowding. Instruction was expanded more readily than housing, through larger lectures, expanded class schedules, and year-round operations. Congress assisted the colleges with supplemental appropriations and provision of army-surplus buildings. The greatest problem was presented by the half of veterans who were married and the one-half of those who had children. Universities created vast trailer parks for these families. Serendipitously, this created supportive communities of highly motivated students. Married students achieved higher average grades than single veterans, who in turn had better grades than regular students.

The veterans were by all accounts exceptionally diligent students. Harvard president James Conant, who had been an initial sceptic, called them "the most mature and promising students Harvard has ever had."[6] In an era when grading was often done on a curve, regular students complained about the competition. Starting at an average age of twenty-five, veterans on the whole were mature, serious, motivated, and in a hurry. In fact, they were self-selected from the 15 million eligible servicemen, which reflected social ambition as much as initial aptitude. Too, their dominant presence on campus created an atmosphere conducive to focused academic efforts. All these factors, no doubt, account for the fact that 79 percent of GI students graduated, compared with a graduation rate of 55 percent for regular students. Legend has it that the veterans flocked to vocational and professional majors, but no comprehensive data exist. Large numbers clearly stud-

---

5   Fraud and waste in vocational education and on-the-job training is covered in Altschuler and Blumin, *GI Bill*; and Frydl, *GI Bill*. Mettler, *Soldiers to Citizens*, is based on a large survey of surviving GI Bill beneficiaries, emphasizing their contributions to civic life.

6   James B. Conant, *My Several Lives: Memoirs of a Social Inventor* (New York: Harper & Row, 1970), 373.

ied engineering, but the numbers of business majors are less certain. Departments of business, or commerce, were not well developed across American universities, and veterans seeking business careers could attend short courses at one of the many proprietary schools. Records from the University of Wisconsin show the largest portion (38 percent) of veterans studying liberal arts, compared to one-quarter of nonveterans. Aside from a predilection for engineering, the veterans seem to have spread themselves across the curriculum.[7] The presence of mature veterans caused the demise of quaint college customs, as well as tolerance of cigarette smoking, but they had little lasting impact on academics. But GI tuitions significantly bolstered the exhausted treasuries of colleges and universities.

How did the college provisions of the GI Bill affect the United States? To what extent did it inspire additional college graduates and augment the educational stock of the country? These questions were first posed as the original bill was winding down. At that time, a representative survey concluded that 10 percent of veteran students would not have attended without the GI Bill and "another ten per cent probably would not have." This 20 percent figure suggests that four-fifths of veteran students either had already begun college studies or would have attended college if the war had not intervened. Polls taken at individual institutions, or much later, yield much higher numbers of additional students, closer to 50 percent. More recently economists have sought to refine these figures. Although the findings are estimates, they suggest substantial effects. Among the older half of WW II veterans, those born before 1921, few used the GI Bill to attend college. The chief beneficiaries belonged to the 1923–1927 birth cohorts, whose college participation was increased by 20–50 percent. The high graduation rates also suggest a net increase greater than 20 percent. In terms of social mobility, despite abundant anecdotes of indigent or working-class veterans attaining college degrees and successful careers, the largest gains were registered by GIs from the fourth income quintile—what was then the middle-middle class, where potential new students might be expected to be found.[8]

Nonetheless, when other factors are considered, the magnitude of effects from the GI Bill appears even larger. Given the fact of war, many prewar expectations of college attendance would not have been realized. The elevated graduation rate of veterans meant that more earned degrees than would have had they attended earlier as civilians. That one-half of veteran students were family heads would have precluded full-time attendance (and diminished completion) without the

---

7 Olson, *GI Bill*, 87.

8 Marcus Stanley, "Education and the Midcentury GI Bills," *Quarterly Journal of Economics* 118, 2 (May 2003): 671–708; also, John Bound and Sarah Turner, "Going to War and Going to College: Did World War II and the G.I. Bill Increase Educational Attainment for Returning Veterans?," *Journal of Labor Economics* 20, 4 (October 2002): 784–815.

bill. And, for those students who had already started college, the GI Bill provided the resources to persist and, for many, to obtain graduate and professional degrees. Hence, the consensus that the GI Bill accelerated the educational advancement and deepened the intellectual capital of the country is not mistaken. According to the Veteran's Administration, degrees were earned under the GI Bill by "450,000 engineers, 180,000 doctors, dentists and nurses, 360,000 school teachers, 150,000 scientists, 243,000 accountants, 107,000 lawyers, [and] 36,000 clergymen."[9]

GHOSTS OF THE NEW DEAL: THE PRESIDENT'S COMMISSION ON HIGHER EDUCATION

The New Deal of President Franklin Delano Roosevelt initially attacked the woes of the Great Depression "in innumerable directions," "a chaos of experimentation."[10] By his second term, New Deal liberalism emerged as a commitment to compensate for the failures of capitalism by expanding the institutions of the welfare state. But higher education was an experiment not attempted, a direction not taken. George Zook, Roosevelt's first commissioner of education, reportedly resigned in 1934 because of this neglect (and a budget cut). The following year, needy students became eligible for work-study assistance, not as students but through Emergency Relief offered by the National Youth Administration (NYA). At the peak year, nearly 140,000 students received an average of $12 per month for performing work assigned by 1,651 participating institutions. But this was the extent of New Deal aid for higher education. The American Youth Congress considered these provisions inadequate, with moral support from First Lady Eleanor Roosevelt. They lobbied unsuccessfully for the American Youth Act in 1936, which would have provided additional benefits for a larger number of students.

University leaders had been eager to promote a New Deal for science. They achieved at least a voice with the appointment of the Science Advisory Board (1933–1935). There MIT president Karl Compton led a campaign for federal appropriations to support nongovernmental scientific research. Although Roosevelt was initially sympathetic, the plan became fatally embroiled in the bureaucracy when the social sciences demanded to be included. Higher education remained on the periphery in the 1930s even as the New Deal itself evolved. From

---

9   Olson, *G.I. Bill*, 109; Michael J. Bennett, *When Dreams Came True: The GI Bill and the Making of Modern America* (Washington, DC: Brassey's, 1996), 277–310.

10   Alan Brinkley, "The New Deal and the Idea of the State," in Steve Fraser and Gery Gerstle, eds., *The Rise and Fall of the New Deal Order* (Princeton: Princeton University Press, 1989), 85–121.

1937, political support waned in Congress while New Dealers in the administration focused on social welfare issues. Both of these dynamics persisted into and through the war years, when higher education and research became part of the war effort.[11]

Higher education's absence from the New Deal agenda can be ascribed to its public image and relative well being. The rapid expansion of enrollments after World War I had been greeted with alarm among much of traditional higher education. The principal concern had been intellectual qualifications—the belief that many newcomers did not possess the intelligence required for college-level work. This mindset was evident in efforts to steer junior colleges toward terminal programs, to exclude the liberal arts from teachers colleges, and in versions of "general education" that emphasized life skills. Higher education largely embraced traditional social and economic values. Demographically, one-half of young people were completing high school by 1940, but only one-third of graduates continued on to college. These students may have struggled to cope with the hardships of the Depression, but only 12 percent qualified for the work-study programs of the NYA. College students were better off than most. In the election of 1936, students voted Democratic for the first time, favoring Roosevelt and the New Deal by a slight margin; but professors and administrators were still largely conservative, especially at private institutions. The American Council on Education (ACE), which was supported by dues-paying institutions, devoted its energies to exempting higher education from New Deal legislation, successfully keeping colleges and universities out of social security. ACE and other higher education bodies basically represented the interests of their membership and in fact were laggards in connecting higher education to larger national purpose. Hence, the most momentous developments for higher education came not from New Deal liberalism or the foresight of the university community but from the war itself.

Although the GI Bill had an enormous impact in repopulating (overpopulating) American colleges and universities, in 1946 there was still no model, policy, or vision for a federal role in American higher education. Into this void stepped the President's Commission on Higher Education.

The idea for the commission came from liberal advisors in the Office of War Mobilization and Reconversion who believed that a greater federal role in higher education was needed to enhance social welfare. This initiative was the product of an internal, New Deal mentality. It was hatched before the deluge of GI Bill

11   Alan Brinkley, *The End of Reform: New Deal Liberalism in Recession and War* (New York: Random House, 1995); Karen Orren and Stephen Skowronek, "Regimes and Regime Building in American Government: A Review of Literature on the 1940s," *Political Science Quarterly* 113, 4 (1998–99): 689–702.

recipients swamped postwar campuses and without input from the higher education community.[12] Several close presidential advisors to President Truman appealed to his liberal inclinations to sell the idea of a thorough inquiry into the role that higher education could or should play in American society. The president's charge asked the commission to examine expansion of educational opportunity, curricula "in the fields of international affairs and social understanding," the feasibility of "intermediate technical institutes," and higher education finance especially for expanding facilities. The commission would take considerable liberty in pursuing these topics. Its membership was carefully managed by its instigators. Chairman George Zook represented both public and private institutions as head of ACE, but he was also known to favor federal aid. Zook and other appointees were sympathetic toward John Dewey's instrumentalist interpretation of general education. The twenty-eight blue-ribbon members were outwardly representative of both sectors, but they had been carefully selected to support the tacit agenda. The administration was assured that "a majority is clearly committed to the principle of the extension of public education through the collegiate level."[13]

The commission began deliberations in July 1946 with abundant staff support and access to data from federal agencies. It reported its findings in December 1947 in some four hundred pages in six slim volumes, released sequentially so that each issue would receive separate public notice. *Higher Education for American Democracy* emphatically defended as its principal findings four controversial positions: the chief purpose of American higher education was the building and strengthening of democracy; enrollments should be greatly expanded; this growth should occur in public institutions, including community colleges; and federal financial assistance was needed and appropriate to achieve these ends. These four objectives were logically related, but the lynchpin of the commission's case was its conception of democracy.

In a horrific war against authoritarian regimes, the United States embraced democracy as its wartime banner and the rationale for postwar world leadership. Every political faction claimed some version of democracy for its cause, and the commission was no different. It envisioned an idealistic reshaping of American

12 This initiative was foreshadowed by a 1943 report from the soon-to-expire National Resources Planning Board, *Equal Access to Education*, which argued the crucial importance of doubling higher education enrollments: John Douglass, *The California Idea and American Higher Education* (Berkeley: University of California University Press, 2000), 190–91.

13 Janet Kerr-Tener, "From Truman to Johnson: Ad hoc Policy Formulation in Higher Education," PhD diss. (University of Virginia, 1985), 50–118, quotes pp. 73, 69. On New Deal authors and the controversy over membership, see Nicholas Strohl, "A Road Not Taken: The Truman Commission as an Alternative Vision of US Higher Education Policy" (paper presented at the annual meeting of the History of Education Society, St. Louis, MO, November 5–8 2015).

society, declaring that the primary purpose of education should be to instill the democratic ideal in citizens in order to transform society into a higher form of democratic community. Thus, for colleges and universities, "education for democratic living ... should become ... a primary aim of all classroom teaching and, more important still, of every phase of campus life." In the rhetoric of the report, democracy assumed an almost mystical quality, essential to confront "the worldwide crisis of mankind," and to guide American leadership in developing "World Citizenship." This vision of transforming society by inculcating democratic ideals through higher education reflected the pragmatist philosophy of John Dewey, although he was not mentioned in the report.[14] His notion of a community unified through democracy was the foundation for the practical recommendations of the President's Commission on Higher Education.[15]

The commission's notion of *general education* was the means to bring about the transformation to a democratic society. Although there were several contemporary versions of this term (discussed below), the commission argued for Dewey's conception of education for human living: "nonspecialized and nonvocational learning which should be the common experience of all educated men and women." The report listed eleven specific objectives, including "ethical principles consistent with democratic ideals," "satisfactory emotional and social adjustment," to "understand and enjoy ... cultural activities," to develop "knowledge and attitudes basic to a satisfying family life," and "skills and habits involved in critical and constructive thinking." General education would thus be the "means to a more abundant personal life and a stronger, freer social order." Remarkably, all the usual functions of higher education were subordinated to general education for democracy. Manpower considerations, which had dominated government thinking during the war, were barely mentioned. Vocational training was less important than the orientation toward work derived from general education. Social mobility was potentially harmful to community unity; in fact, "through education society should come to recognize the equal dignity of all kinds of work, and so erase distinctions based on occupational castes." The advancement of specialized knowledge was described as the bane of the college curriculum, and liberal education dismissed as "aristocratic." Basic research was recognized as a necessary role for universities, but the report emphasized social science research

14   Newton Edwards, consultant for vol. I, was a founding member of the John Dewey Society (1935), as was commission member George Stoddard, president of the University of Illinois: Ethan Schrum, "Establishing a Democratic Religion: Metaphysics and Democracy in the Debates over the President's Commission on Higher Education," *History of Education Quarterly* 47, 3 (August 2007): 277–301, esp. 293.

15   Schrum, "Establishing a Democratic Religion"; Gary E. Miller, *The Meaning of General Education: The Emergence of a Curriculum Paradigm* (New York: Teachers College Press, 1988), chaps. 4, 7.

to advance social reconstruction, and it advocated that federal research support be channeled largely through students.[16]

General education as conceived by the commission was eccentric to the central traditions of American higher education. The approach was staunchly defended nonetheless by T. R. McConnell, an author of the section quoted above. McConnell was the chancellor of the University of Buffalo but had formerly been at the University of Minnesota, where the General College was the most prominent prewar experiment in this type of general education. This unit was created to teach life skills to students who did not qualify for admission to the university's regular programs, and this controversial model had been actively promoted by its organizers. It presaged the commission's vision of higher education serving an expanded pool of terminal two-year students as well as its conception of general education.[17]

A democratic society implied equality of educational opportunity, which was far from the case in postwar America. Socioeconomic factors accounted for the failure of many youth to complete high school, let alone attend college. Large regional discrepancies existed in wealth and educational investment. And the President's Commission on Higher Education directly attacked existing discrimination against Jewish students and segregation in the South.[18] It also criticized the traditional emphasis of colleges on "verbal skills and intellectual interests." In order to estimate the proportion of young people having the ability to benefit from college, the commission turned to the Army General Classification Test—an intelligence test that had been administered to more than 10 million inductees. It determined reference points by comparing these scores with those of entering college students on the ACE psychology tests. This method yielded figures far larger than any previous projection of college attendance: "At least 49 percent of our population has the mental ability to complete 14 years of schooling"; and "at least 32 percent [could] complete an advanced liberal or specialized professional education." These figures were announced as goals for the year 1960—in all 4 million undergraduates compared with 1.5 million students in 1940 and a projected 2.7 million if the prewar growth trend alone persisted. Hence, the commission's

16 President's Commission on Higher Education, vol. I, *Establishing the Goals* (Washington, DC: GPO, 1947), quotes pp. 49, 51–57; Schrum, "Establishing a Democratic Religion," 286–88.

17 T. R. McConnell, "A Reply to the Critics," in Gail Kennedy, ed., *Education for Democracy: The Debate over the President's Commission on Higher Education* (Boston: D. C. Heath, 1952), 105–15; Roger L. Geiger, *The History of American Higher Education: Learning and Culture from the Founding to World War II* (Princeton: Princeton University Press, 2015).

18 President's Commission on Higher Education, *Higher Education for American Democracy*, vol. II, *Equalizing and Expanding Individual Opportunity* (Washington, DC: GPO, 1947), 25–44. Four commission members from southern institutions inserted a note recognizing the inferior educational provisions for Negroes but disagreeing with the recommendation to terminate segregated schooling: 29n.

recommendations aspired to fill by 1960 this substantial "education gap" between projected enrollments and the number of students intellectually qualified for college study.[19]

Community colleges played a key role in the commission's plan, providing a terminal education for one-sixth of all youth. The term "community college" was deliberately substituted for "junior college" because these institutions were envisioned as the means for building democratic communities. The commission wanted free public education to be extended to the thirteenth and fourteenth years because "the complex demands of social, civic, and family life call for a lengthened period of general education for a much larger number of young people." Any vocational instruction was intended to be fully integrated with general education, and community colleges were charged as well with providing adult education—another area recommended for expansion.[20]

Volume V, *Financing Higher Education*, addressed how to pay for this expansion. The cost of providing the first two years free at public institutions would have to be financed by states and localities, but the commission looked to the federal government for the other additional expenditures. These included a national program of scholarships similar to GI-Bill benefits for up to 20 percent of civilian college students, federal support for general educational expenditures funneled through the states, and capital for the expansion of physical facilities. These last two forms of aid would be provided only for public institutions, a specification that provoked a lengthy dissent from two commission members from private universities. The commission somewhat disingenuously assumed that all enrollment growth would occur in public institutions, since the private sector had expressed no intention of expanding. Nor could it imagine privately controlled institutions accepting the equation of democracy with general education. In fact, it ominously warned that acceptance of public funds implied "the right of the people as a whole to exercise review and control of the educational policies and procedures of that institution." The tacit agenda of the commission was to bring the New Deal to higher education: "The time has come," it declared, "for America to develop a sound pattern of continuing Federal support for higher education."[21]

Higher Education for American Democracy was both a forward- and backward-looking document. In positing social reconstruction as a rationale for federal intervention, it mirrored the unrealized aspirations of the late New Deal. By

---

19   President's Commission on Higher Education, *Establishing the Goals*, 32, 41.

20   President's Commission on Higher Education, *Higher Education for American Democracy*, vol. III, *Organizing Higher Education* (Washington, DC: U.S. GPO, 1947), 5–15.

21   President's Commission on Higher Education, *Higher Education for American Democracy*, vol. V, *Financing Higher Education* (Washington, DC: U.S. GPO, 1947), quotes pp. 58, 54; Schrum, "Establishing a Democratic Religion," 282–85.

invoking general education to instill Deweyan democracy, it invoked doctrines with waning currency even in an atmosphere of postwar idealism. However, the issues were real: the federal government had already assumed a role in higher education—but to advance specific national interests (agriculture, health, national defense) rather than the general social welfare. And by the time the report appeared, the country was engaged in a massive natural experiment through the GI Bill, which seemed to demonstrate (at least in retrospect) that a greater portion of the population could succeed in and benefit from higher education. These and other issues raised by the commission would loom large in the immediate future. The strictures against segregation in education dovetailed with the 1947 report of the President's Commission on Civil Rights and the 1948 desegregation of the armed services. The call for a substantial increase in properly trained faculty was an undeniable need. And community colleges would not only assume the title conferred by the President's Commission on Higher Education but also in time some of the roles it envisaged.[22] In other respects, *Higher Education for American Democracy* was hopelessly out of the mainstream of American higher education: the slighting of specialized academic knowledge, the dismissal of the liberal arts as aristocratic, the disregard of academic merit, the demeaning attitude toward the private sector—all ran counter to the prevailing nature and values of American colleges and universities.

In 1949 George Zook could point to general public approval of certain recommendations—a substantial expansion of facilities for higher education, some program of national scholarships, and strengthening the preparation of college faculty. However, the widespread discussion stimulated by the report disputed far more.[23] The two perennial arguments against educational expansion—which have perennially proved false—are that additional students lack the intellect for higher studies and that additional graduates would not find suitable employment. The commission anticipated the first objection by basing its projections on Army testing and sidestepped the second by (unrealistically) elevating democracy above careers.[24] But critics instead argued that lower-middle-class and working-class youth—whose education gap was largest—lacked the motivation to go to college

22   Philo Hutcheson, "The 1947 President's Commission on Higher Education and the National Rhetoric on Higher Education Policy," *History of Higher Education Annual* 22 (2002): 91–109; President's Commission on Higher Education, *Higher Education for American Democracy*, vol. IV, *Staffing Higher Education* (Washington, DC: U.S. GPO, 1947).

23   James G. Harlow, "Five Years of Discussion," *Journal of Higher Education* 24, 1 (January 1953), 17–24; Gail Kennedy, ed., *Education for Democracy: The Debate over the President's Commission on Higher Education* (Boston: D. C. Heath, 1952).

24   The section "The Professional Schools" endorsed limited manpower planning by estimating and publicizing needs in various professions, and also emphasized that professionals should receive general education: President's Commission on Higher Education, *Establishing the Goals*, 75–84.

even if financial barriers could be overcome. In the late 1940s it appeared that low participation by such groups had possibly caused the prewar growth trend to level off and that baseline college enrollments might actually decline after the GIs departed. The Harvard economist Seymour Harris swayed many with a plausible empirical case for the second objection—that suitable jobs would not be available for enlarged cohorts of college graduates.[25]

The most vehement opposition to the report came from the slighted private sector. Its two dissenting members of the commission criticized not just the denial of federal funds (which never materialized) but also the unalloyed statism and the implication that private colleges did not serve the public interest. Beyond these issues lay a huge philosophical gulf, as private institutions strongly identified with intellectual goals, the search for truth, and liberal education. Presidents of private universities—Harold Dodds of Princeton, Charles Seymour of Yale, and Robert Maynard Hutchins of Chicago—defended high intellectual standards and limited social participation. But this general mission was particularly important for the National Catholic Education Association, whose members provided mass higher education to non-elite students. In fact, the commission's desire for free public education for the first two years of college posed a grave threat to the private sector that was not unintentional. The instigator of the commission had originally considered the "struggle between public and private education" to be "the most controversial question," and hence the rationale for a public bias.[26] However, this controversy had been most evident in K-12 education before the war. Insofar as it existed in higher education, the conflict was largely fanned by the commission. In fact, one unforeseen consequence of the commission was to galvanize private sector defenses.

Consideration of the future federal role in higher education extended beyond abstract arguments to politics and policy. The proposal for federal scholarships and fellowships may have received the most favorable reception, being welcomed by institutions in both the private and public sectors. Disagreement existed over whether they should be awarded solely for financial need or for intellectual merit —a controversy that was ultimately moot. President Truman was never enthusiastic about federal initiatives for higher education and failed to exert his (waning) influence for legislation. Proposals for implementing the commission's goals were developed by White House staff. First drafts incorporated the commission's generous recommendations for student scholarships, but they were progressively whittled down as the political climate chilled; and provisions were added for student loans, which the commission had explicitly rejected. Legislation to this

25 Kennedy, *Education for Democracy*, 68–72.
26 Kerr-Tener, *From Truman to Johnson*, 87–103, quote p. 69.

effect was submitted to Congress in August 1950, two months after the outbreak of the Korean War. There it languished, never emerging from committee.[27]

The President's Commission on Higher Education was a product of the evanescent postwar atmosphere of optimism, idealism, and ambitions for the future.[28] Posterity has deemed it prescient for advocating subsequent developments—the expansion of enrollment, federal student financial aid, and the proliferation of community colleges, but there was no direct connection between the commission's report and these later phenomena, as will be evident in later chapters. American colleges and universities shared the postwar euphoria of boundless possibilities, including idealism toward many of the issues considered by the commission. But prevailing beliefs pulled in a different direction. For American colleges, a compelling challenge of postwar education was to formulate a philosophy of liberal education for undergraduate students.

GENERAL EDUCATION AND LIBERAL EDUCATION

Developing a cultural consensus on the nature and role of liberal education was the unfinished business of American higher education between the wars. After 1900 the term "liberal culture," as used by Woodrow Wilson and Abbott Lawrence Lowell, implied a rehabilitation of the liberal arts heritage of the defunct classical course and its implicit social distinctions as well. With the coming of mass higher education after World War I, new initiatives attempted to break with the dominant trend and rekindle the spirit of liberal education. Now, prophets and their projects tended to embrace inclusiveness, advocating practices that claimed to enhance the educational experiences of all students. By the 1930s, would-be reformers preferred the term "general education," in keeping with a consensus that the first two years of college should be oriented to common learning. The majority of colleges, judging from the official publications of institutional associations, still identified with liberal education, however defined. Depictions of liberal and general education overlapped considerably, and both camps harbored contradictory interpretations. Often the same language was used

---

27 John D. Millett, *Financing Higher Education in the United States* (New York: Columbia University Press, 1952), 434–38. In addition, a commission-inspired report of the Office of Education recommended federal support to states to develop plans for community college systems: Kerr-Tener, *From Truman to Johnson*, 95–97, 103–18. Created in an atmosphere of postwar idealism (1946), the commission's reports appeared at the end of 1947 as the Cold War began to dominate American politics and the presidency.

28 Perhaps most evident in the report's endorsement of internationalism: "American institutions of higher education have an enlarged responsibility ... to help our own citizens as well as other peoples to move from the provincial and insular mind to the international mind": President's Commission on Higher Education, *Establishing the Goals*, 14–20, quote p. 15.

for entirely different purposes, and each invoked "baskets" of attributes.[29] But beneath this confusion lay the crucial issue of the future nature of American collegiate education. The World War II raised the ideological stakes.

What liberal and general education had in common was aversion to specialization and vocationalism, two of the most prominent trends of the interwar years.[30] "Specialization" was the pejorative term for the relentless advance of academic knowledge coupled with an elective system that allowed students to choose most of their own courses. Critics recognized these realities and argued further that esoteric academic knowledge had little relevance for collegians in the first two years of college, or even in a four-year bachelor's course. Similar arguments sought to place the study of practical fields for specific careers after general education. What they favored was the desirability of common learning to overcome the fragmentation of the elective system. However, curricular reformers faced the hurdle of existing practice. Many colleges equated liberal education with the mastery of advanced knowledge in academic disciplines and sought to extend their capacity to teach such knowledge. In the median college, barely more than one-third of faculty held PhDs, and only 15 percent of institutions had faculties with one-half or more PhDs. Yet, American science and scholarship had made striking advances prior to the war, and nearly all colleges struggled to catch up by hiring additional faculty with doctorates. Moreover, in 1940 only 43 percent of bachelor's degrees were awarded in the liberal arts and sciences. Despite an outpouring of writing on liberal and general education, American higher education was primarily engaged in teaching the disciplines and professions.

The onset of war kindled an intense focus on democracy and freedom, which carried over into the postwar years. Their survival in the world was truly at issue, along with much else. Colleges and universities were especially fixated on these ideals, which to them embodied the essence of the struggle as it affected their mission. Although heavily engaged with technical instruction for the war effort, institutions soon began pondering how liberal education might best be harnessed to these ends. These efforts generated extensive writings throughout the 1940s. A 1944 bibliography of liberal education contained 289 entries; two bibliographies of general education also appeared, the second with 237 entries.[31] Liberal

29 Bruce A. Kimball, *Orators and Philosophers: A History of the Idea of Liberal Education* (New York: Teachers College Press, 1986), 192–99; Geiger, *History of American Higher Education*. For a critique of contemporary trends and defense of liberal education, see Norman Forester, *The Future of the Liberal College* (New York; Arno Press, 1969 [1938]).

30 Earl J. McGrath issued a manifesto for general education in the first issue of the *Journal of General Education*: "The General Education Movement," 1, 1 (October 1946): 3–8.

31 Kimball, *Orators and Philosophers*, 203; Commission on Liberal Education, *Liberal Education: Ends and Means, Partial Bibliography, 1943–44* (New York: Association of American Colleges, 1944); Earl J. McGrath, "A Bibliography on General Education," *Educational Record* 21 (1940): 96–118; William

arts colleges were particularly invested in liberal education (which only appears to be a truism in retrospect, since most offered vocational majors). The Association of American Colleges, which represented them, sponsored the Commission on Liberal Education, which produced several wartime reports, including the aforementioned bibliography. The American Council of Learned Societies, which spoke for the humanities, published *Liberal Education Re-examined* in 1943. The more ecumenical ACE sponsored two committees on general education. These speculations and pronouncements were prompted not just by the dangers of wartime but also by widespread perception that America and civilization had entered a new era.[32]

In this atmosphere, James Conant in 1942 commissioned a faculty committee to consider the matter of general education not only at Harvard but also for the entire educational system. Conant was a chemist known for his advocacy of research and meritocracy at Harvard and at that moment was teamed with Vannevar Bush to mobilize American science for the war. But he reflected the concerns of the times. He called general education "essential if our civilization is to be preserved." In his oration for the tercentenary of Harvard (1936), he had identified the need for a "modern equivalent" to the former common classical course. While hardly disparaging specialized and professional education, he asserted that they must be complemented by the liberal arts to form an educated person. But the Harvard committee differed from contemporary writings in key respects. It had a concrete mandate to recommend a general education curriculum for Harvard College, and it had to produce a cogent document acceptable to President Conant and the Harvard faculty. Published in the summer of 1945, *General Education in a Free Society* presented a forceful but intellectually nuanced case for requiring a limited number of dedicated general education courses.[33]

The report, known as the Redbook from its crimson cover, summarized five prewar approaches to the problem of general education: "(1) distribution requirements, (2) comprehensive survey courses, (3) functional courses, (4) a great books curriculum, and (5) individual guidance." The first characterized most colleges and universities, including Harvard: a major field of study with electives moderated by some requirement for taking courses in other specified areas. The committee took pains to defend the major field of specialized concentration: "An impressive battery of educational machinery is arrayed in its support: the teach-

---

Nelson Lyons, "A Further Bibliography on General Education," *Journal of General Education* 4, 1 (October 1949): 72–80.

32 Kimball, *Orators and Philosophers*, 195–204.

33 Conant, *My Several Lives*, 363–68, 651–58; Paul H. Buck et al. *General Education in a Free Society: Report of the Harvard Committee* (Cambridge: Harvard University, 1945).

ing departments, prescribed courses, the system of honors, the tutorial system, and the General Examination [for graduation]." The problem was the failure of the elective system to provide general education: for distribution, "the student take[s] two or three courses of something—almost anything." Harvard's four-hundred-some courses taught bits of specialized knowledge but did not provide students with any common learning. As an approach to liberal or general education, the same could be said for elective distribution requirements elsewhere.[34]

Some institutions had addressed the weakness of the elective system by creating survey courses intended to provide students with comprehensive coverage of broad swaths of the humanities, social or natural sciences. Most acclaimed was the Columbia course Contemporary Civilization that evolved from the War Issues course. In 1926 it had been extended to two years, with the first devoted to the history of Western civilization. Other schools instituted similar courses in the following years, and its growing popularity was evidenced by the publication of eight Western Civ textbooks prior to the war (1937–1941).[35] Surveys provided the breadth that specialized electives allegedly lacked, but they were often considered too superficial to elicit the deeper learning goals of liberal/general education. The Redbook felt "a general survey is apt to be a dreary and sterile affair, leaving little residue in the minds of students."[36]

The committee termed the teaching of life skills courses a "functional" approach to general education, also called instrumentalist. It sacrificed intellect to unity and practicality. This was the version of general education subsequently advocated by the President's Commission on Higher Education. The Redbook explicitly repudiated the pragmatism of Dewey and William James as present-minded and incapable of appreciating the Western heritage that informed our civilization. Dewey confirmed this dichotomy as late as 1944, equating the liberal arts with an "older literary and metaphysical point of view" that was inappropriate for modern scientific, technological society. The Harvard committee, on the other hand, insisted on interpreting modernism within the context of Western cultural heritage.[37]

At the opposite pole from Dewey, great books had achieved contemporary notoriety when Scott Buchanan and Stringfellow Barr installed a fixed, four-year curriculum entirely based on great books at struggling St. John's College in 1937.

34   Buck et al., *General Education*, 181, 189, 190.

35   Daniel A. Segal, "'Western Civ' and the Staging of History in American Higher Education," *American Historical Review* 105, 3 (June 2000): 770–805, 781n; Gilbert Allardyce, "The Rise and Fall of the Western Civilization Course," *American Historical Review* 87, 3 (June 1982): 695–725.

36   Buck et al., *General Education*, 215.

37   Ibid., 181, 47–51; John Dewey, "The Problem of the Liberal Arts College," *American Scholar* 13, 4 (Autumn 1944): 391–93.

As originally devised at Columbia University by John Erskine, a great books course was intended to provide students "the advantage of knowing the contents of great books and of discussing them intimately" while also "knowing the same books and ... reading them at the same time." The pedagogy was and remained a distinctive feature. For each two-hour class, two instructors led a Socratic dialogue focused on the meaning and appreciation of a single work without regard for historical context or authorial intent. However, the books were inescapably equated with liberal culture, just as Charles Eliot's five-foot shelf of *Harvard Classics* had promised earlier to provide a liberal education. At the University of Chicago, Robert Maynard Hutchins and Mortimer Adler publicized a more dogmatic version of great books, the approach subsequently employed by Buchanan and Barr. By 1940, Hutchins was dismissed by many as attempting to restore a "medieval curriculum," but Erskine's course, revived in 1937 by his successors, Lionel Trilling and Jacques Barzun, became a fixture for its signature contribution to general education at Columbia College.[38]

Finally, "individual guidance" referred to the experimental approaches of Bennington, Sarah Lawrence, and Black Mountain Colleges, which encouraged students to explore and develop their creativity and personal interests—what would later be called the "aesthetic-expressive ideal."[39] Such approaches required close interactions between students and faculty and could only be implemented on a fairly small scale.

Given these examples to avoid, the committee recommended that Harvard College students take six of their sixteen year-long courses in classes specifically designed for general education in the humanities, social sciences, and natural sciences. In the first two, a single specially designed course would be required of all students; in the sciences, students would take either of two new courses, Principles of Physical Science or Principles of Biological Sciences. The required humanities course would adopt an Erskine-like approach of intensive reading to "Great Texts of Literature." It would "allow the work to speak for itself," eschewing matters covered by literary scholarship. Other humanities offerings in general education might draw from literature, philosophy, or the fine arts. Supplemental courses in the sciences had to differ from specialized introductory courses. President Conant later showed the way by teaching The Growth of Experimental Science, first offered in 1947.[40] However, it was the social sci-

38   Katherine E. Chaddock, *The Multi-Talented Mr. Erskine: Shaping Mass Culture through Great Books and Fine Music* (New York: Macmillan, 2012), 81–100, quote p. 87; Alex Beam, *A Great Idea at the Time: The Rise, Fall, and Curious Afterlife of the Great Books* (New York: Public Affairs, 2008).

39   Gerald Grant and David Riesman, *The Perpetual Dream: Reform and Experiment in the American College* (Chicago: University of Chicago Press, 1978), 21–24.

40   Buck et al., *General Education*, 204–30, quotes p. 205; Conant, *My Several Lives*, 372–73.

ence course that embodied the central objectives of *General Education in a Free Society.*

The social science course recommended for all students was Western Thought and Institutions, a selective historical consideration of the Western heritage from the Greeks to the present day. The course would be "not unlike" Contemporary Civilization at Columbia but would cover fewer topics and use longer portions of fewer books. The "primary emphasis in the course should be placed upon the evolution of such institutions as representative government and the reign of law, the impact of the Reformation ... the growth of religious toleration ... natural rights philosophy, the growing confidence in the power of reason ... humanitarianism, the rise of laissez-faire philosophy, etc." In other words, those aspects of the Western heritage that provided the ideological foundation for democratic citizenship. However, the Redbook called for studying these topics "as great expressions of ideas which emanated from certain historical backgrounds." This implied an objective, scholarly consideration of these issues in their historical contexts. The contradiction between abstract ideas and historical circumstance was not appreciated in 1945, but it was latent in Harvard's conception of general education and in the predominant interpretation of Western Civ that swept American higher education.[41]

The Harvard Redbook sold 40,000 copies and was widely read and discussed. It was credited with strongly influencing the postwar curriculum, an influence that was ascribed to the prestige of its source. Both contentions are exaggerations. The popularity of the Redbook was due, above all, to the fact that other institutions of higher education were preoccupied with the same issues: providing college students with a common core of learning and instilling an ideological foundation for democratic citizenship. These concerns dominated discussions of general education emerging from the Depression and war, and they were soon reinforced by the onset of the Cold War. To address them, the Redbook was an indispensable source—intelligent, sophisticated, and nuanced in its treatment but also consistent with the prewar dialogue. Although it stated at one point, "General and liberal education have identical goals," it posited a vision of general education that avoided the exclusive or "aristocratic," connotations of liberal education as well as the anti-intellectual stance of general education functionalists. It embraced the democratic ideals of the country and sought to enhance the educational system as a whole. The specific recommendations for Harvard courses were a different matter. Each institution reevaluated its curriculum in light of existing curricula, faculty resources, and the common aims of general education. The result was different combinations of core or survey courses. Most colleges

41   Buck et al., *General Education,* 213–17.

and universities reduced electives and expanded common learning in some form in the decade following the war.[42]

Harvard itself illustrated the vagaries of this process. After lengthy deliberations, the Faculty of Arts and Science overwhelmingly approved the report. A trial period followed in which general education courses, like Conant's, were developed and debuted. These efforts depended on the initiatives of individual professors and, given the deep talent pool, produced offerings that were novel, cross-disciplinary, and intellectually challenging. However, this meant that gen-ed courses were shaped as much by professorial idiosyncrasies as by the Redbook. The general education requirement was officially adopted in 1950 for the class of '55, but instead of single prescribed courses, freshmen were given a choice of two to four beginning courses in each of the three basic areas, and a larger list of more advanced courses for their other three gen-ed courses. Over time, the number of items on these menus inexorably grew.[43]

The most distinctive contribution of general education to the postwar curriculum was a required course in the history of Western civilization. Introducing students to the heritage of the West, either in something like Western Thought and Institutions or in Western Civ, spoke directly to the aspiration to form citizens of a liberal democracy. Although it had prewar antecedents, the postwar Western Civ survey was specifically tailored for this purpose. The direction of change was typified at Columbia, where historical continuity in the course Contemporary Civilization was deemphasized in favor of reading and discussing original works. At the University of Chicago, Western Civ was added to general education in 1948 despite President Hutchins's dislike of the subject, but only as a succession of historical case studies. Harvard's adaptation was the most complex, while reflecting, at least initially, the spirit of the Redbook. By 1950 it offered four freshman courses (Social Sciences 1–4), each covering Western history from a different perspective and taught, respectively, by a historian, political scientist, economic historian, and sociologist. Social Sciences 1, Introduction to the Development of Western Civilization, provided somewhat more historical context than the others, but it too stressed ideas and institutions rather than events.[44] With this emphasis on the foundational ideas underlying democratic societies,

---

42   Kimball, *Orators and Philosophers*, 233; Alston Chase, "The Rise and Fall of General Education, 1945–1980," *Academic Questions* 6, 2 (Spring 1993): 21–37; Frederick Rudolph, *Curriculum: A History of the American Undergraduate Course of Study Since 1636* (San Francisco: Jossey-Bass, 1977), 258–62.

43   Conant, *My Several Lives*, 370–71; Morton Keller and Phyllis Keller, *Making Harvard Modern: The Rise of America's University* (New York: Oxford University Press, 2001), 44–46. The general education menu grew to such length that it was scrapped in 1966.

44   Allardyce, "Rise and Fall," 712–15; David Owen, "Harvard General Education in Social Science," *Journal of General Education* 5, 1 (October 1950): 17–30.

and sometimes amalgamated with social science, Western Civ quickly became the most widely taught history course in American colleges and was typically required of freshmen. Hailed as general education, it was actually a repudiation of the instrumentalist interpretation championed by Dewey and the President's Commission. Although it provided common learning and was justified with presentist arguments, it was ultimately rooted in the stuff of history that they had disparaged.[45]

Given the impetus of the Redbook and the President's Commission on Higher Education, the years 1945–1950 were the heyday of the general education movement. Institutions of all types began marching under the banner of general education, but they often marched in different directions.[46] Curricular reforms, extending into the 1950s and beyond, tended to establish various forms of structured core curricula. They divided the undergraduate course into lower and upper divisions, created basic colleges to teach broad surveys of humanities, social sciences and natural sciences, and required some version of Western Civ. They sought to ensure that all students would share some common learning, be exposed to broad coverage of the major fields of knowledge, and acquire an intellectual foundation for citizenship.[47] What they did NOT institute was education for life. The Deweyan instrumentalist version of general education was largely moribund after 1950, despite continued advocacy by dedicated followers in lower schools.[48] The reason was inherent in the make-up of colleges and universities: departments of biology, chemistry, economics, English, history ... and zoology did not teach life skills. They were somewhat willing, given the postwar spirit of reform, to direct their intellectual technologies into new configurations of core, survey, or interdisciplinary courses, especially if it justified hiring more faculty. However, the sine qua non of these endeavors was valuing the intellectual substance of these fields. This was increasingly justified under the rubric of liberal education.

45   Cf. Earl J. McGrath et al. *Toward General Education* (New York: Macmillan, 1949). This suggested curriculum consigns pre-modern thought to philosophy, and dismissed "swiftly moving, superficial survey courses, so productive of manifest evil." Beginning with the Renaissance, it held that the purpose of history is to demonstrate "the present is the product of the past": 143–44. McGrath was founding editor of the *Journal of General Education* (see note 29) and a member of the President's Commission.

46   For examples, see Russell Thomas, *The Search for a Common Learning: General Education, 1800–1960* (New York: McGraw-Hill, 1962); and Willis Rudy, *The Evolving Liberal Arts Curriculum: A Historical Review of Basic Themes* (New York: Teachers College, 1960).

47   Chase, "Rise and Fall of General Education"; Rudolph, *Curriculum*, 256–59. Most authors (Allardyce, Chase, Rudolph) are more concerned with the unraveling of these reforms after 1955, a subject for Chapter 2.

48   Miller, *Meaning of General Education*, 139–42; of course, general education never "died": 143–80.

THE COMMISSION ON FINANCING HIGHER EDUCATION. After 1950 the dialogue on higher education reverted toward traditional roles and away from the more idealistic postwar formulations. Concerns for democracy, internationalism, expansion, and general education were still prominent, and programs still initiated to advance these aims; but the influence of the academic mainstream increasingly predominated. This perspective was articulated in 1952 by the Commission on Financing Higher Education (CFHE). The commission dates from November 1947—the month the President's Commission reported—when the Rockefeller Foundation appointed an exploratory committee to consider these issues. The committee expanded to become the commission eighteen months later, organized under the Association of American Universities and funded by the foundation and the Carnegie Corporation. The commission represented the research universities; it included Harvard Provost Paul Buck and the presidents of Johns Hopkins, Caltech, Stanford, and Brown. The commission's large staff documented the realities of American higher education in eight studies and technical papers, which were condensed into *Financing Higher Education in the United States*—a compendium of the state of higher education at the start of the 1950s. This material was then summarized in the commission's report to the public, *Nature and Needs of Higher Education*.[49] These writings referenced the President's Commission (PC) and addressed the same issues, but largely from the perspective of the research universities and the private colleges. The CFHE sought to counter the PC report on issues central to the development of American higher education.

HOW MANY SHOULD GO TO COLLEGE? Intellectual qualification was posited as the primary criterion for college attendance, and here *Financing Higher Education* repeated the critics' objections to the generous PC estimates. The CFHE applied a slightly higher cutoff on the Army intelligence test and concluded that 25 percent of youth were intellectually qualified to attend and complete college. This still left an enormous "education gap": only 40 percent of those students started college, and just 54 percent of them graduated. These figures were derived from empirical studies by the Commission on Human Resources and Advanced Training, which presented a disturbing picture of American education. Just 28 percent of students with the highest 10 percent of test scores were graduating from college; and for the top 2 percent, the figure was 42 percent. At the other end, half of students entering college fell *below* the top quartile, and one-third of those students managed to graduate anyway. The CFHE urged higher

49   Millett, *Financing Higher Education*; Commission on Financing Higher Education (CFHE), *Nature and Needs of Higher Education* (New York: Columbia University Press, 1952).

education to emphasize recruitment of top-quartile students, especially the most intelligent. However, it failed to acknowledge that factors other than intellectual qualification seemed to determine college-going in America. Worse, it asserted,

> Our colleges and universities enroll a wide representation of American youth.... They promote ... the ideal of the classless society and of careers open to talent. Colleges and universities are among the least discriminatory institutions of American society in so far as race, religion, and nationality are concerned.[50]

This Panglossian view from the commission ignored blatant discrimination against African Americans, as well as a more detailed analysis in *Financing*, based on a commission study. A substantial literature documented the influence of social class on educational attainment, which was cited in the commission study by Byron S. Hollinshead, *Who Should Go to College?* Hollinshead called the phrase "equality of educational opportunity ... more demagogic than rational." The CFHE's avoidance of any potentially negative content reflected the new Cold War mentality.[51]

The uncritical views in *Nature and Needs* reflected contemporary thinking about education in American society. Foremost was IQ determinism—the conviction that tested intelligence was the most important criterion for college attendance and for developing the nation's intellectual resources. Social influences, like parental education and socioeconomic status (SES), were relegated to factors of motivation. The lower participation of women (40 percent of enrollments) was also ascribed to motivation. Hence, "motivation is not just the product of environment, of society and culture. The individual has his own choice to make." Supposedly, individual free will determined whether or not an individual chose to go to college, thus justifying the commission's false assertion of "equality of educational opportunity." Its preferred vision: "A basic challenge to higher education and to our whole society is to interest more of the top students in intellectual promise in attending college."[52]

50 Millett, *Financing Higher Education*, 42–57; CFHE, *Nature and Needs*, 45–54, quote 45–46. Dael Wolfle, director of the Commission on Human Resources and Advanced Training, reported findings in several publications: "America's Intellectual Resources," *NAASP Bulletin* 36, 183 (January 1952): 125–35. Wolfle endorsed the PC figure of 33 percent of youth intellectually qualified for college.

51 Byron S. Hollinshead, *Who Should Go to College?* (New York: Columbia University Press, 1952), 74. The mention of race with non-discrimination reveals a perverse, even mendacious blindness to segregation, which had been criticized by the President's Commission. See Chapter 4.

52 Millett, *Financing Higher Education*, 50–54.

Although the recommended 25 percent participation of the CFHE was somewhat below the 32 percent PC figure, its focus solely on that population muffled arguments for expanding higher education. In fact, it hopefully suggested that greater attendance from the top 25 percent might discourage attendance by "many of those who now go, but fall below that general level of intelligence." *Financing* discussed the goals of the PC under "the dangers in mass higher education," especially the lowering of intellectual standards. Junior colleges were disparagingly excluded from consideration as having a largely terminal vocational mission.[53]

PUBLIC AND PRIVATE INSTITUTIONS. The CFHE sought to counter the PC's negative portrayal of the private sector by emphasizing the value of institutional diversity. *Nature and Needs* called diversity the key to freedom: offering students a multitude of choices, enabling the access of large numbers of students, strengthening institutions through competition, and guaranteeing academic freedom. The two sectors exerted mutually beneficial influence upon one another, such that "our society would be impoverished by the decline in vigor of either."[54] The two sectors were roughly equivalent at this time, but the CFHE addressed the implicit threat to private colleges of public expansion.

FEDERAL SUPPORT FOR HIGHER EDUCATION. The CFHE presented a thorough account and analysis of existing forms of federal support for higher education, which included student support not just for veterans but also for ROTC and some medical students; grants and loans for facilities for veterans and medical schools; grants for research and services for federal agencies; and support through land-grant legislation. While acknowledging the benefits derived from these funds, the commission concluded unanimously that no new federal programs of direct financial aid to colleges and universities should be enacted. Federal funds, it argued, inevitably brought greater control (as advocated by the PC), which in turn would stifle diversity, "and the freedom of higher education would be lost." Additional funds were certainly needed to address the financial plight of higher education: the need created by inflation, capital expansion and modernization, and quality upgrades, especially for private institutions. Enrollment growth would also be a factor when the larger birth cohorts began arriving in the next decade. But the CFHE rather optimistically looked to private philanthropy

53   Ibid., quotes pp. 44, 50–51.
54   Ibid., 44–51; CFHE, *Nature and Needs*, 31–42.

(coupled with economy measures) to address the financial needs of mainly private colleges and universities.[55]

DEMOCRACY AND LIBERAL EDUCATION. The CFHE clearly distinguished its position from that of the PC. Intellectual content was the common denominator: "The liberal arts properly conceived and taught ... is the heart of all higher education." The decadence of liberal education in the 1930s gave rise to the ambiguous notion of general education. However, the PC vision of teaching a "common core" for citizenship and democracy would relegate grades 13 and 14 to the status of high school instruction. The CFHE endorsed the Harvard report's curriculum as a preliminary base of common learning, but it idealized a traditional conception of liberal education as a higher form of learning, fundamental to a free society. Individual freedom was the touchstone, best achieved through the "understanding of man's cultural heritage, an appreciation of the great ennobling sentiments and thoughts of philosophers and scholars, [and] a grasp of the ways in which man's knowledge has accumulated and how it advances." The CFHE thus offered a synthesis of general and liberal education that was perhaps superficial in a philosophical sense, but it privileged the liberal learning that liberal arts colleges and universities now embraced for undergraduate education, and it rationalized that position for contemporaries by identifying liberal education, and the institutions that purveyed it, with freedom.[56]

The copious materials gathered by the CFHE documented conditions in American higher education at the beginning of the 1950s, but the commission's message provided another kind of documentation. Funded by two great foundations, organized by the club of research universities, with membership including university and corporate leaders, the commission spoke for the higher education establishment at the onset of the Cold War. The iterations of *free society* and *freedom* in higher education echoed the identification of the United States as leader of the Free World. The Panglossian assumption about equality of educational opportunity reflected a conscious or unconscious absorption of the preferred self-image of American society, and possibly self-censorship against acknowledging social problems even to the extent that the President's Commission had. The focus on traditional undergraduate education in the liberal arts and a tentativeness

55 CFHE, *Nature and Needs*, 58–89, 150–65, quote p. 159; Millett, *Financing Higher Education* contains an exhaustive analysis of costs, income sources, and possibilities for future finances.

56 CFHE, *Nature and Needs*, 16 & passim.; Millett, *Financing Higher Education*, 11–19, 42–47; Richard Hofstadter and C. DeWitt Hardy, *The Development and Scope of Higher Education in the United States* (New York: Columbia University Press, 1952), 207–25 (a publication of the Commission on Financing Higher Education).

toward federally funded research elevated and in a sense rehabilitated the central historical function of American higher education. *Nature and Needs*, in sum, sanctified the status quo. It identified possible threats to this fundamentally sound system but pointed the way for private actors—not the federal government—to meet these challenges and further strengthen this system. The writings of the CFHE thus signify a transition from the tumultuous postwar debates over the roles and direction of American higher education to an emerging consensus on the "American way of life." Thus, they reflected larger developments within the institutions and in American society.

DEFINING POSTWAR AMERICA: THE COLD WAR AND MCCARTHYISM

James Patterson stated that the end of WWII was met with "grand expectations": "Americans, having fought to win the war, expected to dominate the world order to come.... The future promised a great deal more than the past. In this optimistic mood ... Americans plunged hopefully into the new postwar world."[57] It was soon apparent, however, that formidable fault lines crossed these expectations, domestically and internationally. At home, there was the unsettled legacy of the New Deal. The reform momentum of the New Deal had been blocked by Congressional opposition since 1937, but a reinvigorated coalition, inspired by the scope and authority of the government's wartime powers, envisioned new measures to promote social welfare and regulate capitalism. However, Congress was still dominated by conservatives and anti–New Dealers, who looked to private enterprise to maintain the vitality of the wartime economy. Internationally, strong currents of idealism foresaw a peaceful and cooperative international order under the aegis of American power in conjunction with the newly organized United Nations. Against these internationalist aspirations, United States foreign policy resisted concessions on national sovereignty and national interests, focusing instead on countering the threat of Soviet aggrandizement. The left-liberal position in both these spheres was gradually undermined by a growing opposition to communism—to the actions and influence of the domestic Communist Party and to the hostile policies of the Soviet Union. Anti-communism and the Cold War would both have an immediate impact on American universities and their faculty members. Longer term, these developments exerted a pervasive influence on American higher education in the postwar era.

Official intolerance of communists dated from the Red Scare following World War I. In the public mind, communism was *un-American* and scarcely deserving

---

57 Patterson, *Grand Expectations*, 8–9.

of the protection of civil liberties. But zealots carried such fears much further, applying the label to any groups that advocated enhanced government social programs. In 1938 the House of Representatives established the House Un-American Activities Committee (HUAC) under Texas representative Martin Dies. In the political culture of Texas, "New Deal communist" was a single phrase, with "homosexual" often added for greater odiousness.[58] The Dies Committee targeted labor unions and New Deal Democrats and also inspired "little HUACs" in several states, which sometimes targeted higher education.

The purging of communists from American society passed through three phases. The Dies Committee may be said to have inaugurated the first phase, sometimes called the Second Red Scare. It was led by political entrepreneurs who no doubt genuinely despised communism but also harnessed this issue to discredit enemies and advance their own political ends. The second phase followed the Republican landslide in the 1946 elections. The president soon responded to Soviet provocations by announcing the Truman Doctrine, which committed the United States to opposing Soviet expansion and officially signaled the onset of the Cold War. Domestically, loyalty boards were established to purge the federal government of communists and sympathizers. Suspicion of disloyalty on the part of anyone with present or past associations with communism thus became federal policy, replicated (if not anticipated) in a number of states. Senator Joseph McCarthy only entered the lists of the anti-communist crusaders in 1950, touching off the third and most virulent phase. His sensational charges exacerbated the national paranoia and intimidated reasonable opposition until his downfall in 1954.[59]

The first phase corresponded with a growing wave of anti-communism from the end of the Popular Front in 1939 to the wartime alliance with the Soviet Union, when the Communist Party made expediting the war effort its top priority. The Dies Committee issued charges of alleged communists in federal agencies, and in 1940 the Smith Act criminalized membership in any organization that advocated the violent overthrow of the government. In this atmosphere, little HUACs threatened higher education in several states, but the only consequential investigation occurred in New York City. The state legislature empaneled the Rapp-Coudert Committee in 1940, which sought to expose communists in the city's schools. Like future HUACs, it assumed that exposure was sufficiently damning that other entities, in this case the New York City Board of Education,

58   Susan R. Richardson, "Oil, Power, and Universities: Political Struggle and Academic Advancement at the University of Texas and Texas A&M, 1876–1965," PhD diss. Pennsylvania State University, 2005, 149–52.

59   Larry Ceplair, *Anti-Communism in Twentieth-Century America: A Critical History* (Santa Barbara, CA: Praeger, 2011).

would impose appropriate punishments. Active communists were not hard to find in New York City, where at least one-third of party members resided. The committee focused on the College of the City of New York. Using informants to identify party members, it then called them to testify before the committee. In this initial confrontation the accused compounded their peril by denying they were party members. In protracted proceedings, the board of education dealt harshly with confirmed party members: twenty were dismissed and another eleven resigned under pressure (1941–1942). In addition to lying to the committee and the board, the grounds were that party membership was, ipso facto, incompatible with the responsibilities of a faculty member. No attempt was made to show that party membership had a prejudicial effect on their teaching or students.[60]

At the end of the war, the American Communist Party resumed an aggressive posture, and anti-communist fervor was also reenergized. The election of 1946 signaled a tipping point. Dramatic Republican gains were followed by increasing red-baiting, perhaps most fatefully in Richard Nixon's election to Congress (where he joined HUAC). President Truman reacted to charges that he was soft on communists in government by creating Loyalty Review Boards to vet federal employees. These boards performed the most far-reaching and systematic purge of the entire Red Scare: "During the program's peak between 1947 and 1956, more than five million federal workers underwent loyalty screening, and at least 25,000 were subject to the stigmatizing 'full field investigation' by the FBI. An estimated 2,700 federal employees were dismissed, and about 12,000 resigned."[61] With loyalty enforcement now official policy in Washington, anti-communist initiatives were launched throughout the states.

The anti-communist crusade employed three principal tactics—hearings of legislative investigative committees intended to expose former communists or sympathizers, various forms of loyalty oaths, and communist-control laws, including direct prosecution of party leaders under the Smith Act or the more punitive McCarren Act (1950). By the late '40s, forty-two states had imposed some form of oath on employees that required them to attest to their loyalty, their disinclination to forcibly overthrow the government, and/or their non-membership in the Communist Party. Only in California did a loyalty oath disrupt the university; but the little HUACs during this second phase were drawn to investigate higher education.[62]

60   Ellen W. Schrecker, *No Ivory Tower: McCarthyism and the Universities* (New York: Oxford University Press, 1986), 75–83.

61   Landon R. Y. Storrs, *The Second Red Scare and the Unmaking of the New Deal Left* (Princeton: Princeton University Press, 2013), 2.

62   M. J. Heale, *McCarthy's America: Red Scare Politics in State and Nation, 1935–1965* (Athens: University of Georgia Press, 1998).

The first, pattern-setting investigation occurred at the University of Washington. The Canwell Committee was created in 1947 and investigated the university the next year. Eleven faculty members identified as having communist connections were called to testify before the committee. It was left to the university and its new reforming president, Raymond Allen, to deal with the committee's revelations. The university chose to consider actions against six faculty members—three who admitted to having been party members but refused to "name names" of former associates, and three who had refused to cooperate with the committee. These cases were considered by the university in lengthy, judicious proceedings. President Allen made the final decision to dismiss the three noncooperators and to place the three ex-communists on two-year probation. Two dismissed professors were party members, and the third could accurately be described as a fellow traveler (a much-abused term).[63]

When critics charged a violation of academic freedom and civil liberty, Allen justified the dismissals with a paradigmatic argument in the article: "Communists Should Not Teach in American Colleges." Starting with a paean to freedom, "the keystone of … the American way of life," he asserted that "a member of the Communist Party is not a free man." The university is based on the "free and unfettered search for truth," while a party member "must believe and teach what the party line decrees."[64] This last phrase was a quote from Sidney Hook, the foremost spokesman for this position. This issue was vigorously debated in 1949. Accused professors sometimes claimed that they freely accepted communist viewpoints, so that freedom of conscience was the issue at stake. Both the American Civil Liberties Union and the Association of American University Professors (AAUP) held that communists should not automatically be excluded from teaching, but the educational community, including university faculty, overwhelmingly endorsed the Allen-Hook position that they were unfit to teach. The National Education Association (NEA) voted almost unanimously to back this position. Even faculty at leading universities valued anti-communism over civil liberties. In a secret ballot at the University of California (UC) in 1950, the faculty endorsed the prohibition of communists by four to one, and a 1949 poll of Harvard faculty produced a similar result. Only one in seven Washington faculty protested their colleagues' firings.[65]

---

63   Jane Sanders, *The Cold War on Campus: Academic Freedom at the University of Washington, 1946–64* (Seattle: University of Washington Press, 1979); Schrecker, *No Ivory Tower*, 94–104.

64   Raymond B. Allen, "Communists Should Not Teach in American Colleges," *Educational Forum* 13, 4 (May 1949): the last quote is taken from Sidney Hook, the best-known exponent of this view.

65   Schrecker, *No Ivory Tower*, 106–12; Clark Kerr, *The Gold and the Blue: A Personal Memoir of the University of California, 1949–1967; Volume Two, Political Turmoil* (Berkeley: University of California Press, 2003), 42.

Long after the fact, Clark Kerr, who had been a new faculty member at the University of Washington before the war, noted in his memoir that the same three individuals had harassed him for refusing to join "what was obviously a 'front' organization," calling him a "social fascist." When Nazi Germany invaded the Soviet Union, the same individuals switched overnight from isolationists to interventionists: "They saluted Moscow in unison."[66] Of course, some party members were only nominal communists. Later, as chancellor of the Berkeley campus, Kerr quietly obtained the resignations of three such faculty members, as required by university statute. One remained in the party because his wife, a rabid communist, would break up his family if he left. The other two remained out of fear that the party would expose them if they resigned, leading to a HUAC summons. Still, the majority of American faculty sided with Allen in rejecting communists as colleagues.[67]

The Washington cases were regarded as a victory for the anti-communist forces and as a model purge. Although the Canwell hearings had some of the circus features of the big and little HUACs, the university had given the accused extensive due process and reached reasonable judgments—in fact retaining those faculty with past communist associations, alleged or actual.

The legislative committees investigating un-American activities all operated from the same playbook. They made extensive use of the testimonies of informants, often of "professional anti-communists," that were sometimes dubious or fabricated. Behind all these investigations was J. Edgar Hoover's FBI, with voluminous files on memberships, associations, and alleged subversive activities of hundreds of thousands of Americans, as well as often-fanciful lists of "front" organizations. This information allowed the committees to dredge up and confront witnesses with long-past incidents, especially from the Popular Front era, when the Communist Party had been in the forefront of progressive causes.[68] Questioned about actual or alleged party membership, witnesses who admitted past membership were then pressured to identify former associates. With the proceedings so stacked against them, many resorted to the Fifth Amendment protection against self-incrimination as the only means to avoid acquiescing to these vile tactics. The legality of "taking the Fifth" was contested, but in the

66 Kerr, *Gold and the Blue: Volume Two, Political Turmoil*, 40–41.
67 Ibid., 32, 58.
68 Communist Party membership was characterized by rapid turnover, large fluctuations, and uncertain totals. Maximum membership seems to have been about 80,000, which was reached in 1939, 1944, and 1947, with 33–40 percent in New York City: David A. Shannon, *The Decline of American Communism: A History of the Communist Party of the United States since 1945* (Chatham, NJ: Chatham Bookseller, 1959), 91–97; Guenter Lewy, *The Cause That Failed: Communism in American Political Life* (New York: Oxford University Press, 1990), 307–8.

atmosphere of the Red Scare it was considered tantamount to guilt and inevitably required further explanation to employers under threat of dismissal. The investigating committees also frequently issued dubious indictments of unfriendly witnesses for perjury or contempt of Congress.[69] Given the capriciousness and often downright dishonesty of the investigators, these tactics have rightly been regarded as an abomination of American civil liberties. In addition, the un-American activities committees were led by and filled with some of the most benighted and malevolent members of their respective legislatures—from Martin Dies to Joseph McCarthy. All this was true of the California committee headed by Jack Tenney, a loose cannon who indirectly triggered the loyalty oath fiasco at the University of California.

In 1949 Tenney proposed a constitutional amendment that would have given the legislature the authority to ensure the loyalty of UC employees. To preclude such a drastic intrusion, the administration proposed a special loyalty oath for university employees in which they would swear that they were not members of the Communist Party nor held similar views. This occurred despite an existing loyalty oath for all state employees and a policy since 1940 that no communist could be employed by the university. The faculty was deeply offended and expressed increasing frustration. The regents, feeling their authority threatened, finally issued an ultimatum to sign. For the entire 1949–1950 academic year, this controversy nearly paralyzed the university. When it seemed that a compromise had finally been reached, the regents reneged on the understanding and fired the thirty-one remaining nonsigners. Other prominent professors resigned in protest. None of these individuals were suspected of subversive activities, nor was there any other reason for terminating them. The nonsigners in fact were strongly supported by the national academic community. At the time, many thought that this disaster signaled the fall of the UC from its position as the premier American public university.[70]

From 1947 to 1950, HUAC had searched for atomic spies in the Manhattan Project. Although it found none, it compromised a number of academic physicists, particularly those with past radical associations from their Berkeley days. In these cases, the fact of being called to testify before HUAC threatened their careers. Of the more senior scientists, Martin Kamen suffered years of harassment but retained his professorship at Washington University; and Philip Morrison, the only one who continued to publicly espouse radical views, caused consternation

69   In 1956, 40 percent of Supreme Court cases involved communism or subversive activities: Ceplair, *Anti-Communism*, 106–11.

70   David P. Gardner, *The California Oath Controversy* (Berkeley: University of California Press, 1967); Schrecker, *No Ivory Tower*, 117–25; Kerr, *Gold and the Blue: Volume Two, Political Turmoil*, 27–47.

for the Cornell administration but was not fired. However, the nontenured physicists from this group were all dismissed or resigned under pressure from their
academic appointments.[71]

The years 1949 and 1950 registered a peak of anti-communist fears—though
not without reason. Communist forces led by Mao Zedong gained control over
China in 1949, and the Soviets exploded an atomic bomb. Soviet espionage of
atomic "secrets" was exposed, and in January 1950, Alger Hiss was convicted of
perjury for past espionage. In June, North Korea invaded South Korea. In Washington, HUAC and, after 1951, the Senate Internal Security Subcommittee (SISS)
joined Joseph McCarthy in expanding the scope, intensity, and sheer vindictive-
ness of the exposure hearings.

The Institute of Pacific Relations, which had been the locus of most academic
research on the Far East before the war, was initially attacked by McCarthy, but
SISS followed up with a more thorough inquisition. The intent was to discredit
China scholars with accusations of communist ties, thus blaming them for the
communist victory and vindicating U.S. backing for Chiang Kai-shek's Nation-
alists on Taiwan. The Johns Hopkins scholar Owen Lattimore, a wartime liaison
to Chiang and an outspoken postwar critic of the folly of isolating the Chinese
communists, was the principal target. Although no real evidence was adduced,
trumped-up perjury charges were pursued nonetheless. These charges were repeatedly rejected by the courts, but the prolonged badgering made him an academic pariah.[72] SISS next turned to New York City after a key party member
turned informant, permitting a rehash of the Rapp-Coudert hearings. These new
hearings produced a rash of dismissals under a city rule that invoking the Fifth
Amendment against self-incrimination triggered automatic termination of employment. Rutgers University became involved as well, when the board of trustees on its own initiative fired two faculty members for the same reason, including
Moses Finley, a promising young classicist who subsequently had a distinguished
career in England.

These hearings and their repercussions produced a national controversy over
whether taking the Fifth was an admission of guilt and grounds for firing, as
anti-communists insisted, or a constitutional right, all the more needed in light
of the low tactics of the investigating committees. The urgency of this question prompted the Association of American Universities to take a stand. The
association first endorsed the Allen-Hook injunction: "Present membership in

---

71   Schrecker, *No Ivory Tower*, 194–218.
72   Lionel S. Lewis, *The Cold War and Academic Governance: The Lattimore Case at Johns Hopkins*
(Albany: SUNY Press, 1993).

the Communist Party … extinguishes the right to a university position." Then continued,

> Invocation of the Fifth Amendment places upon a professor a heavy burden of proof of his fitness to hold a teaching position and lays upon his university an obligation to reexamine his qualifications for membership in its society.[73]

The deck was stacked against academic witnesses when HUAC turned its full attention to higher education in 1953.

In 1953–1954 some 150 faculty were interrogated by congressional investigating committees. By now the formula was set. Outcomes were determined by two factors: cooperating or not with the committees and, if not, explaining that noncooperation to their universities. According to Ellen Schrecker, the historian of academic McCarthyism, the largest number of academic witnesses, most of whom had formerly been party members, resisted the committees by invoking the Fifth but then cooperated with university investigators in explaining their actions. Some of this group still lost their positions, but all those who refused to cooperate with both inquiries were fired. All told, Schrecker reports that thirty faculty were dismissed as a result of these hearings alone. During the McCarthy years (1950–1954) the total probably exceeded 100. Few tenured professors at research universities were fired. The strongest private universities, in particular, went to considerable lengths to avoid terminating established professors, sometimes placing them on leave for years. Decisions elsewhere could be more capricious. A survey of social science faculty conducted in the spring of 1955 indicated large numbers of terminations for political reasons unrelated to the congressional hearings. Faculty also reported intrusions by anti-communist zealots into classroom instruction—reading assignments and class discussions—that were egregious violations of academic freedom.[74]

Those who retained their positions, like Lattimore, often paid a heavy price in terms of personal stigma, delayed promotions, and prolonged legal battles. Beyond this population, a much larger number of instructors, graduate assistants, and other fixed-term employees were fired or (more often) not reappointed due to radical views or communist associations. Given the pressures that institutions already had to bear, they were unwilling to risk further embarrassment

---

73 Ibid., 161–93, quotes pp. 188, 189.
74 Paul Lazersfeld and Wagner Thielens, Jr., *The Academic Mind* (Glencoe, IL: Free Press, 1958), 57, 70, 251n, et passim.

from employing such marked individuals, essentially creating an unofficial blacklist.[75]

Historians of academic McCarthyism have placed considerable blame for these outcomes on colleges and universities. Lionel Lewis, who studied 126 cases of accused faculty, concluded that "academic administrators were the creators of the Cold War on campus.... Those responsible for the integrity of academic institutions buckled under, appeased, or bowed to what they believed was the *vox populi*." Since none of the accused were found guilty of any subversive activity, they were judged more "by what they were presumably thinking (or what they may have at one time thought) or by their associations than by their actions."[76] Schrecker charged the entire academic community with contributing to McCarthyism. She lamented that the accused received little support from their faculty colleagues. American faculty on the whole shared the country's aversion to and fear of communism, agreeing that party members should not be hired as teachers and distrusting those who shielded past activities with the Fifth Amendment. But legitimate fears of retaliation for any indication of sympathy for alleged communists was also a factor.

Perhaps the most egregious shortcoming of the academic community was the reluctance of the AAUP to offer any resistance to the assault on academic freedom. The association was asked to investigate the Washington firings, the California Oath dismissals, and other cases, but the general secretary was afraid that criticizing anti-communist measures would taint the organization. "If the Association should get a left-wing or pro-communist tag," he wrote privately, "this would certainly end the effectiveness of the Association." Exhibiting the same intimidation as other institutions at the height of McCarthyism, the AAUP (and Lionel Lewis's administrators) chose to protect the franchise rather than individuals. Beginning in 1955, as hysteria waned, a new general secretary proceeded to complete and publish numerous reports, but these findings concentrated on procedures rather than on substance—whether or not fired faculty had received due process. On this basis, it censured Jefferson Medical College, Ohio State, Rutgers, Oklahoma, and Temple in 1956, and later California, NYU, and Michigan. Besides being years late, these censures had no impact and were soon rescinded.[77]

Schrecker and Lewis held their historical subjects to a contemporary standard of academic freedom. Indeed, any university that treated faculty today as they did during the McCarthy years would incur more public opprobrium for

---

75 Schrecker, *No Ivory Tower*, 194–282.

76 Lionel S. Lewis, *Cold War on Campus: A Study of the Politics of Organizational Control* (New Brunswick, NJ: Transaction Books, 1988), 270–71.

77 Schrecker, *No Ivory Tower*, 308–41, quote p. 328.

violating academic freedom than those institutions would have for harboring communists. Conditions were different in the postwar years. The AAUP guidelines on tenure, or what was then more often called "continuing appointment," were scarcely a decade old. The individuals in question had belonged to or been associated with a secret organization directed by our avowed Cold War enemy. The individuals may have been harmless, blameless social progressives, as Schrecker and Lewis alleged, but it was not unreasonable for their universities to demand a full and sincere explanation of the circumstances of their past association with the Communist Party and how that related to their present politics.[78] To point this out in no way excuses the abhorrent nature and tactics of the investigating committees but instead places the failures of higher education in context. Most of the accused received extensive due process (although they were often fired anyway), and some of the exceptions are alluded to above. In the final analysis, higher education endured nearly a decade of perfervid anti-communist hysteria *with relatively few direct casualties*. Rather, higher education and American society suffered far greater harm from the intimidation generated by the anti-communist crusade.

One objective of the anti-communist crusade from the outset was to discredit the New Deal and liberalism in general. This connection was somewhat plausible during the Popular Front years, when the CP joined with liberals to oppose fascism and also to advance progressive social causes. The postwar era began with a conservative offensive against any recrudescence of the New Deal, against the demands of the labor movement, and against government regulation of the economy. All of this became melded with a renewed crusade against communism. Liberals found themselves subject to red-baiting for espousing any causes that had also been backed by communists. Communists muddied these waters by cynically advocating popular liberal causes, especially through front organizations, stretching back to the 1930s. Thus, liberals became vulnerable to attacks—for advocating civil rights for Negroes, for defending the labor movement, for favoring international cooperation, for seeking to expand social programs, or especially for criticizing the investigating committees. Perhaps the most insidious label was to be called "pink," a charge freely applied that was at once so vague and comprehensive as to be beyond refutation. In defense, liberals strenuously resisted any linkage with communists. In 1947 Americans for Democratic Action was organized to speak for anti-communist liberalism, and in 1948 liberals mobilized to oppose Henry Wallace's presidential bid under the communist-dominated Progressive Party. However, neither the creation of Cold War liberalism nor the staunchly anti-communist policies of President Truman were a

---

78 Cf. Nathan Glazer, "The Professors and the Party," *New Republic* (October 6, 1986), 39–42.

shield against the relentless and irresponsible red-baiting during the height of McCarthyism.

As a result, entire areas of discourse were effectively withdrawn from public discussion, in popular media as well as the academy. In universities, "whole lines of inquiry simply disappeared.... College teachers embraced a cautious impartiality that in reality supported the status quo."[79] A 1955 survey found 46 percent of social scientists to be "apprehensive" (i.e., scared): 25 percent admitted to imposing some form of self-censorship, and Democrats were affected far more than Republicans.[80] Paradoxically, in the case of repression, "the measure of its effectiveness is the scarcity of overt instances." Social science scholarship gravitated toward theoretical themes that vaguely or implicitly validated the status quo, and it largely neglected topics that reflected criticism of American society, past or present.[81]

Thus, the anti-communist crusade was essentially successful. "If nothing else," Schrecker concluded, "McCarthyism destroyed the left." In crushing the Communist Party it also "wiped out the institutional and ideological infrastructure of the old left."[82] McCarthyism, per se, was also dealt a blow in 1954, when the senator was censured by his colleagues and removed from the chairmanship of his subcommittee. But HUAC (and some little HUACs) soldiered on for the remainder of the decade and beyond, holding hearings and citing witnesses for contempt. But there was little left to investigate. The passing of Senator Joe mitigated the pall of intimidation that his fanciful charges had created. And beginning in 1955, a more liberal Supreme Court began to disarm the weaponry of the investigative committees. Interpretation of the Fifth Amendment was strengthened, invalidating, for example, New York City's automatic termination law. The huge backlog of perjury and contempt cases was slowly rejected or abandoned. But public opinion barely changed. The entire anti-communist crusade had been led and conducted by political elites. It succeeded in instilling in the American public an unwarranted fear of domestic communist "subversion." A public consensus instinctively rejected communism and all it stood for, but this was scarcely the chief concern. Americans overwhelmingly embraced cultural values associated with the American way of life.

79 Ellen Schrecker, *Many Are the Crimes: McCarthyism in America* (Princeton: Princeton University Press, 1998), 404.

80 Lazersfeld and Thielens, *Academic Mind*, 85, 156.

81 Peter Novick, *That Noble Dream: The "Objectivity" Question and the American Historical Profession* (New York: Cambridge University Press, 1988), 325–32: e.g., Novick identifies the dominant tendency in postwar American historical writing as "counterprogressive" (325).

82 Schrecker, *Many Are the Crimes*, 369, 413.

★ 2 ★

HIGHER EDUCATION AND THE AMERICAN WAY OF LIFE IN THE CONSERVATIVE 1950s

BY 1950, THE POLITICAL TURMOIL AND INTENSE POLARIZATION of the immediate postwar years were evolving into a powerful consensus over the ascendant values of democracy and freedom. Writers on the left and right emphasized that the United States was defined by a unifying idea: "The American character was spoken of interchangeably with the American mind, the American Spirit, the American tradition, the American creed, the American Civilization ... or the American way of life."[1] Similarly, in higher education, the divergent prescriptions of the 1940s coalesced into a loose consensus over the content and organization of collegiate education, articulated from one perspective by the Commission on Financing Higher Education. In the 1950s, the American way of life became a pervasive cultural framework for American society, a *mentalité*, and higher education became part of the culture in ways that it had never been before.[2]

The idea that the United States embodied a unique expression of democracy and freedom emerged with some urgency in the years preceding the war, when the world appeared to be dividing between communism and fascism. These themes were elaborated extensively during the war. However, unlike the crude "100 percent Americanism" promoted during World War I, scholars and intellectuals produced a stream of wartime publications depicting a more reasoned interpretation of democracy and the American spirit.[3] Far from bringing a fulfillment of these idealistic expectations, victory in 1945 soon brought frustration and disillusionment. Hopes for a new era of world peace were dashed by the

---

1 Philip Gleason, "World War II and the Development of American Studies," *American Quarterly* 36, 3 (1984): 343–58, quote p. 358; Wendy L. Wall, *Inventing the "American Way": The Politics of Consensus from the New Deal to the Civil Rights Movement* (New York: Oxford University Press, 2008).

2 Mentalité: Ensemble des manières habituelles de penser et de croire et des dispositions psychiques et morales caractéristiques d'une collectivité et communes à chacun de ses membres: http://www.cnrtl.fr/lexicographie/mentalit%C3%A9.

3 Gleason, "World War II"; Wall, *Inventing the "American Way,"* Part II.

confrontations of the Cold War and unrest around the globe. Domestically, a striking lack of unity was manifest in the nation's worst wave of strikes, political polarization in Washington, and a growing fear of communism. As late as 1948, Arthur Schlesinger, Jr., in search of a liberal "vital center," could characterize the epoch as "a time of troubles, an age of anxiety."[4] Working through these fundamental issues dominated political conflict in the late 1940s, but after 1950 differences over long-standing public issues were increasingly subordinated to agreement about a transcendent idea of America.

The direction of events in the late 1940s was anything but clear to contemporaries, and those events have been variously interpreted by scholars ever since. However, the consensus on the American way of life was underpinned by several developments. First was the Cold War. Despite the initial appeal of internationalism, the American public soon supported American resistance to communist expansion. Certainly by 1950, after the imposition of Stalinism across Eastern Europe, the Berlin blockade, the victory of the Chinese Communists, and the invasion of South Korea, few doubted that the United States needed to forcefully oppose the policies and aims of communist regimes.

The political mainstream strengthened as heterodox postwar factions were increasingly excluded. Lingering wishes to extend New Deal types of federal intervention in the economy found little support, but neither was much of the 1930s legislation rolled back. New Dealers gradually abandoned federal agencies even as their legacy remained. Liberals found it necessary to redefine their philosophy and reform goals but particularly to make a clear and definitive break with those positions advocated by the Communist Party. The new identity of "cold-war liberal" emerged, one who emphasized individual liberties, was staunchly anti-communist, and accepted the inevitability of American capitalism. Labor peace was achieved, though not without difficulty, as communist influences were largely expunged from trade unions and as the United Auto Workers under Walter Reuther led the general acceptance of collective bargaining and union contracts.[5] Finally, proponents of international cooperation (as echoed by the President's Commission on Higher Education) were discredited by Henry Wallace's 1948 Progressive Party presidential campaign, even as the Cold War was intensifying. The emerging "vital center" was more conservative than Schlesinger had envisioned in 1948. There was still great scope for disagreement in American

---

4   Arthur M. Schlesinger, Jr., *The Vital Center: The Politics of Freedom* (Boston: Houghton Mifflin, 1949), 1.

5   For the often bitter conflict generated by this process, see Nelson Lichtenstein, "From Corporatism to Collective Bargaining: Organized Labor and the Eclipse of Social Democracy in the Postwar Era," in Steve Fraser and Gary Gerstle, eds., *The Rise and Fall of the New Deal Order, 1930–1980* (Princeton: Princeton University Press, 1989), 122–52.

political life, but all major factions could agree on upholding the American way of life.[6]

These developments were all associated with the growing opposition to domestic communism. Indeed, the purge of leftists and former communists discussed in Chapter 1 reinforced consolidation in the political arena. The visceral rejection of communism by the American public conjured up an enemy who could be contrasted with the American way. This popular fear of communism, at home and abroad, peaked around 1950 with the outbreak of the Korean War, but that was only the beginning of McCarthyism. The subsequent four years of heightened paranoia served to further this Manichean view, conjuring imaginary dangers of communist subversion countered by virtues of the American way. Criticism of the real shortcomings of American society was largely silenced.

Finally, and most powerfully, the postwar reality that most affected the large majority of Americans was burgeoning economic prosperity.[7] This too evolved despite immediate postwar shortages, inflation, and intermittent slowdowns. By 1950, Americans were far more prosperous than ever before. And this prosperity was cumulative—increasing at a faster rate in the 1950s, and more so in the 1960s. The historian Alan Brinkley calls these developments "quite simply, the greatest and most dramatic capitalist expansion in American history."[8] Average Americans, especially those connected with the industrial economy, enjoyed a cornucopia of increasingly abundant and affordable material goods. For them, the goodness of the American way of life was manifest in their everyday experience, in the tangible improvement in their standard of living.

During the 1950s, higher education too became an integral component of the American way of life, as the remainder of this chapter will explicate. Colleges and universities expanded in enrollments, faculty, and infrastructure. After 1950, as the GIs graduated, rising participation rates soon supplied new students to replace them. As greater numbers of Americans acquired a middle-class life style, their children attended college in increasing numbers, even before the baby-boom generation reached college in the early 1960s. This was primarily a social demand—an explicit or implicit urge for social betterment that reflected

6   Alonzo L. Hamby, "The Vital Center, the Fair Deal, and the Quest for a Liberal Political Economy," *American Historical Review* 77, 3 (June 1972): 653–78: "The conception of liberalism as a sort of centrism had its liabilities.... It was but a short step from the vital center to the superficialities of the 'New Conservatism' of the 1950s" (657). "The Fair Deal attempted to adapt liberalism to the new conditions.... The political strategy, ambitious but unrealistic, collapsed under the weight of the Korean War" (678).

7   Robert J. Gordon, *The Rise and Fall of American Growth: The U.S. Standard of Living since the Civil War* (Princeton: Princeton University Press, 2016).

8   Alan Brinkley, "The Illusion of Unity in Cold War Culture," in Peter J. Kuznick and James Gilbert, eds., *Rethinking Cold War Culture* (Washington, DC: Smithsonian Institution Press, 2001), 61–73, quote p. 63.

the prosperity of American society—rather than purely economic incentives. In fact, given the booming demand for industrial labor, the wage premium—the difference in earnings of college versus high school graduates—in 1950 was the lowest in the century, and in 1960 it was barely higher.[9]

The consensus on the American way of life defined the "conservative 1950s." It provided an implicit cultural framework through which most Americans interpreted home life, personal relations, daily news, and national issues. Contemporary surveys found "the forces favoring conformity are exceptionally great." There was a "general cultural denial of [the existence of] social classes and [a] cultural ideology of individualized social achievement." In a remarkable mood of social optimism, some "90% reported ... that they believed their children had as good a chance to rise in the world as anybody else."[10] It also validated the role and aspirations of the higher education community. However, to place this era in perspective several caveats should be borne in mind.

The real prosperity of the 1950s brought comfortable life styles, conservative outlooks, complacency, and an overwhelming embrace of traditional family values. This era registered the highest rate of marriage, lowest rate of divorce, and highest fertility rate. It also registered the highest rate of church membership, if not necessarily piety. To one skeptical observer, "The American Way of Life, not Christianity, was the real religion of the country." Religion for the typical American "is something that reassures him about the essential rightness of everything American, his nation, his culture, and himself."[11]

But not everyone enjoyed the benefits of the American way of life. The continuation of rigid segregation throughout the South made a mockery of the clichés about democracy and freedom. Blatant racial discrimination in the North was virtually ignored, being rarely mentioned. Some 30 percent of Americans were poor in 1950, especially in rural areas and inner cities, and although that proportion would decline for the next two decades, a substantial population failed to enjoy the good life and found little succor from the meager provision of welfare services.

Finally, the glorification of the American way of life promoted a kind of national hubris. This was evident in a foreign policy predicated on leadership of the "free world," and in the self-righteousness of Cold War policies. Actual American

9 Claudia Goldin and Robert A. Margo, "The Great Compression: The Wage Structure in the United States at Mid-Century," NBER Working Paper No. 3817 (August 1991).

10 Walter Goldschmidt, "Social Class in America—A Critical Review," *American Anthropologist* 52, 4 (October–December 1950): 483–98.

11 James T. Patterson, *Grand Expectations: The United States, 1945–1974* (New York: Oxford University Press, 1996), 61–81; William L. O'Neill, *American High: The Years of Confidence, 1945–1960* (New York: Free Press, 1986), quote p. 213.

policies scarcely promoted democracy or freedom (although they compared favorably with those of the Soviets). Domestically, the sacred status of such empty phrases precluded honest appraisal of the realities of American society. Only with the 1960s would critical perspectives begin to question the hypocrisy and delusions that accompanied the celebration of the American way of life from roughly 1950 to 1965.

WHO SHOULD GO TO COLLEGE?

The issue of expanding higher education had been raised in unavoidable fashion by the President's Commission. Although its rationale for expansion was subsequently ignored, the tacit expectation endured that more Americans would seek and require accommodation in colleges and universities. Opinion split, however, between those who would simply enlarge existing institutions and more conservative spokespersons who sought growth through differentiation, namely by diverting large numbers to junior colleges. Thus, expansion also involved the curriculum, specifically the assumed dichotomy between liberal arts and sciences for the academically well prepared and terminal two-year programs for the masses.

The rising expectations for college-going stimulated scholarly interest in who attended college and why they did so. Initial data gathered on these questions immediately showed the naïveté of the IQ determinism of both the President's Commission and its critics. Academic ability as measured by the AGCT (Army General Classification Test) scale correlated fairly well with the percentages who graduated from high school, went to college, or graduated from college. But the idea of reserving higher education for the top 25 or 32 percent was chimerical. One-fifth of that group did not graduate from high school, and only one-half of the rest went to college—40 percent. The odds of attending college were determined far more by social and cultural factors. A 1949 study found that 60 percent of high school graduates from the highest income quintile applied immediately to college versus 20 percent from the lowest two quintiles. Students from wealthy families (>$9,000) in the lower half of their graduating class were more likely to attend than poorer students (<$5,000) in the top quarter. But American education was not a caste system. Blue-collar workers and farmers, comprising almost two-thirds of families, produced 39 percent of the college graduates. Moreover, except for farmers, once a student enrolled in college, the chances of graduation were nearly the same regardless of the father's occupation.[12]

12 With an average AGCT score of 100 for the total population, high school graduates averaged 110; college entrants, 115; and college graduates, 121: Dael Wolfle, *America's Resources of Specialized Talent*

Nonetheless, enrollments in higher education were heavily determined by the interaction of academic ability and family background. The effects of social, cultural, and family influences imbued an orientation toward college well before high school graduation. Contemporary observers subsumed these factors under "motivation," as seen in Chapter 1. Indeed, such differences were stark in the 1940s, when large numbers of working-class youth entered the workforce before or upon finishing high school. Factors linked with college-going were evident to contemporaries. Educated parents who encouraged achievement in school and had books in their homes clearly enhanced motivation. Other factors included the geography of college attendance, which varied from 30 percent in Utah to 10 percent in the Southeast. Attendance also varied by ethnic background. These effects reflected socioeconomic circumstances that helped determine social demand, although the substandard schooling received by most African Americans was a special case and clearly depressed participation. Other factors had some independent effects: financial considerations mattered when the cost of residential attendance was beyond the means of most Americans; and propinquity, or the availability of socially amenable local institutions, played a significant role. In the most careful analysis, Dael Wolfle projected the number of college graduates out to 1970. However, actual bachelor's degrees in 1961 were 12 percent higher than his estimate; in 1970, 34 percent more.[13] American higher education proved more expansive than expected.

Fundamentally, the growing prosperity of American society boosted social demand for higher education. Whereas an estimated 17 percent of families had sufficient incomes to afford a residential college education for a child in 1940, a decade later 30 percent did, and this figure continued to rise. Such estimates assumed residential education as the norm, but less expensive opportunities for commuters were increasing. Contemporary studies in the late 1940s nonetheless suggested that social circumstances outweighed financial ones. The middle class, estimated to constitute 40 percent of the population, believed in "the individual's responsibility for his own status" and was driven "to the greatest exertions of effort."[14] Its numbers grew in the 1950s from the increase in white-collar occupations and the burgeoning suburbs. By 1956, white-collar workers outnumbered blue-collars for the first time, and 60 percent of Americans achieved what the government defined as a middle-class standard of living.[15] For middle-class Amer-

(New York: Harper & Brothers, 1954), 146–62; Byron S. Hollinshead, *Who Should Go to College* (New York: Columbia University Press, 1952), 28–41.

13   Wolfle, *America's Resources*, 292–93; Hollinshead, *Who Should Go to College*.

14   Goldschmidt, "Social Class in America," 494.

15   Brinkley, "Illusion of Unity," 66.

icans, new or old, nothing exemplified the American way of life better than sending sons and daughters to college.

Total enrollments in higher education declined only slightly after the veterans graduated and by 1954 surpassed the 1949 peak. Enrollment rates that had
been distorted by the veterans rose rapidly from the early 1950s. Already near
25 percent of the eighteen- to twenty-one-year-olds—the target set by the Commission on the Financing of Higher Education—they reached 31 percent by
1959. Several features of the enrollment growth of the 1950s stand out. In keeping with the trends of an emerging middle class and a high proportion of first-
generation students, this expansion was largely local. At the beginning of the
decade, 96 percent of public and 80 percent of private students attended in-state
institutions, and throughout the decade that figure remained above 90 percent
for public institutions and fell significantly only for the most prestigious private
colleges. New students chose predominantly public institutions. Public and private enrollments were comparable during the GI boom (50:50 in 1950), but the
public share rose to 59 percent by the end of the 1950s. And enrollees were predominantly male: men were 64 percent of students in 1953, and for the rest of
the decade their enrollments increased by 700,000 (64 percent) compared with
400,000 additional women.[16]

Women of the 1950s largely acquiesced in the domestic roles of housewives
and mothers, to the consternation of latter-day feminists. Their putative destinies in the American way of life clearly depressed their level of enrollment, rate
of completion, and choice of curricula. To the historian Paula Fass, this situation
presented a "female paradox: the fact that women were receiving more education
than they seemed to need." This paradox generated an ongoing controversy over
whether a female curriculum should be offered to prepare women for their future domestic roles, or if the liberal arts provided a more general and superior
foundation. Looking backward in 1963, Betty Friedan in *The Feminine Mystique*
excoriated her 1950s contemporaries at elite women's colleges for abandoning
serious studies in favor of social grooming for future family lives.[17]

Seen through the cold lens of demography, collegiate women from 1945 to
the early 1960s were a distinctive generation. Like noncollege women, they married at the highest rate for the twentieth century, married earlier, and had more
children—even while increasing enrollments. Not only were they likely to meet

16 National Council for Education Statistics (NCES), *Digest of Education Statistics: 1967* and *1975*;
Caroline M. Hoxby, "How the Market Structure of U.S. Higher Education Explains College Tuition,"
NBER Working Paper No. 6323 (December 1997), Table 1a.

17 Paula S. Fass, *Outside In: Minorities and the Transformation of American Education* (New York:
Oxford University Press, 1989), 156–88, quote p. 157; Betty Friedan, *The Feminine Mystique* (New York: Norton, 1997 [1963]), 227–38.

their husbands in college, one-half married before or during their graduation year. Marriage took precedence over careers for these cohorts. The median college woman married a college graduate, worked for four years (usually teaching), exited the labor market for eight years to raise her children, and then again entered the workforce—most likely for a job rather than a career. Given the lower pay and interrupted employment, the rate of return on their college investment averaged 5–6 percent compared with better than 10 percent for males. But women doubled their total return in the marriage market, enhancing income by another 5 percent by marrying a college graduate—and the earlier the better, since those marrying during or shortly after college snagged higher-earning spouses.[18]

The pattern of college-marriage-employment was evident to contemporaries. Female participation in the workforce continued to rise in the postwar years and soon affected thinking about collegiate education. Rather than being exclusively homemakers, educated women could be expected to work outside the home at various stages of their lives. At first, official commissions acknowledged this trend by praising the valuable contributions working women made to the economy, but they always added the qualification that "the lives of most women are fundamentally determined by their functions as wives, mothers, and homemakers." This cultural presupposition conditioned official positions about women's education. The Commission on the Education of Women of the American Council on Education advanced the discussion somewhat by suggesting that women passed through different "life phases." This approach implied not only that women should acquire a solid educational foundation but that continuing education programs could facilitate such transitions. However, the life-cycle model was also used to buttress the growing consensus that a liberal education was the most effective preparation for the several phases of a woman's life. Thus, liberal education was linked "to the traditional female concern for family life and community service."[19]

On actual college and university campuses, evidence was lacking to support such views. The vast majority of women showed little interest in preparing for the phases of their future lives, nor did they find much inspiration in liberal arts courses. Their chief preoccupation in the 1950s was finding a marriage partner before they graduated—"a ring by the spring." Institutions, for their part, rationalized the efficacy of the liberal arts throughout the postwar era, perhaps because it was the subject matter they were best suited to teach. The disconnect

18   Claudia Goldin, "The Meaning of College in the Lives of American Women: The Past One-Hundred Years," NBER Working Paper No. 4099 (June 1992).

19   Linda Eisenmann, *Higher Education for Women in Postwar America, 1945–1965* (Baltimore: Johns Hopkins University Press, 2006), 19–28, 96–106, quote p. 24; Fass, *Outside In*, 170–73.

between these two viewpoints was obvious in surveys of coed opinion. But Fass noted a deeper dysfunction:

> A liberal-arts program for women ... allowed women to invest all their eager expectations in marriage because their studies, good in themselves, bore no clear fruit in long-term preparation.... Without the immediate prospect of marriage, the liberal-arts degree in itself directed women after college only to their traditional outlets—teaching or the typewriter.[20]

The powerful orientation toward marriage and family clearly overshadowed the restricted employment opportunities for this generation of college women. This pattern, as did the pattern of enrollments, remained largely unchallenged until Friedan issued her clarion protest in 1963. From the 1950s through the early 1960s, two women enrolled in college for every three males, which testified to the stability of cultural values regarding college-going. Only with the arrival of the baby-boom generation in the mid-1960s would the ratio of women students slowly begin to rise.[21]

In other respects, the 1950s saw the onset of significant demographic changes in enrollment patterns. In the last half of the decade, eighteen-year-olds graduating from high schools rose from 63 to 70 percent; total graduates increased from 1.4 million to 1.7 million; more students achieved high test scores and more went to college. The latter developments inaugurated a process that the economist Caroline M. Hoxby has termed the "re-sorting" of American higher education.[22] Basically, higher education shifted at the margins from predominantly local to more national patterns of attendance. Stronger students, in particular, broadened their horizons to attend higher-quality, selective colleges at greater distances. This enhanced mobility in the market for higher education was facilitated not only by improvements in transportation and communication but also by increased information about the nature and quality of colleges and their students. The latter came from widespread adoption and publication of results of the Scholastic Aptitude Test (SAT) and the National Merit Scholarship Examinations (1957–), as well as the appearance of college guidebooks. However, the key factors were the increasing population of high-ability students and the impact they brought to selective institutions.

---

20   Fass, *Outside In*, 187. A "Vassar study, like that at Berkeley, reinforced the image of marriage-hungry undergraduate women": 177.

21   The ratio of first-time female degree enrollments was 38 percent in the mid-1950s and 42 percent in 1963—and 48 percent in 1975: NCES, *Digest of Education Statistics: 1980*, Table 82.

22   Caroline M. Hoxby, "The Changing Selectivity of American Colleges," NBER Working Paper No. 15446 (October 2009).

The inadequacies of American schools were the target of innumerable publications from the early 1950s. Clearly some school districts responded with such innovations as college prep tracks in high schools and special programs for talented and gifted students, as well as a general upgrading of curricula.[23] An increased emphasis on college-going, possibly stimulated by the example of the GI Bill, was also evident. These efforts were redoubled after the panic over the Soviet launch of Sputnik in 1957. Although diffuse, such measures had an apparent impact, especially on students with the highest tested abilities. At the beginning of the decade just 60 percent of the top 2 percent entered college (and only 70 percent of them graduated), but at the end of the 1950s, 96 percent of National Merit finalists and semifinalists (roughly the top 2 percent) attended.[24] Although previous college attendance had been determined by family income far more than academic ability, the 1950s witnessed an upsurge in the attendance by the top-quartile students, with students in the top decile of ability reaching saturation levels.[25] Thus, American schools became more effective in channeling intelligent students toward college, and selective colleges unexpectedly found themselves with growing numbers of highly qualified applicants. Colleges, for their part, furthered this process by extending admissions recruitment geographically.

Hoxby presents a theoretical model of colleges' response. High ability students gravitated toward higher quality institutions, that is, those with greater resources. Improvements in student body quality translated to rising prestige, which in turn attracted additional resources. In addition, better students were themselves an important input to quality through peer effects, advancing the effectiveness of the institution further. In other words, wealthier institutions were able to become more selective and better resourced while, conversely, the average ability levels of students at weaker institutions tended to decline. Hoxby's empirical data showed that this is precisely what occurred: the process of re-sorting produced a gradual divergence between stronger and weaker colleges and universities. This process began in the mid-fifties and accelerated through the 1960s. After a hiatus in the 1970s, this trend predominated after 1980 (Chapter 7).[26]

23   Patricia Albjerg Graham, *Schooling in America: How the Public Schools Meet the Nation's Changing Needs* (New York: Oxford University Press, 2005), 103–24.

24   Seymour E. Harris, *A Statistical Portrait of Higher Education* (New York: McGraw-Hill, 1972), 50–52.

25   Paul Taubman and Terence Wales, *Mental Ability and Higher Educational Attainment in the 20th Century*, National Bureau of Economic Research, Occasional Paper 118 (Carnegie Commission on Higher Education Technical Report, 1972).

26   Robert J. Havighurst identified these forces to be creating a "bimodal" distribution between high-status and low-status institutions in 1960: *American Higher Education in the 1960s* (Columbus: Ohio State University Press, 1960).

In actuality, this path of development presented colleges with a succession of organizational choices. Public universities expanded as they accepted increasing numbers of qualified students, and eventually those institutions tended to raise minimum requirements. Private institutions had to decide how to allocate their limited places. Hence, re-sorting had the greatest impact on private colleges and universities. Liberal arts colleges, post-GIs, almost all sought to return to prewar dimensions and campus traditions. By the late 1950s, however, they reacted to the surge in applicants by raising the bar for admissions. Typically, this meant eliminating what had been the bottom fraction of a class. Academic advancement for most required increased scale, which became feasible with more well-qualified applicants. Small colleges (ca. 500 in 1955) grew the most, more than doubling by 1970; mid-sized colleges (1,000+) tended to expand by about 50 percent; and large colleges (2,000) added around 25 percent. Initially, the first new buildings were usually dormitories. A surfeit of applicants also allowed private colleges to raise tuition, slowly to begin with and aggressively from the late 1950s. Inevitably, the growing applicant pool raised issues of whom to admit—a clash of academic and collegiate values. These decisions were more difficult than Hoxby's scheme would imply. According to one admissions officer, "Colleges are fighting harder than ever, with no holds barred for top candidates."[27] But these were not necessarily the smartest.

THE EXPANSION OF PUBLIC HIGHER EDUCATION

In 1951, enrollments in public and private institutions of higher education were virtually equal at just over 1 million students. A decade later, before the arrival of the baby boom, the public sector had added an additional 1.3 million and the private sector less than one-half million. When the baby-boom generation arrived, enrollments in the public sector more than doubled from 1962 to 1969, adding 2.8 million students versus 470,000 in private institutions. Thus, the great postwar expansion of American higher education took place largely in the public sector, but in two stages. During the first—between the GIs and the baby boomers—growth occurred largely within gradually changing institutional types, with increasing tension between traditional practices and the attempted adaptations. During the second stage, the pace of change was almost breathtaking, as the balance of enrollments shifted toward new and transformed institutions. These dramatic changes, the subject of Chapter 4, tend to obscure the more measured

27   Elizabeth A. Duffy and Idana Goldberg, *Crafting a Class: College Admissions and Financial Aid, 1955–1994* (Princeton: Princeton University Press, 1998), 4–15, 35–37.

evolutionary developments of the 1950s; but the latter formed the bridge from the traditional institutions that emerged from World War II to the new configurations of American higher education in the 1960s.

The description of the organization of American higher education compiled by the Commission on Financing Higher Education at the end of the 1940s employed categories from the prewar era. It identified four types of institutions: universities (121), which enrolled 53 percent of students; liberal arts colleges, which accounted for 23 percent; separate professional schools, 15 percent; and junior colleges, 9 percent. Universities offered undergraduate programs in arts and sciences and professional degrees but were distinguished by participation in graduate education and research. By no means could they all make that claim: "The aspiration, if not always the fact, of the university is to advance the frontiers of knowledge."[28] The liberal arts college was a default category for 453 institutions teaching basic arts and sciences. However, the commission felt compelled to distinguish 61 "complex" liberal arts colleges that offered numerous professional courses but without aspiring to advance knowledge. These were fairly large (avg. 3,000 students), mostly public institutions. Simple liberal arts colleges, the traditional type under private governance, averaged only 800 students, with two-fifths under 600. The 493 professional schools encompassed 193 small theological seminaries (avg. 200 students). The bulk of professional students attended 170 teachers colleges (avg. 1,000 students), which in most states were appended to state boards of education that governed the schools. Thirty engineering schools or technical institutes (avg. 2,500 students) were highly vocational. Finally, 474 junior colleges were considered by the commission as belonging only marginally in higher education. Mostly tiny, three-quarters of them had less than the mean of 400 students. Across all institutions, 227 were for men only, 266 for women, and 103 were historically black colleges and universities (HBCUs) of all types. The commission, as seen in Chapter 1, was a strong proponent of the liberal arts, and this was generally considered the distinguishing criterion for colleges and universities. But they composed just 37 percent of institutions of higher education, and liberal arts accounted for about the same percentage of degrees.[29] The subsequent expansion of higher education took place in institutions that scarcely fit into this configuration, which in fact was soon obsolete.

---

28   John D. Millett, *Financing Higher Education in the United States* (New York: Columbia University Press, 1952), 71–92, quote p. 73. Mary Irwin, *American Colleges and Universities, 1952* (Washington, DC: ACE, 1952) lists 99 institutions that conferred doctoral degrees from 1940 to 1950, only 72 of which were universities (pp. 54–57).

29   Millett, *Financing Higher Education*, 71–92.

URBAN UNIVERSITIES. State universities had an additional characteristic omitted from the CFHE definition—an inherent proclivity to expand geographically to provide educational services to a larger number of citizens. This incentive was present from the beginning of the century in the Wisconsin Idea and the growth of extension education. It was then by no means limited to public universities but was also exemplified at New York University and the Universities of Pennsylvania and Chicago. University extension expanded in the 1930s to meet the needs of local students who could not afford to reside at colleges. When the GIs inundated state universities, extension campuses were widely employed to meet this pressure. Extension centers were usually welcomed in smaller towns or cities, the locus of 1930s initiatives; but for large cities they affected established vested interests. Local politicians often sought the prestige of the state-supported flagship university; existing colleges lobbied to restrict the scope of such branches; state legislators often divided along regional lines; and the main campus was seldom supportive toward such branches, although sometimes it regarded branch campuses as preferable to the creation of separate rivals. The GI crunch brought a flurry of branch activity, but public institutions for urban populations could be a difficult sell in the 1950s.

Rutgers acquired the struggling private University of Newark in 1946; the University of Minnesota annexed the teachers college in Duluth in 1947; and the University of Illinois established a two-year undergraduate division at the Chicago Navy Pier in 1946. The latter campus enrolled 4,000 students, but unlike other improvised branches, enrollments did not decline when the GIs departed. Even though it was the nation's second largest city, Chicago had no public university and just two teachers colleges, which labored under the smothering bureaucracy of the Cook County Board of Education. In 1951, Chicago's state legislators managed to pass a mandate for the university to establish a full four-year course, but this was resisted by President George Stoddard, who was focused on academic development at Urbana and feared a diversion of resources. Stoddard was fired in 1953, and in 1955 David Dodds Henry (1955–1971) assumed the presidency. Formerly the president of Wayne University, Henry was an articulate proponent of the urban service university, emphasizing its contribution to the community through applied research and part-time evening programs, in addition to liberal and professional degrees. Not until 1960 did the state supply funding for a true urban campus in Chicago, but downstate opposition limited its scope. Even more restrictive was a "gentleman's agreement" that was made to placate the city's private colleges and universities and that precluded dormitories, evening classes, and programs in business or law. The Chicago Circle Campus finally opened in 1965 and quickly became one of the fastest-growing institutions in the country. However, this development occurred during the second stage of expansion, when urban universities became a priority everywhere.[30]

The best exemplar of an urban service university in the 1950s was the institution over which David Henry had presided from 1945 to 1952. Wayne University had been cobbled together from various schools in the interwar years and derived its meager budget from the Detroit Board of Education. When Henry departed, Wayne was educating 11,000 undergraduates, 3,000 graduates, and more than 4,000 nondegree students. One-half studied liberal arts, and the others, professional subjects. Wayne operated like a traditional university but in ways that accommodated its urban clientele. Almost all students commuted and many worked full or part time, attending intermittently. Almost two-thirds resided in Detroit and one-third in the surrounding suburbs—an area that contained one-half of the state population. Michigan had the same kind of budgetary struggles as every other state but was more farsighted than most in its policies toward higher education. After the requisite blue-ribbon study, in 1956 it assumed complete financial responsibility for Wayne *State* University.[31]

Despite this ostensible promotion, the university continued to embrace an urban-service identity and thus sought to strengthen its academic profile within that context. Under President Henry it had established its first doctoral programs and began to establish a research role, even if largely confined to chemistry and the medical school. The state study commission had recommended an enrollment balance of one-third in each of lower division, upper division, and graduate programs. In the 1950s it gradually jettisoned lower-order service courses that taught remedial or elementary subjects, and it moved nondegree students into an adult education unit. At the end of the decade, it sought to create a liberal education curriculum similar to those of traditional colleges and universities, but in a separate unit—Monteith College.

The inspiration may have reflected the quickening national interest in bolstering undergraduate education, but the initiative came from a set of Wayne old-timers. They envisioned offering a solid core of general education in the humanities, social sciences, and natural sciences to average Wayne students, including those who typically aimed for professional careers. With the aid of the Ford Foundation Fund for the Advancement of Education, the college admitted its

30   Fred W. Beuttler, "Envisioning an Urban University: President David Henry and the Chicago Circle Campus of the University of Illinois, 1955–1975," *History of Higher Education Annual* 23 (2003–2004): 107–42.

31   Leslie L. Hanawalt, *A Place of Light: The History of Wayne State University; A Centennial Publication* (Detroit: Wayne State University Press, 1968); Roger L. Geiger, *The History of American Higher Education: Learning and Culture from the Founding to World War II* (Princeton: Princeton University Press, 2015), 440–41.

first class in 1959 and grew over four years to its intended size of nearly 1,000 students. The aims of Monteith resembled those of the Harvard Redbook. However, many new faculty came from the University of Chicago and brought with them much of its general education curriculum. Monteith was unique in its students, but not its curriculum. They were essentially self-selected and resembled the demography of Wayne State undergraduates. However, they formed a cohesive group, attended special Monteith classes for up to half of their credit hours, and had closer interactions with faculty. Monteith was an honors college for average students. In the last half of the 1960s, David Riesman led a thorough study of Monteith as an experiment in "mass" undergraduate education. It found perceptible intellectual gains from the Monteith curriculum and that graduates more closely resembled those of elite liberal arts colleges than those from other public universities. But it also registered uncertainty about the viability of the college. As a unit dedicated to a superior liberal arts education, it was resented by the College of Liberal Arts and out of step with the blue-collar ethos of the campus.[32] The termination of Monteith was announced in 1975, allegedly for budgetary reasons.

The tension between the liberal arts ideal and the urban service ideal was inherent in the new University of South Florida (USF), which was chartered in 1956 and opened in 1960. The fact that it claimed to be the first public four-year university created de novo in the twentieth century underscored how much the expansion of the public sector relied on the branching, annexing, or elevation of existing institutions. Founding president John Allen committed USF to providing an education for citizenship based on a core of arts and sciences requirements that filled most of the first two years. He envisioned an undergraduate teaching-learning community, with no intercollegiate athletics and a faculty recruited for their dedication to teaching, not research. Allen's vision was one interpretation of the 1950s liberal arts ideal. However, it ill-served the Tampa community for whom the university had been created. A survey of prospective applicants revealed mostly first-generation commuter students who above all sought preparation for employment. The survey's author could only conclude that "students will need to be shown the explicit relevance of courses in the Liberal Arts for their personal aspirations."[33] The contrast with Monteith College is instructive. There a general education of similar intent and nature was successfully offered to small numbers of urban students on a voluntary basis. Like other

32   David Riesman, Joseph Gusfield, and Zelda Gamson, *Academic Values and Mass Higher Education: The Early Years of Oakland and Monteith* (Garden City, NY: Doubleday, 1970).

33   Charles Dorn, "'Education for Citizenship ... Is Too Important to Leave to Chance': John Allen and the University of South Florida, 1956–1970," *Perspectives on the History of Higher Education* 32 (2017): 50–78.

urban universities, USF experienced burgeoning growth in the 1960s but was always plagued by the cross-purposes inherent in its creation. When Allen retired abruptly in 1970, his liberal arts core was retired as well.

TEACHERS COLLEGES. Like urban universities, the expansion of teachers colleges represented greater participation in higher education by a particular demographic. From an average size of 1,000 students in 1948, these institutions grew to 2,200 by 1960. Such averages mask different velocities of growth, but they were all moving in the same direction. Until 1951, teacher education programs at all institutions were represented by the American Association of Colleges for Teacher Education. That year, the Association of Teacher Education Institutions was organized to represent just these colleges. A decade later, that organization was superseded by the Association of State Colleges and Universities, thus abandoning identification with teacher education and heralding an era of meteoric growth and institutional transformation. In their truncated existence, the teachers colleges of the 1950s remained close to their roots even while widening access to mass higher education.

The students who filled the teachers colleges were in some respects rural counterparts to those attending urban universities. Most teachers colleges were located in towns or small cities where they largely served a rural or semi-rural hinterland. But unlike in cities, these students had lacked alternatives. Few of these students' parents had attended college, and a large proportion were "working class." They sought, above all, educational pathways to good jobs. As a student at Ball State Teachers College explained, "It was close to home; it was a choice of going to Ball State or not going at all." In these relatively homogeneous communities, the comfort of the familiar was an important factor in attendance. This might be called the "propinquity effect"—not only physical proximity but also social compatibility signaled by friends and family familiarity with the institution. Some students commuted, but the majority tended to be resident students; and although some may have worked part time, most attended full time. These institutions were thus able to nurture a rich extracurricular life, including intercollegiate athletics. College life at a teachers college was much like traditional college life elsewhere—except for the curriculum. Students at most schools could study only for education degrees. Most teachers colleges were controlled by state or local boards of education, which supported them only to educate teachers. As enrollments grew in the 1950s, students seemed to accept an education degree as the means for acquiring a college education. At Ball State in the 1950s, 90 percent of graduates took education degrees even after other courses became available. At Brockport State Teachers College in New York, only education degrees were offered until 1963. Ball State began the postwar era with 1,000 students in

1945 and reached 5,000 in 1958. Most graduates of Ball State and Brockport spent at least part of their careers as teachers. Since many teachers colleges were in state systems, the nominal change into state colleges occurred through legislation, as it did in Pennsylvania in 1960. Internally, teachers college practices persisted into the 1960s at many of these institutions, regardless of names, until being overwhelmed by baby-boom growth.[34]

JUNIOR COLLEGES. Two-year, or junior, colleges wrestled with an ambiguous status in postwar higher education. Considered by some to be the "capstone" of K-14 education systems, they were regarded as marginal to higher education by traditionalists. These institutions had an energetic champion in the American Association of Junior Colleges (AAJC), which sought to project a more positive image. Since before the war, it had emphasized terminal vocational programs to provide students with livelihoods and local industry with workers. The President's Commission had christened them community colleges, and the AAJC was happy to embrace this comprehensive mission. Education-policy pundits accepted this interpretation as complementing their concerns for upholding high standards for four-year colleges and universities. James Conant, for example, looking to maximize meritocracy and social opportunity, envisioned a fairly high threshold of aptitude for study at traditional colleges, with everyone else consigned to junior colleges. This was little different from the recommendations of the President's Commission, which, with more generous thresholds, would have junior colleges serve one-sixth of cohorts with intelligence above average but below college levels (34th to 49th percentile). This consensus view of the 1950s implied that junior college students would take terminal vocational courses, not academic subjects for transfer to four-year schools. However, no one informed the students. After the war, two-thirds of junior college students enrolled in transfer curricula, and this figure rose to three-quarters in the 1950s.[35]

Four possible reasons have been offered for why students would choose to attend a junior college: (1) Location-bound, either by choice or necessity: this would be a factor for more rural junior colleges but less so for urban sites where other alternatives existed; (2) Financial, including low or no tuition and living at home: junior college students on average came from families with lower SES and parental education, but this in itself does not prove financial hardship;

34 Anthony O. Edmonds and E. Bruce Geelhoed, *Ball State University: An Interpretive History* (Bloomington: Indiana University Press, 2001), quote p. 148; W. Bruce Leslie and Kenneth P. O'Brien, "The Surprising History of the Post-WWII State Teachers College," *Perspectives on the History of Higher Education* 32 (2017): 23–49.

35 Steven Brint and Jerome Karabel, *The Diverted Dream: Community Colleges and the Promise of Educational Opportunity in America, 1900–1985* (New York: Oxford University Press, 1989), 67–101.

(3) Unable to qualify academically for a four-year institution: since admissions criteria at public teachers colleges and many universities were minimal, 1950s students in this situation would have had poor high school records indeed, most likely below a C average; and (4) Preference for a two-year, vocational degree: always true for some, this segment continued to shrink in the 1950s and 1960s. Evidence suggests that junior colleges expanded access only moderately in these years—that lower SES students in particular substituted a junior college for a possible four-year institution, most likely because they too felt propinquity effects.[36]

An empirical study of a mid-fifties junior college by the sociologist Burton R. Clark revealed complications unmentioned in the policy literature. His subject, San Jose Junior College, was located next to a state college and not far from the state university. It was the bottom rung of mass higher education. Administrative weaknesses exacerbated this situation. It was governed by a superior organization—the local school board—that had other priorities; and open admissions afforded no control over whom it taught. Although the college enrolled some strong students, the average verbal ability was at the tenth-grade level, and quantitative skills were lower still. Yet three-quarters of these students hoped to transfer to a BA program. Clark called a good portion of them "latent terminal students," meaning that they intended to transfer but lacked the aptitude or motivation to achieve a C average. The college made considerable effort to counsel these students into vocational courses, but the majority dropped out without obtaining any degree. As for more capable students, those who qualified for admission to four-year institutions but attended a junior college instead reduced their odds of obtaining a bachelor's degree.[37] Thus, junior colleges in the 1950s increased educational opportunity somewhat less than enrollment numbers might indicate. For the decade, two-year enrollments grew in line with higher education totals. However, there was an obvious role in American mass higher education for two-year institutions—for community colleges. In the 1960s and beyond, they would grow at nearly twice the rate of colleges and universities, spurred by favorable public policies.

THE CALIFORNIA PARADIGM. California was the birthplace of junior colleges and harbored by far the largest number of such institutions and students. California also had a distinctive organizational structure of higher education that differed from the official categories described above. Its six teachers colleges had

36   Christopher Jencks and David Riesman, *The Academic Revolution* (Chicago: University of Chicago Press, 1977 [1968]), 485–87; Brint and Karabel, *Diverted Dream*, 90–92; for propinquity effects, see Howard B. London, *The Culture of a Community College* (New York: Praeger, 1978), 1–27.

37   Burton R. Clark, *The Open Door College: A Case Study* (New York: McGraw-Hill, 1960); Brint and Karabel, *Diverted Dream*, 90–92.

been renamed state colleges in 1935 and quickly developed into diversified under-graduate institutions. The flagship University of California (UC) was unique in replicating itself on additional campuses, beginning with the Southern Branch, in Los Angeles. Californians referred to this as the "tripartite" system, but it might also be called the California paradigm—the pattern of public higher education that would soon characterize American public higher education. But it first required refinement in its home state.[38]

Faced with a rising demand for higher education from a burgeoning population, California commissioned a thorough postwar study. The 1948 Strayer Report defined the respective roles of the three sectors. For junior colleges, it foresaw what amounted to a community college slate of comprehensive programs with recognition of the importance of the transfer function. For state colleges, it confirmed their diversification into liberal arts and applied fields, as well as aspirations to offer master's degrees in those fields. The University of California was guaranteed its monopoly over the major professions, doctoral education, and basic research. Expansion was imperative across the board—the continued building of new junior colleges, several new state colleges to meet regional demand, and the development of UC campuses at the Riverside research station and Davis.

The University of California, led since 1929 by Robert Gordon Sproul, zealously guarded its privileged roles and corresponding claims on state higher-education funds. It had adamantly opposed any elevation of the functions of teachers/state colleges and even resisted new campuses of the university. Sproul's leadership had also made UC Berkeley into the nation's premier public research university, aided by the division of labor in the tripartite system that allowed it to concentrate on research and advanced studies. Constitutionally independent under the board of regents, the UC consistently obstructed efforts to expand public higher education in order to protect its advantages. Because the state population grew faster than projected, and with it the need for more public institutions, the recommendations of the Strayer Report quickly became glaringly inadequate. The Restudy Report reiterated these views with more data but satisfied no one. Growing urban centers around the state were demanding local colleges to bolster development, and powerful state legislators threatened to provide them. Discontent centered on the state colleges, which were chafing under the Department of Education bureaucracy and seeking to expand their roles and

38   The following draws on John Aubrey Douglass, *The California Idea and American Higher Education: 1850 to the 1960 Master Plan* (Stanford, CA: Stanford University Press, 2000); and Simon Marginson, *The Dream Is Over: The Crisis of Clark Kerr's California Idea of Higher Education* (Berkeley: University of California Press, 2016).

campuses. This was the situation when Clark Kerr became president of the UC in 1958. The state faced an unprecedented increase in demand for higher education from immigration and the impending baby-boom cohorts. If this challenge was resolved by the politicians instead of the higher education community, the academic excellence of the UC might well be jeopardized.

Kerr informed the regents that planning for this growth was impossible given the prevailing uncertainty, and he received their blessing to seek an accommodation with the other sectors. He joined forces with the superintendent of Public Instruction to gain legislative approval for yet another planning commission. An experienced negotiator, Kerr enhanced its credibility by including the community colleges and the private sector, making the latter's representative the chair of the committee. Negotiations were often difficult, but by early 1960 they produced the Master Plan for Higher Education in California, which was adopted by the legislature with a near unanimous vote.[39]

The Master Plan, Kerr later emphasized, was not a plan as such but rather a treaty defining the relative roles of the principal sectors of higher education. It succeeded at the time largely because it brought concrete benefits to each. The state colleges—the most aggrieved party—received a significant upgrade. They were emancipated from the schools through a promised independent governing board, allotted four new campuses, given carte blanche for establishing master's degrees in any subject, and accorded the possibility of limited funds for applied research and joint doctorates (with the UC) in education. The community colleges were slated for almost unlimited expansion, so that one would be within commuting distance of all Californians. The private sector was given a seat on the Coordinating Council, and hence a voice in future public policies. And the UC, above all, protected "what were called its 'crown jewels'—the Ph.D. and other advanced degrees beyond the M.A., and basic research"—as well as getting three additional campuses. Admission caps were tightened, with the UC taking the top 12.5 percent of high school graduates and the state colleges the top 33 percent. By raising the floors for student qualifications, the ceilings were effectively raised for the state and community colleges. Community colleges were open to all high school graduates, and transfer rights were guaranteed to successful students.[40]

---

39 Clark Kerr, *The Blue and the Gold: A Personal Memoir of the University of California, 1949–1967; Volume One, Academic Triumphs* (Berkeley: University of California Press, 2001), 172–90; Douglass, *California Idea*, 223ff.

40 Clark Kerr, "The California Master Plan of 1960 for Higher Education: An Ex Ante View," in Sheldon Rothblatt, ed., *The OECD, the Master Plan and the California Dream: A Berkeley Conversation* (Berkeley, CA: Center for Studies in Higher Education, 1992), 47–60.

By providing something for everyone, the Master Plan reflected the emerging realities of American higher education as it entered a period of accelerating growth. The academic excellence and large expenditures of the UC were preserved, and the opportunities it offered to Californians would expand with the population—but no more. The state-college sector was freed to develop full-fledged regional universities, accommodating a rising share of students at lower unit costs. The low-cost community colleges would be the default institutions, absorbing any and all students wishing to enter higher education. California led the nation in the demographic expansion of higher education, but other states faced the same situation and would gravitate toward the same pattern. *Time* magazine in 1960 featured Kerr in an October cover story, lauding his acumen and negotiating skills but also sending a message to other states: "The problem of all U.S. state universities in the 1960s is to keep mass education from becoming mob education."[41] Public higher education in most states had been developing in various degrees toward the California paradigm. In the 1960s, other states would adopt their own master plans, usually without committing to the clear demarcations adopted in California. The result, however, would be unequivocal: the California paradigm would become the American paradigm for the structure of higher education.

A UNIVERSITY FOR NEW YORK. Nowhere did this evolution have a longer path to travel than in New York, the only state without a public university. This glaring lacuna became a political issue as the GIs returned. Governor Thomas Dewey deflected criticism by appointing the Temporary Commission on the Need for a State University in 1946, which laid the groundwork for legislation establishing the State University of New York (SUNY) in 1948. This act merely swept all the existing state postsecondary institutions into the new entity—seven state-funded units contracted to private universities, eleven teachers colleges, eleven two-year vocational schools, and three temporary centers for GIs. Even this modest effort enraged the New York State Board of Regents, which coveted responsibility for all education in the state and blatantly favored private colleges and universities. A modus vivendi was reached: the official role of SUNY was to "supplement" the private sector, not compete; it would refrain from establishing any liberal arts colleges for ten years; and the teachers colleges would offer no liberal arts, engineering, or secondary school preparation (excepting Albany). And there would be no actual university. A 1957 report began, "State University

41 "Education: Master-Planner," *Time* (October 17, 1960).

is an academic animal without a head." When the president openly favored establishing such a head, that is, a university, he was summarily fired.[42]

SUNY's fortunes brightened in 1958 when Nelson Rockefeller was elected governor. Higher education was among the new governor's (many) priorities, especially the building of a great state university. Another commission was naturally required, this one chaired by Ford Foundation president Henry Heald. The 1960 Heald Commission foresaw a transformation of public higher education in New York; no longer a supplement, it should assume a major responsibility for providing educational opportunity for state students. Legislation the following year implemented these recommendations. The teachers colleges would develop strong liberal arts programs and award liberal arts degrees; two (later four) "university centers" would be established; and the City University of New York became an autonomous system. Any resentment in the private sector was assuaged, in typical New York fashion, with public money for student aid and construction loans. SUNY soon became the largest university system in the country, and one that conformed to the California paradigm.[43]

The expansion of public higher education in the 1950s involved a complex interaction of vocationalism and liberal arts. An analyst summarized the former in 1960: "The principal appeal of higher education to youth of lower-middle and working-class status, and to their families, [is] ... economic and social advancement.... This is the main reason for the great increases since World War II."[44] Indeed, the institutions reviewed here expanded the supply of higher education, and they were patronized overwhelmingly by first-generation students from these social strata. However, their alleged careerism had some paradoxical features. Community college students largely eschewed vocational programs in favor of the lure of transfer and a four-year degree. Teachers college students were willing to accept education degrees in order to become college graduates. And new urban students tended to divide between liberal and professional courses. Students and institutions were affected by the superior status accorded to the liberal arts. Traditional defenders, especially in the private sector, actively sought to deny these upstart institutions the ability to teach liberal subjects—at Georgia State, Chicago, SUNY, and to some extent at California State Colleges. John Allen sought to distance his new university from such strictures by requiring a solid academic core for all students, and Wayne State opted to provide a pure

42   Sidney Gelber, *Politics and Public Higher Education in New York State: Stoney Brook—A Case History* (New York: Peter Lang, 2001); John B. Clark, W. Bruce Leslie, and Kenneth P. O'Brien, eds., *SUNY at 60: The Promise of the State University of New York* (Albany: SUNY Press, 2010).

43   Judith S. Glazer, "Nelson Rockefeller and the Politics of Higher Education in New York State," *History of Higher Education Annual* 9 (1989): 87–114.

44   Havighurst, *American Higher Education*, 58.

liberal education for at least some students in Monteith College. The California and SUNY colleges achieved emancipation after 1960. In fact, as the California paradigm superseded the old structure, institutions were no longer pigeonholed into ascribed roles. Instead, the new pattern across public colleges and universities would be to offer liberal and professional courses of study side by side. This pattern was less evident in the private sector, where the liberal education ideal was nurtured and embellished during the 1950s.

PRIVATE COLLEGES AND UNIVERSITIES IN THE 1950S

Private colleges and universities in the 1950s were pulled in three different directions. Within the colleges and their leadership, liberal education strengthened as a compelling ideal. Liberal education (entangled with general education) had been a preoccupation since before the war, but only afterward were institutions able to take concrete steps to realize these aspirations. They sought, above all, to elevate the level of undergraduate attainments while according the liberal arts, especially the humanities and Western heritage, with transcendent intellectual powers. An implicit bond seemed to connect this ideal with the American way of life. A liberal education was assumed to provide the foundation for future leadership in American society.

But the strong desire to elevate undergraduate education in practice conflicted with entrenched traditional practices unique to each school. Colleges depended upon constituencies that might be religious, regional, cultural, or social. As alumni, these constituents provided vital donations and helped to govern the colleges as trustees. They were a crucial source of students and thus had a vested interest in admissions. Their view of the college was strongly colored by the extracurriculum and the intangible personal qualities of "character" thought to be instilled in its graduates. The conservatism of the American way of life was a factor here as well, because institutions were reluctant to take initiatives that would disturb these comfortable relationships.

A third orientation emanated from the academic perspective of the faculty. While many shared commitments to the traditional instructional and liberal arts missions, they were beholden as well to the knowledge imperatives of their respective academic disciplines. Their specific interests lay with the intellectual capital of the colleges—laboratories and libraries—but above all with the opportunity to teach their subjects at levels commensurate with advanced knowledge in their fields. As the professionalism of faculties increased during the 1950s, their voices became more insistent and their priorities more compelling.

The dynamics of these contending interests were conditioned everywhere by financial considerations. Initiatives were tightly constrained after 1945 by the tsunami of veterans and by the paucity of resources following two difficult decades. After 1950, the financial outlook improved, slowly at first but accelerating after mid-decade, allowing institutions a greater measure of choice in planning their development. But money was only one aspect of feasibility. The development of colleges and universities was conditioned by the market for undergraduates, the availability of faculty, the predilections of their leaders, and the prevailing conservatism of the decade.

LIBERAL EDUCATION IN THE COLLEGES. The concept of liberal education served as both a pedagogical goal and an affirmation of Americanism, but over time the latter predominated. At Amherst College, a faculty committee in 1944–1945 sought to address the challenge of a small private college with a public mission of educating an intellectual elite—its self-proclaimed historical mission. Focusing on the first two years, they identified three objectives: to continue and supplement the foundational education acquired in secondary school; to provide "a common body of knowledge in the three great fields of the curriculum; and ... [to] make a sufficient beginning in work preparatory to the major, or major with honors ... during the last two years." At the end of these two years, the college would be able to separate students into regular and honors groups. To accomplish this, the committee proposed, and the college implemented, a common two-year curriculum that consisted of one course each semester in science, history (Western Civ; Problems in American Civilization), English/humanities, and a foreign language or elective. An evaluation of the new curriculum after seven years (1954) was quite positive, although not self-congratulatory. An abundance of empirical information described the impact on the achievement of Amherst students and provided a basis for fine-tuning these courses. A commitment to strengthening liberal education at Amherst seemed to bring noticeably better students and outcomes.[45]

The Commission on Financing Higher Education imposed a patriotic interpretation on liberal education. Encompassing all nonvocational undergraduate education, liberal education sought "to liberate the study of man ... through studying the great artistic and intellectual achievements of man." Furthermore, "the qualities which liberal education would cultivate in all students with intellectual aspirations are the very qualities which the world most needs from its educated citizens." Thus, "a liberal education is also vital to a free society"—that is,

---

45   Gail Kennedy, ed., *Education at Amherst: The New Program* (New York: Harper & Brothers, 1955), quote p. 39. Less sweeping than the Harvard Redbook, the Amherst Report and New Program was practical and internally focused.

the United States.[46] Clearly by 1952, at least for educators, a grandiose and uncritical notion of liberal education had been annexed to the American way of life.

Liberal education interacted with collegiate and academic forces in the postwar experience of Wesleyan University, in Middletown, Connecticut.[47] A formerly Methodist liberal arts college, it was challenged to compete with Amherst and Williams as a member of the Little Three. Under its revered president, Victor Butterfield (1942–1967), the college was continually focused on defining and devising a liberal education ideal. As at Harvard and Amherst, a wartime faculty committee was appointed to recommend a curriculum that would enhance liberal learning. They proposed a great books type of course, Humanities 1 and 2, which was subsequently required of all freshmen. After the war, President Butterfield advocated a two-year common liberal arts curriculum for all students, like Amherst's; but the faculty largely resisted, prescribing only a course in Western Civilization. Butterfield persisted in pursuing this ideal, writing *The Faith of a Liberal College* (1955) largely for internal circulation. But as Wesleyan grew wealthier, a larger and more professional faculty preferred to move in the direction of a "little university."

An additional impediment to the aspirations for liberal learning was presented by Wesleyan students. After the GIs departed, they were replaced by what *Time* magazine dubbed the Silent Generation, which was evident at Wesleyan in "academic apathy, low marks, and slack spirit."[48] The college's response was to revamp the admissions process to recruit better students. The president and trustees insisted that character and social responsibility should be given equal weight with academic promise, but the faculty favored the latter. Over time, faculty preferences tended to prevail for two compelling reasons. The liberal education goals of the president and the faculty could be achieved (or approximated) only with students of relatively high academic ability. And, as competition for prestige and national standing rose, it was now measured by metrics for SAT scores and the proportion of students with high class rankings. In the long run, institutional incentives compelled and conditions favored recruiting better students. More students were going to college, and more capable matriculates could be culled from this growing population by professionalizing the admissions office, mobilizing alumni, expanding recruitment geographically, and offering financial aid. Wesleyan hired a director of admissions who employed all these

46   Commission on Financing Higher Education, *Nature and Needs of Higher Education* (New York: Columbia University Press, 1952), 15–18.

47   The following draws on David Potts, *Wesleyan University, 1910–1970: Academic Ambition and Middle-Class America* (Middletown, CT: Wesleyan University Press, 2015).

48   Ibid., 295.

means and soon raised the qualifications of its incoming classes to match those of archrivals Amherst and Williams.

These developments were not entirely welcome by old grads. In 1955 they organized the Committee of One Hundred to formally register their unhappiness. With the spirit of McCarthyism still strong, they disapproved of the trends toward secularism and humanism in the college. They objected to the waning Methodist heritage, especially optional attendance at chapel services. They sensed that the admissions office was forsaking "integrity and sturdy character." And perhaps most shocking were rumors of abolishing the fraternities.[49] This minor insurrection died out over the next three years, but the existence of such attitudes served as a lasting brake on college policies. President Butterfield attempted to unite these factions by positing a higher goal in the *Liberal College*, an ideal that might be honored by teachers, alumni, and occasionally even students.

HARVARD, YALE, AND PRINCETON. Tensions in the 1950s over who would attend and what they would be taught were more acute for the nascent Ivy League, and particularly at the Big Three of Harvard, Yale, and Princeton.[50] In the most detailed study, Jerome Karabel termed the era to 1965 as "the struggle over meritocracy."[51] These schools were dependent for their wealth, traditions, and campus culture on bonds with the Northeastern Protestant upper class, who prepared their sons in the elite boarding schools of the region. Beyond this core constituency, often referred to as "the gentlemen," they looked to their far-flung graduates to support and preserve their unique brands. Notorious for their discriminatory Jewish quotas during the interwar years, they liberalized admissions considerably after 1945 while still keeping a lid (not a "quota") on the number of Jewish students.[52] But they were also leading research universities—Harvard per-

---

49   Ibid., 333–35. At Wesleyan and other institutions opposition to fraternity charter restrictions barring Jews and African-Americans was a long-running issue, but Wesleyan, like other Eastern men's colleges, could hardly abolish fraternities since 85 percent of the undergraduates belonged and 40 percent resided in fraternity houses (346). It seems likely that the alums had read William F. Buckley, Jr., *God and Man at Yale* (1953), which blames secularism for the decline of religion (discussed below).

50   The eight institutions once called the Ivy Colleges signed an intercollegiate agreement in 1945 pledging to field football teams that were representative of their student bodies. The Ivy League is officially known as the Ivy Group Presidents and has offices at Princeton University. Besides the Big Three, it includes Brown, Columbia, Cornell, Dartmouth, and Penn: Roger L. Geiger, "The Ivy League," in David Palfreyman and Ted Tapper, eds., *Structuring Mass Higher Education: The Role of Elite Institutions* (New York: Routledge, 2009), 281–302.

51   The following draws upon this comprehensive study: Jerome Karabel, *The Chosen: The Hidden History of Admission and Exclusion at Harvard, Yale, and Princeton* (Boston: Houghton Mifflin, 2005).

52   Indignation over discrimination against Jewish students after the war led to laws forbidding such practices in New York, New Jersey, and Massachusetts; complaints of discrimination under these laws were made by individuals and were readily defended by institutions, which were never charged with sys-

haps the national leader, with Yale and Princeton committed to the same standards of excellence, only in somewhat fewer fields. Given their prominence and prestige, they were initial beneficiaries of the "re-sorting" with a growing surge in applicants. As research universities they sought to enroll academically talented students from across the nation (but not too many from eastern cities); but as elite colleges they were loath to lessen their connections with the prep-school crowd.

Harvard president James Conant (1933–1953) was known for tilting Harvard admissions in a meritocratic direction by instituting national scholarships, and Yale and Princeton followed with their own efforts at national recruitment. In all cases the numbers were small and were chiefly aimed at smart WASPs vetted by loyal alumni.[53] Academic ability could be readily measured with SAT scores and class standing, especially for the right tail of extraordinary talents. But measures of "character" and "leadership" were more problematic but yet essential for identifying the future achievers most valued by these institutions. Yale approached this challenge analytically, believing that the students it preferred were truly superior and that these qualities could be measured. After 1950, every non-prep applicant was interviewed by members of Alumni Schools Committees spread across the country. Yale devised a detailed scorecard on which traits associated with leadership and character could be given numerical ratings. The sociologist Joseph Soares has shown that these alumni ratings were the most important criterion for the ultimate admission decision: "For Yale, intellectual selection and social selection went together as institutional policies"; however, "character was never more important to admission than after the Second World War."[54] The same could be said of the other Ivy League schools. The increasing numbers of quality applicants made it easier to choose students on other than academic criteria. The relative weight of academic and social factors in this subjective process was deliberately obscured from the public. But at Harvard these trade-offs could not be kept entirely under wraps.

When Wilbur Bender was named the director of Harvard admissions (1952–1960), nearly two-thirds of applicants were admitted, including nine-tenths of alumni sons. With unusual candor, he penned a formal statement of admission policy that attempted to sort out the multiple objectives involved. Realistically,

---

tematic discrimination: Harold S. Wechsler, "The Temporary Commission Surveys Bias in Admissions," in John B. Clark, W. Bruce Leslie, and Kenneth P. O'Brien, eds. *SUNY at Sixty: The Promise of the State University of New York* (Albany: SUNY Press, 2010), 29–38. For Yale, see Dan A. Oren, *Joining the Club: A History of Jews and Yale* (New Haven, CT: Yale University Press, 1985), 173–214. After the quota was abandoned, the percentage of Jews at Yale remained about 12 percent until 1966 (320–21).

53   Morton Keller and Phyllis Keller, *Making Harvard Modern: The Rise of America's University* (New York: Harvard University Press, 2001), 22–26, 32–35.

54   Joseph A. Soares, *The Power of Privilege: Yale and America's Elite Colleges* (Stanford, CA: Stanford University Press, 2007), 36–52, quote p. 51.

he acknowledged the importance for Harvard of the social elite it had traditionally served and the necessity of preserving ties with the prep schools by according their graduates preference in admission. Similar considerations applied to sons of the national alumni. On the other hand, Harvard's strong appeal to "the studious, the intellectuals, the aesthete" could be a problem. He insinuated that such students were more likely to have character flaws and that excessive intellectualism could alienate the gentlemen. Overall, Bender favored raising the academic level somewhat: he thought the proportion of "top brains" might be expanded from 5 to 10 percent. However, as Karabel pointed out, this left "90 percent of the students … to be selected on other grounds."[55]

During Bender's tenure, the number of top brains applying to Harvard rapidly increased, including winners of national scholarships, who favored it over all other schools. Especially after Sputnik, demands were raised for greater recognition of academic merit for Harvard College students, particularly by Harvard scientists. The dean of Harvard College, McGeorge Bundy, a blue blood who was fiercely meritocratic toward the faculty, appointed a committee of distinguished professors to mull these issues. Scientists on the committee, and no doubt most of the faculty, favored a greater emphasis on academic merit. One committee member felt that Harvard students should be drawn from the top 1 percent of American high school graduates, or, at the very least, that the current bottom 10 percent should be eliminated in future classes. Seeing the writing on the wall, Bender tendered his resignation, but he defended his regime with an artfully crafted guide for his successor. He explicitly rejected a "top-one-percent Harvard" with arguments similar to those he had used in 1952: students chosen solely for academic ability might lack creativity, be grade-grubbers, or "bearded types"; and without the social elite, the "traditional pattern of extracurricular life [might] disintegrate."[56] The faculty committee's report contained considerable meritocratic rhetoric but in effect only nudged admissions policy in that direction. Ignoring the extreme position of its scientists, the report acknowledged that institutional interests required continuing ties with alumni and boarding schools. In eight years under Bender, Harvard had raised the SAT scores of its incoming classes almost 200 points, but the socioeconomic diversity of its students rose hardly at all.[57] The former was the result of market forces, the latter of admissions policy.

55   Karabel, *Chosen*, 248–71, quotes pp. 252, 254.

56   Ibid.; William J. Bender, "A Report on the Admission and Scholarship Committee for the Academic Year 1959–1960," in *Report of the President of Harvard College, 1959–1960* (Harvard University, 1960), 52–62.

57   From 1952 to 1960, the percentage of rejected applicants rose from 30 to 63 percent; median SAT scores rose from 1181 to 1377, and the 90th percentile student of 1952 would have been at the 50th percentile in 1960: Karabel, *Chosen*, 282.

Harvard, Yale, and Princeton faced the same admissions issues, each in its own unique manner. The Princeton faculty pressured the admissions office to accept all applicants with high SATs, and a committee convened at the same time as Harvard's produced similar recommendations. A subsequent faculty committee at Yale made even stronger recommendations in 1962, but here too implementation would take several years. Both public opinion and faculty sentiment favored admissions based chiefly on academic ability, which is why Bender had warned that preferences for alumni, athletes, and prep-school gentlemen could be "sources of potential embarrassment if discussed candidly in a public document." For the first half of the 1960s, as pre–baby boom cohorts applied in ever greater numbers, all three schools quietly resisted these pressures. That is, each institution adjusted its admissions procedures to accord greater weight to nonacademic criteria. In doing so, they largely reacted to institutional interests— financial incentives to enroll full-payers and limit scholarship expense, to ensure alumni loyalties, and, especially, to compete among themselves for the prep-school gentlemen whom they considered vital to their mission and traditions.[58]

Yale, Harvard, and Princeton each named new presidents in the 1950s who reflected in different ways the conservative tenor of the times as well as institutional priorities. Yale in 1950 replaced the superannuated Charles Seymour with A. Whitney Griswold (1950–1963), a forty-three-year-old history professor with strong convictions and a forceful personality. Griswold passionately upheld his views on the dual missions of college and university. The former, above all, was intended to provide a liberal education through dedicated teaching, while the latter advanced learning, but exclusively in the basic arts and sciences. He believed that applied subjects had no place at Yale, and he succeeded in purging research institutes and professional undergraduate programs (nursing, education). In an attempt to reinforce the liberal arts in Yale College, he presided over a committee that recommended an Amherst-like reworking of the first two years, but with a separate liberal arts faculty. This initiative was rebuffed by the

58   Karabel, *Chosen*, 285–345, quote p. 281. Need-based scholarships are an important component of admissions policy, since many high-ability students could not afford private colleges, and private colleges could not afford too many scholarship students. Private colleges kept the percentage of scholarship students stable from the 1950s to the 1970s. The Big Three tended to support 20–25 percent of their students, many of whom were not below median income: Duffy and Goldberg, *Crafting a Class*, 172–79; Karabel, *Chosen*, passim.

The assumptions governing selective admissions would change abruptly and decisively in the midsixties. The Big Three became aware—and concerned—that while they were competing among themselves for prep-school students, other institutions were enrolling more of the nation's brightest students: Soares, *Power of Privilege*, 40. The recruiting weakness reported in this account is not consistent with the SAT scores reported for 1966–1967 in *American Universities and Colleges, 1968* (Washington, DC: ACE, 1968).

Yale faculty, who defended the prerogatives of the departments and disciplines. Griswold made extensive and needed investments in the academic strengths of the university, particularly in the natural sciences, while doing all he could to fortify the traditions of Yale College.[59]

In 1953 Harvard replaced James Conant with Nathan Pusey (1953–1971), a classicist and Harvard grad who was then presiding over Lawrence College in Wisconsin. The anti-Conant, Pusey was personally devoted to Harvard College, liberal arts, humanities, and the church.[60] But he quickly appreciated the emerging meritocratic nature of the faculty and, increasingly, students. He was greatly assisted in this respect by the wunderkind McGeorge Bundy, whom he appointed dean of the Faculty of Arts and Sciences. Bundy possessed the Brahman background helpful in dealing with the old guard and the academic acumen to impose rigorously high standards on the faculty. Pusey projected a conservative facade while presiding over the relentless expansion of Harvard's academic prowess.

When Princeton replaced Harold Dodds (1933–1957) with Robert Goheen (1957–1972), the choice signaled continuity rather than change. As the smallest of the Big Three, Princeton under Dodds had consistently sought to bolster academic programs and was receptive to the postwar expansion of sponsored research. When Griswold banished the Institute of International Relations, for example, Princeton readily adopted it. A classics professor with three Princeton degrees, Goheen had administered the Woodrow Wilson Fellowship Program. That experience, as well as his own distinguished scholarship, gave him an innate appreciation of high academic standards. His administration extended the academic rigor of his predecessor while belatedly overseeing a modernization of the college.

The institutional conservatism of the Big Three was most evident in the undergraduate colleges. Harvard, garnering the lion's share of very high ability students, moved furthest toward a new temper of campus life. By the late 1950s, Harvard College was more meritocratic and affluent, with fewer commuters and a prevailing culture that was becoming more middle class. To some, the old Harvard of the gentlemen and the final clubs had not disappeared but instead "gone underground." Above ground, academic attainments became more conspicuous. For the class of 1960, one-half received honors degrees, and 82 percent planned on further graduate studies. Just 1 percent chose banking. As Harvard graduates

59 Geoffrey Mark Kabaservice, "Kingman Brewster and the Rise and Fall of the Progressive Establishment," PhD diss., Yale University, 1999.

60 "The most conspicuous dynamic in the Harvard presidential selection process—get someone as unlike his predecessor as possible—had once again kicked into gear. This was true of the choice of Eliot in 1869, of Lowell in 1909, of Conant in 1934; it was true of Pusey in 1953": Keller and Keller, *Making Harvard Modern*, 175.

won the largest numbers of prestigious national fellowships, Wilbur Bender's fear of intellectuals appeared increasingly anachronistic.[61]

The situation was quite different at Princeton, where the junior-senior eating clubs made social hierarchy a formal feature of campus life. The seventeen clubs had a hierarchy of their own, but club membership was considered an essential component of the Princeton experience. The selection process ("bicker") submitted the entire sophomore class "to judgments on the basis of well-defined social and cultural criteria"—"the qualities that Princeton's student culture most valued and most scorned." In recognition of this institutionalized status, the clubs in 1950 had agreed to accept 100 percent of sophomores who sought to join, which meant that thirty or so "unclubbables" would be distributed among them. In 1958, however, when a bare majority of freshmen were public school graduates, and 14 percent of students were Jewish, this inherently unstable compromise collapsed. Widely publicized, the "dirty bicker" of 1958 was a public relations disaster. Nevertheless, the clubs were vehemently defended by President Goheen, the first Princeton president to have belonged to an eating club. He echoed even stronger alumni sentiments, which had previously opposed the 100 percent plan. But the discriminatory nature of Princeton culture further weakened its applicant pool vis-à-vis Harvard and Yale. The faculty demanded that the admissions office accept more high-ability students, but fewer were applying, and alumni preferences were largely continued. Goheen addressed the crisis by creating a special facility for upperclassmen not in the clubs. But a decade after the dirty bicker, Princeton had fewer Jewish students, and 90 percent of upperclassmen belonged to eating clubs.[62]

Yale was most conservative politically of the Big Three, but in 1951 it was rocked by a polemical attack—from the Right! *God and Man at Yale: The Superstitions of "Academic Freedom"* was written by William F. Buckley, Jr., a 1950 grad and former editor of the *Yale Daily News*. He excoriated his alma mater for failing to inculcate religion and individualism. Instead, he alleged, the faculty promulgated secularism and collectivism, which were defended under the pretense of academic freedom. Most outrageous, Buckley called on the trustees to impose the values of the alumni on teaching in Yale College—"a belief in God and a recognition of the merits of our economic system."[63] The university appointed a blue-ribbon committee to gauge its "intellectual and spiritual welfare" and sent the resulting apologia to all alumni—without mention of Buckley's book. More

61 Keller and Keller, *Making Harvard Modern*, 290–97.

62 Karabel, *Chosen*, 294–320, quote p. 307.

63 William F. Buckley, Jr., *God and Man at Yale: The Superstitions of "Academic Freedom"* (Washington, DC: Regnery, 2002 [1951]).

effective was a savage attack in the *Atlantic* on the book and its author by Mc-George Bundy (Yale, '40), which supplied point-by-point refutations of this "assault on the freedom of one of America's greatest and most conservative universities."[64] Still, coming at the height of McCarthyism, allegations of "collectivism" made Yale nervously defensive for some time.

Not surprisingly from his perspective, Buckley felt that politically active students at Yale were predominantly "left-wing," supposedly reflecting the collectivism of their economics texts. More accurately, he judged "the student body as a whole to be apathetic to politics." The culture of Yale College in fact reflected the gentlemanly culture of the prep-school students that the admissions office sought to nurture. Unlike at Princeton, President Griswold was adamantly opposed to ethnic or religious discrimination. Although the admissions door was opened wider in the 1950s, the "new" students that Yale recruited immediately felt the pressure to conform to this dominant culture. Little changed before the late 1960s. Outsiders in the class of 1964 perceived Yale as "a place where 'the likes of us' were pressed ... to turn into 'the likes of them.' "[65]

For liberal arts colleges and private universities, the tensions signaled at the beginning of this section were starkest at the Big Three, where many of the nation's most talented students applied for admission, where alumni were most powerful in supporting collegiate tradition, and where the faculty consisted of productive scholars and scientists. Yet, nowhere were these tensions so overt as to cause a crisis. Rather, several positive trends propelled the rapid development of these institutions.

Probably the most beneficial national trend was the increasing academic attainments of prospective students, which allowed admission offices to operate on a rising gradient. As more selective schools eliminated their weakest students (the bottom tenth, or fifth, or quarter) those applicants cascaded down a tier, bolstering the pool at less selective schools. Thus, the effects were felt throughout higher education but were most apparent at private colleges because of their restricted size. The more selective colleges opened enrollments significantly after the war in response to the GIs, anti-discriminatory legislation (enacted or threatened), and a democratic spirit. However, from the mid-fifties through the early sixties, there was little advance in social inclusion. The rising qualifications of applicants gave admissions officers the best of all worlds—more applicants, better applicants, and the preservation of preferences.

---

64   McGeorge Bundy, "The Attack on Yale," *Atlantic* (November 1951). This article apparently convinced Nathan Pusey to appoint Bundy as dean of the Faculty of Arts and Sciences.

65   Buckley, *God and Man*, 95–96; Howard Gillette, Jr., *Class Divide: Yale '64 and the Conflicted Legacy of the Sixties* (Ithaca, NY: Cornell University Press, 2015), 6.

Rising student abilities complemented the other pervasive trend of this era, the ascendancy of faculty professionalism known as the academic revolution (Chapter 3). Commitments to graduate education and research grew relentlessly at universities, and young PhDs brought fresh disciplinary perspectives to liberal arts colleges. With these developments, faculty prerogatives became unassailable in areas like curriculum and admissions. The preferences of faculty for meritocratic admissions have been noted, but the increasing abilities of students for the most part kept faculty content. In the curriculum, the rhetorical endorsement of liberal education was pervasive in this era. Significant innovations meant to counter the academic disciplines, such as those at Harvard and Amherst, occurred early in this period. Subsequently, the never-ending urges for such reforms were largely diverted to distribution requirements. Faculty prevailed in defining liberal education as a scattered collection of disciplinary courses across the major fields of knowledge.

The traditional features of college life treasured by alumni tended to be defended by relatively conservative administrations—with ongoing tension. In an era of expanding financial ambitions and increasing willingness of alumni to make significant donations, presidents were sensitive to issues affecting image, culture, and established practices. A smoldering issue throughout this era was official discrimination in campus organizations, particularly fraternities. The issue largely persisted into the 1960s, as administrations tended to drag their feet on the issue (as at Princeton), but responded to public pressure when these practices became publicized. After the unruly GIs departed, administrations sought to control student behavior with a philosophy of in loco parentis, another area of alumni concern. On the whole, private colleges and universities of the postwar era wholeheartedly embraced the American way of life, leading them at times to act on principle and at other times to adopt expediency. Relatively conservative presidents and administrations presided over institutions that were rapidly evolving with more and better students, a larger and more professional faculty, and expanding campuses. In time, quantitative changes would produce a cultural transformation as well.

Observers of American higher education at the end of the 1950s perceived an apparent division developing. Traditional colleges and universities comprised one sector. They were becoming increasingly selective in admissions, drawing their students predominantly from the upper-middle class, graduating most of them in four years, and sending half of their graduates on to graduate or professional education. The other sector was open to most high school graduates, attracted largely first-generation students from the middle or working classes, and trained many in technical or specialist skills, if in fact they graduated, which many did not. This sector consisted of the expanding public institutions reviewed in the previous section; the first sector largely consisted of the private colleges just described. These developments threatened "to stratify higher education along socio-economic lines." Not only had selective private colleges raised tuition and become unaffordable for most families, but "youth from lower-status families do not do as well on the measures of selection as youth from middle-class families."[66]

In other words, contemporaries were perceiving a differentiation of markets for higher education that Caroline Hoxby would later model as a "re-sorting" of American higher education. These conditions were experienced by the more selective private colleges and universities. By the mid-sixties, many of them felt that they had reached a meritocratic plateau. The most selective private colleges charged much higher tuition and matched it with growing income from other sources. Less selective colleges enrolled "average" students, charged half as much tuition, and had few additional resources. Market forces were thus making colleges more homogeneous internally while increasing stratification across institutions.[67] But higher education as a whole was not yet ready to bifurcate. The public sector in 1960 was on the cusp of significant qualitative upgrading. And although two "segments" were evident, there was a very large middle to the American system. American universities in 1960 enrolled 43 percent of students from all social backgrounds, at all levels, and in virtually all courses of study.

POSTWAR UNIVERSITIES

In 1955 the director of the College Education Examination Board articulated an increasingly apparent fact: "The university ... has now replaced the undergraduate college as the dominant unit in higher education[,] ... [dominating] educational thought, the setting of academic patterns, determination of intellectual goals, the capacity to create an atmosphere of stability or change."[68] The implied referent here is not the 121 institutions the Bureau of Education classified as universities, but rather those that would later be called research universities—the institutions that were setting the standard for research, doctoral studies, and educational depth at all levels—and additionally, by the mid-fifties, the institutions that sought to emulate them.

In 1910 Edwin Slosson published detailed portraits of fourteen "great American universities," the success stories of the previous generation's efforts to build universities of distinction in the United States. Five were founded as colonial

---

66   Havighurst, *American Higher Education*, 70.
67   Hoxby, "Changing Market Structure."
68   Frank Bowles, quoted in Bernard Berelson, *Graduate Education in the United States* (New York: McGraw-Hill, 1960), 38–39.

colleges—Harvard, Yale, Princeton, Columbia, and Pennsylvania. Five were western state universities—California, Illinois, Minnesota, Wisconsin, and Michigan, all but the last land-grant designees. And four were philanthropic creations of the age of university building—Cornell, Johns Hopkins, Stanford, and Chicago. Massachusetts and (later) California Institutes of Technology were of comparable stature in science and engineering. These sixteen were largely unchallenged in terms of research, doctoral education, and academic reputation during the interwar years and through the 1940s.[69] In 1950 they produced 47 percent of science PhDs, most with more than 2 percent of the total.[70] As academic leaders, they naturally stimulated imitators, but emulation had been exceedingly difficult before the postwar era. During the 1950s, becoming a research university became increasingly feasible—and imperative for institutions wishing to keep abreast, let alone advance, academically. Besides the sixteen prewar research universities, twenty more institutions belonged to the exclusive Association of American Universities (AAU) and its adjunct Association of Graduate Schools and were thus officially committed to fostering research and doctoral education. Beyond these groups, another twenty to thirty institutions had varying degrees of involvement in doctoral education and research—some rapidly growing state universities, some more cautious privates, some engaged in a few specific fields, and some with more balanced portfolios.[71] All faced similar challenges in adapting to the new research economy, but with vastly different means at their disposal.

The postwar research economy evolved out of the massive federal support of research during the war.[72] Under wartime pressure technological advances of enormous significance had been achieved. First and foremost was atomic energy, but almost as many dollars had been invested in the development of radar. Jet and rocket propulsion, radio technologies, computing, and medical advancements also headed a long list of breakthrough technologies. There was no question of abandoning their further development after the war ended, since they were essential for the nation's future defense and held great potential for civilian industries as well. Clearly this would have to be a federal responsibility, but there were few models for how this might be done.

69   Edwin Slosson, *Great American Universities* (New York: Macmillan, 1910). These sixteen institutions are the focus of Roger L. Geiger, *To Advance Knowledge: The Growth of American Research Universities, 1900–1940* (New York: Oxford University Press, 1986).

70   Also attaining 2 percent of PhDs in 1950 were the less prestigious New York University, Ohio State, and Iowa State, while Caltech and Princeton awarded fewer PhDs: Irwin, *American Colleges and Universities, 1952*, 58–59.

71   Berelson, *Graduate Education*, 109–16, 280–81.

72   For the following and for additional sources, see Roger L. Geiger, *Research and Relevant Knowledge: American Research Universities since World War II* (New York: Oxford University Press, 1993), 3–40.

CHAPTER 2

Vannevar Bush, director of the Office of Scientific Research and Development (OSRD), which organized wartime research, prompted President Roosevelt in 1944 to request such a plan. Bush believed that a large investment in basic scientific research would be needed to maintain the momentum of wartime progress and that such research should take place largely in universities. The resulting document, *Science, the Endless Frontier* (1945), embodied these views in a proposed national research foundation that would oversee all federal funding of external research. Congress had already broached this issue. It favored a more bureaucratic arrangement that would ensure an accountable and somewhat equitable distribution of such funds. However, Bush was adamant that the effectiveness of federal support required an independent governing board of eminent scientists who alone could ensure that funds were directed to the most competent investigators—to the "best science." President Truman was not averse to best science, but he was insistent that any unit that disbursed public funds must be accountable to elected officials, namely himself.

In the aftermath of the war, the considerable funds still in the pipeline and other stopgap measures sustained many wartime projects. More permanent arrangements could be made only by Congress, and they found a place on a crowded docket late in the summer of 1946. At this juncture, an administration bill for a national science foundation was countered by a Bush-inspired measure with an autonomous governing board. No reconciliation was attempted in this hectic session, and the matter was tabled. It would be another four years until the National Science Foundation was founded, and nearly another decade before it would be given significant funds. At the same time, legislation was passed covering other federal commitments to research. The Manhattan Project,, which had produced the atomic bomb,, ceded its monopoly over all things nuclear to the Atomic Energy Commission. Contracts for medical research were assumed by the Public Health Service and joined to the National Institutes of Health. And the armed services continued lines of research relevant to their responsibilities. Only one original organization was authorized—the Office of Naval Research. Independent of previous Navy research, the ONR was specifically intended to create access to and foster relations with university scientists.

The young officers who inspired the ONR sought to expand a naval research portfolio that had been constrained by wartime limitations. Their first hurdle was to overcome resistance to working for the Pentagon. Scientists were eager to return to university laboratories and, like their universities, chafed under wartime restrictions and red tape. In 1945 naval officers visited the principal universities engaged in wartime research—MIT, Caltech, Harvard, and the Universities of California and Chicago. They proposed ideal terms: investigator-initiated proposals for basic research, full cost reimbursements, and freedom to publish findings. All signed contracts with the ONR. Research proposals accepted by the agency would be attached to these master contracts as task orders. With the leaders in the fold, other universities had no qualms about joining as well. The ONR supported research projects at some 200 universities in the 1940s, creating an entirely new dimension of federal science policy. It funded small science rather than huge projects—most in the range of $12,000 to $40,000 and running for less than a year. Its chief scientist, Alan Waterman, came via the OSRD and the Yale physics department. He established panels of experts to evaluate proposals, as the OSRD had done, to ensure that ONR funds would support the best science. Waterman and the ONR consciously assumed the role of a substitute for the missing national science foundation. The approximately $20 million it disbursed annually made a substantial contribution to the vitality of postwar academic science. It also signaled that federal research funds were available to any university that could offer worthy proposals.[73]

The postwar federal research economy ignited an unprecedented degree of competition among universities for academic talent, especially in federally supported fields. Previously, universities had competed for faculty to some degree, but in the interwar years the largesse of foundations was awarded chiefly on the basis of comparative advantage in existing capabilities. Now, new conditions created a fluid situation. Most academic scientists had relocated during the war, and many younger ones had acquired intensive research experience; where they would find academic homes was in many cases open. Furthermore, new fields gained prominence, first and foremost atomic physics. Research now would be pursued and supported in places having the appropriate expertise and facilities. The advancement of knowledge had simply accelerated, not only through wartime discoveries but also in the emergence of new understanding across academic fields. Finally, after all the dislocations of the war and the GI invasion, every university faced the challenge of reconstituting itself, rebuilding their faculties and their treasuries as well. In this initial turbulence, only one thing was clear: the desirability of hiring and retaining the best scholars and scientists possible. But how to do so and how much to adapt to the federal research economy was for long unclear to universities and their leaders.

Research universities were still primarily teaching institutions, and they primarily taught undergraduates. The crush of postwar GIs temporarily reinforced this emphasis, and financial limitations forced difficult choices. President Conant was typical in declaring that at Harvard, "we had better concentrate all our

---

73 Harvey M. Sapolsky, *Science and the Navy: The History of the Office of Naval Research* (Princeton: Princeton University Press, 1990). Waterman became the first director of the National Science Foundation in 1950.

thoughts on this transitional period, as it may well last until 1950." The department was the foundation of university organization, and it consisted of professors whose first obligation was teaching, whether or not they preferred scholarship and research. The introduction of federal research funds challenged this
model. It gave rise to widespread university misgivings, which were expressed as
the four Ds: distortion of academic research, displacement of other university
functions, dependence on federal research funding, and domination by the federal government. Federal support was concentrated in the physical sciences and
engineering, and most sponsored research was what Conant called "programmatic" in nature—motivated by ulterior practical applications rather than basic
scientific understanding. Sponsored research projects diverted professors from
teaching and other academic chores. As recipient departments became increasingly dependent on federal funds, there was widespread apprehension about their
future availability. And, as the CFHE warned, the outsized federal role might
lead to "direct federal control [that] would in the end produce uniformity, me-
diocrity and compliance."[74]

Hence, universities proceeded into this brave new research economy with
both eagerness and trepidation. Guidelines had to be devised on faculty time
commitments to teaching versus sponsored research, how outside support affected salaries, the disposition of overhead revenues, the organization of separate
research units, and the university's ultimate fiscal responsibility for all such activities. Principle and practice were often at odds. President Conant declared in
1947 that no secret research would be conducted on the Harvard campus, and
most other universities concurred. However, there were several degrees of secrecy or classification, and in the key field of nuclear studies, all research was
classified. For all of their high-minded intentions, universities had little control
over such matters. Federal funders set the rules, and academic scientists drove the
practices of research universities. If universities wished to retain their most valuable scientists—in reputation and grantsmanship—they had to acquiesce in necessary arrangements and adjust policies accordingly. The continuation of wartime research projects, and the acceleration of external funding after the Korean
War began, made research into an increasingly autonomous university activity.
Those universities that adapted to this reality tended to lead the postwar research
economy; others adjusted sooner or later to these new realities.

The universities in the postwar research economy might be grouped as follows.
The six institutions that performed more than $10 million of wartime OSRD

74 Keller and Keller, *Making Harvard Modern*, 166; Geiger, *Research and Relevant Knowledge*, 58–
61, CFHE quoted on p. 60. Federally supported medical research increased rapidly in the 1950s but posed
fewer concerns.

research contracts had an initial advantage. They were the universities (mentioned above) first contacted by the ONR, plus Columbia and Johns Hopkins.[75] The other ten prewar research universities conducted far less contract research, but many of their scientists were involved with wartime research on large projects elsewhere. These institutions were committed to academic distinction in scholarship and research and thus were compelled to take measures to establish and enhance their participation. Other AAU universities were generally involved to a lesser extent, depending on their capabilities. And finally, more marginally involved state universities soon developed the scale and ambition to join the research economy. Research supported by the armed services was heavily concentrated in the physical sciences and engineering but also tapped social and psychological disciplines.[76] The other source of federal funds was the growing support for medical research, which accelerated in the mid-1950s. Despite the concentrated nature of federal research funds, research universities were committed to high standards across all academic fields, including the humanities and social sciences. For almost every university, improving their academic profile and participating in the research economy required extraordinary efforts.

MIT was the foremost university in which postwar research was substantially a continuation and elaboration of wartime activities. Home to radar research in the Radiation Laboratory, MIT's $100 million of OSRD contracts far surpassed all other universities. Although eager to return to education and basic research, MIT accepted that its contributions to national security were too vital to abandon, and the armed services agreed. It began plans for postwar conversion even before VJ Day by committing institutional funds to sustain the Radiation Lab before new federal funds materialized. MIT recruited future faculty aggressively from Rad Lab personnel and war research projects elsewhere. Before 1945 ended, it secured federal funding to reconstitute the Rad Lab as the Research Laboratory of Electronics (RLE) and to establish a laboratory for nuclear science and engineering. Where many universities, like Harvard, expressed a desire to withdraw from weapons-related or classified research, MIT not only continued such research but agreed to serve as a resource on call for the special needs of the defense establishment. Provost Julius Stratton explained, "Several projects under MIT management ... are of such critical national significance as to transcend our own, local, institutional interests." In many ways, the MIT formula succeeded in advancing academic science *and* military technology. The RLE, in particular,

---

75 National Science Foundation, *The State of Academic Science and Engineering* (Washington, DC: NSF, 1989), 48–59.

76 Mark Solovey, *Shaky Foundations: The Politics–Patronage–Social Science Nexus in Cold War America* (New Brunswick, NJ: Rutgers University Press, 2013), 56–102.

spawned a succession of new and innovative lines of research. When a defense commitment proved too large—like the design of a system for early-warning strategic radar defense—it was hived off to create the Lincoln Laboratory as a federal contract research lab administered by MIT. The expenditures for sponsored research soon dwarfed the educational budget, and the institute prospered as never before.[77]

MIT did not forsake traditional academic values but instead tried to honor them as well as fulfill its new national role. In 1946 it authorized a faculty committee to make a thorough study of all aspects of education and research at the institute. The resulting report noted all the caveats about distortion and displacement of fundamental investigations and sought to promote a balance between education and sponsored research. To provide a more fully rounded education for MIT students, it recommended creating the School of Humanities and Social Studies, which was promptly done. However, it acknowledged that "in the final analysis, the scope and character of sponsored research at MIT is determined by the faculty."[78] The same year the report was accepted by the MIT faculty (1950), the State Department asked MIT to lead a study on international communications. It resulted the next year in creation of the Center for International Studies, funded by the Central Intelligence Agency. The center was the first research unit attached to the School for Humanities and Social Studies, but to enter its offices required a security clearance. In the next decade, MIT's subservience to the defense establishment would become a source of considerable embarrassment,[79] but in the 1950s the institute served both academic and federal masters.[80]

The second-largest beneficiary of war research was the University of California at Berkeley. Under longtime president Robert Gordon Sproul, the UC had consciously sought academic distinction and become the most highly rated state

77   Geiger, *Research and Relevant Knowledge*, 63–73, quote p. 71. James R. Killian, Jr., *The Education of a College President: A Memoir* (Cambridge, MA: MIT Press, 1985), 22–76.

78   Geiger, *Research and Relevant Knowledge*, 65.

79   Stuart W. Leslie, *The Cold War and American Science: The Military-Industrial-Academic Complex at MIT and Stanford* (New York: Columbia University Press, 1993).

80   The Korean conflict caused a large increase in defense research, as President James Killian explained in 1952: The "Korean conflict produced an abrupt and compelling demand for the Institute and its staff to make their special competence further available to aid the rearmament program": David Kaiser, ed., *Becoming MIT: Moments of Decision* (Cambridge, MA: MIT Press, 2010), 105. For defense policy and research, see David M. Hart, *Forged Consensus: Science, Technology, and Economic Policy in the United States, 1921–1953* (Princeton: Princeton University Press, 1998), 175–205; for the defense establishment and university research, see Roger L. Geiger, "Science, Universities, and National Defense," *Osiris* 7 (1992): 26–48.

university.[81] Its brightest star was E. O. Lawrence, whose invention of the cyclo-tron earned the 1939 Nobel Prize in physics. The Berkeley physicist J. Robert Oppenheimer directed the Manhattan Project, and Lawrence played a key role. Immediately afterward, project funds allowed Lawrence to expand his Radiation Laboratory, completing a large cyclotron and two additional accelerators. Berke-ley emerged as the world leader in high energy physics. The eminence of physics inspired academic ambitions across the university. In some cases, Lawrence pro-vided tangible assistance. In setting up an isotope lab for the future Nobel Lau-reate Melvin Calvin, he explained, "Don't worry about the money. I'll take care of that, you just do the science." The UC quickly became wholly engaged in the postwar research economy, but with an inherent focus on promoting basic aca-demic science. Like MIT, it created numerous "organized research units" (known locally as ORUs) that received external support and performed appropriate ser-vices, while faculty in their departmental roles focused on disinterested inqui-ry.[82] The UC quickly grasped the logic of an autonomous research role: "[If the] size of staff is ... determined primarily by teaching requirements ... the extent of research activity is limited accordingly.... On the other hand, with an expanding national program of research, the research activities of the university will be ex-tended to the extent necessary to meet public demands."[83]

Soon Berkeley committed to attaining the highest level of academic distinc-tion. After Clark Kerr became chancellor in 1952, it formulated the Academic Plan for the Berkeley Campus, which envisioned a concentration on upper-division and graduate education, a doubling of the faculty, and a standard of quality equal to that of the best universities. Kerr personally scrutinized all ap-pointments and promotions with the goal of having each department rank no lower than sixth nationally.[84]

81 C. Judson King, *The University of California: Creating, Nurturing, and Maintaining Quality in a Public University Setting* (Berkeley, CA: Center for Studies in Higher Education, 2018), passim.

82 Organized research units existed since the nineteenth century, but they played an indispensable role in the organization of postwar research. Generally created to manage sponsored research supported by external funds, some were established with state, institutional, or private funds to emphasize particular lines of research. Large capital research facilities required separate professional staff, as did units providing applied research and services. Each ORU tended to be an "organic" creation, adapted to unique combina-tions of mission, funding, and professional leadership, but all of them forced postwar universities to de-vise personnel policies for researchers who were not teachers: Carlos E. Kruytbosch, "The Organization of Research in the University: The Case of Research Personnel," PhD diss., University of California, Berkeley, 1970; Geiger, *Research and Relevant Knowledge*, 47–57.

83 Quoted from *Report of a Study Committee on Contract Research* (Berkeley, CA: 1950), 22, in Charles V. Kidd, *American Universities and Federal Research* (Cambridge, MA: Harvard University Press, 1959), 36.

84 Geiger, *Research and Relevant Knowledge*, 73–82.

Other universities were less successful in translating large OSRD contracts into postwar academic research. The wartime laboratories managed by these institutions were converted into federal national laboratories and were generally effective in developing their respective technologies, but with few of the academic spillovers achieved at Berkeley and MIT. A spokesman for Caltech called the Jet Propulsion Laboratory "an inheritance from the war days.... Three-hundred and fifty persons, roughly, are on the ... pay roll. Exactly three of our permanent faculty have [a] part-time connection." At Johns Hopkins, half-hearted efforts were made to integrate personnel from the Applied Physics Laboratory with the faculty, but it too remained peripheral to the somewhat hidebound academic units. The Argonne National Laboratory, which developed from Chicago's role in the atomic bomb project, was dedicated to reactor development and loosely connected with the physics department. Chicago employed a number of atomic physics luminaries, but academic development was compromised by the president's preoccupation with undergraduate education (the Hutchins College), which inhibited enrollments, revenues, and academic stature.[85]

If they wished to be at the forefront of scientific advancement, research universities all faced the challenge of adapting to the postwar federal research economy. Impeding them were the scarcity of funds, competing priorities like undergraduate instruction, misgivings about the four Ds, and often the ingrained myopia that accompanied institutional inertia. What was needed was leadership at the highest level committed to scientific excellence, particularly in faculty hiring. Opportunism could be vital as well given the rapidity of developments immediately after the war. Opportunities were apparent to individuals such as Stanford's Frederick Terman (below) and Illinois's F. Wheeler Loomis, both of whom had worked on wartime projects and were familiar with networks of scientists and funders. There was a price of admission to the research economy, but once it was paid, the returns were substantial and soon multiplied.

Developments at Cornell exemplified this process. President Edmund Ezra Day (1937–1949) joined the university from the Rockefeller Foundation and valued both academic excellence and public service. Late in 1945 the possibility arose of acquiring the multimillion-dollar Curtiss-Wright aeronautical laboratory in Buffalo. Located far from campus and engaged in applied, secret research for manufacturers and the Air Force, its huge budget posed a significant financial risk for the university. But the lab would be a bonanza for the new School of Aeronautical Engineering. Facing an end of year deadline, Cornell took the plunge although, if it "had been put to a faculty vote, it would certainly have

---

85   Kidd, *American Universities*, 186; John W. Boyer, *The University of Chicago: A History* (Chicago: University of Chicago Press, 2015), 314–15.

been rejected."[86] But air travel was a burgeoning industry, and the laboratory found numerous patrons and fruitful lines of research. Another fateful commitment was required in atomic physics. Professor (and future Nobel laureate) Hans Bethe had been chief of the theoretical division at Los Alamos, and he returned with a complement of talented nuclear scientists, including Richard Feynman. Receiving an offer from Berkeley in 1946, he informed Day that nuclear studies required an investment of up to $2 million for the necessary facilities. Day later called this commitment "perhaps the most momentous decision" of his administration: "If we did not create a laboratory of Nuclear Studies, we would lose most of our key physicists, jeopardize not only our position of leadership in the physical sciences, but also, in consequence, the strength of our programs in engineering and other areas of applied science."[87]

Research competitiveness in the postwar research economy required continual investment, but the demands of nuclear physics were particularly onerous. Yale physics was a laggard before the war and did not participate in wartime science. To catch up it managed to hire a theoretical physicist who was well supported by the ONR. But it soon confronted the same dilemma as Cornell—the need to devote scarce institutional funds to building a laboratory for atomic physics. The decision to scrape together funds for this project was especially difficult for the new president, Whitney Griswold, an academic purist who disdained federal research funding. He ultimately accepted that for Yale to remain a great university, modern laboratories were needed for first-rate scientists. Still, a freeze on faculty salaries and promotions in 1952 made this move widely unpopular. The University of Michigan found a more creative way to establish itself in nuclear physics. Wartime and postwar research was driven by the university faculty in multiple areas, despite President Alexander Ruthven's (1929–1951) distrust of federally supported research and worries over the four Ds. As a memorial for the university's war dead, it launched the Phoenix Project in 1948 to raise funds privately for the peaceful use of atomic energy. With these two laudable aims, it garnered a remarkable $7.5 million over several years, with the final $1 million gift coming from the Ford Foundation for purchase of a nuclear reactor. Federal funds naturally followed, but the private endowment supported a broad spectrum of research applications across the university.[88]

86   Morris Bishop, *A History of Cornell* (Ithaca, NY: Cornell University Press, 1962), 580–81.

87   Glenn C. Altschuler and Isaac Kramnick, *Cornell: A History, 1940–2015* (Ithaca, NY: Cornell University Press, 2014), 13–14.

88   Geiger, *Research and Relevant Knowledge*, 82–85; Howard H. Peckham, *The Making of the University of Michigan, 1817–1992*, edited and updated by Margaret L. Steneck and Nicholas H. Steneck (Ann Arbor: University of Michigan Press, 1994), 240–63.

The University of Pennsylvania was another institution afflicted with lethargic postwar leadership. Its administrators and trustees were perceived as "unimaginative and unduly cautious," in keeping with "the general conservatism of the Philadelphia environment."[89] Its medical school was an exception, advancing under a research-savvy dean, but the Wharton School declined after the departure for the Rockefeller Foundation of its guiding spirit, Dean Joseph Willits (1933–1939). The malaise was particularly evident in the College of Arts and Sciences, where prewar weaknesses persisted into the 1950s. In this respect, Penn was representative of many American universities facing the challenge of raising academic standards to compete in the postwar environment. In 1953 the trustees elevated the physics professor Gaylord Harnwell (1952–1972) to the presidency, finally providing a leader determined to address Penn's many problems.[90]

Among his first acts, Harnwell commissioned the Educational Survey, directed by Joseph Willits, which over five years and multiple studies examined every aspect of the university's operations. The studies of the faculty and graduate school identified core weaknesses, even though conditions were beginning to improve by the time they appeared in 1958. Faculty inbreeding was one problem, as it was at many universities: over half the Arts and Sciences faculty had Penn PhDs, 76 percent in the Wharton School. Home-grown faculty "resisted change, were distrustful of experiments performed elsewhere, and viewed critics as disgruntled or disloyal." They were also complacent about their relative standing. In fact, aside from President Harnwell, the only distinguished scientists were in the medical school. Relatively unselective admissions of undergraduates, especially in the Wharton School, diminished university prestige and faculty morale. For graduate programs, most departments admitted 85–100 percent of applicants, and they neither attracted applicants from top schools nor placed graduates in such places. Only half were bona fide graduate students studying full time. Penn, in fact, ranked seventeenth in PhDs awarded before the Harnwell era. Money, of course, was a serious limitation in that higher salaries and stipends were needed to attract better faculty and support graduate students. But universities had to

89   Richard H. Shryock, *The University of Pennsylvania Faculty: A Study in American Higher Education* (Philadelphia: University of Pennsylvania Press, 1959), 111. Under President Harold Stassen, who was preparing for a presidential run in 1952, Penn was aggressive in promoting big-time football and possible lucrative TV contracts: Ronald A. Smith, *Play-by-Play: Radio, Television, and Big-Time College Sport* (Baltimore: Johns Hopkins University Press, 2001), 66–72.

90   Steven A. Sass, *The Pragmatic Imagination: A History of the Wharton School, 1881–1981* (Philadelphia: University of Pennsylvania Press, 1982), 233–63. Overcoming the handicap of location in a "blighted area" was a vital and indispensable achievement of the Harnwell administration: John L. Puckett and Mark Frazier Lloyd, *Becoming Penn: The Pragmatic American University, 1950–2000* (Philadelphia: University of Pennsylvania Press, 2015); Margaret Pugh O'Mara, *Cities of Knowledge: Cold War Science and the Search for the Next Silicon Valley* (Princeton: Princeton University Press, 2005), 142–81.

improve their reputations in order to raise revenues. The Educational Survey was clear about the goal: "Pennsylvania, like other leading universities, is thoroughly committed to the research objective." Reflecting changing national priorities, it added a sentiment that would resonate in the next decade: "Efforts to improve teaching in the undergraduate colleges, desirable in themselves, should not be permitted to interfere with a university's prime purpose."[91]

Perhaps as an antidote to complacency, the Educational Survey sought to gauge Penn's relative standing by conducting a rating of arts and sciences departments. This was the first systematic ranking of universities and departments since that done by Raymond Hughes in 1925.[92] Penn ranked itself a charitable eleventh, buoyed by several minor humanities departments. It consoled itself that its position had not changed since 1925, but it was conspicuously weak in the largest, most competitive departments. Overall, the Keniston ratings confirmed the university groupings identified at the start of this section. The prewar research universities were still on top, except that UCLA was rated no. 14 and Johns Hopkins slipping to no. 16 (MIT and Caltech were omitted as technical schools). California now challenged Harvard as the leading university; Chicago declined to no. 6; and Columbia's weaknesses had not yet registered. Keniston only considered twenty-five institutions worth rating, a reflection of the state of academic development in the mid-1950s. Below the prewar research universities, he included Indiana, Northwestern, Ohio State, NYU, and Washington. Beyond them and not ranked (having few departments in the top fifteen) were Catholic University, Duke, Iowa, North Carolina, and Texas. Clearly in 1957, the year of the Keniston surveys, most of these universities shared Penn's problems with faculty inbreeding and weakly organized graduate programs.

The Keniston ratings failed to detect the rising academic strength of Stanford. Rated at the bottom of the research universities (no. 13), as it had been in 1925 (no. 14), Stanford was already well launched on the most remarkable of all postwar institutional transformations. The initial strategic steps were taken by Frederick Terman and ably promoted by President Wallace Sterling (1949–1968). Terman spent the war directing the Radio Research Lab at Harvard, which developed radar countermeasures and communications. He returned to Stanford as dean of engineering with the avowed ambition of building the top engineering

91   Hayward Keniston, *Graduate Study and Research in the Arts and Sciences at the University of Pennsylvania* (Philadelphia: University of Pennsylvania Press, 1959); Shryock, *University of Pennsylvania Faculty*, 112, 237, 255.

92   Keniston, *Graduate Study*. Hughes conducted a rating in 1934 that sought to avoid ranking. In 1946 the AAU conducted an unpublished ranking among its members, Columbia did so in 1954, and the *Chicago Tribune* in 1957 attempted rankings—indications of a growing preoccupation with academic standing: Shryock, *University of Pennsylvania Faculty*, 105–10.

school on the West Coast. He was certain that federal support of defense research, especially electronics, would continue, and he consciously sought to use these research contracts to advance his school and Stanford University. He brought back a contingent of scientists from the Harvard Lab, aggressively sought contracts from the ONR, and shaped the engineering school to perform this research. In rapid succession, he created laboratories to consolidate research on microwaves, electronics, and applied electronics, while also working closely with local industries. In 1955 Terman was elevated to provost, in which position he oversaw hiring and promotions for the entire faculty. His ambitions now transcended engineering and sought to emulate the practices he had observed during his time at Harvard.[93]

These ambitions were fully shared by President Wallace Sterling, who was instrumental in achieving them. What distinguished Stanford from other rising research universities was, foremost, a determination to emulate the best. For engineering research that meant MIT, but for university advancement the model was Harvard, particularly its capacity to sustain the highest levels of quality through planning and foresight. These high ambitions fostered an internal mentality at once critical in seeking improvement and coldly realistic in judging existing conditions. Stanford consistently related the ends they wished to achieve with the means necessary to attain them, which in most cases meant a lot more funding. This mind-set allowed Stanford to create and exploit potential opportunities and made possible what may have appeared in retrospect to be good fortune. Sterling had served on the CFHE, where he became plugged in to the foundation world and cognizant of the financial exigencies of private universities. This experience may have reinforced an eagerness to work with private industry, which many universities were reluctant to do (Penn, for example). Such ties not only brought additional research, but also stimulated a rising tide of gifts especially from wealthy industrialists of the Bay Area. Stanford benefited greatly from its affinity with the Ford Foundation: its own goals for carefully planned academic advancement were precisely those of the foundation. And, as the university's accomplishments became manifest, Sterling's success in fund-raising from all sources multiplied. Stanford's progress was piecemeal before 1955, although the changing character of the institution was increasingly apparent. After that date, resources and academic milestones accumulated. When the next rating survey was conducted in 1964, Stanford vaulted to no. 5.[94]

93   Geiger, *Research and Relevant Knowledge*, 118–22; Rebecca S. Lowen, *Creating the Cold War University: The Transformation of Stanford* (Berkeley: University of California Press, 1997); Leslie, *Cold War*; C. Stewart Gillmor, *Fred Terman at Stanford: Building a Discipline, a University, and Silicon Valley* (Stanford, CA: Stanford University Press, 2004).

94   Geiger, *Research and Relevant Knowledge*, 122–35.

Stanford stands out as the only private research university to increase its relative standing between the 1957 and (far more thorough) 1964 surveys.[95] The research economy of the 1950s and 1960s tended to favor public universities. Wisconsin, Michigan, Illinois, and UC Berkeley (no. 1) achieved their highest rankings in these years, along with burgeoning doctoral programs. State universities tended to have large departments in the physical sciences and engineering. Their large and growing undergraduate enrollments supported a departmental scale that could absorb the expense of PhD instruction. In a significant development, a growing number of state institutions increasingly embraced the university mission of graduate education and research. From 1945 to 1965, eighteen land-grant "colleges" changed their appellation to "university." The nomenclature spanned different degrees of internal development but signaled a singular identification with the "mainstream" idea and mission of universities.[96]

Most of these schools were former "A&Ms" that had been defined by a different mission from the states' flagship universities. What research they performed originated in agriculture and spread to other applied fields. They were slow to develop colleges of arts and sciences, and these units tended to remain underdeveloped. Postwar enrollment growth helped to fill out these other curricular areas, which was a first step toward a university mentality. Arizona State, for example, felt it had become a university in all but name when it was reorganized in 1954 into four colleges—Liberal Arts, Education, Applied Arts and Sciences, and Business and Public Administration. These units in fact reflected the distribution of undergraduates in most land-grant institutions.[97] Half of these schools did not award a PhD until the 1950s, but several had engaged in research and graduate education in the interwar years. Iowa State was the first to become so engaged, and it was one of the handful of this group that had become research universities in fact as well as name. In 1958 the AAU conferred membership on Iowa State, Penn State, and Purdue (always named a university, but part of the A&M group), the first former A&Ms to be so honored.

95   Allan M. Cartter, *An Assessment of Quality in Graduate Education* (Washington, DC: ACE, 1966); David S. Webster, "America's Highest Ranked Graduate Schools, 1925–1982," *Change* (May–June 1983): 13–24.

96   Univ. of Massachusetts (1947), Florida State Univ. (1947), Penn State Univ. (1953), Michigan State Univ. (1954), Rutgers—The State University (with a public board: 1956), Utah State, Oklahoma State, and Colorado State Universities (1957), Arizona State, New Mexico State, and Mississippi State Universities (1958), Iowa State and Washington State Universities (1959), Auburn Univ. and N. Dakota State Univ. (1960), Oregon St. Univ. (1961), N. Carolina State Univ. (1963), Clemson Univ. (1964).

97   Roger L. Geiger, "Land-Grant Colleges and the Pre-Modern Era of American Higher Education, 1850–1890," in Alan I. Marcus, ed., *Science As Service: Establishing and Reformulating American Land-Grant Universities, 1865–1930* (Tuscaloosa: University of Alabama Press, 2015), 9–32; Ernest J. Hopkins and Alfred Thomas, Jr., *The Arizona State University Story* (Phoenix: Southwest Publishing, 1960), 284–89.

Each conferral of a university title was a unique event, but in all cases it signified joining the modernization of American higher education. In some states legislation was required, often after a review of the state's entire system of higher education. In others, boards of trustees acted alone, often after a blue-ribbon commission report. In Kansas, Michigan, and Washington, the colleges were initially given the condescending title of "university of agriculture and applied science," but these demeaning tags were soon dropped. At Penn State College, President Milton Eisenhower carefully canvassed all interested parties on a name change and discovered that ... no one really cared. The university's lawyer filed the necessary paperwork at the county courthouse. In Arizona, however, the University of Arizona opposed the ambitions of the state college and also dominated the state board of higher education. A grassroots movement organized a 1958 referendum in which voters approved the title Arizona State University by a two-to-one margin. By this date, universities and modernization drew growing popular support. Ten of these eighteen name changes occurred between 1957 and 1960.

Penn State's development benefited somewhat indirectly from the war, but here again personal connections were important. The seventh-largest engineering school before the war, it devoted most of its wartime efforts to sizeable education programs. The engineering dean played an important role in the national organization of these efforts, but he also recognized that research would need to be expanded afterward. He hired Eric Walker from the Harvard Underwater Sound Lab, and Walker was soon asked to continue the lab's research at Penn State. The Navy then expanded the project into the Ordnance Research Laboratory, with a large water tunnel for underwater testing. Although engaged in classified weapons research, the lab was integrated with the engineering college, where Walker became dean, and it provided a wellspring for further research. Walker also used wartime connections to establish the first college nuclear reactor to be licensed by the AEC. Penn State committed to academic modernization when Milton Eisenhower became president (1950–1956). In seven years as head of Kansas State, he had injected a liberal arts curriculum into a typically applied land-grant college. Now he took the reins of a more developed institution that suffered from a cow-college image and low morale. Eisenhower was an adept administrator and an inspiring leader (being the president's brother didn't hurt), but he conceded academic affairs to the deans, especially Walker, who subsequently became vice president for research and the heir apparent. Achieving a name change to Penn State University was symbolic, but it represented a real transformation to the mentality of a full-fledged academic institution. Penn State research retained the science and engineering orientation of a land-grant school, with the College of Liberal Arts and the library relatively neglected, but academically it found a viable niche in the postwar research economy.[98]

In the last half of the 1950s, the main features of a federally dominated postwar research economy had become manifest, but academic leaders were by no means pleased. With more than half of research expenditures coming from the federal government, and half of those from the Pentagon and the AEC, they repeatedly expressed a litany of worries. Prevailing conceptions of the traditional university seemed threatened. Of the university's fundamental mission of preserving, transmitting, and creating knowledge, federal research dollars supported only the latter. Free inquiry, the most essential quality of a university, might possibly be compromised by the requirements of federal research contracts. And the programmatic ends of federal agencies threatened to displace the university mission of advancing knowledge through basic research.[99] These normative concerns stemmed from the academic zeitgeist of the 1950s. As critiques, they were not entirely accurate at the time, but more important, they distracted contemporaries from appreciating a far larger phenomenon that would only be apparent in retrospect: American postwar academic research had evolved the most powerful system for advancing knowledge that the world had ever seen.

The sponsors and performers of research had coalesced into a *self-organizing system*. Extremely decentralized, a multitude of actors and actions were coordinated by positive-feedback mechanisms that oriented and stabilized the research processes and validated the outputs. This system presented research sponsors with an amazingly rich palette of possibilities. They could draw upon the entire population of academic researchers, awarding support to the most promising proposals, whether independently submitted or solicited. If their objective was to develop products or weapons, they could assign such projects to specialized laboratories—federal, industrial, or university-managed. Could sponsors identify and secure the most competent investigators? They relied on the scientific community to identify the best science. The efficiency of the funding process was scarcely an issue: valuable findings were retained and built upon; disappointing results were dismissed. Did academic researchers forfeit their freedom by accepting the terms of sponsored research? By no means. Their behavior was shaped by positive feedback from three separate but interrelated reward systems. Research grants provided resources—for their labs, their students, and themselves.

98   Michael Bezilla, *Engineering Education at Penn State: A Century in the Land-Grant Tradition* (University Park: Pennsylvania State University Press, 1981); Stephen E. Ambrose and Richard H. Immerman, *Milton S. Eisenhower: Educational Statesman* (Baltimore: Johns Hopkins University Press, 1983).

99   Geiger, *Research and Relevant Knowledge*, 157–58; Kidd, *American Universities*, 25–38.

Universities rewarded academic achievement with promotion and tenure. And the academic disciplines conferred professional recognition and prestige. Academic scientists were strongly motivated to advance their field in ways that earned professional advancement as well as garnering research grants. Large funders like the ONR, AEC, or Ford Foundation could and did dominate selected fields, but these were only small pieces of the research economy, and they mirrored these same merit-based processes. Irregularities in any case tended to be self-correcting. With a common objective, the multitude of participants in this self-organizing system generated increasing amounts of knowledge—theoretical, basic, programmatic, technical, and/or applied.

At the end of the 1950s the power and efficacy of this system quelled the doubts and fears of academic traditionalists. A transformation took place in perceptions and support for universities and the academic research system. Misgivings, trepidation, fear of the four Ds all gave way to a social and political endorsement of the processes just described—what soon would be recognized as the academic revolution.

PART II

THE LIBERAL HOUR

1957–1968

THE ASCENDANCY OF
THE UNIVERSITY

THE HISTORIANS CALVIN MACKENZIE AND ROBERT WEISBROT have dubbed the 1960s the Liberal Hour—a time in which Americans entrusted the federal government to rectify the country's social ills and accepted "a ferocious gust of reform that swept across a broad plain of issues, some old and some new."[1] It was a period of gradually accelerating awareness of the need for change—in public attitudes and in government actions. Recognition of the need for reform emerged in a meaningful way with the 1960 election of John F. Kennedy. Fairly conservative politically, Kennedy nevertheless conveyed a spirit of reform in the appointment of academic scholars to his administration, the rhetoric of a New Frontier, and not least in the Camelot image. Frustrated during the Kennedy years by Congressional roadblocks, the "ferocious gust" of liberal reform burst forth in a hurricane of legislation during the first half of Lyndon Johnson's presidency (1963–1969). Monumental breakthroughs were enacted for civil rights, the War on Poverty, cities, the environment, and education, all of which expanded the scale and scope of the federal government. From 1966, however, Johnson's Great Society met growing resistance that challenged and ultimately undermined the short-lived hegemony of the Liberal Hour. But by then the American state had been transformed, and so had American higher education.

During the conservative 1950s, a "liberal accord" had embraced the American way of life while accepting the postwar status quo, particularly the coexistence of industrial capitalism and the New Deal accommodation of organized labor. Efforts toward social amelioration aimed to "uplift the poor without unduly burdening the wealthy," and the general good was equated with achieving "full employment."[2] This consensus began to be challenged beginning in 1957. The need to mobilize troops to integrate Central High School in Little Rock, Arkansas,

---

1   G. Calvin Mackenzie and Robert Weisbrot, *The Liberal Hour: Washington and the Politics of Change in the 1960s* (New York: Penguin, 2008), 5.

2   Ibid., 42–43; Richard H. Pells, *The Liberal Mind in a Conservative Age: American Intellectuals in the 1940s and 1950s* (New York: Harper & Row, 1985), 147–62.

was a premonition that liberal avoidance of deep-seated contradictions would not long persist. But the greatest shock to public complacency was delivered in October, when the Soviet Union launched Sputnik I. Americans were unprepared for the possibility that the Soviets might be ahead of us in the space race, in science generally, and possibly in military hardware. It provoked a decided shift in the public mood. For many this became a clarion call to address the challenge, strengthen the country, and overcome the shortcomings of education, while still upholding the American way of life.

The following year, the prevailing social consensus was challenged by John Kenneth Galbraith's best-selling book, *The Affluent Society*. Witty and iconoclastic, Galbraith's critique of growing private affluence amid public penury questioned the very core of the American way of life at the end of the 1950s. The Achilles' heel of the Affluent Society was its obsession with the continuous expansion of economic output. Everyone seemingly had a vested interest in growth, but America's newly achieved affluence left American consumers with few pressing needs (a shortsighted view in retrospect). Instead, advertising contrived demand for additional goods, and the crusade against communism stimulated extravagant expenditures on military hardware. At the same time, the public sector was starved of resources. Growing private consumption was accompanied by stagnation or deterioration of the public aspects of American life, including the condition of cities, transportation, the environment, medical care, and education. On this last point Galbraith emphasized the emergence of a New Class of workers whose labors were based on technical and intellectual skills—a vision that foreshadowed what would later be called postindustrial society. To join the New Class, "overwhelmingly, the qualification is education." Instead of investing in increased production, he advised, America should invest in the schools and universities that were needed to educate this New Class.[3]

Of all the potential areas for liberal reform, expanding and improving education probably had the widest potential for popular and political support. But at this juncture there was little agreement on how that might be done or who might pay for it. In the mid-fifties, the nation was faced with the challenge of supplying classrooms and teachers for the burgeoning cohorts of baby-boom pupils, and awareness was growing that these same students would seek places in higher education in the next decade. The 1955 "White House Conference on Education" aired the problems facing primary and secondary education, but its recommendation for "emergency" federal aid for school construction was ignored, victim

---

3 John Kenneth Galbraith, *The Affluent Society*, 4th ed. (Boston: Houghton Mifflin, 1984), 263; Pells, *Liberal Mind*, 162–74.

of the Congressional impasse over federal involvement with education. Its sequel the following year was the President's Committee on Education Beyond the High School. The still dismal climate for federal educational initiatives was apparent when Congress withdrew the committee's funding in 1957. Its final report nonetheless boldly portrayed the approaching Tidal Wave—a doubling or tripling of students by 1970. It further detailed the immediate needs: raising abysmal faculty salaries to competitive levels; providing counseling and financial aid to encourage more academically superior students to attend college; and broadening educational opportunity by building more community colleges.[4]

Sputnik transformed the nation's willingness to address the challenges facing higher education. David Henry, president of the University of Illinois and a member of the presidential committee, later noted the "enormous boost" given by "the favorable public evaluation of higher education that prevailed from roughly 1958 to 1968.... That educated men and women are the chief resource of America became an article of faith, a faith widely shared even [though it] was not measurable in specific terms." The reaction to Sputnik at the federal level included the National Defense Education Act (NDEA, 1958), which implemented some of the committee's recommendations for student aid by establishing graduate fellowships and student loans.[5] However, Sputnik diverted federal attention from the Tidal Wave to the state of American science. The enormous investment that followed will be examined below. The burgeoning cohorts of college students were accommodated instead by the American public through state and local governments and private donors. From 1956 to 1970, enrollments nearly tripled, but educational expenditures at colleges and universities grew sixfold. Donations in the decade after 1955 more than quadrupled. Public favor and faith propelled the transformation of American higher education.[6]

The transformation had multiple dimensions—enrollment growth, institutional proliferation and adaptation, expansion of scientific research, and intellectual advancements across the academic spectrum. These developments occurred nearly simultaneously. The Liberal Hour encompassed these parallel stories: academic developments (in this chapter) and the multiple consequences of the Tidal Wave (in Chapter 4).

4   David D. Henry, *Challenges Past, Challenges Present: An Analysis of American Higher Education Since 1930* (San Francisco: Jossey-Bass, 1975), 99–107; Janet Kerr-Tener, "From Truman to Johnson: Ad hoc Policy Formulation in Higher Education," PhD diss., University of Virginia, 1985, 131–221.

5   Wayne J. Urban, *More Than Science and Sputnik: The National Defense Education Act of 1958* (Tuscaloosa: University of Alabama Press, 2010), 176–78.

6   Henry, *Challenges Past*, 106–21, quotes pp. 106, 112.

THE FEDERAL RESEARCH ECONOMY

The immediate reactions to Sputnik emphasized space, science, and education. For education, the NDEA was the contribution to higher education, while other efforts sought to address the deficiencies of K-12 schooling, largely through the Office of Education. For space, the National Aeronautics and Space Administration (NASA) was formed in 1958 and would soon become another channel for federal support for university science. For science, Sputnik quickly affected the national dialogue on scientific research. [7]

When the National Science Foundation was created in 1950, 87 percent of federal funds for university research came from the Pentagon and the Atomic Energy Commission. Academic and scientific leaders complained in the ensuing years of the dominance of defense research to the neglect of basic research. Vannevar Bush had argued the essential role of basic science in *Science, the Endless Frontier* (1945). The NSF was the direct legacy of Bush's report, and its director, Alan Waterman, was a consistent advocate for basic research in these years. However, the defense establishment grew increasingly skeptical of basic academic science, favoring instead programmatic research for weapons systems at its own centers. The Sputnik crisis reversed the relative standing of these two positions, elevating basic research as a national priority both to best the Soviets and to undergird the nation's scientific efforts. An immediate response was bolstering scientific input to the executive branch. MIT president James Killian was appointed to the new post of presidential science advisor, assisted by senior scientific statesmen in the new President's Science Advisory Committee. PSAC advised Eisenhower on issues such as the design of NASA, and it also used its national forum to articulate and embellish an ideology of basic research—meaning principally university research. PSAC issued reports in 1958 and 1959 that made the case for strengthening academic science, and proponents reinforced this message by organizing the Symposium on Basic Research, which Eisenhower not only attended but also used to endorse the $100 million Stanford Linear Accelerator.[8]

PSAC issued an even stronger statement in 1960. A panel chaired by Berkeley chancellor (and discoverer of plutonium) Glenn Seaborg asserted that research was above all an investment in our economic self-interest and that "our proper

7   Roger L. Geiger, *Research and Relevant Knowledge: American Research Universities Since World War II* (New York: Oxford University Press, 1993), 161–66; Geiger, "What Happened after Sputnik? Shaping University Research in the United States," *Minerva* 35 (1997): 349–67; Barbara B. Clowse, *Brainpower for the Cold War: The Sputnik Crisis and the National Defense Education Act of 1958* (Westport, CT: Greenwood Press, 1981); Urban, *More Than Science and Sputnik*.

8   Geiger, *Research and Relevant Knowledge*, 166–69.

course is to increase our investment in science just as fast as we can, to a limit not yet in sight." Basic research and graduate education, it stressed, "*belong together* at every possible level." And given the "critical importance to the national welfare," the resources to permit universities to flourish are "inescapably a responsibility of the federal government." The Seaborg Report called for the implementation of the ideology of basic research. It exhorted the government not simply to fund research contracts but also to take responsibility for building the research capacity of universities with support for graduate students, faculty, new fields of study, and facilities. In addition, it set a goal of doubling the number of "first-rate centers of science ... to thirty or forty in another fifteen years." Amazingly, this blueprint was largely followed in the 1960s.[9]

Support for universities and academic research epitomized the transformation of the national zeitgeist to the Liberal Hour. The Seaborg Report appeared just weeks after the election of John F. Kennedy, who would appoint Seaborg chairman of the Atomic Energy Commission. During these years science achieved a level of influence and prestige in the executive branch unequaled before or since. The machinery for supporting academic science was largely in place, with NASA and the NDEA providing minor additions. The appropriations forthcoming from a previously parsimonious Congress were an uncritical endorsement of science. From 1958 to 1964, federal funds for university research quadrupled—from $200 to $800 million. In this "great inflation," almost three-quarters of the increase was allocated to NSF (+$110 million) and the National Institutes of Health (+$329 million). Competition with the Soviets may have triggered this surge, but the ideology of basic research provided the sustaining rationale. NSF sought to uphold the world-leading stature of all sciences, and NIH appropriations reflected domestic backing for advancing health care. The Soviet challenge was largely addressed by NASA with the pledge to send an American to the moon— and develop intercontinental ballistic missiles in the process.

The great inflation of the research economy occurred in two phases. From Sputnik to the mid-sixties, the influence of the scientific establishment was ascendant, the ideology of basic research unchallenged, and the growth of federal research support geometric. The national expenditure for academic R&D doubled from 0.1 to 0.2 percent of GDP, all the more impressive in an expanding economy. All federal science agencies benefited. NSF budgets averaged 20 percent annual growth during these years, reaching 15 percent of the federal support for academic research. Embodying the ideology of basic research, it aspired to become the "balance wheel" for stable support of American science. As its budget

9   Ibid., 169–70. The following draws from ibid., 170–97.

expanded, so did its roles. In addition to providing research grants to individuals, it assumed greater responsibilities for Big Science projects and their costly facilities, and it also sought to assist universities with institutional support and equipment.

Still, the National Institutes of Health under James Shannon (1955–1968) was the greatest beneficiary, becoming after 1960 the largest funder of academic research. As the research arm of the Public Health Services, NIH's mission was to investigate the "cause, prevention, and method of diagnosis and treatment of diseases." A coalition of lobbyists advocated this unimpeachable cause to Congressional committees and achieved a gusher of appropriations. Given this mandate, NIH had little need for the ideology of basic research, even though nearly 90 percent of the research it sponsored was of this character. As its budgets grew in the 1960s, NIH too used a substantial portion for traineeships and institutional support.

The agencies of the "defense establishment" all contributed to the post-Sputnik inflation. The Department of Defense (DoD) responded to the crisis by establishing the Advanced Research Projects Agency to attack high-risk technological challenges that transcended the purview of the individual services. ARPA began as an ideal funder of academic research, seeding long-term university projects on computers and materials science. The Atomic Energy Commission under Glenn Seaborg naturally embraced the spirit of the Seaborg Report. The main research efforts of the AEC rested with the national laboratories, but it also was responsible for sustaining atomic sciences in universities. NASA, as a latecomer, had to purchase the attention of academic researchers, much as the ONR had done in 1945. Once the budget was sufficient, NASA spread its grants widely. Space science was a part of the raison d'être for building space rockets and essential for holding the interest of Congress and the public. All told, the defense establishment increased support for academic research from $124 to $309 million (1958–1964).

The second phase of the great inflation spanned the last half of the 1960s. Growth rates slowed to a halt, and expenditures for academic research peaked in 1968 at 0.25 percent of GDP. The dizzying pace of the first phase stimulated ambitions across the scientific community. Future annual increases of 15 percent were now expected. A 1965 survey of science disciplines produced extravagant estimates for "essential" additional support. But enthusiasm in Washington was cooling. PSAC and the scientific establishment exerted less influence in the White House of Lyndon Johnson. In particular, the president began to ask for practical benefits from the burgeoning scientific expenditures, and he criticized the concentration of federal support in the leading research universities. Initiatives for science policy largely shifted to Congress, which shared Johnson's concerns. In

1964, Congress scuttled two multimillion-dollar research projects,[10] and the assumptions of the basic research ideology began to be scrutinized. However, the overheated research economy of the mid-sixties brought more federal money for more science-related purposes to more recipients.

A distinctive feature of federal support in the 1960s was the eagerness of funding agencies to enhance the research capacity of universities so that they might perform more and better investigations. In 1965 the NSF extended this logic by launching the Science Development Program, which allocated five-year grants of $4–6 million to 32 universities. This initiative seemed to address the Seaborg Report's call for additional performers of "first-rate science." More relevant, perhaps, it answered Congressional pressures to spread research funding more widely around the country. President Johnson endorsed this policy by instructing other federal agencies to do the same, prompting science development initiatives by NASA, NIH, and the DoD. NSF adjusted to the inherent expansiveness of such commitments, since judgments of merit are difficult for prospective "development." In the next two years it mollified supplicants (and Congress) by creating two smaller programs that benefited 73 more institutions. NASA was eager to seed space science widely for its own purposes, making "sustaining grants" to 175 recipients. The DoD, feeling the effects of antiwar sentiments on many campuses, funded 82, mostly lower-ranking universities, to develop expertise in relevant fields and attract new researchers. NIH, which had already provided abundant institutional support, made development grants to only 11 medical schools. All told, 216 colleges and universities received development funding. Since the effect of science development was to allow supplicants to develop and submit viable research proposals, the overall effort represented a major expansion of participants in the university research economy, a conjuncture at once of federal policy and local ambition. But the underpinnings of the ideology of basic research were eroding.

In 1966 the DoD released results from Project Hindsight, which sought to measure the nature and sequence of "research events" leading to major technological innovations. It found the contributions of basic research to be miniscule. NSF countered with its own study that, unsurprisingly, concluded that longer-term academic research was the chief factor driving technological advancement. A draw perhaps, but the mystique of basic research was tarnished. Besides seeking new academic partners through the science development program, DoD largely

---

10   Project Mohole was an ill-advised attempt to drill through the earth's crust—potentially a subterranean NASA; MURA was a contentious proposal for a particle accelerator for Midwestern universities, later approximated in Fermilab: Daniel S. Greenberg, *The Politics of Pure Science* (New York: New American Library, 1967).

withdrew ARPA funding from universities in favor of government and private laboratories. However, a decisive change of policy was enacted by the 1969 Mansfield Amendment, which restricted the department's research funding to "a specific military function or operation." Senator Mike Mansfield claimed to be closing "a second and a backdoor National Science Foundation which has grown up in the Department of Defense," but in fact the Senate reflected the fading ideology of basic research, as well as antiwar agitation. This legislation sent a message to all federal agencies to avoid supporting research that was not explicitly mission related. For the DoD, which had supported 34 percent of federally sponsored university research in 1960, that figure declined to 15 percent in 1970 and 8 percent in 1975.[11]

Appropriations for NSF plateaued at $480 million from 1966 to 1968. In that last year, after a lengthy review, Congress instructed the foundation to include applied research in its mission. But now, there were no additional funds for an additional mission. Appropriations for 1968 were the high-water mark for academic research. The levels of real appropriations for NSF and the percentage share of GDP would not be surpassed for two decades. Actual academic research expenditures declined modestly until the mid-1970s, only buoyed by the continuing strength of NIH funding. Federal agencies absorbed much larger cuts; however, they tended to protect actual research funds as much as possible while cutting institutional support for graduate students, facilities, and science development. The science development programs were phased out entirely by 1971. Thus, the impact on institutions was greater than on research budgets. Universities abruptly had to adjust from expectations and plans for growth to "retrenchment," as the supplemental support that had fueled a robust research role disappeared.

FOUNDATIONS AND UNIVERSITY RESEARCH

Prior to World War II, the Carnegie Corporation and the Rockefeller Foundation had provided the bedrock of extramural support for university research and academic advancement. With the enlargement of federal programs after 1945, both had to rethink the role of foundations in higher education for the postwar world. One conspicuous area was the social sciences, which had been deliberately excluded from the proposed national science foundation.[12] Here foundations re-

---

11   Roger L. Geiger, "Science, Universities, and National Defense, 1945–1970," in *Science after '40*, Arnold Thackray, ed., *Osiris* 7 (1992): 26–48.

12   Mark Solovey, *Shaky Foundations: The Politics-Patronage-Social Science Nexus in Cold War America* (New Brunswick, NJ: Rutgers University Press, 2013), 20–55.

furbished their prewar efforts both to strengthen the scientific basis of these fields and to mobilize social science for social amelioration. A second broad area was the private sector of higher education, a traditional concern of foundations, now emerging from depression and wartime in parlous condition. The seeming disadvantage of private institutions had prompted both foundations to sponsor the Commission on Financing Higher Education. Their special concern with academic excellence also favored the private research universities. These basic interests were shared by the new colossus of American philanthropy, the Ford Foundation, which soon eclipsed the efforts of the Carnegie and Rockefeller Foundations. Foundation giving to higher education was more narrowly tailored than federal programs. Foundations were especially generous to research universities, and they reacted more quickly to the same developments that affected federal programs.

New leaders at the Carnegie Corporation after the war deliberated over how to achieve a significant impact with constrained resources. They determined that the foundation should aim for strategic interventions of limited duration and maintain a rigorous programmatic focus on goals. Reasoning that the United States lacked knowledge commensurate with its new global responsibilities (a common postwar theme), it chose to establish area-studies programs at universities to treat every region of the world. Centers were established in 1947–1948 to study Russia at Harvard, Japan at Michigan, Southeast Asia at Yale, and eleven others. Not all were renewed, but this initiative institutionalized international area studies in American universities.[13] The foundation also sought to discover "how the social sciences can be put to work" to assist governments in their expanded slate of activities. That could be accomplished only by strengthening social science in universities, which Carnegie, like others, assumed would require interdisciplinary syntheses. Area studies sometimes achieved this, since area expertise often took priority over disciplinary specialties. However, explicit interdisciplinary efforts, such as support for the Harvard Department of Social Relations, proved disappointing. The Carnegie Corporation president, Charles Dollard, concluded that "a great deal of time is wasted on premature attempts to produce very large 'syntheses' or 'integrations' of social science fields." The Carnegie Corporation also supported academic excellence, funding the Woodrow Wilson program of graduate fellowships in 1949 and the National Merit Scholarships for undergraduates in 1955 and providing strategic support for the honors program

---

13   Robert McCaughey, *International Studies and Academic Enterprise: A Chapter in the Enclosure of American Learning* (New York: Columbia University Press, 1984), 113–40.

movement in 1958. It also sponsored Bernard Berelson's comprehensive study of graduate education (1960).[14]

The Rockefeller Foundation Social Science Division had been led since 1939 by Joseph Willets, former head of the Wharton School and a leading figure of prewar economics. Willets knew academic social science thoroughly and was aware of its deficiencies. However, when challenged over its scientific validity, he named thirteen locations where conditions existed for fruitful social science research. All but one were special programs or organized research units, mostly in economics and international relations, the single exception being the heavily patronized Chicago sociology department. Under Willets, the division tended to support such specialized research institutes as the loci of the most scientific work in the social sciences and the best positioned to produce applicable social knowledge. Economics, in which he felt the United States had become preeminent, was well supported, as was international relations, the older handmaiden of area studies. When Willets retired in 1954, the division faced the reality that "the Ford Foundation had moved into the social sciences in a large way financially." The foundation and the division redirected resources to focus on the problems of underdeveloped countries. Thus, Rockefeller and Carnegie ceded initiatives in the social sciences, including area studies, to the new giant of American philanthropy.[15]

Henry Ford's death in 1947, four years after his son Edsel's, transferred ownership of 90 percent of the Ford Motor Company to the family foundation. Now the largest in the world, its primary purpose had been to avoid taxes. It was devoid of social mission or philanthropic principles. A study commission resolved this lacuna by 1950, defining five areas of action—promoting world peace, democracy, economic well-being, education, and "knowledge of factors that influence or determine human conduct." After a tumultuous beginning, by 1953 the foundation had settled upon five divisions to address these activities. Only the last of these explicitly concerned academic knowledge. The Behavioral Sciences Program aspired "to acquire scientific knowledge of human behavior and to apply such knowledge to human affairs." It was also the only major section to be terminated (1957). However, other divisions of the Ford Foundation eagerly sought to acquire and apply academic knowledge in their respective spheres. The Ford Foundation thus had a huge impact on universities, supporting research and academic programs in international affairs, economic modernization, urban

---

14 Geiger, *Research and Relevant Knowledge*, 92–98, quotes pp. 96, 97. The Carnegie Corporation supported the "Inter-University Conference on the Superior Student" in 1958, which popularized the honors movement (discussed in Chapter 6).

15 Geiger, *Research and Relevant Knowledge*, 98–99, 361n28.

studies, and business administration, among others. The historian Robert Mc-Caughey noted that one-half of the $1.3 billion the foundation disbursed in the 1950s went to American universities: "Over and above their spongelike qualities, universities became the foundation's favorite beneficiary because Ford officials, like many other Americans in the 1950s and 1960s, became increasingly persuaded by the argument that universities deserved all the support they could get." Moreover, Ford Foundation president Henry Heald (1956–1965) believed that the kinds of change the foundation was "capable of effecting in society could and would be done through the university."[16] Hence, the foundation invested in the academic development of institutions as well as grants designed to accomplish the instrumental social purposes of specific foundation programs.

The Ford Foundation in these years sought to induce fundamental change in American higher education in four areas—promoting the behavioral sciences, overhauling education for business, expanding the graduate education of faculty, and elevating the academic profile of private research universities. Like previous foundation efforts in the social sciences, the Behavioral Science Program sought to remedy existing weaknesses and make these disciplines more scientific, more integrated, and more useful for attacking social problems.[17] However, it also aimed to alter the basic organization of the disciplines, believing them too isolated and overspecialized. In 1953 it made grants to Chicago, Harvard, Michigan, North Carolina, and Stanford Universities to survey their behavioral science departments and propose measures to achieve closer integration. The program also sponsored knowledge inventories of the behavioral sciences and interdisciplinary awards to span the humanistic and social science realms. All these efforts were deemed "particularly disappointing" in its five-year report. What proved effective were programs that supported the best of existing social science. Such was establishing the Center for Advanced Studies in the Behavioral Sciences at Stanford, which, despite its name, became a retreat for academics to write and think. In its last years, the BSP resorted to grants to eminent scholars to do whatever they pleased. The program was an asset for social science in the lean mid-fifties, even though it failed in its original intention to reshape them. It was not terminated for this failure, but because foundation trustees did not appreciate its rather abstract academic mission.

16 McCaughey, *International Studies*, 171, 181.

17 Geiger, *Research and Relevant Knowledge*, 99–105. Ford Foundation trustees avoided the term "social" for fear of connotations of socialism or social reform. The program sought to promote behavioral approaches that were developing tangentially to the rather unreceptive social science disciplines (below). Behavioral sciences included psychology and all the social sciences in theory but centered on sociology and social psychology.

In 1953 the foundation resolved to reform business education. An advisory committee recommended a "trickle-down" strategy of supporting a small number of university centers selected for their problem-oriented research and graduate training in economics and administration.[18] A substantial fellowship program was also intended to recruit top students into the field and produce research-trained faculty. Harvard was naturally one such center: it was the leading business school—the exemplar of the case method of teaching management—and whose dean was a powerful foundation trustee. The second, portentous choice would become the poster child for the Ford-inspired revolution in business education. The four-year-old Graduate School of Industrial Administration of Carnegie Tech was committed to rigorous scientific doctoral education employing economics and behavioral science. Later grants designated Chicago, Stanford, and, less successfully, Columbia for reformation. The New Look that Ford imposed emphasized research and doctoral programs. Above all, it promoted quantitative methods drawn from the social science disciplines, especially economics: operations research, game theory, systems analysis, and decision science. To bolster faculties, the foundation created generous doctoral and postdoctoral fellowships for social scientists who would address business issues and join business schools. Summer institutes introduced large numbers of business school faculty to the New Look methodologies. The gospel of the new scientific approach to business graduate studies was presented in a foundation-sponsored volume, *Higher Education for Business* (1959), which established the preferred standard for faculty and curriculum.[19]

The revolution in business education was intended to "trickle down" from the top business schools. It included curricula on accounting, statistics, decision science, behavioral applications to management, and heavy doses of economics. New Look faculties became heavily populated with economists engaged in both theoretical and applied topics. The original intention of the Ford program was to foster a scientifically rigorous curriculum that would yield a new type of manager. What it produced was a new type of business school faculty member. By the 1960s, the business faculties at major universities had become academicized. Faculty were recruited from social science disciplines primarily for their research

18   For Ford's business programs, see Rakesh Khurana, *From Higher Aims to Hired Hands: The Social Transformation of American Business Schools and the Unfulfilled Promise of Management as a Profession* (Princeton: Princeton University Press, 2006), 195–290; Mie Augier and James G. March, *The Roots, Rituals, and Rhetorics of Change: North American Business Schools after the Second World War* (Stanford, CA: Stanford University Press, 2011), 94–185; Steven Schlossman, Michael Sedlak, and Harold Wechsler, *The "New Look": The Ford Foundation and the Revolution in Business Education* (Los Angeles: Graduate Management Admission Council, 1987).

19   Robert Aaron Gordon and James E. Howell, *Higher Education for Business* (New York: Columbia University Press, 1959).

expertise, and their subsequent orientation was predominantly toward research. That aspect of their productivity was furthered, no doubt, by the founding of new academic business journals—8 in the 1950s and 126 in the 1960s. Their research tended to be highly theoretical, involving quantification and modeling; academic knowledge was assumed to inform business practice, not learn from it as intended in the case method.[20]

Ford exited the field of business education in 1962 with generous three-year terminal grants. The New Look was now ascendant at the leading business schools, but an extensive internal postmortem study revealed limited trickle-down to the typical business school. Contemporaries generally recognized 25 major business schools, headed by the 8 elite schools that Ford had supported. The eight "significantly increased the quality and quantity of their research and incorporated developments from mathematics, statistics, psychology, sociology, and economics."[21] Each had assimilated the New Look into existing traditions while enhancing academic rigor. The next 17 schools showed "great promise" as they sought to compete in the same arena, although with fewer resources. Beyond these institutions, however, another 182 business schools awarded MBAs in 1961. They may have had more MBA students and more PhDs on the faculty, but little had occurred (as of 1965) to raise the intellectual level of students or to enrich the curriculum.

The upgrading of American higher education, particularly the private sector, was an ongoing mission of the Ford Foundation. It early endorsed the belief in a crisis of faculty numbers and qualifications (PhDs), publicizing this problem in its annual reports and through a 1955 blue-ribbon conference. That same year, circumstances afforded an opportunity to ameliorate what was widely agreed to be an underlying cause: abysmal faculty salaries. Ford was exhibit number one in a congressional crusade to reign in the unaccountable economic power of foundations. In light of this threat, the foundation in 1955 began divestment of its 88 percent ownership of the now-thriving Ford Motor Company. With assets hugely augmented, the trustees thought it prudent to downsize. They awarded some $260 million in endowment grants to 630 private colleges and universities, pegged to each institution's instructional budget, to be used to raise faculty salaries.[22] The foundation consistently sought to augment the supply of PhDs by including ample support for doctoral fellowships in program grants, and a 1957 grant to the Woodrow Wilson Fellowship Program increased the number of awards from 200 to 1,000. As late as 1967, Ford sought to augment PhD numbers

20   Khurana, *From Higher Aims*, 305–17.
21   Augier and March, *Roots, Rituals*, 180–87, quote p. 184.
22   The foundation made similar capital grants to nonprofit hospitals and medical schools.

by shortening the time to degree. It awarded grants of $4 million to the ten lead-ing doctoral universities to be used, with matching funds, to graduate PhDs in humanities and social sciences in four years. During the seven years of this pro-gram, the PhD shortage turned into a glut, and the foundation's house history concluded that "this large program did not have a significant effect on the ways major universities conduct their Ph.D. training programs."[23]

The fourth major initiative to shape higher education sought to elevate the financial health and academic stature of private research universities. The Chal-lenge Grant Program (1960–1967) aimed to promote a "second tier" of private universities to create "regional peaks of excellence." The underlying assumptions of this program revealed the foundation's stance toward higher education: the private sector was essential to excellence and academic freedom; its beneficent influence required a regional presence; and although private institutions had re-covered from their postwar poverty, they still needed the foundation's patronage to hold their own against the expansion of publicly supported universities. Recip-ients were expected to devise plans, with foundation guidance, for fund-raising (to meet the matching requirements) and academic advancement. Stanford was the first and most exemplary recipient, already committed to and acting upon the foundation goals. Other universities found Challenge Grants more challeng-ing. The initial recipients included Johns Hopkins (Capital area), Vanderbilt (the South), Notre Dame (Catholic), and in a stretch the University of Denver (Mountain West). Development programs were inherently expansionary since differences among institutions are subtle and based on future projections. In this respect, Ford's experience mirrored that of NSF. The original rationale was stretched or ignored to extend Challenge Grants to another 11 universities, in-cluding Chicago and Columbia, and 68 colleges—in all, an outlay of $347 mil-lion. These funds were no doubt welcome, even at the height of 1960s prosperity. But aside from exemplary Stanford, only Notre Dame and Vanderbilt met foun-dation expectations. For most others, meaningful improvements in academic qual-ity would wait two decades, until the 1980s efflorescence of the private sector.[24]

In area studies and urban affairs, Ford investments in university capacity were intended chiefly to foster practical results, though they too had an impact on universities. The Ford Foundation had an international outlook from its modern inception. In 1953 it consolidated several disparate initiatives into the Interna-

23   Geiger, *Research and Relevant Knowledge*, 111–13, 219–20, 227–29; Richard Magat, *The Ford Foun-dation at Work: Philanthropic Choices, Methods, and Styles* (New York: Plenum, 1979), 32–33, 97–108, quote p. 99.

24   Geiger, *Research and Relevant Knowledge*, 111–16; most Challenge Grant universities failed to gain research share (206–9).

tional Training and Research (ITR) Program. Its original mission was to increase "the number of Americans trained [in foreign affairs] for service in government, education, and business" and "to broaden the base of public understanding of international problems." Thus, ITR intended to work domestically, which quickly involved universities. Ford took responsibility for funding the area studies centers started by Rockefeller and Carnegie, and through the 1950s it increased support for the study of more regions at more universities. However, the inherent bias toward excellence favored the leading universities and well-studied regions. One-third of ITR university grants went to Harvard, Chicago, and Columbia. In 1959, grant-making was simplified by adopting block grants to universities, which could then apportion support among their multiple centers. In the next three years (1960–1962), ITR awarded $41 million in single block grants to thirteen universities, bringing ITR's total expenditures above $100 million. A second round of funding added $71 million to the coffers of eleven universities (1964–1965), which included establishment of forty-nine endowed professorships of international studies. In addition, Title VI of the NDEA was now providing $13 million annually for language and area centers. It was, indeed, a golden age—international studies were now institutionalized and thriving across American research universities. The number of PhDs granted reached 550 in 1966, a 144 percent increase in fifteen years. With little presence in undergraduate education, international studies depended on external patronage. Predictably, it requested and expected much more. Hopes focused on the International Education Act before Congress and the continuing largesse of the Ford Foundation. But the legislation failed to pass, and McGeorge Bundy, the new president of the Ford Foundation, abruptly terminated the ITR Program.[25]

In 1959 the foundation focused on the problems of American cities. Urban and regional studies had long existed in American universities,[26] but Ford hoped to invigorate this field by promoting research and graduate studies on urban problems and connecting university scholarship with local governments. Its first initiative was an experiment to create "urban extension" modeled on the effective agricultural extension programs of land-grant universities. (see Chapter 4). The foundation also pursued a more typical course in supporting economists and their doctoral students to concentrate on urban topics. With the urban crisis of the mid-sixties, Ford focused additional funds on a dozen leading universities, creating urban studies centers and endowed professorships. Like other Ford

25   McCaughey, *International Studies*, 167–235, quote p. 212.

26   Ethan Schrum, *The Instrumental University: Education in Service of the National Agenda after World War II* (Ithaca, NY: Cornell University Press, forthcoming).

programs, the urban initiatives had little discernible effect on ameliorating the ills of American cities, but they did produce an abundance of academic scholars, research, and doctoral degrees.[27]

McGeorge Bundy's presidency of the Ford Foundation (1966–1979) marked the end of an era of philanthropy for higher education. His 1967 graduate education grants were the last foundation tonic for university research, even while it withdrew from business schools, international studies, university building, and several other fields.[28] In a decade and a half it had infused more than $1 billion into American higher education, mainly research universities. If the results were often somewhat oblique to the original intentions, they nonetheless accelerated and influenced academic development, especially during the Liberal Hour.

In the 1920s, Wycliffe Rose's motto in disbursing Rockefeller dollars was "Make the peaks higher." The Ford Foundation admitted no such intention but largely furthered the same result. When it sought "excellence," it looked to the academically strongest, mostly private, research universities. Whatever the purpose, Harvard would likely be judged the most effective vehicle. The rise of Stanford was deliberately and materially assisted. The University of California, although public, was frequently tapped. The foundation no doubt helped to maintain the academic eminence of Chicago and Columbia, considering their underlying financial weaknesses. To compensate, Ford consciously sought to "broaden the resource base" with Challenge Grants and some dispersion of grants from well-funded programs. But the foundation's officers were often disappointed in the second-tier universities. According to one, "If we had had less money to spend, we would have done well to concentrate our support in the major research universities." Where the foundation sought to achieve specific objectives, it had no qualms about supporting public universities. These included the stalwarts like Michigan and Wisconsin, but also newcomers like Indiana, Michigan State, and the University of Washington. Although these institutions received smaller awards, Ford grants helped to embed them into the research economy, where they also pursued federal grants.[29]

Ford philanthropy contributed substantially to the advancement of knowledge, but not in the manner originally intended. The subject-focused programs were formulated to produce practitioners and practical knowledge of foreign affairs, business and public administration, or American cities. Instead, these funds

27   Magat, *Ford Foundation at Work*, 99–101.

28   Support for urban studies continued into the 1970s, and Ford launched an initiative to promote public policy studies in 1972, establishing eight graduate-level schools or institutes. Bundy initiated a major initiative (c. $100 million) for minority graduate fellowships and support for private black colleges (1967–1977): ibid., 57, 101–2, 178–79.

29   Ibid., 104–6, quote pp. 105–6; McCaughey, *International Studies*, 197–211.

produced what McCaughey has termed "academic enclosure": the multiplica-
tion of academic scholars and theoretical publications. "With virtually all the
growth and dispersion of international studies ... occurring within universities,
the entire intellectual enterprise came to be regarded as, and to be, synonymous
with its academic component." An abundance of fellowship money lured master's students—potential practitioners—to continue into PhD programs, from
which two-thirds of graduates took academic appointments.[30] Nor was academic enclosure confined to international studies: it was a phenomenon inherent to the era. Disciplinary scholars recruited to give analytic capacity to business schools sought professional recognition through academic publication in
disciplinary journals. Economists subsidized to study urban problems "produced
considerable discipline-oriented research of merit, but [their] output in terms of
research applicable to urban policy was negligible."[31] The situation could hardly
have been otherwise, given the foundation's reliance on expert knowledge, given
the locus of expertise in universities and the commitments to expanding that
expertise, and given the demand for scholarly faculty in a rapidly growing system
of higher education. Academic departments, above all, acted to replicate themselves in their doctoral programs and to enhance their professional standing
through academic research and scholarship—a process known as the academic
revolution of the 1960s. The Ford Foundation scarcely triggered the academic
revolution, but the billion dollars lavished on American universities, on top of
copious federal funding, clearly furthered it.

THE ACADEMIC REVOLUTION

To gauge the state of American higher education in the mid-sixties, Christopher
Jencks and David Riesman published a richly detailed overview of its many components. The title conveyed their conclusion—*The Academic Revolution* (1968).
The phrase captured the remarkable development of the previous decade. The
graduate schools of arts and sciences and the specialized academic departments
they contained had become the dominant influence in universities and throughout much of higher education. Academic research was alluded to throughout
as the activity that informed and sustained the departments and their graduate programs. This had produced an "academic imperium" in which the "academic profession had freed itself from effective lay control." In their view, "the
graduate academic departments are for the most part autotelic. They resent even
being asked whether they produce significant benefits to society beyond the

30 McCaughey, *International Studies*, 211–14.
31 Khurana, *From Higher Aims*, 305–7; Magat, *Ford Foundation*, quote p. 100.

edification of their own members, and mark down the questioner as an anti-intellectual."[32]

The authors articulated a widespread concern—soon the conventional wisdom—that the growing research prowess of American universities was causing an alleged neglect of undergraduate education.[33] Professors absorbed in research and scholarship supposedly placed a lower priority on instruction, and curricula reflected the esoterica of graduate seminars. Jencks and Riesman sympathized with students, not professors. The bulk of their volume consisted of historically grounded depictions of the diverse institutional types that composed the higher education system, its implicit and explicit stratification, and the consequent implications for the educational and career opportunities of students. However, this account failed to credit the root of the academic revolution, the forces impelling the explosion of graduate study, the proliferation of research, and the hegemony of the professoriate. This, quite simply, was the accelerating advancement of knowledge—the process by which faculty research and graduate instruction sought to contribute to and keep pace with the growth of knowledge.

Jencks and Riesman provided some insight into these activities. The higher education system now privileged talent and ability, as "universities, especially their graduate professional schools, have become pacesetters in the promotion of meritocratic values." Further, "the academic profession places little weight on knowledge derived from individual subjective experience. It insists on knowledge that is objective in the sense that others can be told how it was acquired, can repeat the operation, and can be expected to arrive at the same result." Hence methodology was key for producing objective knowledge: "Government agencies and foundations subsidize academic research primarily because they are impressed by the methodological competence of university professors."[34] An understatement, to say the least! Meritocratic processes tended to direct the finite resources of research grants and university positions toward the most competent investigators. Scientific methods—that is, those that yielded reproducible results—ensured that research findings would be cumulative, hence valid contributions to knowledge. The extraordinary proliferation of these processes (later called "sci-

---

32   Christopher Jencks and David Riesman, *The Academic Revolution* (Chicago: University of Chicago Press, 1977 [1968]), 236–50; 541, xiv, 250.

33   Similar observations, including the weakening of undergraduate education, had been made earlier in 1963 by Edward Shils in "Observations on the American University," *The Intellectuals and the Powers and Other Essays* (Chicago: University of Chicago Press, 1972), 298–306.

34   Ibid., 18, 517, 516. Jencks and Riesman had slight regard for these fundamentals of the scientific method that made knowledge cumulative, even joking that "this book is in this sense largely non-academic" (517).

entization")[35] in postwar American universities, especially after the late 1950s, was the true academic revolution.

But these phenomena were scarcely new. Laurence Veysey famously pronounced that there was only one academic revolution in American higher education and it had occurred in the 1890s. True, the emergence of the American university in that era brought some recognition and reward for academic achievement at the leading universities, and American scholars consciously sought to implant the rigor of German empirical sciences in their disciplines and institutions. In the ensuing decades, research and scholarship built further upon these efforts and made impressive gains.[36] Hence the questions: To what extent did the huge expansion of postwar American research and scholarship alter higher education? How did quantitative growth induce qualitative change? The answers lie in the transformation of the academic knowledge base, the predominance of disciplines and departments, the mushrooming of graduate education, and the embrace by growing numbers of institutions of the academic revolution—and how these developments reinforced each other.

Advances in disciplinary knowledge were evident before the war in growing academic publications and a trickle of new faculty trained in the latest theories, but the overall impact on the higher education system was muted. These developments had little impact on undergraduate education, where the animus against specialization was reflected in the preoccupation with liberal or general education (Chapter 1). And only the handful of prewar research universities had doctoral programs of any size. Wartime research and postwar research funding tipped the balance, as seen in Chapter 2. Name changes from "college" to "university" symbolized the growing identification with graduate education and research. More significant than names was the establishment of PhD programs. Before 1950, just over 100 regular universities awarded doctoral degrees, but by 1970 the number had almost doubled: 35 institutions awarded their first PhD in the 1950s, and 45 did so in the 1960s. By 1970, many of these new entrants were graduating large numbers of PhDs.[37]

These developments were led by the natural sciences but not confined to them. In fact, wartime agencies conducted a great deal of social science research, and afterward, like the natural scientists, those researchers migrated to university

---

35   Gili S. Drori et al., *Science in the Modern World Polity: Institutionalization and Globalization* (Stanford, CA: Stanford University Press, 2003).

36   Roger L. Geiger, *The History of American Higher Education: Learning and Culture from the Founding to World War II* (Princeton: Princeton University Press, 2015), 326–48, 528–32.

37   E.g., the University of Utah, (first PhD 1947), 248 in 1970; Florida State (1952), 286; Southern Illinois (1959), 129: Geiger, *Research and Relevant Knowledge*, 218–19.

posts.[38] In the humanities and social sciences new paradigms opened new vistas for investigation and explication. These were exciting times across all disciplines as new theories, discoveries, and methods promised significant advancements in knowledge. The fields developed by Ford Foundation initiatives, described in the previous section, exemplified this process. New knowledge was embodied in the newly minted PhDs, who were hired by colleges and universities as they expanded and replaced the aging prewar generation of faculty. Motivated to continue their research and scholarship, these cadres filled the academic departments in their disciplines.

Andrew Abbott has called these disciplinary departments "the essential and irreplaceable building blocks of American universities." Disciplines became "uniquely powerful [b]ecause of their extraordinary ability to organize in one single structure research fields, individual careers, faculty hiring, and undergraduate education."[39] Thus, the powerful incentives for research and careers imposed a disciplinary agenda that carried over to undergraduate education. In the mid-1950s these forces were still coalescing for most universities. The Keniston Report and a coeval study of graduate education revealed these efforts before 1960 to be somewhat inchoate at all but the leading institutions.[40] But now the imperative for more ambitious and competitive approaches was increasingly evident, and specifically enjoined by the Seaborg Report. Colleges and universities were compelled to enhance their capacity to incorporate the new academic knowledge, and such steps were the very actions underlying the academic revolution. In fact, each discipline experienced its own intellectual revolution.

English literature may not appear an obvious subject for charting the advancement of knowledge, but it typified the process by which intellectual innovation and professional consolidation reinforced one another. Prewar departments taught two distinct aspects of their subject: undergraduates were entertained with literature courses while graduate studies and faculty scholarship were devoted to literary history, biography, and philology—chiefly the history of the English language. The field was challenged at the end of the 1930s by the New Criticism, which asserted that a poem was a discreet work of art to be analyzed for its intrinsic qualities and that the circumstances of its creation were of little or no

---

38   Roger E. Backhouse and Philippe Fontaine, "Toward a History of the Social Sciences," in Backhouse and Fontaine, eds., *History of the Social Sciences since 1945* (Cambridge: Cambridge University Press, 2010), 184–233; Andrew Abbott and James T. Sparrow, "Hot War, Cold War: The Structure of Sociological Action, 1940–1955," in Craig Calhoun, ed., *Sociology in America: A History* (Chicago: Chicago University Press, 2007), 281–313.

39   Andrew Abbott, "The Disciplines and the Future," in Steven Brint, ed., *The Future of the City of Intellect: The Changing American University* (Stanford, CA: Stanford University Press, 2002), 205–30.

40   Bernard Berelson, *Graduate Education in the United States* (New York: McGraw-Hill, 1960): discussed below. The Keniston Report is discussed in Chapter 2.

importance. In a seminal piece, John Crow Ransom argued further that the existing preoccupation with historical philology undermined the autonomy of English, making it virtually "a branch of the department of history." In placing literary criticism at the center of the discipline, Ransom thus "redefined both the object of study and the skill required for studying it in terms that fully satisfied the professional requirements of distinctive knowledge—knowledge carefully set off from that of all the adjoining academic disciplines."[41]

Thus, both intellectual revolution and professional identity energized postwar English departments and stimulated an outpouring of scholarship. Alvin Kernan, who imbibed the New Criticism at its hearth in the Yale English department, testified that "we thought we were building up an accurate reading of literature, and our formalist methodology concentrated unbiased attention on the objective literary text in the same way that the scientist looks closely and without bias at nature." The New Critics had enemies to overcome (literary historians) and new worlds to conquer, namely reinterpreting the entire corpus of English literature. Although its inherent aestheticism and subjectivity carried the seeds of its own destruction by the mid-sixties, the New Criticism moved the object of English studies from language to literary texts, their techniques, and their elucidation by the critic.[42]

Other disciplines experienced their own postwar intellectual revolutions. These new paradigms may not have monopolized their respective fields, but they dominated to a greater or lesser extent depending on the coherence and cohesiveness of the subject. They generally promised to make investigations more "scientific" (the anti-scientistic reactions would come later), attracted talented neophytes entering the field, opened whole new realms of research, established disciplinary identities with paradigmatic norms, and garnered institutional prizes in research patronage and faculty positions. Among historians, generally a diffuse lot, "there was a deep and widespread conviction that the profession was moving steadily in the direction of establishing objective historical truth." Political science sought to become more scientific by embracing behavioralism, which demanded the testing of clearly formulated theories using quantitative, empirical data. In economics, Keynesianism became the dominant paradigm in postwar

41 M. H. Abrams, "The Transformation of English Studies, 1930–1995," in Thomas Bender and Carl E. Schorske, eds., *American Academic Culture in Transformation: Fifty Years, Four Disciplines* (Princeton: Princeton University Press, 1997), 123–50; Catherine Gallagher, "The History of Literary Criticism," in ibid., 151–72, quotes pp. 154–55.

42 Alvin Kernan, *In Plato's Cave* (New Haven, CT: Yale University Press, 1999), 109; Roger L. Geiger, "Demography and Curriculum: The Humanities in American Higher Education from the 1950s through the 1980s," in David A. Hollinger, ed., *The Humanities and the Dynamics of Inclusion since World War II* (Baltimore: Johns Hopkins University Press, 2006), 50–72; Gallagher, "Literary Criticism," 157–58.

America by incorporating large-scale data and mathematical modeling.[43] Such developments were intrinsically linked with a revolution in graduate studies.

In 1960 Bernard Berelson published *Graduate Education in the United States*, the most thorough examination to date. Gathering data from 1957 to 1959, he portrayed conditions in doctoral education just prior to the revolution of the 1960s. Recruitment into PhD programs was weak, with most students deciding to attend sometime after college graduation. The supply of programs exceeded student demand, so that "everybody who wants to get into graduate school does get in." Various forms of financial support were sufficient to cover almost all full-time students, but still only an estimated half of students completed their PhDs. Berelson estimated that 10,000 of them had become ABDs (all but dissertation), while more than 9,000 PhDs were awarded annually in the years of the study. And, despite the shortage of faculty, there was general concern that a large portion of PhDs chose nonacademic employment rather than poorly paid faculty positions.[44]

After 1960 the numbers of graduates surviving the PhD gauntlet accelerated. This growth occurred in two phases, driven first by increasing percentages of college graduates obtaining PhDs, and then by much larger student cohorts. The 10,000 PhDs granted in 1960 rose by 50 percent by 1964, then doubled by 1970 (29,866). The increment of additional PhDs awarded each year surpassed 1,000 in 1962 and increased steadily to 3,700 in 1970, the largest annual jump. Large cohorts and a full pipeline carried this growth to a peak of 34,777 PhDs awarded in 1973, a level unsurpassed for fifteen years. In the mid-sixties, Jencks and Riesman ascribed this phenomenon to the postwar emergence of "university colleges": liberal arts colleges or the undergraduate units of research universities "whose primary purpose is to prepare students for graduate work of some kind—primarily in the arts and sciences but also in professional subjects." These colleges attracted the most academically able undergraduates and either drew upon university graduate faculties or (for colleges) professors who were products of those departments. They estimated that there were 100 such colleges, "the most prestigious ... [having] the ablest faculty and administrators and the most generous philanthropists." The university college was "the fruition of the academic revolution at the undergraduate level" and "a model which many of the other 1,900 colleges regard as desirable."[45]

43 Peter Novick, *That Noble Dream: The 'Objectivity Question' and the American Historical Profession* (New York: Cambridge University Press, 1988), quote p. 362; Robert M. Solow, "How Did Economics Get That Way and What Did It Get?," in Bender and Schorske, *American Academic Culture*, 57–76; Hunter Crowther-Heyck, "Patrons of the Revolution: Ideals and Institutions in Postwar Behavioral Science," *Isis* 97, 3 (September 2006): 420–46.

44 Berelson, *Graduate Education*.

45 Jencks and Riesman, *Academic Revolution*, 24–25.

The years in which Jencks and Riesman characterized university colleges were in fact the zenith for the attraction of graduate studies. The "propensity" of college graduates to obtain PhDs turned up sharply after 1960, rising from roughly 4.4 percent to over 6 percent for the PhD classes of 1970–1972.[46] Thus, the most intense pursuit of doctorates began, on average, with college graduates of the class of 1961 and continued through 1967. Subsequently, the ever-larger size of graduating classes propelled further increases in the number of PhDs for several more years, but propensity fell into a prolonged decline, which was greater for men than women.[47] The PhD cohorts of this growth period thus preceded the first baby boomers, who arrived in 1964 and graduated in 1968. The first of the peak doctoral cohorts would have entered college, on average, around 1957 and the last around 1963. It seems likely that intrinsic motivations inspired them. These ten years coincide with what has just been described as the Liberal Hour, an era of remarkable idealism, intellectual ferment, and optimism about progress. First-year graduate enrollments as a proportion of college graduates increased by 38 percent in those years, reaching an all-time high in 1967. These years also marked the apex of commitments to the liberal arts, their highest-ever proportion of BAs and PhDs. Professional schools did not share in this popularity. Professional degrees increased by 45 percent in the 1960s, compared with the tripling of PhDs.[48]

Any explanation for this surge in arts and sciences PhDs must credit the liberal idealism of the era and the academic revolution. The former infused a spirit of critical, yet optimistic, desire for social, economic, and intellectual progress. The latter saw the university as a fount of new ideas, both practical and theoretical. The academic revolution was thus a prime draw for a growing proportion of college graduates choosing academic careers. This phenomenon is conventionally ascribed to the burgeoning demand for college teachers and rising salaries. However, doctors and lawyers had more lucrative career prospects. Further, doctoral

46   "Propensity" is calculated here by dividing the number of doctoral degrees by the number of bachelor's degrees five years earlier. One can object that average time to degree is longer and that many students do not go "straight through." However, this estimate is probably more accurate for the 1960s than for any other era, and any lengthier assumptions make the date of the bachelor's degree earlier and smaller, yielding higher propensities (Jeffrey A. Groen and Michael J. Rizzo, "The Changing Composition of American-Citizen PhDs," Cornell Higher Education Research Institute, March 2004). In any case, the shape of the propensity curve is accurate, although absolute values may be uncertain. Propensity is calculated more precisely for several disciplines by William G. Bowen and Neil L. Rudenstine in *In Pursuit of the PhD* (Princeton: Princeton University Press, 1992).

47   The propensity of males and females to earn PhDs peaked in 1971 at 9.2 and 2.2 percent, respectively; in 1974 it was 7.7 and 2.0. See Alan M. Cartter, *Ph.D.s and the Academic Labor Market* (New York: McGraw-Hill, 1976), 204–20.

48   For data on graduate and professional enrollments and degrees, see Cartter, *Ph.D.s and the Academic Labor Market*, 73–87.

education in other decades has shown a muted response to conditions in the faculty labor market. The commitment to undertake years of intensive study with little remuneration requires, above all, intellectual commitment, which suggests why the PhD supply was little affected by negative market conditions. After 1967 the idealism of the Liberal Hour and the academic revolution waned. Subsequent cohorts of undergraduates experienced a climate of growing disillusionment and negativism on campuses. Disciplinary paradigms were in increasing disarray, challenged in disparaging terms by both academics and external critics.[49] Many remained in graduate school out of an aversion toward bourgeois society—or the Army. Nonetheless, enrollments in graduate schools ballooned into the early 1970s for reasons both good and bad.

The conditions favoring graduate education persisted throughout the 1960s. From the mid-1950s, the shortage of faculty prompted dire warnings of a looming crisis for the country's colleges and universities. Annual reports from the National Education Association warned that just 40 percent of faculty possessed doctorates, and only 30 percent of new hires did, which implied that quality was deteriorating.[50] The Ford Foundation responded by boosting the number of Woodrow Wilson Fellowships, and passage of the NDEA created generous three-year fellowships for students committed to college teaching or international studies. With increasing support from the NSF, federal fellowships and traineeships reached 15,000 by 1961. Still, a 1962 report of the President's Science Advisory Committee called for explicit federal programs to address the nation's growing needs for scientific manpower. Specific programs to fund fellowships and facilities were not enacted until the Johnson administration, but then on a grand scale. Federal support for graduate studies peaked in 1966–1967, when 60,000 students were recipients. In 1967 the Ford Foundation reflected this enthusiasm with the program to expedite PhD completion in the humanities and social sciences.[51]

Copious funding for graduate education persisted until the end of the decade, which was justified as alleviating the faculty crisis. Given this goal, funders were concerned with the quality of graduate education as well as the quantity. Universities benefited from "cost of instruction" supplements attached to fellowships and traineeships from federal agencies and Ford. To prevent monopolization of these plum awards by the most prestigious universities, quotas were applied to spread this bounty. As with research funding, graduate student support was widely dispersed across research universities, providing a further incen-

49 For these conditions and the precipitous drop in academic attainments, see Chapter 6.
50 Cartter, *Ph.D.'s and the Academic Labor Market*, 11–17.
51 Geiger, *Research and Relevant Knowledge*, 217–21.

tive to develop and expand graduate programs. A 1968 study found that 80 per-cent of doctoral students across all institutions were benefiting from fellowships and research or teaching assistantships. The first two forms of support were most prevalent at the academically strongest institutions, but subsidized graduate study was the rule across American higher education. Not only could "every-body who wants to get into graduate school," but they could find support there as well.[52]

By the mid-sixties, more than three-quarters of new PhDs intended to pur-sue careers in academe. They were readily hired (many while still ABD) across the academic spectrum, but especially by the expanding institutions described in Chapter 4: aspiring research universities, new urban institutions, former teachers colleges cum regional universities, and expanding liberal arts colleges. The number of full-time faculty doubled from 1963 to 1970—from 184,000 to 368,000. These were the cadres of the academic revolution, trained in the latest theories and methodologies of university graduate schools. In 1968, by one esti-mate, 58 percent had been hired in the previous five years. They represented the youngest faculty in the nation's history, 49 percent were aged 40 or younger.[53] These were halcyon days too for those already established in academic careers. In 1963, faculty mobility registered an unprecedented 8 percent—one of every twelve faculty changed schools. Faculty mobility, which remained elevated for the rest of the decade, also furthered the academic revolution. Faculty who showed any scholarly promise could readily move to institutions offering better resources and more supportive environments. And the connection between scholarship and advancement could only encourage neophytes. What was not obvious to policymakers, graduate schools, or their progeny, was that the golden-age conditions of the 1960s could not last.

The curmudgeon who delivered this message was Allan M. Cartter, an econ-omist with ACE who later became chancellor of New York University. His data revealed that in 1965 half of American faculty in fact possessed PhDs and that academic quality had been improving, not deteriorating, since the early 1950s. Many had obtained their degrees *after* assuming faculty positions, and attrition of non-PhDs was double those with degrees. He assessed the demographic evi-dence and foresaw that the rising tide of PhDs and the leveling of college-age cohorts would cap the demand for faculty by the end of the decade. As he pub-licized these findings, Cartter "became a missionary for what then seemed like a

---

52   Ibid., 222–24. The 1964 rating of graduate programs reported the ages of the 4,000 respondents: chairmen and senior scholars were 46–52, junior scholars, 33–38: Allan M. Cartter, *An Assessment of Quality in Graduate Education* (Washington, DC: ACE, 1966).

53   Cartter, *PhDs and the Academic Labor Market*, 109, 165. These outsized cohorts would dominate the demography of the academic profession into the next century.

radical point of view." The PhD juggernaut rolled on for the remainder of the decade on the assumption of a faculty shortage and predictions for 50–70,000 annual PhDs by the end of the 1970s. But Cartter was correct. A rising number of new PhDs and declining openings for new faculty hires intersected around 1970, and the surplus of new PhDs expanded thereafter.[54] Still, it would take several years to slow the momentum of the academic revolution.

The overriding mentality of the academic revolution extended the fixation on graduate education from the pinnacle of the academic hierarchy and the university colleges, where it originated, through the gamut of universities. From 1968, when the impending imbalance should have been apparent, to 1974, forty additional universities launched doctoral programs, 10,600 additional PhDs were awarded annually, and graduate enrolments grew by 155,000. Growth at this stage was concentrated in newer and lower-rated programs. Considering only the three-quarters of graduates who envisioned academic careers, the top thirty universities, based on the 1965 ratings, granted 1,602 additional doctorates from 1968 to 1973 (+19 percent); the next 35 (roughly the second quartile), 1,769 (+40 percent); the lower half of rated universities, 3,102 (+87 percent); and new or unrated programs, 1,191 (+102 percent). Where did they go? Cartter's data showed that academic PhDs were largely hired within their own quality stratum or below, including the college sectors. By 1973, larger numbers of these graduates were accepting employment even further down the academic hierarchy.[55] These were institutions that previously had relatively few PhDs on their faculty. Thus, by hiring teachers with extended academic training, they raised, on balance, their academic competence. Faculty in these schools might have relatively little opportunity for scholarship or research, but this pervasive upgrading of the lower reaches of the higher education system was also part of the academic revolution.

The dynamics of this quantitative expansion during the academic revolution can only be understood in relation to the quest for knowledge—a compulsion to embrace more subjects, extend knowledge frontiers, and above all to enhance the quality of academic endeavors. Given this intense focus, the American Council on Education in 1964 sponsored a state-of-the-art assessment of the quality of graduate programs. Penn's Keniston ratings, which appeared five years previous, had aroused wide interest. However, that study was conducted for internal purposes, included just 25 universities, and excluded engineering. The ACE survey, entrusted to Allan Cartter, rated 106 universities in twenty-nine disciplines for a total of 1,663 departments. Responses were obtained from 4,000 academics—

54   Ibid., 18, 129–43.
55   Ibid., 196–201.

junior, senior, and department chairs. The resulting ratings were subject to statistical tests, which supported their validity, and provision was made for a follow-up survey in five years.

More than 1,000 of these departments had never been rated, so the ACE survey provided the first objective measure of their relative standing in the increasingly competitive academic marketplace. Deans and department heads employed the ratings to argue for "reallocation of financial support." And students also made use of them in selecting graduate programs. Cartter was scrupulous in reporting only departmental ratings and refusing "to aggregate scores to arrive at university-wide ratings." However, he did provide a rank order by division of the top universities that had at least two "distinguished" departments in a division. UC Berkeley was alone in being represented in all five divisions, ranked second in each, and was anointed "the best balanced distinguished university in the country." Harvard was first in four divisions (but deficient in engineering), and Stanford was prominent in four as well; "Columbia, Illinois, Yale, Princeton, Michigan, and Cal. Tech. [were] in three; M.I.T., Chicago, and Wisconsin in two." These institutions represented only a slight juggling of the peak of Keniston's hierarchy. Contemporaries in the 1960s were fixated on the elevation of more "first-rate" research universities, as called for in the Seaborg Report, but sentiment throughout the country envisioned far more. One typical view: "With essentially our whole population flooding to the hundred or more metropolitan areas ... it seems clear that our economic and social health will require in each metropolitan area at least one great university." And President Johnson noted, in calling for greater dispersion of federal research funds: "We want to find excellence and build it up wherever it is found so that creative centers of excellence may grow in every part of the Nation."[56]

These expectations were addressed by H. W. Magoun, who used Cartter's data to identify the top fifty research universities and potential future leaders. His top twenty-five were identical to the institutions Keniston surveyed with only two exceptions.[57] As one moved down this list, quality became thinner, distinguished departments rare, and strong ones less frequent. This pattern is all the more apparent in the next twenty-five institutions, which had fewer strong departments and more "adequate" ones. It should have been apparent that the

56 Kenneth D. Roose and Charles J. Anderson, *A Rating of Graduate Programs* (Washington, DC: ACE, 1970), 2; Cartter, *An Assessment of Quality*, 106–7; H. W. Magoun, "The Cartter Report on Quality in Graduate Education," *Journal of Higher Education* 37 (1966): 481–92, quotes pp. 486, 488.

57 Magoun, "Cartter Report," 484: from Keniston's list, the University of Iowa and Catholic University were dropped. And Brown and the University of Washington were included in Magoun's top twenty-five. Of the top seventeen universities, eleven were private; the next thirty-five, using Magoun's list, were evenly divided between public and private.

university distribution resembled a bell curve, with institutions on the right tail readily identified but an increasing muddle as one moved toward the median. By implication, it was unrealistic to expect institutions to cross a threshold to become a "great university" or a "center of excellence" (with Stanford the clear exception).[58] Nor were gradations of rank meaningful beyond the right tail, since different universities were good at different things. Rather, if they were able, universities struggled to enhance the quality of their faculty and graduate programs and move perceptibly to the right on the bell curve. What did this take? The most significant causal factor for the quality of graduate faculty, Cartter determined, was high salaries for tenured professors. Data on general income for the top twenty-five universities was more ambiguous but seemed to show economies of scale for institutions with large incomes, whether from large enrollments or ample per-student wealth.[59] The intangible factor that could not be measured was the institutional priority placed on graduate faculty quality. Successful research universities needed both resources and a commitment to excellence, while average universities, both public and private, had to juggle competing missions and priorities.

The second ACE rating by Kenneth D. Roose and Charles J. Anderson provided a fuller picture of American universities. Conducted in 1969, the twilight of the academic revolution, a change in tone was already notable. The authors expressed "serious misgivings about the apparent endorsement a study of this kind gives to the primacy of the university and, more particularly, to a hierarchy of university prestige and influence." They consequently withheld raw scores and simply ranked departments achieving scores of 3.0 or above (combining the "strong" and "distinguished" Cartter categories). In light of the "serious problems affecting undergraduate education," the authors were "deeply concerned lest this 1969 rating ... might contribute to some further distortion of effort in the university ... to shift resources and attention in excessive amounts to the development of quality in graduate programs."[60] By the time they wrote, the PhD glut was also becoming evident, and they advised states to eliminate weak and duplicate programs. Research and graduate education were no longer preeminent in public attitudes toward American higher education.

Roose and Anderson rated thirty-six disciplines in 130 institutions, almost 1,000 more programs than the Cartter study. Their results showed an overall improvement in the programs rated in 1964. An additional 72 of those departments were rated 3.0 or better, an increase of 13 percent. Average results for the

---

58 For the rise of Stanford and UCLA, see Geiger, *Research and Relevant Knowledge*, 118–46.

59 Cartter, *Assessment of Quality*, 111–14.

60 Roose and Anderson, *Rating of Graduate Programs*, 24.

entire sample were reduced by new institutions entering the lower ranks: 31 percent of departments were above 3.0, compared with 34 percent in 1964; 30 percent were below 2.0 (inadequate), compared with 28 percent in 1964. The bell curve had, if anything, shifted slightly leftward. The twenty-five new institutions rated in 1969 were nearly all public: five flagships (e.g., Georgia, Hawaii, South Carolina, Mississippi), five second state universities (e.g., Auburn, Arizona State), and six regional (e.g., Southern Illinois, Ohio University, Texas Tech). For middling institutions, in the 2.0 range, the study reported departments that were rated "better than 5 years ago" by 20 percent of respondents. Some 85 percent of these departments were in public universities. Public universities also contained 58 percent of the departments that rose across the 3.0 threshold.[61] Among the stronger universities, private institutions held their own, with the traditional leaders undiminished in prestige. In the middle and lower ranks, fast-growing public universities, especially in the South and West, benefited from rising state appropriations and a buyer's market for PhDs to enter the ranks of research universities and establish credible graduate programs. Drawing on the federal research economy, their exertions added significantly to the breadth and depth of academic research. Only a few would develop the scale and resources to be considered centers of excellence, but all these universities were the progeny of the academic revolution.

UNIVERSITIES AND AMERICAN SOCIETY

The text for the academic golden age was *The Uses of the University*, by Clark Kerr, president of the University of California. Delivered at Harvard as the 1963 Godkin Lectures, he depicted the contemporary research university at the apex of its prestige and influence. He called it a multiversity in recognition of the multiple domains of knowledge it now incorporated, the multiple tasks it had assumed, and the many publics to which it related. This enlarged scale and scope was part of a postwar transformation, still ongoing. To a large extent, he noted, the university had been transformed by external forces: the enlarged postwar responsibilities of the "federal-grant" university, and the "enormous" influence of foundations to induce "new developments." But within higher education, "interuniversity rivalry has become so intense that the rate of acceptance of change has been accelerated." *The Uses of the University* offered wise and telling observations about life in the multiversity, for students, faculty, and administrators charged with managing these dynamic, fragmented institutions. Kerr offered sensible reflections on current "imbalances" and likely future developments. He also offered

---

61 Ibid.: calculations by author.

a deeper conception of the university's distinctive contributions to modern American society.[62]

The "great transformation" of the postwar era had made universities into "a prime instrument of national purpose." Driving this change was the ascendancy of the "knowledge industry." Kerr cited a study by Fritz Machlup that calculated that "the production, distribution, and consumption of 'knowledge' … account[ed] for 29 percent of gross national product." Knowledge had become "the focal point for national growth. And the university is at the center of the knowledge process."[63] He rejected the idealistic and inward-looking characterization of the university as a "house of intellect." Rather, the modern university resembled an outward looking "city of intellect" that included multiple, disparate, unrelated parts—a multiversity. The university had thus become inexorably involved with and central to society: knowledge "is wanted, even demanded, by more people and more institutions than ever before." Hence, the responsibility of the multiversity was not only to engage in the challenging task of creating knowledge but also to assist it being "put into use better and faster."[64]

Clark Kerr had both the intellectual and administrative standing to make such sweeping pronouncements. A labor economist trained at Berkeley, he rejoined the university in 1945 as director of the new Institute of Industrial Relations. Appointed chancellor in 1952, he led an already strong faculty toward being named the country's most distinguished university in the 1965 Cartter ratings. Elevated to the presidency of the UC system (1958–1967), Kerr negotiated the 1960 Master Plan, which reconciled access to mass higher education with academic excellence at the University of California. At the time of the Godkin Lectures, he was supervising the building of three new campuses to join the university's six existing ones.[65] Kerr was intimately familiar with the imperatives of growth and the changing demands confronting higher education, but he was also an active agent shaping those forces. One means was forming centers and institutes to mediate between knowledge users—external funders and their objectives—and the knowledge creators—academic scholars and scientists. Such organized research units (ORUs) proliferated across the University of California.

---

62   Clark Kerr, *The Uses of the University* (Cambridge, MA: Harvard University Press, 1963), 107 et passim. Kerr added additional chapters until the fifth edition in 2001.

63   Ibid., 86–88; Fritz Machlup, *The Production and Distribution of Knowledge in the United States* (Princeton: Princeton University Press, 1962).

64   Kerr, *Uses of the University*, 94, 114, 124; reference is to Jacques Barzun, *The House of Intellect* (New York: Harper, 1959), which was critical of the realities that Kerr described.

65   Clark Kerr, *The Gold and the Blue: A Personal Memoir of the University of California, 1949–1967; Volume One, Academic Triumphs* (Berkeley: University of California Press, 2001); "Education: Master Planner," *Time* (October 17, 1960).

By 1963 few would question the contributions to society made by university science, technology, medicine, and the ORUs that they spawned. Kerr extended that vision of social involvement to applied social science, beginning with his initial position as director of a social science ORU. He was among postwar leaders who sought to develop effective social science methods and apply them to social issues, efforts soon spearheaded by the Ford Foundation. Kerr himself was a principal in a multiyear, Ford-funded, comparative study of industrialism that contributed to now-obsolescent modernization theory. Largely through his efforts, the Institute of International Studies, the Survey Research Center, and the Center for Research on Management Science joined the Institute of Industrial Relations as problem-oriented Berkeley ORUs. In this respect, Kerr exemplified a far larger movement to harness the social sciences to address and resolve an array of pressing postwar issues.[66]

The historian Ethan Schrum has characterized these developments as defining the "instrumental university," which sought to harness academic social science to inform and guide measures to address national needs.[67] Although such efforts had existed before the war, they became prominent features of American multiversities after 1945. These fields included urban planning, industrial relations, administration, and economic modernization. As already seen, the Ford Foundation played a prominent role in all these fields, but other interested parties also supported them, including the federal government. For some topics, the Cold War competition with the communist world was a more or less explicit rationale. In addition, the social science disciplines were generally regarded as inadequate to address real-world problems, so that interdisciplinary approaches were required. But this still left the central problem: what instrumental knowledge could social scientists offer? Here two approaches were evident—grand theory that could analyze problems and possible courses of action, or tools that could solve problems.

The intellectual and methodological development of postwar social science is enormously complex, but three threads were germane to developing applicable methodologies. Survey research was a practical tool that developed intellectually, methodologically, and institutionally after the war. Rensis Likert's wartime

---

66 Ethan Schrum, "Clark Kerr's Early Career, Social Science, and the American University," *Perspectives on the History of Higher Education* 28 (2011): 193–222; Geiger, *Research and Relevant Knowledge*, 47–57 (on ORUs), 73–82 (on Berkeley); Clark Kerr et al., *Industrialism and Industrial Man* (Cambridge, MA: Harvard University Press, 1960); John T. Dunlop et al., *Industrialism and Industrial Man Reconsidered: Some Perspectives on a Study over Two Decades on the Problem of Labor and Management in Economic Growth*, Final Report of the Inter-University Study of Labor Problems in Economic Development (Princeton: 1975).

67 Schrum, *Instrumental University*.

survey unit in the US Department of Agriculture found an academic home at the University of Michigan in 1946, but with no university support. The Institute for Social Research was thus compelled to be problem-oriented to obtain contracts and income. Highly successful, it earned more than $800,000 in 1950 and acquired a national reputation for leadership in survey research and social psychology. Paul Lazarsfeld's Bureau of Applied Social Research at Columbia (founded 1944) also supported itself by survey research for commercial clients. It too endeavored to improve the art while also inspiring fundamental sociological studies. The National Opinion Research Center, founded at the University of Denver in 1941, moved to the University of Chicago in 1947, where it became a predominantly academic ORU. Survey research provided far more than information on opinions. It applied survey sampling techniques to a variety of human behaviors from several social science perspectives.[68]

In 1946 the Air Force, unlike ONR's outreach to universities, funded what became the RAND Corporation to provide independent research pertinent to air warfare and national defense. Originally staffed by scientists and mathematicians, it soon focused on operations research (a valuable wartime mathematical methodology) and game theory (to model decision-making). RAND quickly established relationships with university scholars. With a particular interest in how nations make decisions about war, it sponsored breakthrough work on decision sciences that included university-based mathematicians and social scientists. Increasingly incorporating economics, it became a leader in the development of systems analysis. From the academic periphery and for its own purposes, RAND furthered the emergence of behavioralism in social science—an approach that was mathematical, problem-centered, interdisciplinary, and focused on behavioral functions.[69]

In 1945 the publication of Herbert Simon's *Administrative Behavior* illuminated decision-making by offering a new conceptual framework for organizational phenomena. Simon's work was rigorously quantitative. He was associated with the Cowles Commission at Chicago, an influential center advancing mathematical economics, and was a close consultant to RAND. At the center of behavioralism, he championed these approaches at Carnegie Tech's Graduate School of Industrial Administration, which became the template for the Ford Foundation's New Look in business education. However, strengthening public administration

68   Jean M. Converse, *Survey Research in the United States: Roots and Emergence, 1890–1960* (Berkeley: University of California Press, 1987); Geiger, *Research and Relevant Knowledge*, 53–56.

69   Bruce Kuklick, *Blind Oracles: Intellectuals and War from Kennan to Kissinger* (Princeton: Princeton University Press, 2006), 22–36; Crowther-Heyck, "Patrons of the Revolution," 420–46; Backhouse and Fontaine, "Toward a History," 184–233.

—Simon's original focus—was also a postwar concern. Cornell founded a school that combined business and public administration, and in the spirit of promoting scientific rigor, it launched the *Administrative Science Quarterly*. Organizational studies represented the theoretical side of administration, such that Kerr felt "the social sciences might be unified around the study of organizations and the relations of individuals to and within them."[70]

Kerr's casual insight in fact reflected the underlying direction of the postwar transformation of the social sciences. The historian of social science Hunter Heyck identified the emergence of a unifying theme that he dubbed "high modern social science": the conception of society as complex, hierarchical, structured systems. Several fundamental works related to systems thinking came to fruition in the mid-fifties: Simon's notion of bounded rationality; W. W. Rostow's stages of economic growth; Talcott Parsons' *Economy and Society*; the founding of the journal *Behavioral Science*; and synthetic works summarizing operations research and game theory. These and other seminal works viewed society as an interrelated system in which behavior could be measured and analyzed. Propelling these developments was a patronage system based on an instrumental rationale for developing academic social science. These themes of high modern social science and instrumental patronage were well supported until roughly 1965. In the twenty years since the Second World War, 250 interdisciplinary social science research institutes had been created.[71] However, by that year a second patronage pattern overshadowed instrumental patronage, one that favored the elaboration of theory and methods within the academic disciplines.

The shift toward support for disciplinary development began after Sputnik, and it was directly related to rising federal appropriations for social science and the heightened value accorded basic research. This trend occurred in the patterns of research support by NSF and the National Institute of Mental Health, which after 1958 became the largest supporter of psychology and a patron as well of other social sciences. Both agencies supported basic and applied research but with less interest in interdisciplinary behavioralist approaches. According to Heyck, these federal funders viewed applied research as the application of existing social science knowledge, whereas behavioralists had emphasized that problem-based research set in system-based frameworks was in itself a means for advancing

70   Hunter Crowther-Heyck, *Herbert A. Simon: The Bounds of Reason in Modern America* (Baltimore: Johns Hopkins University Press, 2005); Kerr, *Uses of the University*, 119–20. Simon had published *Organizations* in 1958 with James March and Harold Guetzkow (New York: Wiley), a seminal synthesis of postwar organizational theory.

71   Hunter Heyck, *Age of Systems: Understanding the Development of Modern Social Sciences* (Baltimore: Johns Hopkins University Press, 2015), 81–83.

social science knowledge.[72] As budgets soared in these civilian federal agencies, their preference for basic research and their use of discipline-based review panels all favored research within the social science disciplines. However, this development only mirrored more powerful forces within universities.

With the academic revolution at flood tide in the mid-sixties, academic departments focused their energies on research and graduate education, as Jencks and Riesman had lamented. American higher education had a seemingly insatiable appetite for discipline-trained PhDs to fill the faculty ranks of new and growing institutions. Feeding that hunger was the preferred mission of academic departments, in the social sciences as elsewhere. The appearance of the Cartter ratings in 1965 increased the stakes in the intense "inter-university rivalry" that Kerr had noted. In this case, the rivalry was among departments for prestige, recognition, and resources; and the stakes were grants, publications, faculty hires, and PhDs. In American higher education, disciplinary departments possessed the advantages already noted by Andrew Abbott, namely, uniting research fields, individual careers, faculty hiring, and undergraduate education. In contrast, each of these can be problematic for the ORUs of the instrumental university. Unlike the university's instructional budget for departments, support from external patrons is temporal and conditional in nature. Research themes can run their course or go out of fashion. And research units are dependent to some degree on departments for appointments or new hires. ORUs and instrumental purposes have remained essential and intrinsic components of American research universities, but at the height of the academic revolution, their influence tended to be eclipsed by the vitality of disciplinary departments, especially in the social sciences.

Both instrumental social science and academic social science were part of a larger transformation taking place in the roles of universities, university training, and university knowledge in American society. In the late 1950s, social commentators took note of the growth of white-collar positions in the workforce. Peter Drucker noted the large numbers of people now employed in "knowledge work," and Galbraith noted the New Class of workers whose technical and intellectual skills were acquired in higher education. More theoretical, University of Chicago economists first articulated the notion that productivity was related to human capital acquired largely through education. In the 1960s greater recognition was directed toward knowledge per se. Besides Machlup's inventory of knowledge contributions to the economy, the science historian Derek de Solla Price calculated that scientific knowledge roughly doubled every fifteen years.

---

72 Crowther-Heyck, "Patrons of the Revolution," 434–38.

Kerr was not alone in envisioning not just a knowledge economy but also a knowledge society. Foremost among such theorists was the sociologist Daniel Bell, whose conception of a postindustrial society was first floated in 1962. Elaborated in subsequent essays, the full development of these ideas was published in 1973 as *The Coming of Post-Industrial Society*.[73]

Postindustrial society for Bell was characterized by the rise to preeminence of not just the service economy but also the knowledge-based sector that encompassed health, education, research, and public administration. What was truly distinctive was the *"centrality* of theoretical knowledge"—"the source of innovation and policy formulation for the society." Hence, Bell pronounced the university to be "the primary institution of the post-industrial society." Moreover, granting the importance of higher education in general, the "axial" institutions were those in the knowledge-producing sector—the research universities. Bell referenced Machlup and Price, and he presented numerous tables showing the exponential growth of education, college degrees, PhDs, research, etc., but he also noted the concentrated nature of the latter items in the twenty-some leading research universities. The centrality of universities did not give them a causative role. Rather, the products they generated—academic experts and theoretical knowledge—were necessary facilitators of inherent features of the social transformation that Bell described. Besides the expansion of the service sector, postindustrial society included the democratization of higher education, the rising importance of the professional/technical class, rational planning in the organization of society, new intellectual technologies, and much more. Bell had little to say about universities themselves or higher education, subjects he had discussed in an earlier volume. The crucial role Bell ascribed to universities reflected a new reality of American society, the product perhaps of a lengthy evolution, but one which burst forth to unmistakable prominence in the 1960s.[74]

The growing impact of science and technology and their roots in academic research, which Bell described at length, was evident to any sentient observer. More subtle were the ways that theoretical knowledge informed thinking about everyday social life. Consider terms such as "self-fulfilling prophecy," "relative deprivation," "role model," "focus group," "opportunity cost," "free rider." These concepts, and innumerable others, originated in social science studies and became

---

73 Peter F. Drucker, *Landmarks of Tomorrow* (New York: Harper Brothers, 1957), 122; Schrum, *Instrumental University*, chap. 3; Daniel Bell, *The Coming of Post-Industrial Society: A Venture in Social Forecasting* (New York: Basic Books, 1973): Price is discussed on 178–85.

74 Bell, *Coming of Post-Industrial Society*, 14, 245–46 et passim. Bell had discussed higher education in *The Reforming of General Education* (New York: Columbia University Press, 1966), but with less emphasis on the university's distinctive role.

familiar in public discourse. Yet they would be unintelligible without the larger theoretical constructs emanating from university knowledge, and they would have been obscure to the public before the 1960s.[75]

More consequential—and controversial—examples can be drawn from the 1960s linkage of social science and public policy. President Kennedy sought to tap academic expertise directly by recruiting scholars into his administration. W. W. Rostow, who developed his theories of modernization at the MIT Center for International Studies, became the White House national security advisor. His conception of the stages of economic growth was the most prominent among the variants of modernization theory that rationalized U.S. policy toward developing countries.[76] Secretary of Defense Robert F. McNamara was strongly influenced by RAND and introduced New Look management and systems analysis to the DoD. In 1965 President Johnson generalized such approaches to all federal agencies with an executive order mandating the "planning-programming-budgeting system." It required policy analysis and evaluation for all government programs—and an abundance of government work for social scientists. The Office of Economic Opportunity (1965), in particular, was given responsibility for evaluating the programs of Johnson's War on Poverty. Finally, passage of the Civil Rights Act (1964) was followed by a survey to determine the lack of educational opportunity for racial minorities and its effects. The study, *Equality of Educational Opportunity* (1966), led by James Coleman, surveyed 650,000 school children and concluded, contrary to expectations, that differences in educational resources had small effects on educational achievements but that socioeconomic background was responsible for large effects.[77]

In none of these cases, or any others, did social science findings determine government policies. Rather, they served to buttress and rationalize what Henry Aaron called "the simple faiths of the early 1960s."[78] When these simple faiths were undermined at the end of the decade, so too was their social scientific baggage. Modernization theory was discredited, McNamara's planning systems abandoned, the OEO was eliminated by Nixon, and the issues raised by Coleman are still being disputed. What was challenged, but not displaced, was what Bell had

75   Jonathan R. Cole, *The Great American University: Its Rise to Preeminence, Its Indispensable National Role, Why It Must Be Protected* (New York: Public Affairs, 2009), chap. 10.

76   Rostow was regarded as too academic in the Kennedy administration but had considerable influence under Johnson: Kuklick, *Blind Oracles*, 146–50.

77   Michael E. Latham, *Modernization as Ideology: American Social Science and "Nation Building" in the Kennedy Era* (Chapel Hill: University of North Carolina Press, 2000); Kuklick, *Blind Oracles*, 97–101; Robert H. Haveman, *Poverty Policy and Poverty Research: The Great Society and the Social Sciences* (Madison: University of Wisconsin Press, 1987).

78   Henry J. Aaron, *Politics and the Professor: The Great Society in Perspective* (Washington, DC: Brookings Institution, 1978), 159.

perceived as the new centrality of theoretical knowledge for informing social organization. When a theory, with logical and empirical foundations, is discredited, whether by experience or a superior theory, knowledge is not lost, but modified. This amounts to progress, a net intellectual gain. Commentators of the 1960s knew, or sensed, or assumed that scientific knowledge was cumulative, which was perhaps too simplistic a view. They failed to appreciate the full ramifications of the impact of university knowledge in American society.

Sociologists have recently recognized the extent to which universities actually create knowledge. The modern knowledge society is "distinguished by the degree to which society is organized around the university's abstracted and universalized understandings of the world and its degree-certified graduates."[79] In the natural sciences, one might still say that scientists "discover" relationships in the natural world, but in technology, social and behavioral science, and the humanities, knowledge is embedded in paradigmatic constructs that are developed and elaborated in academic settings. How? Academics acquire expertise through years of specialized study; faculty positions allow, in fact require, them to enlarge that expertise through further research and study; and they share it with others through publication—new knowledge—in thoroughly vetted, publicly circulated journals and books. The great majority of university knowledge is of interest only to specialists. But modern society has become dependent on such knowledge since it intersects a variety of needs and interests. Society turns to university knowledge precisely because it is authoritative. That is, academic knowledge is objective, in that academic writings must present the premises on which they are based and the evidence that supports their findings; and academic knowledge is abstract and universal, in that the proposed knowledge pertains to a general class of phenomena. The objective nature of academic knowledge permits evaluation and challenge. In fact, important findings are sure to be contested by academic peers and often in the wider society. This process is indispensable for establishing and augmenting university knowledge. It is the foundation of its cultural authority.[80]

Universities have always fulfilled this role to some extent—providing a site and a culture for generating authoritative knowledge. Before World War II, American universities nurtured, in some cases, world-leading disciplinary advances,

79   David J. Frank and John W. Meyer, "University Expansion and the Knowledge Society," *Theory and Society* 36, 4 (2007): 287–311, quote p. 287; David P. Baker, *The Schooled Society: The Educational Transformation of Global Culture* (Stanford, CA: Stanford University Press, 2014).

80   For John Meyer and associates, "the authority of science in modern societies ... operates as the secular equivalent of a 'sacred canopy' for the modern order, generating a modern rational interpretation of world order, and offering this logic as a secular interpretive grid for natural and social life": Drori et al. *Science in the Modern World Polity*, 23.

but American society and polity did not look to universities for intellectual sustenance. Academic expertise was largely ignored, for example, by the New Deal. This changed after the war, dramatically in the sciences but only gradually in other realms. Universities were regarded primarily as educational institutions by the President's Commission and considered faintly subversive during the McCarthy era. By the end of that decade, however, the growing salience of university science, the incipient knowledge explosion of the academic revolution, and the catalyst of Sputnik, all contributed to the profound cultural shift of the Liberal Hour and the growing social utilization of university expertise. The authors of the three principal documents discussed in this chapter all reacted to this change, albeit from somewhat different perspectives. From the standpoint of undergraduate education, Christopher Jencks and David Riesman viewed with trepidation the university's obsessive fixation with advancing knowledge through research and graduate training. From a university standpoint, Clark Kerr conceived of a knowledge industry that looked to universities for multiform useful activities and outputs. Daniel Bell attempted to portray a new social order that would encompass capitalism, social classes, and government. With a somewhat longer perspective, he posited theoretical knowledge and the universities that produced it as driving the transformation from industrial society. In addition, they and others were in fact witnessing an additional dimension of this phenomenon: that the new era had brought a massive increase in the number of young people attending institutions of higher education.

★ 4 ★

EXPANSION AND
TRANSFORMATION

T HE DECADE OF THE 1960S WAS THE MOST DYNAMIC PERIOD IN the long history of American higher education. The ramifications of Sputnik, described in Chapter 3, opened the academic world to the need for progressive change, and the spirit of the Liberal Hour raised expectations of substantial, if uncharted, advancement. The baby boom generation arrived simultaneously with President Johnson's Great Society, accelerating an already substantial rate of growth.

From fall 1959 to fall 1969, total enrollments grew from 3 million to 7 million (122 percent); college-age cohorts grew from 9 million to 14 million, and the proportion of them in college rose from 31 percent to 44 percent. High school graduates rose by 1 million, and those continuing on to college peaked at 60 percent for men and nearly 50 percent for women. And these growth dynamics persisted into the early 1970s. But mere numbers mask significant qualitative developments. New institutions provided new pathways, affecting who went to college, as well as how and where. Many of these developments constituted additions to the postwar system of higher education that had evolved since 1945, but they also reflected changing assumptions. The new demography of higher education stemmed from alterations in social behaviors and cultural values. The enlarged institutional base of higher education stemmed from an endorsement by democratically elected governments of the desirability of providing higher education to a large proportion of young people.

A TIDAL WAVE OF STUDENTS

Observers of American higher education marveled at how enrollments had "skyrocketed" in the 1950s. As undergraduate enrollments rose from a post-GI low of just over 2 million in 1951 to 2.9 million in 1959—a rise from 24 to 31 percent of the 18–21 age cohort—three factors were at work.[1] An additional 800,000 high

---

1   Enrollments from National Council for Education Statistics (NCES), *Digest of Education Statistics*, various years. Discrepancies exist in these data, but the general trends are stark.

school graduates in these years supplied more potential students, although in 1959 more students still dropped out of high school than continued to college. Some of the enrollment growth came from more effective identification of high-ability students and encouragement for them to go to college. In addition, rising family incomes swelled the number of middle-class and suburban households that were more likely to send children to college. However, during this expansion the socioeconomic patterns of college attendance were remarkably stable. They were also highly skewed. Males from the top income quintile were more than three times as likely to attend college than their counterparts from the lowest quintile. Well-off females were five times more likely to attend. This pattern reflected the mentality of the American way of life and persisted until the arrival of the baby-boom generation.

The disparity between male and female enrollments is a telling indicator of the stable relation to American society that prevailed simultaneously with significant growth. Through the 1950s, about 35 percent of female high school graduates continued to college, while the corresponding figure for males was 50–55 percent. (Throughout the twentieth century, more women graduated from high school than men.) Project Talent, a survey of 1960 high school seniors, depicted the relationships between academic aptitude and socioeconomic status (SES) at that juncture.[2] Overall, 49 percent of males and 35 percent of females attended college. Differences in attendance were least for women in the top ability quintile (76 vs. 85 percent of men) and the top SES quintile (75 vs. 81 percent). Differences were also small for the opposite quintiles where college attendance was lowest. The largest differences in college attendance were located precisely in the middle quintiles—middling aptitude and middling SES (25 vs. 46 percent). Thus, college-going was strongly influenced by SES. Performance in school could counteract much of this effect, but more so for men than for women. However, for every cell of this five-by-five matrix, parents were more likely to send a son to college than his sister. The creeping growth in middle-class incomes, values, and life styles in these years helped the girls but favored the boys.

These attitudes were reflected in a 1960 attempt by an old-school sociologist, Robert Havighurst, to predict how higher education might adapt to the challenges of the new decade. He foresaw the current era, in which the demand for college graduates exceeded the supply, persisting until the boomers arrived. Then, the situation would reverse, and college graduates would outstrip the supply of college-level jobs. He expected the number of male graduates to increase as cohorts grew but predicted that the rate of attendance would have to decline. Col-

---

2　Christopher Jencks and David Riesman, *The Academic Revolution* (Chicago: University of Chicago Press, 1968), Table V, p. 103.

lege selectivity would consequently tighten, favoring the intelligent and the well-born. Working-class students, who were less prepared and more sensitive to job prospects, would probably suffer. And so would women. He projected no increase in college-level jobs for women, and hence no increase in their relative attendance. He assumed that only half of women graduates would work and that many of them would "take jobs as stenographers or as salesclerks." He feared that current growth was unsustainable, "since under present conditions about three times as many girls enter college as can be accommodated in occupations of 'college level.'" Havighurst's faulty crystal ball reflected contemporary thinking. He extrapolated from the data available in 1960 and applied the conventional wisdom as well: namely, that college-going was determined by academic aptitude and labor markets and that the 1950s status and behavior of women would not change.[3]

The anticipated Tidal Wave of baby boomers arrived on schedule in 1964. Rather than favoring men, as Havighurst forecast, the gender balance began a prolonged shift in favor of women. From 1964 to 1969, more than one million additional high school graduates increased first-year enrollments by two-thirds. Male enrollments surged, but the share of women slowly rose to 44 percent, compared with less than 40 percent in the 1950s. Then, first-year enrollments of men stagnated while those of women continued to grow. After 1975, more women than men entered college, where they formed the majority of students by 1980. The transformation of feminine roles in America is a story of the 1970s and will be examined in Chapter 6. The 1960s was a transitional decade in which the rigid gender stereotypes of the 1950s gradually dissolved. Greater participation in higher education served as both cause and consequence of this development.

When the great expansion of higher education is viewed in relation to American society, the obvious questions are what motivated increasing proportions of students to attend college, and how were they absorbed into the labor market? That they were absorbed is an undisputed fact: until the end of the 1960s college graduates had little difficulty finding suitable employment—available places exceeded the supply. In the 1950s, male college graduates in the workforce increased from 6.9 to 9.7 percent. They were widely diffused. In terms of *additional* graduate workers, 60 percent were broadly "professional." The largest category of additional workers was engineers, who accounted for 12 percent of the total increase, followed by teachers (9.5 percent). But 28 percent were spread over twenty-three professional categories. Salaried white-collar employees added 10 percent; clerical and sales workers, 13 percent. Knowledge workers (natural and social scientists, college faculty), the presumed core of the knowledge society, composed just 6 percent of additions. College graduates in the female workforce only grew from 7.7 to 7.9 percent, but the number of working women grew by 35 percent. Although 70 percent of additional graduates were professional, most of those were teachers (42 percent). Clerical workers comprised 17 percent, and nurses another 6 percent. Women generally made substantial gains in employment in the 1950s, but two-thirds of additional college graduates found work in these three typically female occupations.[4]

In the 1960s, the college-educated workforce increased to 15 percent for men and 12 percent for women. The proportion of college graduates in professional occupations increased for women, but barely for men. Graduate jobs in managerial/administration positions were a major source of growth for both sexes.[5] However, it was evident by the end of the decade that the traditional view of the labor market failed to explain how the great expansion of higher education affected jobs. The assumptions of neoclassical economics—that employees (college graduates) were added when their marginal productivity exceeded marginal costs and that wages were determined by the supply and demand of labor—shed little light on actual developments. The definition of jobs requiring a college degree had become ambiguous, as well as the premise that preparing for such positions was the principal motivation driving college attendance. Finally, ascribing "overeducation" to market imperfections merely rationalized an outworn model.[6]

By one estimate, 60 percent of the increased employment of men and women college graduates in the 1960s was attributable to growth in college jobs as the economy expanded and modernized. The other 40 percent could be ascribed to educational upgrading. Economists dismissed this phenomenon as "credentialism." They identified various market imperfections that would allow it to occur, including a nonrational preference of managers for college-educated employees.[7] This view sought to account for evidence that social forces drove the expansion of higher education independent of the labor market demand for college-trained workers. Hence, even though graduates exceeded college jobs, credentialism explained why "excess" graduates found employment. The economist Lester Thurow provided a more plausible explanation for this phenomenon. Since most

4   Margaret S. Gordon, "The Changing Labor Market for College Graduates," in Gordon, ed. *Higher Education and the Labor Market* (New York: McGraw Hill, 1974), 33–45. Graduate women were far outnumbered by nongraduates in nursing and clerical positions.

5   Gordon, *Higher Education*, 55.

6   Douglas L. Atkins, *The Great American Degree Machine* (Berkeley, CA: Carnegie Commission on Higher Education, 1975), 165–78.

7   Ibid., 55; V. Lane Rawlins and Lloyd Ullman, "Utilization of College-Trained Manpower in the United States," in Gordon, *Higher Education*, 195–236.

productive skills were learned on the job, prospective workers competed for job opportunities. Educational credentials provided a screen that identified more-trainable employees, and employers relied on such signals to advance college graduates in the "job queue."[8] Such a process reflected both credentialism and substantive educational upgrading, since college-educated employees were not only more readily trained but probably more productive as well. Subsequent analyses have established that better-educated workers indeed have substantial positive effects on upgrading workplaces.[9] Thus, in assimilating increasing cohorts of college graduates in the 1950s and 1960s, labor markets made functional reactions to the surge in college graduates. They were not the cause of that surge.

Instead, the transformative agent in the great expansion of higher education was social demand. Demographic variables played a role. Larger cohorts and more high school graduates supplied more bodies, but social aspirations lured increasing proportions of them to enroll. Families sought higher education for their children because it provided opportunities for better life prospects, a relative advantage in economic opportunities, social status, and cultural distinction.[10] The critical development of the 1960s was a changing mentality as increasing numbers of families embraced these aspirations. Martin Trow observed that as participation levels rose, higher education evolved from a privilege to a right for all having the requisite qualifications and then to an obligation essential for maintaining social status.[11] Thus, economic development played a crucial role in elevating families above that aspirational threshold. Governments responded by making places in higher education available to meet popular demand (see next section). And public attitudes also changed. In the 1960s, earlier postwar convictions about higher education were conveniently forgotten: notions that only the most intelligent quartile should go to college (IQ determinism), that working-class youth and most women lacked the motivation to attend, and that overeducation in relation to college jobs posed a social threat. In their place emerged "a new model of society" in which the university constituted a central institution, education and individual development were basic human rights for all, and

8   Lester C. Thurow, "Measuring the Economic Benefits of Education," in Gordon, *Higher Education*, 373–418. This model was elaborated in Thurow, *Generating Inequality: Mechanisms of Distribution in the U.S. Economy* (New York: Basic Books, 1975).

9   David P. Baker, *The Schooled Society: The Educational Transformation of Global Culture* (Stanford, CA: Stanford University Press, 2014), 139–53 et passim.

10   Simon Marginson, "Universal Higher Education in the Global Era" (paper presented at The Dynamics of High Participation Systems, Higher School of Economics, Moscow, September 26, 2013). My thanks to Simon Marginson for sharing this paper.

11   Martin Trow, "Problems in the Transition from Elite to Mass Higher Education," in Michael Burrage, ed., *Martin Trow: Twentieth-Century Higher Education, Elite to Mass to Universal* (Baltimore: Johns Hopkins University Press, 2010), 86–142.

expanded human capital contributed to a more rationally managed society.[12] This new model of society was both advocated and contested with considerable passion, as will be seen below. Several features of the expansion help to clarify its nature.

One seemingly anomalous development was the rising proportion of students studying and graduating in the liberal arts (humanities, social sciences, and psychology). First-generation students typically were vocationally oriented, but the share of bachelor's degrees earned by baby boomers in these academic subjects was the highest ever attained, rising from 30 to 41 percent (1960–1970). Science and engineering degrees lost more than 5 percent of their share, which might be expected of demanding, math-based subjects given wider participation, but education shed the same amount, and business lost half that much.[13] These choices reflected the preferences of both institutions and students. With the liberal arts enjoying peak prestige, new and expanding institutions emphasized these subjects, some offering little else. Vocational curricula were available but, outside of education and engineering, were weakly developed, as was the case with business education. For students, the academic revolution generated exciting new content in these subjects. More generally, liberal arts were identified with latent aspirations for social and cultural betterment. A college education and degree were still associated in America to some extent with liberal learning. Nor were these beliefs misguided: the degrees and cognitive abilities of liberal arts majors were validated in the wide availability of jobs. In addition, by the end of the decade the spreading propensity to disassociate from bourgeois society further favored academic over professional subjects.[14]

In the early 1960s, the average scores of prospective students on the Scholastic Aptitude Test attained their highest levels. After 1963, when the boomers began to be tested, average scores declined, though not by much. After 1970, scores plunged. An inquiry commissioned by the College Board determined that the drop from 1963 to 1970 was due to a wider and less select population of test-takers. Recall that expanding access previously had increased the partici-

12   Evan Schofer and John W. Meyer, "The Worldwide Expansion of Higher Education in the Twentieth Century," *American Sociological Review* 70 (December 2005): 898–920. These conclusions are based on international trends that have formed modern global society, largely through isomorphism. The expansion, however, occurred first in the United States, accompanied by these contested traits.

13   Author's calculations from Atkins, *Great American Degree Machine*.

14   Roger L. Geiger, "Demography and Curriculum: The Humanities in American Higher Education from the 1950s through the 1980s," in David Hollinger, ed., *The Humanities and the Dynamics of Inclusion since World War II* (Baltimore: Johns Hopkins University Press, 2006), 50–72; Steven Brint et al., "From the Liberal to the Practical Arts in American Colleges and Universities: Organizational Analysis and Curricular Change," *Journal of Higher Education* 76 (March–April 2005): 151–80.

pation of high-ability students, so that average SAT scores actually rose slightly even as many more students were tested. A ceiling was reached by 1963, when nearly all high-achieving students were now going to college.[15] For the remainder of the 1960s, rising social demand meant that additional students were comparatively less able. Nor did participation decline after 1970, when academic ability declined across the board, with no change in the composition of test-takers. Going to college was now regarded as a human right.[16]

But graduation from college was not. Historically, the college graduation rate has been less than 50 percent, but in the 1960s it appeared to be appreciably higher.[17] However, college completion varied widely across institutions. For the entering class of 1966, one-third of community college students failed to enroll for a second year. Four-year institutions lost about one-fifth of freshmen the first year, and another fifth of the class before graduation. Colleges with below-average students graduated just over half; highly selective institutions graduated 70–80 percent of their freshmen. For students, the clearest predictors of college graduation were good high-school grades and high test scores, which was consistent with earlier postwar patterns. Women averaged better grades and lower scores, and they had lower graduation rates (56 percent)—a condition that would change in the next decade. Several factors may have buoyed graduation rates in the late 1960s. Average academic ability was still relatively high. After 1965, the impending threat of the draft encouraged men to stay in school.[18] Academically, college became easier. These years experienced the steepest grade inflation ever recorded, as As increased by 15 percent and Cs fell by an equal amount (1966–1974), even as student qualifications were declining. And college was eminently

15   Paul Taubman and Terence Wales, *Mental Ability and Higher Education Attainment in the 20th Century*, NBER Occasional Paper No. 118, (December 1972).

16   *On Further Examination: Report of the Advisory Panel on the Scholastic Aptitude Test Score Decline* (New York: College Entrance Examination Board, 1977); Roger L. Geiger, "The Case of the Missing Students," *Change* 10, 11 (December 1978–January 1979): 64–65.

17   Graduation rates are usually calculated by comparing census categories for "1–3 years of college" with college graduates, but even this method suggests higher rates for the 1960s: Martha J. Bailey and Susan M. Dynarski, "Inequality in Postsecondary Education," in Greg Duncan and Richard Murnane, eds. *Wither Opportunity? Rising Inequality, Schools, and Children's Life Chances* (New York: Russell Sage, 2011), 117–32. The following data are from an institutional survey of the class of 1970 (entering in 1966): Alexander Astin, *College Dropouts: A National Profile*, ACE Research Reports, vol. 7, no. 1 (Washington, DC: ACE, February 1972).

18   By one estimate, 6–7 percent of males were attending "involuntarily"; however, far more altered enrollment plans or attended graduate school to avoid the draft: Lawrence M. Baskir and William A. Strauss, *Chance and Circumstance: The Draft, the War, and the Vietnam Generation* (New York: Vintage, 1978), 28–32. A later economic analysis suggested 4–6 percent: David Card and Thomas Lemieux, "Going to College to Avoid the Draft: The Unintended Legacy of the Vietnam War," *American Economic Review* 91 (May 2001): 97–102.

affordable. For the class of 1970, there was no discernible relationship between family income and persistence to graduation.[19]

Mass higher education in the 1960s followed traditional patterns in most respects, but now included a wider swath of the American population. Freshmen entering four-year colleges in 1968 were overwhelmingly recent high school graduates—96 percent were age nineteen or younger. They were middling in many respects. In high school, one-quarter had less than a B average and just 15 percent earned As. Their origins, roughly in even thirds, were rural/small town, medium-sized towns, and large cities and their suburbs. One-third came from families earning $8,000 or less, below the family mean. Slightly more than one-quarter of fathers had graduated from college, the same portion that had not finished high school.[20] As a whole, mass higher education represented massive participation by the broad middle class. However, significant differences existed in where students went to college. Mass higher education in the 1960s was made possible by the development of institutions consciously addressed to serving the masses.

MASS PUBLIC HIGHER EDUCATION

From fall 1959 to fall 1969, only 12 percent of 1.1 million additional beginning students enrolled in private colleges, and all private growth occurred in the first half of the decade. Eight of nine new places were in public institutions: five in community colleges and three in four-year colleges. These places were made possible by an enormous increase in the public investment in higher education—part federal, part local, but mostly from state appropriations.[21] The rate of growth varied across the fifty states, but every state multiplied its investments several times over. This robust public support continued, with greater irregularity, into and through most of the 1970s, despite a weaker economy and increasing disenchantment with many aspects of higher education.

19   Stuart Rojstaczer and Christopher Healy, "Where A Is Ordinary: The Evolution of American College and University Grading, 1940–2009," *Teachers College Record* 114, 7 (2012): 1–23; Astin, *College Dropouts*, 38; Claudia Goldin and Lawrence F. Katz, *The Race between Education and Technology* (Cambridge, MA: Harvard University Press, 2008), 271–77.

20   American Council on Education, Office of Research, *National Norms for Entering College Freshmen—Fall 1968*. When fathers with "some college" are added to graduates, five of nine entering students were first-generation college attendees.

21   State appropriations to public higher education for current operating funds increased from $1,129 million in 1958 to $2,927 million in 1966; state appropriations as a percentage of personal income in the United States increased from 0.4 to 0.6 percent: Selma J. Mushkin, "A Note on State and Local Financing of Higher Education," in *The Economics and Financing of Higher Education in the United States* (Washington, DC: GPO, 1969), 518–40.

The landscape of public higher education in the 1960s largely conformed to the California paradigm described in Chapter 2—one or more state research universities, regional colleges or universities, and community colleges. Research universities tended to enroll as many undergraduates as was feasible but largely focused growth on graduate education and research. Demographic expansion was concentrated in the other two sectors. The former teachers colleges, dispersed throughout small towns and cities, were expanded and upgraded to offer a wider curriculum to larger numbers of their traditional clientele. The community college movement experienced mushroom growth in the 1960s. By the end of the decade, new community colleges opened at a rate of better than one per week. Public urban universities filled multiple roles that are less readily categorized. Their prominence in the decade stemmed from a belated realization that for higher education to serve a wider public, universities had to be located where populations lived.[22] Branch campuses filled out this picture, in some cases providing urban access and in others substituting for community colleges. Together, these institutions provided the places that made the United States the first society to achieve mass higher education.

REGIONAL COLLEGES AND UNIVERSITIES. Former normal schools that had become teachers colleges and then public colleges and universities formed the core of this sector. These institutions acquired a new identity in 1961 with the establishment of the more inclusive American Association of State Colleges and Universities (AASCU). The Office of Education, still using the old designation, in 1963 counted 186 teachers colleges enrolling 10 percent of U.S. students. By 1969 the AASCU had 231 members, 166 of which were former teachers colleges. This expanded group enrolled 21 percent of all students, 42 percent of students in public four-year institutions.[23]

In 1968 Alden Dunham surveyed the AASCU schools for the Carnegie Commission on Higher Education. He described what he found as "a spectrum from single-purpose teachers colleges to multipurpose universities." Among the former, the New Jersey state colleges had just escaped from the thumb of the state board of education and still operated like teachers colleges. And twenty-four

22   By one estimate, 47 percent of Americans lived in SMSAs of 500,000 or more, which contained 30 percent of FTE enrollments (1965). The largest number and proportion of higher education students were found in SMSAs of 100,000–250,000: Seymour E. Harris, "Financing Higher Education: An Overview," in *Economics and Financing*, 467–506.

23   Totals include forty-four kindred nonmember institutions on the AASCU mailing list, including a number of technical institutes. These public schools did not identify with the AASCU model: E. Alden Dunham, *Colleges of the Forgotten Americans: A Profile of State Colleges and Regional Universities* (New York: McGraw-Hill, 1969).

colleges had fewer than 1,000 students, the smallest being in New England. Four-fifths of the schools, with more than two-thirds of students, had enrollments between 1,000 and 10,000, and most were experiencing rapid growth. A tenth of schools exceeded that size. The largest had gotten an earlier start toward university status and by that date were feeling the lure of the academic revolution. All types envisioned doubling undergraduate enrollments by 1975 and increasing graduate students even more. Coming to terms with growth, past, present, and future, was the dominant condition as they navigated the transition to the new academic norms of the 1960s.[24]

One thing that changed more slowly was the students. Although there were more of them, they still resembled the traditional clienteles. Largely first-generation college-goers from working or lower-middle class families, they had middling abilities, on average, and came predominantly from surrounding regions. One-quarter failed to return after their first year. More than 40 percent intended to become teachers even late in the 1960s. As the decade wore on, community college transfers supplied additional upper-division students. Most students lived on campus and participated in extracurricular life, but many retained local ties and traveled home for weekends. In the radical sixties, students at non-urban campuses were decidedly moderate. They registered high on practicality, low on national or international awareness, and low on commitment to scholarship. Dunham concluded: "The state college population more nearly resembles the community college student population than it does other four-year colleges and universities."[25]

New faculty drove the modernizing movement. Growth brought new recruits in the arts and sciences, fresh from university graduate schools, who soon overwhelmed the ed-school old guard. In the late sixties, one-half of faculty members commonly had been on campus for three years or less. These cadres brought the culture of the graduate schools and the academic revolution, and they soon chafed against the mores and leadership of teachers colleges. They considered research and scholarship to be essential for the faculty role and favored the expansion of graduate education. New leadership supported these values, a means to advance an institution's image and prestige. But limited facilities and heavy teaching loads were constraining and a source of faculty frustration, as was the task of teaching provincial, uninspired students. Faculty typically sought a greater voice in governance and often established faculty senates. Later they would opt for collective bargaining (Chapter 5). Despite the powerful academicizing trend, many AASCU institutions, especially smaller and more rural ones, had difficulty up-

---

24 Ibid., 40–43.
25 Ibid., 94: a rather gross generalization considering the variety of circumstance among this type.

grading their faculties with PhDs. As of 1966, nearly half of regular faculty were assistant professors, and less than one-quarter of them had doctorates (though many were no doubt ABD). Schools commonly sought to address this lacuna by recruiting PhDs from the third-tier universities described in Chapter 3.

Some of the larger AASCU institutions made concerted efforts to emulate research universities. By 1966, eight of them were awarding PhDs, although that was not in itself a distinguishing feature of university status.[26] The impact of the academic revolution was evident on upwardly mobile hopefuls, like Northern Illinois University, and the tensions just described were if anything more acute. A teachers college with 1,800 students in 1951, NIU grew tenfold by the end of the 1960s. In the mid-sixties, the state designated NIU a liberal arts university, and it became self-governing with its own board of regents. A "euphoria of rapid growth" followed, accompanied by copious state appropriations that not only accommodated growth but also funded academic upgrades as well. Resources were devoted to expanding arts and sciences departments, and a majority of faculty held doctorates. By the end of the decade the chief preoccupation was to build doctoral programs and enhance NIU's status as a true university. Weaknesses tended to be ignored. A record of publication was now required for promotion, but only to full professor. Otherwise, the requirements for gaining tenure and associate professor status were reputedly lax. Externally funded research was virtually nonexistent. Little thought was given to improving undergraduate teaching and learning. First- and second-year students were consigned to large lectures with teaching assistants and audio-visual aids. In 1967 a majority of bachelors still earned degrees in education. Admissions requirements to NIU, like most state colleges, were minimal. Students were conventional and vocational, though possibly improving by the end of the decade.[27]

The most academically advanced subset of AASCU institutions were the California State Colleges, which were precluded from having doctoral programs by the Master Plan. The four that had begun as normal schools had been converted to state colleges in 1935. Seven were established as general purpose state colleges by 1950. Four more were added in the 1950s, and three after the Master Plan. Chartered in response to population pressure, most were urban or suburban institutions. Enrollments rose from 95,000 to 242,000 in the 1960s; five of the eighteen colleges exceeded 20,000. The largest institution, San Diego State College, was a university in all but name. They were more selective than other AASCU

26 Doctorates were awarded by numerous small colleges and professional schools. Accreditation for doctoral programs was a more stringent criterion. The eight AASCU doctoral-granting universities: Colorado State College; the Universities of Akron, Northern Illinois, and Southern Mississippi; Bowling Green, East Texas, North Texas, and Ball State universities.

27 Harold L. Hodgkinson, *Institutions in Transition* (New York: McGraw Hill, 1971), 183–95.

members, drawing students from the top third of high school classes. PhDs composed a substantial majority of the faculties, and they too responded to the siren song of the academic revolution. By the end of the 1960s, the state colleges were near open revolt over the "second-class" citizenship imposed by the Master Plan. Compared with the University of California, they had heavier teaching loads, lower salaries, fewer opportunities for research (or travel), and a prohibition of doctoral programs. In 1967 the state system launched a concerted effort to achieve more parity with the university. This campaign was stonewalled by the UC and, given the potential expense, had little appeal for the legislature as the fiscal picture darkened. In 1972, as a costless concession, the system was permitted to become the California State *Universities*, with no change in function.[28]

At the end of the 1960s, when the Carnegie Commission on Higher Education published the complete *Classification of Institutions of Higher Education*, the AASCU institutions were labeled Comprehensive Colleges. Less than ten of them attained the level of Doctorate-Granting Colleges and Universities, and none ever graduated to become a research university. In the mid-sixties, when state appropriations seemed to have no limits, aspirations for academic distinction seemed attainable and desirable. Only after decade's end did it become apparent that the essential features of a research university were inherently scarce and competitive. Research grants were awarded to the most scientifically promising proposals; academics who produced significant publications were few in number and concentrated in settings that favored research; and the supply of talented, full-time doctoral students, which may have seemed unending circa 1970, was actually finite. The former teachers colleges were ill-equipped to compete with established universities for these crucial inputs. Rather, they supplied access to a college education for a large swath of the population that had previously attended sparsely, whether for reasons of social class, culture, or economics. And, through concerted academic upgrading, they enhanced the quality of instruction that those students now received. Going forward, as will be seen, they would abandon the aspirations of the academic revolution and of necessity focus institutional priorities on serving their existing constituency.

PUBLIC URBAN UNIVERSITIES. Worldwide, great universities are associated with great cities. A peculiarity of American academic history has been the predominance in American cities of private institutions under a varied sponsorship:

---

28   Dunham, *Colleges of the Forgotten Americans*, 51–56; Neil J. Smelser and Gabriel Almond, *Public Higher Education in California* (Berkeley: University of California Press, 1974), 9–141; Françoise Alice Queval, "The Evolution toward Research Orientation and Capability in Comprehensive Universities: A Case Study, the California State University System," PhD diss., UCLA, 1990.

Colonial (Columbia, Pennsylvania, Brown), philanthropic (Johns Hopkins, Chicago, MIT), YMCA (Northeastern, Youngstown). The Catholic Church maintained educational systems from primary grades to universities that served its community, and municipalities filled higher educational voids, often with private assistance (e.g., Cincinnati). The City University of New York was a unique pioneer in inaugurating all types of higher education for city students (in 1964 it awarded the nation's largest number of bachelor's degrees). The postwar expansion revealed that the hodge-podge of existing institutions could not accommodate the rising urban demand and that public initiatives were required. Some progress was made in the 1950s, often resisted by established rivals, as happened at Georgia State in Atlanta and the University of Illinois at Chicago. After 1960, though, these pressures could no longer be ignored. Cities contained both population and jobs. The baby boomers needed places to study; existing institutions lacked capital to grow or remained identified with insular groups; and urban taxpayers demanded a share of the state's educational spending. The 1960s witnessed the creation or transformation of a new type of public urban university— by whatever means seemed feasible. State universities established branches in cities; municipal universities were adopted and financed by states; struggling private universities were converted to large state campuses; and a few urban universities were established de novo.

In many ways these new or transformed institutions resembled (or in fact had been) state regional colleges. They were tasked with educating first-generation college-goers, many with weak academic preparation. The new faculty they recruited were products of the academic revolution with the usual aspirations of research. But universities in urban settings were more complicated institutions. Cities provided abundant prospects for professional and graduate education, as well as for vocational programs beyond teacher education. And the urban student was likely to be a transient on campus—a commuter, often an adult, studying part-time and possibly employed. A potential tension existed between the traditional conceptions of a college education based on arts and sciences, and the interests, orientations, and capacities of this new wave of urban students. In the first years of the 1960s, liberal arts inclinations exerted a powerful influence, as seen in different ways at the University of South Florida and Monteith College. After mid-decade, however, an entirely different conception of the urban university became dominant. Urban service became the watchword for accommodating any and all students, addressing the crisis of the cities, and providing services for the surrounding environment.

Traditional liberal arts, fortified by the academic revolution, soon proved almost antithetical to the urban service roles of older city institutions. The University of Buffalo was a representative private urban university in 1952: just 18 percent of its 9,600 students were in arts and sciences, 42 percent in the Evening Division, and the remainder in eight professional schools. With no residence halls, it served a local population. In 1962 it was incorporated into the State University of New York and designated one of four graduate centers. A report chaired by Indiana University president Herman Wells then urged SUNY to emphasize high-quality graduate education and scientific research, including building "peaks of excellence." In 1966 Martin Meyerson was named president (1966–1970). A scholar of urban planning who was then acting chancellor of UC Berkeley, he was eager to fulfill that mandate and make Buffalo "the Berkeley of the East." Meyerson accelerated a breathtaking transformation already underway, recruiting large numbers of research-minded faculty to staff prestige-minded departments. Admissions became selective as resident students were drawn predominantly from elsewhere, especially from the New York City area. Meyerson paid lip service to serving the Buffalo community, but his goal—and SUNY's—was to create a national research university. However, in the polarized atmosphere of the late 1960s, a profound gulf developed between the academic cosmopolitanism of the new students and faculty and the largely blue-collar Buffalo community, with consequences that will be seen in Chapter 5.[29]

Similar tensions beset the new Boston campus of the University of Massachusetts. The long-starved flagship campus in Amherst (designated a "university" in 1947), along with other state colleges, benefited from an uncharacteristic burst of state support in the 1960s. A shortfall of student places raised the smoldering issue of creating a public university in Boston, which alarmed private colleges and was opposed by many within UMass. Quite abruptly, legislation creating a Boston campus was passed in 1964, stipulating that UMass Boston would begin offering classes the following fall. In the haste to organize the institution, the curriculum was left to the faculty, whose natural proclivities favored the kind of liberal arts course offered in small New England colleges. However, in the dense collegiate marketplace of metropolitan Boston, the new institution served the marginal students of mass higher education. Forty percent came from the lowest economic quartile of Massachusetts families, and many older students worked part time. They were offered a full-time, daytime liberal arts course that was admirable for its intellectual fidelity, but which often presented logistical and academic difficulties for commuter students. This disjunction persisted until

29   Warren Bemis, *The Leaning Ivory Tower* (San Francisco: Jossey-Bass, 1973); Patricia A. Maloney, "Presidential Leadership, Change, and Continuity: SUNY Buffalo from 1966 to 1981," in John B. Clark, Bruce Leslie, and Kenneth P. O'Brien , eds., *SUNY at Sixty: The Promise of the State University of New York* (Albany: State University of New York Press, 2010), 144–58; Roger L. Geiger, "Better Late Than Never: Intentions, Timing, and Results in Creating SUNY Research Universities," in ibid., 171–83.

1968, when a new campus head began to forge links with the Boston community, including planning for the College of Public and Community Service.[30]

Boston already possessed an urban university, but it was private. Northeastern University was begun in 1896 as the Evening Institute of the YMCA. It grew into a degree-granting university by focusing on cooperative programs (alternating work and study) in professional fields for regular students and on part-time evening programs for adults. A religious commitment to serve the needs of working-class students animated the school and was melded with business acumen toward the educational marketplace. Northeastern prided itself on eschewing the trappings of academic status and educating students that traditional institutions neglected. By the 1960s the success of its vocational and professional programs generated revenues for developing the arts and sciences and erecting residence halls. But Northeastern remained a paradigmatic urban-serving university and, with 45,000 students in 1967, the country's largest private university.[31]

In 1962 the future governor of Ohio James Rhodes proposed that every Ohioan should be within thirty miles of a state university. With four existing state universities located in small cities, and the flagship Ohio State in the capital, he fulfilled this pledge by establishing six state universities in major cities. Three had been municipal universities, one had been private, and two were basically new ventures. The University of Cincinnati was the country's first municipal university, and it retained that tie by becoming state affiliated (1968); but the municipal universities of Toledo and Akron were annexed outright, as was the YMCA university in Youngstown (1967). Cleveland State University (1965) filled a public education void in the state's largest city, and Wright State (1967) supplanted extension courses in Dayton. The first five of these enrolled 77,000 students in 1966, an increase of 77 percent in just four years. Four were already well-established urban universities, now able to expand with state largesse. But Cleveland State faced the challenge of forging an urban role. Besides being constrained by a cramped downtown campus, it sought to maintain academic respectability by upholding "competitive" admissions. The university initially had little rapport with the city's large African-American population and would soon need to develop this dimension of service.[32]

---

30   Richard M. Freeland, *Academia's Golden Age: Universities in Massachusetts, 1945–1970* (New York: Oxford University Press, 1992), 327–37.

31   Ibid., 260–68.

32   Cleveland State was rated "competitive" in admissions by *Barron's Profiles of American Colleges, 1969*; Dunham, *Colleges of Forgotten Americans*, 142–43. Missouri also addressed the dearth of public higher education in cities, establishing a new branch of the University of Missouri in St. Louis and converting the private University of Kansas City into another branch, both in 1963.

In the early 1960s, a dogma grew that urban universities should do more for their cities than provide additional seats for local students. These sentiments were advanced by a Ford Foundation program to direct university resources toward addressing the increasingly glaring problems of American cities. The program drew inspiration from the land-grant movement, and particularly agricultural extension. With grants totaling $4.5 million (1959–1966), it asked eight land-grant universities to devise "urban extension experiments." Rutgers and the Universities of Wisconsin and Delaware, with the largest grants, established Urban Affairs units. UW Milwaukee sought to train urban teams and agents. A small grant to UC Berkeley was used to mobilize black communities against the Oakland city government. Ford's evaluation of these efforts was reserved. Academic studies of urban problems, it seemed, provided "no direct benefits ... from even a first-rate research monograph." Universities were not structured to make "an across-the-board commitment," because academic departments tended to "insulate themselves from community involvement." Politics and "disputes with city officials and other local powers" presented additional pitfalls. These caveats were uttered far too late: by 1966 the urban extension train had already left the station.[33]

Lyndon Johnson's declaration of the War on Poverty raised the urban crisis to a national crusade in 1964, and both politicians and university leaders were eager for urban universities to enlist. In the following year's Higher Education Act, Title I endorsed the notion of urban land-grant extension by authorizing funds for universities to provide community service and continuing education, with $10 million appropriated for 1966.[34] By then, rioting across American cities transformed a latent urban crisis into a dire one in which universities were inescapably involved. Clark Kerr in 1967 called for the federal government to establish sixty-seven "urban-grant universities" (to parallel the existing sixty-seven land-grant institutions) "where the city itself and its problems would become the animating focus." Rhetoric escalated more than funding. The Kerr-led Carnegie Commission on Higher Education pronounced, "Colleges and universities ... recognize that their fate and the fate of the cities are inextricably linked. The call for a new and massive commitment of higher education to the problems of the city is strong both from within the academic community and from within the city."[35] Such

33 *Urban Extension: A Report on Experimental Programs Assisted by the Ford Foundation* (New York: Ford Foundation, October 1966), quotes pp. 6–7.

34 Hugh Davis Grant, *The Uncertain Triumph: Federal Education Policy in the Kennedy and Johnson Years* (Chapel Hill: University of North Carolina Press, 1984), 80–83.

35 Clark Kerr, *The Urban-Grant University: A Model for the Future* (New York: City College, 1968), 6; Carnegie Commission on Higher Education, *The Campus and the City: Maximizing Assets and Reduc-*

exhortations were usually followed by numerous practical reservations. But universities were compelled to respond to these challenges.[36]

Foremost was the challenge of expanding access. By the late 1960s, the problem of serving the population of black ghettos, soon called the inner city, dominated all others. Effective urban universities had made programs available to local students through part-time study, continuing education, and extension centers, but such efforts had not reached black communities. These students were largely precluded by inadequate schooling or intimidated by a less-than-welcoming atmosphere. Now, higher education (not only in cities) was charged with rectifying these conditions—*immediately*. Active recruitment in inner-city schools brought some students but scarcely addressed the limitations of preparation, the barrier of selective admissions, and poor retention. Urban universities consequently reached out to the high schools with compensatory programs to enhance college readiness, although such efforts could reach only a handful of potential students. Open admissions was everywhere advocated as a remedy. This was best accomplished in community colleges, but those campuses had to be built among the affected populations. Universities that were semi-selective quickly devised special admissions programs for inner-city youths that were tantamount to open admissions. At the same time, academically able black students were aggressively recruited by more selective colleges and universities, as will be seen below.[37] These urban efforts contributed to the incorporation of African-Americans into the mainstream of higher education, however limited. Much of this demographic expansion of American higher education occurred in the cities where they resided. In addition, these developments were a powerful component of the cultural shift by which the rightful availability of higher education for all took precedence over academic qualifications.

A second challenge to universities was to apply their expertise toward resolving the urban crisis. Universities had long harbored urban planning units, and academic studies of city issues were redoubled in the 1960s. By the end of the decade, 300 university research centers were devoted to studying urban issues. In the prevailing atmosphere, such centers and their universities were increasingly urged to address pressing practical problems. That pressure posed a classic

---

ing Liabilities (New York: McGraw-Hill, 1972), 14–15. The Carnegie Commission later recommended a $10 million federal investment in urban grants for ten universities: ibid., 115–18.

36 Carnegie Commission on Higher Education, *Campus and the City*; George Nash, *The University and the City: Eight Cases of Involvement* (New York: McGraw-Hill, 1973).

37 Suddenly eagerly sought after, black students soon gained the confidence to seek changes in the institutions. Black students demanded measures that would enroll more of them, provide courses in black studies, and hire teachers and administrators of their own race. The confrontations generated by these demands are considered in Chapter 5.

dilemma. University knowledge was by nature theoretical and universal and, as the Ford Foundation observed, capable of supplying few direct solutions to social problems.[38] The best academic studies brought enlightenment after the fact, and not always the conclusions that urban activists desired.[39]

Applied social science blended into a third challenge to universities: providing community services. Once again, service had been a longstanding mission of universities, but the 1960s added a distinct urban twist. Many such services depended on volunteers, especially students. In this respect, they complemented the educational mission and would later be officially sponsored as service learning. Special efforts were made to bring university expertise into urban communities through arrangements such as storefront educational centers or the Urban Corps of work-study students. Programs of any scale had financial implications. The Ford Foundation found that the most successful contribution of its grantees was helping communities apply for War on Poverty funds. A great many initiatives were possible when Great Society and foundation resources were available. The president of Northeastern characterized university behavior as "getting on the bandwagon because they know that is where the money is."[40] When external support for organized urban service efforts dried up, neither cities nor universities had funds in their regular budgets to sustain such projects.

Urban universities emerged in the 1960s as a distinctive, if ill-defined, component of American higher education. Research universities in cities endured an inherent conflict between academic aspirations and new imperatives arising from their urban milieu. These tensions were generally accommodated by having an urban focus in a few of their multifarious undertakings. The emerging urban universities of the 1960s were more stretched, maintaining wide access and selective graduate programs, vocational majors and an arts and science core, extension centers, professional schools, and commitments to community service. They contributed substantially to the demographic expansion of higher education in the 1960s, but in terms of sheer growth, they were overshadowed by community colleges.

38 Academic social scientists study problems by reducing them to puzzles that are solvable within paradigms with restricted numbers of variables. The calls for applied social science broached subjects that encompassed personalities, social groups, vested interests, and local politics.

39 E.g., the report by James S. Coleman et al., *Equality of Educational Opportunity* (Washington, DC: National Center for Education Statistics, 1966): Henry J. Aaron, *Politics and the Professors: The Great Society in Perspective* (Washington, DC: Brookings Institution, 1978), 75–81. One of the most valuable contributions to public policy from this era was Aaron Wildavsky's analysis of inept federal demonstration projects in Oakland: Jeffrey L. Pressman and Aaron Wildavsky, *Implementation: How Great Expectations in Washington are Dashed in Oakland* (Berkeley: University of California Press, 1973).

40 Nash, *University and the City*, 94. A common sentiment in those years: "poverty is where the money is."

COMMUNITY COLLEGES. In the 1960s, four-year public enrollments increased by 142 percent, while community college students rose from a smaller base by 314 percent. Still, four-year public institutions added two additional students for each new community college student. Enrollments of entering first-year students provide a more sensitive barometer for these changes. For the first half of the decade, new enrollments in both sectors grew at comparable rates, with four-year schools maintaining their two-to-one advantage. After 1965, new entrants to the four-years topped-out around 700,000, while community-college entrants more than doubled. In 1969, more first-time students entered two-year institutions. To 1975 (the enrollment peak for both sectors), the two-years added 360,000 annual entrants to 46,000 for the four-years. The decade of the community colleges was not the 1960s, but from 1965 to 1975. Even in that period, growth was driven by several factors.

In the last half of the 1960s, as the crush of baby boomers applied to colleges, public institutions raised their admission thresholds, many for the first time. In 1969 a few flagship universities had become "very competitive," and the majority of the fast-growing public institutions described above were rated "competitive," which meant requiring a B average and SAT or ACT scores near or above the national median.[41] High school graduates with C averages had few alternatives to a community college. In the first half of the 1970s, the downturn in the economy dampened job prospects for college graduates (Chapter 6). This affected perceptions of higher education and further energized the powerful community college movement. Publications both scholarly and popular portrayed the over-supply of college graduates and praised the virtues of "practical" community colleges. At the same time, academic achievement in high schools was plummeting. And so was the earnings premium for college graduates.[42] High school graduates in these years had plausible reasons for choosing the convenience of enrolling in a local community college.[43]

The incidence and role of community colleges varied across states, although the influence of the community college movement promoted convergence over time. California was the originator of junior colleges, and it always had the highest number and percentage of students in the sector. The Master Plan dictated

41 *Barron's Profiles of American Colleges, 1969*, 748–52. Median test scores for "competitive" colleges were "upper 400's" to 550; national medians for 1969 were V463/M493.

42 Few eighteen-year-olds read the economics journals in which earnings premiums were reported, but this phenomenon was publicized—and exaggerated—in popular media.

43 Steven Brint and Jerome Karabel, *The Diverted Dream: Community Colleges and the Promise of Educational Opportunity in America, 1900–1985* (New York: Oxford University Press, 1989), 102–16; Carnegie Commission on Higher Education, *The Open-Door Colleges* (New York: McGraw-Hill, 1970); Richard Freeman, *The Overeducated American* (New York: Academic Press, 1976).

that two-year institutions were the only public alternative for the lower two-thirds of high school graduates. California had sixty-seven community colleges at the time of the Master Plan and built twenty more in the next seven years. With an average enrollment of 6,000, they were by far the largest of any state, and enrolled 61 percent of state undergraduates. In Michigan, as in many other states, public school systems organized the first junior colleges, eight before the war and three after. Community college districts were then formed and created eighteen more independent institutions (1954–1968). By 1968, 31 percent of undergraduates enrolled in community colleges. Massachusetts was a latecomer to publicly supported higher education. It passed legislation enabling community colleges in 1960, and started fifteen in that decade. This process was centrally orchestrated and funded by the state legislature. These schools enrolled 18 percent of state undergraduates by 1968.[44]

A few broad generalizations can be made across the forty-nine diverse state systems (Nevada had none). Initiatives to found community colleges evolved from localities to states. In the 1960s, states essentially took control through laws, boards, and authorizations. They assumed responsibility for a significant portion of the funding for community colleges, which in itself made hosting these institutions far more attractive for localities. The student composition of these institutions was shaped by locally available educational opportunities. Semi-isolated institutions might draw location-bound students with a range of abilities and motivations, but schools in more densely served locales largely drew poorly prepared students who lacked the qualifications or ambition to go elsewhere. The community college movement of the 1960s navigated three large issues: how great the demand was; what should be taught; and how best to deal with the distinctive clientele.

Enrollments in two-year institutions grew in large part through their proliferation: 315 in 1960; 603 in 1970; 763 in 1974. Martin Trow wrote early in the 1960s that "where there is a local public junior college in the community, half of the boys from lower-class backgrounds went on to college, as compared with only 15% of boys from similar backgrounds ... with no local college."[45] Whether or not those percentages were representative, *if you build it they will come* became

44 Ben E. Fountain and Terrence A. Tolefson, *Community Colleges in the United States: Forty-Nine State Systems* (American Association of Community and Junior Colleges, 1989); Brint and Karabel, *Diverted Dream*, 143–63; Leland L. Medsker and Dale Tillery, *Breaking the Access Barriers: A Profile of Two-Year Colleges* (New York: McGraw-Hill, 1971), 24–25.

45 Martin Trow, "The Democratization of Higher Education in America," *European Journal of Sociology*, 3, 2 (1962): 255–56, quoted in Daniel Bell, *The Coming of Post-Industrial Society* (New York: Basic Books, 1973), 241. In the 1960s, the number of community colleges roughly doubled and so did the average enrollment (from 1,200 to 2,400).

an article of faith buoying the community college movement. The standard of a community college within commuting distance of all citizens was adopted as state policy in California, New York, and Florida, among others. The Carnegie Commission, on this ambitious basis, calculated in 1968 a need for 230–280 additional community colleges to be built by 1980.[46] By that date, 310 had been added.

Scholars have debated the underlying cause of this surge of new community colleges. Was it the desire of business for cheaply trained workers? Parental demand for inexpensive, local access? The design of foundations, especially Clark Kerr at the Carnegie Commission, to keep the masses from inundating elite research universities? Evidence can be adduced for all such arguments, since these actors in various ways supported the movement. However, scholars have determined that the chief *instigators* were, first, local school administrators and, second, state governments.[47] For educational administrators, establishing a community college not only enhanced educational opportunity in their district, it enhanced their careers. It was the era's most fashionable innovation, bringing the prestige of higher education, college-level teaching positions, and higher administrative positions. State governments were generally eager to provide the legal structures necessary to accommodate local initiatives. They too endorsed the expansion of educational opportunity, especially if it could be done more cheaply than in universities. They also were affected by the enthusiasm propelling the community college movement. And legislators relished opportunities to direct state funds to their districts. By 1963, forty-four states had enacted legislation for systems of community colleges, including provisions for state funding. The AAJC, besides publicizing the virtues of two-year institutions, assisted states in formulating these laws. It effectively encouraged the universal adoption of the "comprehensive community college" model, that is, an institution devoted to general education for college transfer, vocational education, and adult education. Lobbying by the AAJC won the inclusion of special provisions for community colleges in the 1963 Higher Education Facilities Act and the 1965 Higher Education Act, both of which added to the incentives for launching new institutions.[48] The community college movement in the 1960s had a phalanx of supporters and

---

46   Medsker and Tillery, *Breaking the Access Barrier*, 32–34.

47   This institutional interpretation has been documented by Kevin Dougherty, who emphasized the role of school administrators and state governments in foundings, in *The Contradictory College: The Conflicting Origins, Impacts, and Futures of the Community College* (Albany: SUNY Press, 1994); and Brint and Karabel, *Diverted Dream*, who focus on institutional reasons for promoting vocationalism (below). For a longer perspective on these issues: Steven Brint, "Few Remaining Dreams: Community Colleges Since 1945," *Annals, AAPSS* 586 (March 2003): 16–36.

48   The Higher Education Facilities Act (1963) and its renewals encouraged and contributed to the higher education building boom of the 1960s but has not been analyzed.

virtually no consequential detractors, and it would gain even greater traction in the early 1970s.

External enthusiasm for community colleges masked a host of internal weaknesses. Most of their students had not done well in high school. Whereas the postwar consensus had designated (albeit unrealistically) the top quarter of students as fit for college, three-quarters of community colleges students in 1968 came from the bottom three-quarters of their class. Seventy percent earned less than a B average.[49] Regardless of IQ, these students were on average deficient in academic skills or motivation—usually both. Like the students Burton Clark found at San Jose Junior College in the 1950s, they had vague aspirations to earn bachelor's degrees, but many were what he called "latent-terminal." The community college environment provided little assistance to overcome these handicaps. For commuting students, the colleges offered little academic or social integration. Completion or transfer rates are difficult to determine. Nationally, associate degrees amounted to 36 percent of community college entrants the previous year. In the fairly closed world of California public higher education circa 1972, 3 percent of students transferred to UC, and 11 percent to the California State Colleges.[50] More discouraging, a longitudinal study found that for students of equal ability, enrollment in a junior college lessened the probability of eventual college graduation.[51]

The weaknesses of community colleges may well have been exacerbated for new institutions in previously unserved areas. The sociologist Howard London studied the culture of a new college in a white working-class district of a northeastern city. Students came from weak high schools and tested at seventh- to eighth-grade levels for reading and math. Yet, their chief deficiency was a working-class ethos that, at once, feared a recurrence of academic failure and defensively disdained academic achievement. This hostility was expressed in chronic absence from classes, low levels of effort, cheating, and incivility. For the males, over half of course grades were D or failure. But there were exceptions. Current and aspiring firemen in the fire science course, though decidedly anti-intellectual, applied themselves to obtain tangible rewards from employers. Secretarial students were motivated by the prospect of attaining white-collar office jobs and middle-class

49   Not that high intelligence is required to earn a BA, but these students lacked the social and cultural capital associated with the tenacity to persist and overcome obstacles; three-fourths had parents with a high school education or less: American Council on Education, *National Norms*.

50   Dougherty, *Contradictory College*, 83–106; Brint and Karabel, *Diverted Dream*, 128–32; author's calculations from NCES, *Digest of Education Statistics*.

51   Brint and Karabel, *Diverted Dream*, 90–92. However, by choosing a two-year rather than a four-year institution, students of equal tested ability were likely not equal in aspiration and motivation.

status. And older students knew firsthand the kind of menial labor they wished to escape.[52] Access for everyone provided benefits for some, not all.

London's study revealed a dichotomy between the liberal and vocational tracks that was fully apparent by 1970. In the original surge of community college enrollments, students had heavily favored a transfer curriculum. For them, a two-year college was *higher* education—a stepping stone to the university, a BA, and the middle class. Since the interwar years, the AAJC and the movement it led had promoted terminal, vocational courses, despite contrary student sentiment. After 1960 the AAJC redoubled its vocational advocacy, assisted by grants specifically for this effort from several foundations. This campaign intensified during the decade, with increased backing from the college administrators. They embraced the role and public image of training students for immediate employment in the local community. Mindful of the poor record for retention and completion—let alone transfer and subsequent college graduation—they favored being the pinnacle institution for a system of practical education rather than the bottom rung of higher education. With the encouragement of the AAJC, they canvased local employers and devised increasing numbers of vocational curricula (e.g., fire science). Students were then recruited into these curricula. Supply preceded demand. In the late 1960s, the percentage of vocational associate degrees began to rise, topping 40 percent by 1970 and rising much higher in that decade.[53]

BRANCH CAMPUSES. In 1968, 127 two-year branch campuses of colleges and universities provided an alternative to community colleges.[54] Generally, branch campuses were not open access, but they had forgiving admissions requirements for degree courses. And they did not aim to be comprehensive but emphasized a transferable liberal arts curriculum. Pennsylvania had the largest number (23), but the state was not immune to community college fever. From 1957 to 1963 the legislature debated a succession of proposals before finally passing the Community College Act. By then, Penn State had organized fourteen branch campuses and the still-private University of Pittsburgh had four. Penn State campuses had evolved from a mixed collection of engineering extension centers, terminal associate degree programs, and continuing education. They had been organized into

---

52 Howard B. London, *The Culture of a Community College* (New York: Praeger, 1978). Social integration at this school occurred in preexisting neighborhood cliques and had a decidedly negative influence.

53 Brint and Karabel, *Diverted Dream*, 92–134, 164–81. Occupational associate degrees reached 62.5 percent in 1980 (117); Dougherty, *Contradictory College*, 189–242. For the ascendancy of vocationalism in community colleges and job markets, see Brint, "Few Remaining Dreams."

54 Medsker and Tillery, *Breaking the Access Barrier*, 169–70.

the Commonwealth Campus system in 1959, chiefly to accommodate the enrollment growth that could not be absorbed by the main campus. Eight of the campuses offered lower-division baccalaureate courses, but the aim was to replicate these transfer courses at all campuses. The state, however, commissioned successive studies to devise a "master plan" for higher education, and both studies recommended converting some Penn State branches to community colleges. Penn State vehemently objected, arguing that the branch campuses were more effective than community colleges. Further, it proceeded to establish four more two-year campuses. By 1970, Pennsylvania had fourteen community colleges under the 1963 act, and Penn State had nineteen Commonwealth Campuses enrolling 20,000 students. Citizen support had rarely been a factor nationally in the community college boom of the 1960s, but the Penn State campuses were all products of local initiatives, local financial support, real-estate donations, and in one case a petition signed by 10,000 residents. For students, the Penn State connection represented real higher education, a path to a bachelor's degree. Like community colleges elsewhere, the Pennsylvania institutions drifted toward vocationalism, while the Commonwealth Campuses focused on leading students toward college graduation.[55]

These institutions—regional colleges, urban universities, community colleges, and branch campuses—provided the places that allowed more than 50 percent of American high school graduates to attend higher education by the end of the 1960s. This remarkable expansion carried American society beyond mass higher education to the cusp of what Martin Trow called universal higher education. Quantitative change, as he showed, entailed qualitative change.[56] While growth more than doubled the number of students, qualitative changes transformed the premises underlying American higher education. By the mid-sixties, higher education was no longer conceived as an activity that should be confined to those with above-average IQs destined for certain occupations. The social norms for higher education had been reformulated by some unconscious process into a right for all who wished to make use of it. In California, for example, community colleges were open to any person over eighteen years of age who could benefit from the instruction, a formula widely copied. Governments at all levels had responded to this new imperative and made it possible by investing prodigious sums in building out the institutions just reviewed. They served, as has been seen, the middling ranks of American society—first-generation students from middle-

55   Michael Bezilla, *Penn State: An Illustrated History* (University Park: Pennsylvania State University Press, 1985), 323–37; Fountain and Tollefson, *Community Colleges*, 189–93; Dougherty, *Contradictory College*, 22–24, 175–78.

56   Martin Burrage, ed., *Martin Trow: Twentieth-Century Higher Education, Elite to Mass to Universal* (Baltimore: Johns Hopkins University Press, 2010), 511–610.

to working-class families—that in the past had attended sparingly or not at all. Now a new mentality prevailed, one that asserted that they and others like them not only could go to college but also that they should go for their own benefit and that of the country. The culture had changed, but it would be a long road before these new social norms would be assimilated and their consequences apparent.

DESEGREGATION IN THE SOUTH, DIVERSITY IN THE NORTH

Nowhere was the notion that higher education was a right open to all Americans more fiercely resisted than in the states of the former Confederacy. In 1935, in seventeen southern and border states, no black and white students were educated in the same classrooms or schools, from kindergarten to graduate school.[57] That year, an NAACP suit forced the University of Maryland to enroll Donald Murray in its law school, the first slight crack in the edifice of educational segregation. Still, African Americans in the South had no choice but to attend historically black colleges and universities (HBCUs), and enrollments in those institutions grew from 65,000 in 1950 to 110,000 when the Civil Rights Act was passed in 1964. At that date, the most intransigent universities in the Deep South had begun to admit black students in token numbers. However, as Peter Wallenstein emphasizes, desegregation was not an event but a process, one that began after the war and continued even after black students were allowed to matriculate in formerly all-white institutions.[58]

Blacks were first admitted, like Donald Murray, under actual or threatened court orders to graduate and professional programs that were not available in HBCUs. Later, the same principle opened a few specialized undergraduate programs like engineering. These individuals—usually a single person—attended under severe restrictions, a situation Wallenstein calls "protodesegregation." They were not allowed to reside on campus, eat in college dining halls, and initially were restricted to designated "colored" facilities. The acceptance of undergraduates to unrestricted programs was a huge hurdle. Even early acceptors, like the University of Texas (1955), imposed restrictions, stating "that Negro students will be integrated ... for educational purposes but will be segregated for residential

57   Marybeth Gassman and Roger L. Geiger, eds., *Higher Education for African Americans before the Civil Rights Era, 1900–1964*, Perspectives on the History of Higher Education, vol. 29 (New Brunswick, NJ: Transaction, 2012).

58   Peter Wallenstein, "Black Southerners and Nonblack Universities: The Process of Desegregating Southern Higher Education, 1935–1965," in Wallenstein, ed., *Higher Education and the Civil Rights Movement* (Gainesville: University Press of Florida, 2008), 17–59.

purposes."[59] Thus, breaking the so-called color barrier was just the beginning of the process of desegregating campuses. Barriers to residence, social activities, and athletics were only overcome after 1970, when most southern colleges and universities could be said to have become substantially integrated.

The legal wedge used by the NAACP to pry open segregated public universities was the manifest hypocrisy of the "separate but equal" doctrine. Not only were public HBCUs grossly unequal in facilities, funding, and faculty, but none had schools of law or medicine or PhD programs, and few offered much science or any engineering. States offered black aspirants meager scholarships to study these fields at northern institutions. In the 1938 *Gaines* decision, the Supreme Court rejected such measures and instructed Missouri to admit Lloyd Gaines to the university law school or create a new publicly funded law school for Blacks. Missouri chose the latter course, as did Louisiana, Texas, and South Carolina, but subsequent court decisions ruled against these Potemkin law schools in all but South Carolina.[60] After 1945 the *Gaines* precedent was accepted voluntarily or after litigation in the border states and upper South. Individual black students were accepted to schools of law or medicine or graduate study at the Universities of Delaware and Arkansas (1948), Kentucky and Oklahoma (1949), Virginia and Texas (1950), and Tennessee and North Carolina (1952). Similar developments followed with undergraduate admissions to special programs in Delaware and Maryland (1950), and Oklahoma State, Virginia Tech, and Louisiana State (1953). The pioneer students in these states confronted inhospitable conditions—isolated, ignored, and restricted—but their presence provoked little controversy and no violence.[61]

In May 1954, Chief Justice Earl Warren and the Supreme Court issued the epic *Brown* decision: "The doctrine of 'separate but equal' has no place. Separate educational facilities are inherently unequal."[62] In the subsequent rulings (*Brown II*, 1955) and in a decision against the University of North Carolina (*Frasier*, 1956), the court held that the prohibition of segregation applied to public higher education as well. In the short run, *Brown* affected higher education for better and for worse. For better, the states that had already accepted protodesegregation now acquiesced in admitting Blacks as undergraduates. They included Del-

---

59   Ibid.

60   Henry H. Lesesne, *A History of the University of South Carolina, 1940–2000* (Columbia: University of South Carolina Press, 2001), 70–71.

61   Wallenstein, "Black Southerners." An example of the difficulty and slow pace of protodesegregation: John A. Hardin, *Fifty Years of Segregation: Black Higher Education in Kentucky, 1904–1954* (Lexington: University Press of Kentucky, 1997), 85–112.

62   James T. Patterson, *Grand Expectations: The United States, 1945–1974* (New York: Oxford, 1996), 385–99.

aware, Maryland, West Virginia, Kentucky, Missouri, Arkansas, Oklahoma, and Texas, followed by North Carolina after the *Frasier* decision.[63] For worse, holding out were the most intransigent Deep South states—from South Carolina to Mississippi—and strongly recalcitrant states that had accepted some protodesegregation—Florida, Louisiana, Tennessee, and Virginia. Across the South, but particularly in these states, the *Brown* decision provoked "massive resistance." Race was always highly politicized in these states, but *Brown* caused its hypertrophy. As the resistance built, progress toward desegregation in higher education was frozen for the rest of the 1950s.

Brown advanced an unequivocal principle, but the court was somewhat tentative about enforcement, since it had few means to counter outright defiance. *Brown* II consequently urged desegregation to take place "with all deliberate speed," which sounded resolute but in fact left broad scope for equivocation and evasion. Politicians pandered to the worst racial prejudice of constituents. Legislatures passed admissions requirements, like letters of character from local sheriffs, that were impossible for Blacks to comply with. Local courts imposed seemingly endless delays. Florida blocked a black applicant to the university law school for nine years through litigation; Georgia did the same for seven years. Yet, some signals were mixed. Virginia closed public schools rather than allow them to be integrated but tolerated token integration at the state universities. Alabama admitted Autherine Lucy in 1956 then quickly expelled her for causing disorder.

A singular exception occurred in Louisiana. In 1953 the suit that admitted the first black undergraduate to LSU was, typically, reversed on a technicality, followed by his expulsion. However, in Lafayette Parish a class action complaint was filed to gain admission to Southwestern Louisiana Institute (later, the University of Southwestern Louisiana). This suit succeeded on straightforward Fourteenth Amendment grounds that the state provided Whites but not Blacks with access to regional state colleges. As a result, sixty-eight black students registered for the 1954 fall term—far more than token integration. The school deliberately suppressed publicity. White students were unhappy, but there were no protests or incidents. In the backlash following *Brown*, the legislature passed a law requiring character references with prohibitive conditions. Black admissions virtually ceased for a year, but the blatantly unconstitutional law was quickly annulled. SLI and two other regional colleges that had followed its precedent remained the only integrated state colleges in the Deep South.[64] At the flagship Louisiana State University, another black undergraduate was not admitted until 1964.

63   Wallenstein, "Black Southerners."

64   Michael G. Wade, "Four Who Would: *Constantine v. Southwestern Louisiana Institute* (1954) and the Desegregation of Louisiana's State Colleges," in Wallenstein, *Higher Education*, 60–91. If this

Massive white resistance stalled any progress on desegregation in holdout states for the rest of the 1950s. The event that tipped the balance in the other direction originated with higher education and, surprisingly, with students. In 1960, four freshmen from black North Carolina A&T sat in at the lunch counter of the local Woolworth store to protest the Whites-only policy that prevailed there and throughout the South. This gesture, at once defiant and just, spread like wildfire. Within two weeks, fifty-four sit-ins were taking place in fifteen cities and nine states. This was the spark that reignited the civil rights movement. In April, activists energized by the sit-ins met and organized the Student Nonviolent Coordinating Committee (SNCC), which would play a prominent role on and (mostly) off campuses. The events of the next five years, quashing segregation and bringing basic rights of citizenship to African Americans, were a saga in which higher education was just one chapter. Still, gaining unrestricted access to higher education was one of the most important rights achieved in this struggle. How this was achieved was largely beyond the control of the institutions involved, especially the violent confrontations that became the best known and least representative episodes in the process of desegregating higher education.

In January 1961, following the court-ordered registration of Hamilton Holmes and Charlayne Hunter at the University of Georgia, an angry mob attacked and damaged Hunter's dormitory, prompting Holmes and Hunter to be temporarily removed from campus. On September 30, 1962, the day before James Meredith was registered at the University of Mississippi, a nightlong riot resulted in gunshot injuries and two fatalities. In June 1963, Governor George Wallace stood in the "schoolhouse door" ostensibly to block Vivian Malone and James Hood from registering at the University of Alabama. In these cases, the decision whether or not to admit black students had been usurped by the states, and the resistance was led by governors. Georgia governor Ernest Vandiver had been elected on the slogan No, Not One. Georgia had erected an obstacle course of admissions regulations to trip up black applicants while asserting preposterous claims that no one was denied admission because of race. Georgia law gave the governor the authority to close any state school that integrated white and black students, and Vandiver voiced his intention to close the University of Georgia after Holmes and Hunter were admitted. Only after the riot did Vandiver desist from fomenting further violence.[65] Mississippi governor Ross Barnett chose rhet-

---

decision had been appealed, Louisiana would probably have been ordered to build regional colleges for Blacks.

65   Governor Vandiver's fear of violence in reaction to the riot made the admission of Holmes and Hunter a turning point in Georgia. Atlanta public schools were integrated soon afterward, and Georgia Tech and Emory accepted desegregation as unavoidable: Thomas G. Dyer, *The University of Georgia: A Bicentennial History, 1785–1985* (Athens: University of Georgia Press, 1985), 303–34.

oric over reality in encouraging the illusion that desegregation could be resisted. After the final court order for Meredith's admission, he told Mississippians in a statewide televised address to "stand like men and tell [the federal government] NEVER!" The day before the riot, after he had agreed to admit Meredith, he misled a football crowd to believe otherwise. His most cowardly act, which assured violence, was to break his promise to provide security in order to transfer all blame to federal forces.[66] George Wallace stood in the schoolhouse door not to prevent desegregation, which was already decided, but to uphold a campaign promise and salvage his reputation as a staunch segregationist.

These examples were object lessons for other state universities. After the events at the University of Georgia, Georgia Tech felt it could no longer obstruct black applicants and admitted three for the fall semester. The university's entire concern was to defuse any possible violence or disruption, not to take positive steps toward integration. In South Carolina, Harvey Gantt was admitted for the 1963 spring semester at Clemson by court order but without incident. Desegregation at the University of South Carolina was clearly next. It was a more polarized campus, where a faction had supported Ross Barnett and the Mississippi rioters, but other groups worked toward racial conciliation. The university consulted President Harrison of Georgia Tech for guidance to ensure a peaceful process. Three black students enrolled by court-order in the fall amid massive security and no hostile incidents. The president revealed what was no doubt a widespread attitude when he asked a critical alum for greater understanding and support for an institution that "has fallen into misfortune through no fault of [its] own."[67] Indeed, the state universities of the South had desegregated through no fault of their own; the decision had been taken from their hands. If it had not been, the universities would not have done it on their own. A majority of students opposed desegregation but were generally resigned and responsible, though often rude, in accepting the inevitable. Universities accommodated their black students by isolating them as much as possible. White students responded by ignoring their presence.[68] By the late 1960s, the generation of students who had originally entered all-white state universities passed from the scene, and the prospects for real integration improved.

66   David G. Sansing, *Making Haste Slowly: The Troubled History of Higher Education in Mississippi* (Jackson: University Press of Mississippi, 1990), 156–95.

67   Robert C. McMath, Jr., et al., *Engineering the New South: Georgia Tech, 1885–1985* (Athens: University of Georgia Press, 1985), 312–19; Lesesne, *History of the University of South Carolina*, 138–50, quote p. 149.

68   This was not difficult because there were not very many of them. In 1967 the number of black students at formerly white state colleges and universities were 181 in Mississippi, 222 in South Carolina, 435 in Alabama, and 550 in Georgia: Frank Bowles and Frank A. DeCosta, *Between Two Worlds: A Profile of Negro Higher Education* (New York: McGraw-Hill, 1971), 76.

The private colleges and universities of the South were independent actors in that they were not subject to *Gaines* or *Brown* or governors. However, they were steeped in regional culture and ruled by boards of trustees drawn from regional elites. Trustees were successful professionals and businessmen, deeply attached to their alma maters and their traditions. They were embedded in local communities where attitudes on race affected personal relationships. Such leadership was most problematic at the region's would-be research universities—Duke, Emory, Rice, Tulane, and Vanderbilt. All conducted federally sponsored research, and all save Rice included academically ambitious medical schools. They were the principal beneficiaries of foundation efforts to modernize southern higher education. As such, they valued their academic reputations and, like other universities, sought to enhance their national standing through research, faculty distinction, graduate education—and foundation patronage. At the same time, they wished to be the leaders of higher education in the South by educating the region's social, intellectual, and professional elite. The responsibility for balancing these conflicting roles of national academic distinction and regional leadership fell upon the respective presidents.

The presidents of these universities, as portrayed by the historian Melissa Kean, were well suited for this role. They combined Deep Southern roots with experience in northern academic venues. By the early 1950s they saw that desegregation in some shape or form would become legally unavoidable, but also necessary for acceptance as research universities. The more progressive presidents envisioned the kind of protodesegregation that was occurring in the upper South—the admission of a small number of highly qualified Blacks to graduate or professional schools. The obstacle was convincing university boards of trustees, which contained few sympathizers with Blacks or research. For Vanderbilt chancellor Harvie Branscomb (1946–1962), this delicate matter could best be resolved behind closed doors by "the intelligent white men of the South."[69] Indeed, by cajoling his board Branscomb maneuvered them into accepting an exemplary black graduate candidate into the School of Divinity (1953), probably the only unit that favored desegregation. Using the same approach, his friend Rufus Harris, president of Tulane, brought his board to the verge of admitting black graduate students the next year. But the *Brown* decision unleashed "segregationist rhetoric [that] ... escalated over the next several years to a fever pitch of hysteria and hatred." Integration was impossible in the Deep South and put on hold elsewhere. Branscomb still managed to obtain board approval for admitting

69   The leitmotiv of Melissa Kean's definitive study: *Desegregating Private Higher Education in the South: Duke, Emory, Rice, Tulane, and Vanderbilt* (Baton Rouge: Louisiana State University Press, 2008), 15–24.

a black student to the law school in 1956. However, the inability to advance de-segregation for the rest of the 1950s revealed the impotence of intelligent white men to guide this process, and it set the stage for crises at all these universities.[70]

The conflict was most dramatic at Vanderbilt. The 1960 sit-in movement was quickly emulated in Nashville, where it was led by a black divinity student, James Lawson. The consternation of the city's business community was communicated directly to the board, which expelled Lawson. This action provoked a huge pro-test, locally and nationally, including the resignation of most of the Divinity School faculty. Facing an impasse that threatened the future of the university, Branscomb placated the faculty and got rid of Lawson by granting his degree, despite the disapproval of the board. From this point, the tide relentlessly turned against segregation, in national opinion and within these universities. Founda-tions threatened to withhold badly needed gifts; federal agencies refused to con-sider grants to segregated institutions; faculty recruits declined appointments; and their own faculties began to demand an end to segregation. Ostracism from the national academic community was now at issue.

By 1962 all five universities had capitulated by at least endorsing desegrega-tion, though some legal hurdles remained. Duke admitted its first black graduate students in 1961 and opened its doors to black undergraduates in 1963. The Van-derbilt faculty in 1962 passed a resolution for undergraduate admissions that was ultimately accepted by the board. Emory had to overcome a Georgia law that could have removed its tax exemption (1961–1963). Tulane actually sought a court order to integrate so that the board could be held blameless, which delayed the first admissions to 1963. And Rice, probably the most eager to transcend segregation in order to develop as a technological university, was blocked by an alumni lawsuit over charter language until 1964.

The Civil Rights Act of 1964 required institutions to sign a statement of compliance with desegregation to be eligible for federal aid. By this date, the major universities of the South had all crossed that Rubicon, with the putative leaders of southern higher education among the last. Indeed, compliance could hardly mask the sorry record of those institutions. Their capitulation to unre-stricted admissions based on merit was in all cases coerced. Their concerns were with local reputations—of the institution and the trustees—and above all the effects on their white students. Absent were any concerns with the rights of black students to a university education or the conditions imposed on their pursuit of one.

Nonetheless, the process of desegregation expanded access for Blacks in the South. Their enrollments in formerly white southern colleges and universities

70   Ibid., quote p. 112.

grew from approximately 3,000 in 1954 to 38,000 in 1967. Four-year public institutions accounted for 17,000; private ones for 4,000; the rest attended junior colleges. Texas accounted for nearly one-quarter. During those same years, HBCUs grew from 63,000 to 134,000, roughly one-half of the national black enrollment. Outside the formerly segregated states, black enrollments had doubled in those years, from 45,000 to 97,000. But enrollments in historically white institutions, North and South, remained at less than 2 percent in both years. [71] However, in the North, an entirely different mindset arose in the mid-sixties. Providing more black students access to higher education became a priority at increasing numbers of institutions, public and private. And the need for special measures to assist their success in college was recognized as well.

INTEGRATION IN THE NORTH. The treatment and experience of black students outside the South differed in public universities, where they attended in sufficient numbers to form separate communities, and private schools, where they attended largely as individuals, if at all. In both sectors, postwar conditions were considerably better than before the war and improved steadily in the 1950s. Blacks then became the focus of special concern after 1960, parallel with the development of the civil rights movement. For the first half of the decade, institutions took increasing measures to attract more black students and to address deficiencies, although the numbers admitted were still small. In the Liberal Hour, it was an article of liberal faith that eliminating inequalities in education was the path to resolving the civil rights crisis. With the violent events of 1965, the realization spread that special measures were necessary to mobilize higher education to ameliorate conditions for African Americans. The events of 1968 raised these concerns to crisis dimensions, intensified by the rise of the Black Power movement on campuses (Chapter 5).

Northern prewar flagship universities were internally segregated institutions. They varied in the degree and extent of segregation—in the mix of custom and official proscriptions—but the pattern was consistent. Black students had to live off campus, usually in the local black community, and they were segregated or restricted for dining, social life, and athletics. Segregation extended to college towns, where Blacks were excluded from restaurants, movie theaters, and residential areas. White students, especially fraternities, freely indulged in demeaning

---

71   Bowles and DeCosta, *Between Two Worlds*, 61–83. Based on these uncertain estimates, black undergraduate enrollments lost ground during 1954–1967, from 4.5 percent of national enrollments to 3.9 percent, with the relative shrinkage coming from HBCUs. Christopher Jencks and David Riesman report higher estimates, in the 4–5 percent ranges for various years of the 1960s: *Academic Revolution*, 440n.

caricatures of Blacks in campus newspapers, yearbooks, and minstrel shows.[72] After the war, universities rapidly disavowed institutional discriminatory practices, possibly embarrassed by the presence of black GIs. Dormitories, cafeterias, social activities, and athletics were integrated in stepwise fashion. Townies were more resistant, but during the 1950s pressure was applied by sympathetic faculty and students, sometimes assisted by the NAACP. Some practices were difficult to alter—for example, discrimination in off-campus housing and restrictive clauses in Greek charters. The persistence of off-campus discriminatory practices in hiring and accommodations became the target of campus activists. On campus, however, universities by 1960 were officially committed to treating all students equitably, and forms of overt discrimination that had existed before the war had effectively disappeared.[73] But the beneficiaries were few.

The civil rights movement had increasing resonance on major northern campuses. Beginning with the 1960 lunch-counter sit-ins, the succession of confrontations and atrocities in the South was reported in campus newspapers and motivated student groups and liberal faculty. When well-known campus graduates became victims, their plights were prominently publicized: Michigan's Tom Hayden (1961), beaten in Mississippi; Rutgers' Donald Harris (1963), imprisoned for three months in Georgia; Cornell's Michael Schwerner (1961), murdered in Philadelphia, Mississippi. Prominent civil rights workers, led by Dr. Martin Luther King, spoke often on northern campuses. By 1963 there was substantial sentiment among faculty and students that universities had a duty to help rectify the racial inequities of American society, and administrators agreed. An obvious target was the low enrollments of black students, typically 1 percent or less at flagship universities. The University of Michigan began the Opportunity Awards Program in 1964 to admit disadvantaged black students, recruiting 70 the first year and 63 the next, but retention was poor. The University of Illinois made similar initiatives, raising its black enrollment in 1967 to 330, or 1 percent—the same as in 1929.[74]

---

72   Richard M. Breaux, "Nooses, Sheets, and Blackface: White Racial Anxiety and Black Student Protest at Six Midwest Flagship Universities, 1882–1937," *Perspectives on the History of Higher Education* 29 (2012): 43–74; Clifford S. Griffin, *The University of Kansas: A History* (Lawrence: University Press of Kansas, 1976), 626–32: a candid institutional history.

73   Recent accounts have alleged with vague chronology and documentation that discrimination was still prevalent after 1960 and was a serious detriment to black experiences at Indiana and Illinois: Mary Ann Wynkoop, *Dissent in the Heartland: The Sixties at Indiana University* (Bloomington: Indiana University Press, 2002); Joy Ann Williamson, *Black Power on Campus: The University of Illinois, 1965–75* (Urbana: University of Illinois Press, 2003). Both studies focus on subsequent confrontations.

74   Howard H. Peckham, *The Making of the University of Michigan, 1817–1992*, edited and updated by Margaret L. Steneck and Nicholas H. Steneck (Ann Arbor, MI: Bentley Historical Library, 1994),

1965 was an inflexion point nationally and on campuses. The report of the Kerner Commission concluded that the U.S. was "moving toward two societies, one black and one white—separate and unequal." This dire warning was soon punctuated by Bloody Sunday in Selma and the summer riot in Watts. In Washington, the Voting Rights Act and the Higher Education Act followed the previous year's Civil Rights Act. Federal programs like Upward Bound now sought to bolster the academic preparation of disadvantaged students. By 1965, if not before, virtually all northern universities instituted policies for the active recruitment of minority students. And they all faced the same conundrum: given the substandard educational preparation of most black high school graduates, standards had to be loosened to admit them and special measures taken before or after admission to improve their chances of success, including financial aid (of which public universities had little to offer). Initially, universities faced difficult decisions on these matters, given the weight of traditional practices. But the crisis atmosphere of 1965 and increasing pressure from groups on campus left little choice. The admission of black students increased dramatically but, as at Illinois, the numbers were still relatively small.[75] Universities would soon reach another inflexion point in 1968, when far more would be asked—and granted (Chapter 5).

Private colleges and universities, especially in the East, were more liberal in their racial attitudes, but their numbers of Blacks were in the low single digits. In 1947, a Smith graduate, Felice Nierenberg Schwartz, distressed by their rarity, started a writing campaign asking colleges if they were willing to admit qualified black students. Their replies defined the situation at that juncture: they reported that they rarely received such applications but would not discriminate if they did. Schwartz then organized the National Scholarship Service and Fund for Negro Students (NSSFNS) to serve as a liaison, contacting potential students and encouraging them to apply to what were termed interracial colleges. By 1955, the NSSFNS had placed 4,000 students in 300 non-southern colleges. An evaluation found that these students earned average grades, but an above-average 80 percent graduated. The organization thus seeded nearly all-white colleges with highly qualified Blacks, providing those students with an educational upgrade and the institutions with a small black presence.[76]

278–79; Richard P. McCormick, *The Black Student Protest Movement at Rutgers* (New Brunswick, NJ: Rutgers University Press, 1990); Williamson, *Black Power*, 17, 65.

75 In 1968 a special program at Illinois aimed to increase admissions of black students from 200 to 400, in a freshman class of almost 6,000: Williamson, *Black Power*, 64.

76 Linda M. Perkins, "The First Black Talent Identification Program: The National Scholarship and Service Fund for Negro Students, 1947–1968," *Perspectives on the History of Higher Education* 29 (2012): 173–97. The HBCUs and the United Negro College Fund regarded the NSSFNS as a competitor for students and foundation philanthropy, of which it received little. It continued this mission until 1968.

Eastern private colleges did not go beyond admitting the "qualified Negro" applicant until after 1960. That year, Harvard enrolled nine in its incoming class, Yale five, and Princeton one. More representative, Wesleyan averaged two black students in its 1950s classes, Union College one. These schools had been striving to overcome reputations for discrimination against Jewish students, and admissions at all these schools might be described as parochial—tailored to their traditional constituencies. All had broadened their applicant pools geographically in search of high achievers. These efforts had raised the average SAT scores of entering classes to the highest levels ever—a hurdle of rising qualifications. The conviction spread, nonetheless, that admissions recruitment should be extended to urban high schools, which they had traditionally avoided, to identify high-achieving Blacks. In 1962, President Kennedy summoned five university presidents to the White House and charged them to "do something" to address the impending racial crisis. Yale's Kingman Brewster returned from the meeting determined to act. Yale extended its recruitment to high schools with high-performing Blacks. This approach was then shared with the Ivy League and the Seven Sisters through formation of the Cooperative Program for Educational Opportunity. This effort sought to identify and recruit black students who met the stringent admission standards of these schools.[77] The implicit role that these institutions embraced went beyond equality of opportunity; it was to provide well-educated leaders to further the assimilation of the black community with American society.[78]

Cornell's new president James Perkins (1963–1969) was also personally committed to increasing black enrollment. He hired a new admissions director and established the Special Project to proactively recruit black students. Working through the NSSFNS and the Cooperative Program, black matriculates increased from the average 3–4 to 20 in 1964 and 35 the next year.[79] Others were close behind. Wesleyan, Princeton, and Yale hired new admissions directors committed to proactive recruitment, and Yale managed to enroll 23 black students in 1966. The lofty admission standards of the elite eastern colleges made the admissions conundrum all the more challenging. All emphasized the verbal SAT, the most

77   Geoffrey Mark Kabaservice, "Kingman Brewster and the Rise and Fall of the Progressive Establishment," PhD diss., Yale University, 1999, 353–65. Provost Brewster became president in 1964 after the death of the ailing Whitney Griswold. Admissions dean Arthur Howe, Jr., (1957–1964) employed a strategy of actively discovering black candidates who met Yale admission standards.

78   Jerome Karabel, *The Chosen: The Hidden History of Admission and Exclusion at Harvard, Yale, and Princeton* (Boston: Houghton Mifflin, 2003), 378–81; Elizabeth A. Duffy and Idana Goldberg, *Crafting a Class: College Admissions and Financial Aid, 1955–1994* (Princeton: Princeton University Press, 1998), 76–84, 137–40.

79   Glenn C. Altschuler and Isaac Kramnick, *Cornell: A History, 1940–2015* (Ithaca, NY: Cornell University Press, 2014), 155–59.

culturally biased of all measures of achievement. Yale estimated that only 400 black high school seniors in the country exceeded its cut-off score of 550. Yale and the elite colleges all reached the same conclusion: other criteria would have to be employed to estimate potential, motivation, and leadership. As in the public sector, 1965 marked the juncture when new criteria and more aggressive forms of recruitment were adopted. All these colleges commenced searching for the "uniquely qualified applicant ... who presents evidence of academic potential [and] a strong desire to be useful to society [and] unusual talents or skills, frequently of nonacademic nature." The quest for such applicants quickly became highly competitive, and fortunate candidates were now able to compare offers of admission from several schools. The sense of social mission led institutions to focus on finding talent among disadvantaged, inner-city candidates, who required full financial aid. Federal programs were supplemented by foundation assistance for private colleges, but soon Cornell was devoting 52 percent of its financial aid budget to minority students, and other Ivies committed from 15 to 30 percent.[80] As with public universities, soon much more would be asked.

Two decades after World War II, enormous progress had been made in the provision of higher education for African Americans. This progress accelerated in the mid-sixties, attaining undergraduate black enrollments of 267,000 in 1967, almost 5 percent of the total.[81] However, these students reached the thresholds of college, for the most part, despite cultural deprivation and poor preparation in substandard schools—and these handicaps were reflected in the schools they attended. The predominantly white institutions just discussed accepted a small share of these students. The 2,500 in highly selective private colleges, North and South, compared with 2,800 at Los Angeles City College, 3,650 at Chicago City College, or 1,700 at Highland Park in Detroit, all community colleges. Major public universities enrolled 7,500 black students in the South and 17,000 in other states. Thus, 10 percent of Blacks (27,000) attended selective institutions that prepared students for graduate and professional schools. Another 14,000 attended the eight to ten moderately selective HBCUs. Two-thirds of black students attended unselective HBCUs (120,000) or community colleges (60,000). The remainder (60,000) attended public or private colleges or commuted to urban service universities. This snapshot of enrollments captures a fleeting point in the midst of a rapid transformation. College attendance for black high school graduates was increasing, financial support was expanding, and aspirations were

---

80   Duffy and Goldberg, *Crafting a Class*, 142–5; Karabel, *Chosen*, 380–85; Altschuler and Kramnick, *Cornell*, 156–58; Joseph A. Soares, *The Power of Privilege: Yale and America's Elite Colleges* (Stanford, CA: Stanford University Press, 2007).

81   Estimates for undergraduates from Bowles and DeCosta, *Between Two Worlds*, 83–103.

rising. Educational opportunities for Blacks in 1967, relative to Whites, were skewed toward lower-status institutions. But they were opportunities nonetheless, most of which had not previously existed.

CURRICULUM, QUALITY, AND MASS HIGHER EDUCATION

The vast expansion of American higher education sometimes appeared to overshadow the perennial concern for quality. In fact, two dimensions of quality were always relevant: the advancement and incorporation of knowledge and the learning and intellectual growth of college students.

The growth of knowledge in the academic revolution compelled institutions to upgrade quality or fall behind. They had to add PhDs to their faculties, expand existing academic departments and add new ones, institute credible graduate programs, and engage in respectable amounts of research. For institutions these were not idle predilections; they were market-driven imperatives necessary to compete for students and generate the revenues that such investments required. Andrew Greeley has described these pressures on Catholic universities as they evolved "from backwater to mainstream." Indeed, the mainstream is where reputable institutions had to be. This was the case for old and new urban universities and newly emergent regional universities.[82] However, these efforts were increasingly interpreted as detracting from the second dimension of quality—student learning. This notion, with antecedents stretching from early in the century, became conventional wisdom by the late 1960s. Jencks and Riesman invoked what might be called the Pavlovian theory of faculty behavior: faculty "have only a limited amount of time and energy, and they know that in terms of professional standing and personal advancement it makes more sense to throw this into research rather than teaching." This ever-popular theory would seem to ignore the fact that most faculty performed little or no research.[83] There were numerous factors behind what Clark Kerr called the "general deterioration of undergraduate teaching," including logistical problems with overcrowded classrooms and dependence on teaching assistants.[84] However, a root cause stemmed from

---

82 Andrew M. Greeley, *From Backwater to Mainstream: A Profile of Catholic Higher Education* (New York: McGraw-Hill, 1969), 120–27; Jencks and Riesman, *Academic Revolution*, 356–75; Freeland, *Academia's Golden Age*, describes this process at several Massachusetts universities.

83 Oliver Fulton and Martin Trow, "Research Activity in American Higher Education," in Martin Trow, ed., *Teachers and Students: Aspects of American Higher Education* (New York: McGraw-Hill, 1975), 39–83.

84 Jencks and Riesman, *Academic Revolution*, 532; Clark Kerr, *The Uses of the University* (Cambridge, MA: Harvard University Press, 1963), 65.

the divergence between faculty professionalism and instruction in the first two years of college, the prime focus for this critique. Faculty who were products of the academic revolution spent their careers developing high levels of expertise in specialized subjects, and they lacked enthusiasm for general education courses that aimed to synthesize or summarize or simplify complex topics. Yet, such courses were championed by educators as the foundation of a liberal education.

Chapter 1 reviewed the postwar quest for a core curriculum that would instill common learning, intellectual development, citizenship, love of freedom, and democracy. The best that could be said of the multiple interpretations of a liberal or general education would be that some seemed more effective than others, but none emerged as a model for achieving those purposes. Thus, by the late 1950s, discontent with the state of undergraduate education was again prevalent, but now a greater willingness existed to attack this problem, to undertake significant reform. These efforts produced three kinds of initiatives. Honors education, which had a checkered history in the U.S., was reinvented in a form appropriate for burgeoning state universities. New forms of liberal education, both partial and pure, were devised to revive and hopefully fulfill the postwar quest. And the notion spread that learning could be improved through downsizing, creating smaller units within large universities.

HONORS PROGRAMS. Honors in American higher education was long associated with Frank Aydelotte and the program he created at Swarthmore in the 1920s. A Rhodes scholar, Aydelotte was inspired by the rigorous studies and examinations required for honors degrees at Oxford. When named president of Swarthmore (1921–1939), he instituted and gradually expanded an adaptation of honors work for juniors and seniors while also becoming its national spokesperson. The honors program thrived at Swarthmore, becoming the college's signature and solidifying its reputation for an exemplary liberal education.[85] It was widely imitated, but with much less success. By the 1940s, *departmental* honors programs of this type existed on paper at a large number of colleges and universities. They allowed juniors and/or seniors release time for researching and writing an honors thesis. But most had too few takers for separate seminars or merely awarded honors degrees on the basis of grade-point averages. Outside this pattern, the University of Colorado experimented with various honors colloquia and devised a *general* honors program for lower-division students. The director of this program, the philosophy professor Joseph Cohen, sought to develop and

85   Frank Aydelotte, *Breaking the Academic Lockstep: The Development of Honors Work in American Colleges and Universities* (New York: Harper & Brothers, 1944); Frances Blanshard, *Frank Aydelotte of Swarthmore* (Middletown, CT: Wesleyan University Press, 1970).

perfect honors education and soon became its advocate.[86] He surveyed 110 institutions in 1952 and found just 20 that extended honors beyond the departmental approach. Cohen failed at this time to attract foundation support, but in 1956 he obtained a small grant from the Rockefeller Foundation. It allowed him to visit numerous campuses to proselytize for honors and to host a large conference the following year on the "superior student." The enthusiastic response to the conference led to a larger grant from the Carnegie Corporation and the formation in January 1958 of the Inter-University Committee on the Superior Student (ICSS).

The formation of ICSS, shortly after Sputnik, reflected the spreading awareness of high-ability students and a budding consensus that they deserved special accommodation. ICSS served this swelling interest as a clearinghouse of information on honors education and the sponsor of additional conferences. As its director, Cohen served as a peripatetic ambassador spending much of his time traveling to interested campuses. Its newsletter, *The Superior Student*, reached 3,000 recipients in its first year. The ICSS proffered guidelines for a successful honors program, but aside from favoring general honors, it was never prescriptive; rather, it appreciated that every program had to be adapted to an institutional context. Some targeted incoming freshmen; others, like Michigan State, made students prove themselves in their first year before admission to honors. Required introductory courses might be waived or offered in honors sections. Additional privileges were another local decision. And wisely, no attempt was ever made to define a "superior student."

More than 100 honors programs were begun in the first three years of the ICSS (1958–1960). The organization's role might best be described as midwife. Launching such programs was a major institutional undertaking involving leadership, politicking, and financial backing. They were opposed on some campuses as elitist, divisive, and expensive. ICSS excelled at providing information, moral support, and personal visits to assist local champions to make their case, but it never transcended that role to become an asset for operating programs. By 1961 virtual saturation had been achieved, with honors programs at all but a few state universities, 80 percent offering general honors work. By that year, ICSS was operating on its second and final Carnegie grant. When that concluded in 1962, it struggled to be self-supporting before closing shop in 1965. The honors movement lost favor amid the egalitarianism of the late 1960s, but its reinvention had made general honors a permanent feature of American higher education. The ICSS was succeeded by the National Collegiate Honors Council, a membership association that still represents a thriving honors movement.

---

86   The following draws on Julianna K. Chaszar, "The Reinvention of Honors Programs in American Higher Education, 1955–1965," *Perspectives on the History of Higher Education* 32 (2017): 79–115.

The rise and proliferation of general honors fit the unique conditions of American higher education in the late 1950s. The movement spearheaded by Joseph Cohen and ICSS originally aimed particularly at large state universities. The many private colleges and universities that started honors programs in these years revealed their broad appeal, but public universities had several specific concerns that general honors addressed. Rapid growth brought increasing awareness of the heterogeneous composition of their student bodies. Critics alleged that introductory classes geared to median students fostered laziness or loss of interest among the brighter ones. Public universities also complained that they lost high-achieving candidates to the private sector, where talented students could receive financial aid. At Michigan State, recruitment was specifically mentioned as a reason for establishing the Honors College in 1958. Going one step further, MSU began offering scholarships to National Merit Scholars, with the result that it enrolled the most in the country for several years. The momentum for honors began to build before Sputnik, but the ensuing emphasis on developing the nation's talent was clearly an additional stimulus. For one perfervid commentator, "It is not overstatement to say that our very survival depends on excellence in higher education."[87] Finally, never very far in the background was the commitment to liberal education. Honors education was largely confined to the liberal arts and specifically rejected by professional fields. An additional motive, frequently voiced, sought to focus the intellect of superior students and the rarified settings of honors seminars on achieving a higher form of liberal education. But honors was not the only means by which this goal was pursued.

LIBERAL EDUCATION REDUX. The years of the Liberal Hour were a golden age for liberal arts colleges. Most entered the postwar era as largely regional institutions, but by the mid-fifties, the stronger schools had extended recruitment over a wider geographical area. All the demographic trends favored such a strategy, allowing these schools (and private universities) to attract a good portion of the "cream" of high-ability, well-off high school graduates. The academic credentials of their students rose while the percentage of nearby or in-state students plunged. By the mid-sixties, the strongest colleges felt they had reached a meritocratic plateau—that it was pointless to seek ever-higher SAT averages and that applicants could be judged on other criteria as well (including those facilitating recruitment of African Americans). Ten colleges averaged median combined SAT scores at or above 1,350; forty-five more were above 1,200. All these schools now enrolled the most highly qualified students in their histories, although the

---

87   Ibid., quote p. 84; Paul L. Dressel, *College to University: The Hannah Years at Michigan State, 1935–1969* (East Lansing: Michigan State University, 1987), 139–46.

latter group no doubt aspired to rise further. But for American higher education, the outstanding success of these colleges seemed to be an unequivocal endorsement of the value of and demand for a liberal education.[88]

This message might seem to be at odds with the academic revolution, but contemporaries did not yet interpret it that way. Given the great prestige of liberal education, they sought curricular arrangements that could achieve the advantages of both. Honors education was one of these. Colleges felt pressures on both fronts. For them too, academic distinction was an imperative, which meant building a strong disciplinary faculty. But there was also a tacit model of liberal education by which they were likely to be judged. Amherst and Williams commonly served as exemplars, having small classes, close interaction with faculty, a heritage-based core, and provisions for advanced projects or examinations. Franklin and Marshall College, like many, felt the pressure to improve its standing by enhancing liberal education. In a lengthy process of renovating the curriculum, it examined practices at forty other liberal arts colleges. The New Curriculum (1960) it devised replaced credits with course units, as at prestigious eastern colleges; core requirements were expanded, especially in the humanities; and more personalize work was injected into concentrations. F&M also distanced itself from nonliberal subjects, eliminating vocational majors in education and business. This effort to elevate the intellectual level encountered difficulties. Students disliked it. A subsequent Middle States review found the academic programs to be inadequate in several areas. The college then felt the need to institute an honors program to attract "extraordinarily able students who will leaven the entire student body" and draw "high-quality faculty." Advancing academically and educationally was a continual challenge.[89]

The gravitational pull of both ideals was particularly evident at Wesleyan University. By the late 1950s it equaled perennial rivals Amherst and Williams in student quality and had become the wealthiest liberal arts college in the country. President Butterfield regarded liberal education as an ideal toward which the college should constantly strive, while academic faculty envisioned expanding advanced work to the graduate level. As the Wesleyan historian David Potts explained, these two visions contended for Wesleyan's future:

> One vision would restructure the first-rate national liberal arts college to make undergraduate liberal learning even more intellectually exciting and

---

88   Duffy and Goldberg, *Crafting a Class*; *Barron's Profiles of American Colleges, 1968* (Woodbury, NY: Barron's, 1968), 748–49.

89   Sally F. Griffith, *Liberalizing the Mind: Two Centuries of Liberal Education at Franklin & Marshall College* (University Park: Pennsylvania State University Press, 2010), 259–94.

educationally effective. The other would develop ... a little university with doctoral-level graduate programs that augmented research opportunities.[90]

Both visions moved forward: the president's College Plan to strengthen liberal learning and the New University plan favored principally by scientists. In 1962 the faculty and the trustees accepted both plans, but with different results. Two of Butterfield's colleges were created but had little impact. The first doctoral program was approved in 1963, but the university proponents then received a huge boost from a financial windfall in 1965,[91] and more PhD programs soon followed. Wesleyan largely embraced the academic revolution as a little university. In a decisive break with the past, the faculty voted to abolish all general education requirements (1968). Students would be liberally educated through advanced courses of their own choosing.

The forces acting on Wesleyan were prevalent elsewhere. Wesleyan's development as a liberal arts college, despite Butterfield's aspirations, had reached a degree of success from which it seemed little further could be accomplished. (The admission of women in 1968 was not yet on the horizon.) An academically strong faculty, its members products of the academic revolution, had come to dominate institutional policy, eclipsing the leadership of the president. They sought involvement in research and graduate education not only for their own careers but also in the conviction that it would enhance student learning and institutional stature. But unique to Wesleyan was the financial windfall that provided the resources for a major thrust into doctoral education. This same temptation was widely felt, albeit without the same wherewithal. Bowdoin College sponsored a conference in 1967 on "the development of doctoral programs by small liberal arts colleges." After hearing blandishments from university and foundation speakers, the general conclusion was that in terms of costs and benefits, these colleges should retain their focus on undergraduate liberal education.[92]

By the mid-sixties, the ideal of liberal education may still have been honored, but its content was increasingly muddled. In practice, however, postwar forms of liberal or general curricula had substantially eroded. The chief culprit was academic expansion—more disciplines with much greater content demanded more space in the curriculum. But students too were increasingly dismissive. In one

90   David B. Potts, *Wesleyan University, 1910–1970: Academic Ambition and Middle-Class America* (Middletown, CT: Wesleyan University Press, 2015), 328: the following draws on this exemplary history.

91   Potts provides a unique account of the investments of postwar colleges, desperate for income, in commercial enterprises, and subsequent complications with the IRS. Wesleyan purchased *My Weekly Reader*, which subsequently prospered. In 1965 it was sold to Xerox for 400,000 shares of stock, which also appreciated, making the university "rich"—at least until the 1970s: 302–10, 391–92.

92   Ibid., 366–415.

institution after another, general education courses were replaced by distribution requirements, which in theory brought some acquaintance with major domains of knowledge but did little to further the goal of common learning. Daniel Bell offered a rearguard attempt to resuscitate general education that was more acute in diagnosing the problem than offering a cure. He documented the decline of general education at Harvard, where the Redbook approach had been eclipsed by departmental courses, and Columbia, where such courses displaced the second year of the famed Contemporary Civilization. At Chicago, what had been a four-year general education course in the Hutchins College was reduced to two years in 1958 and to a single year in 1966. Besides common learning, Bell identified the basic aims of general education as instilling "comprehensive understanding of the Western tradition" and combatting "intellectual fragmentation with interdisciplinary courses."[93] Heritage-based courses—the humanities, great books, and Western Civ—were losing favor everywhere.

The elimination of the Western Civ requirement was emblematic of the bankruptcy of general education. It was not killed by animus against the West (that would come later), but rather by professionalized historians who no longer believed in the ideological justification. Western Civ had been the most popular undergraduate course in the 1950s at Amherst and Stanford, for example. Essentially European history, it was taught there and elsewhere as a succession of colorful episodes deemed significant for the evolution of the liberal democratic tradition. In the 1960s, specialists rejected such an idealized version of the European past. At Amherst, Western Civ was replaced by a "less-Eurocentric" course in historiography. Stanford resisted wholesale change until it conducted a review published as *A Study of Education at Stanford* (1968). The objective of the curriculum now became "to encourage the faculty member to teach what he likes to teach...and the student to learn what seems vital to him." This was just what had been happening. The required Western Civ course had become dominated by the teaching assistants, who assigned their own readings and ignored lectures. The course conveyed neither common learning nor a cultural rationale. The history department offered no defense to critics, and the course was dropped in 1969. The study concluded, "The general education ideal is totally impractical as a dominant curricular pattern in the modern university"—a statement that summarizes the fate of prescribed curricula at the culmination of the academic revolution.[94] Indeed, by the end of the 1960s any notion that an educated person

93   Daniel Bell, *The Reforming of General Education: The Columbia College Experience in Its National Setting* (New York: Columbia University Press, 1966), 183–208, 282, et passim; John W. Boyer, *The University of Chicago: A History* (Chicago: University of Chicago Press, 2014), 365–68.
94   Gilbert Allardyce, "The Rise and Fall of the Western Civilization Course," *American Historical Review* 87, 3 (June 1982): 695–725.

ought to know certain things was no longer credible. Distribution requirements, if any, were all that remained of what students called "gen ed." Institutions remained rhetorically committed to liberal education but avoided any recognition that its virtues were no longer connected with any specific content.

FROM LIBERAL TO LIBERATING EDUCATION. Residual discomfort with intellectual fragmentation still existed and attracted both university leaders and reformers to the idea of cluster colleges within larger institutions. Such units were justified with several rationales: as a source of community, they might counteract the anonymity of monolithic universities; distinctive curricula or curricular focus promised to rekindle common learning; small size allowed for innovation, and thus the possibility of recovering the ideal of liberal education, or perhaps, its essence. A contemporary interpreter noted that cluster colleges were typically committed to "what they loosely call liberal education," which they associate with "a host of 'good' outcomes for students." More accurately, liberal education meant a rejection of vocational preparation in favor of learning for its own sake and a liberation from "conventional requirements," which often meant heritage subjects. Most fundamental, a liberal education in cluster colleges of the late 1960s implied cultivating "any experiences that help students to broaden their range of ideas, values, or skills," in short, "liberating education."[95]

Advocates of cluster colleges had no lack of attractive models. Invariably mentioned were the Oxbridge colleges, though the modern university had developed around them, not vice versa. The Yale Colleges and Harvard Houses were admired residential units but had little curricular input. The five Claremont Colleges were a federated university with a graduate school at the center. Wayne State's Monteith College was a spontaneous innovation but it was nonresidential with little internal cohesion. A true innovation was Raymond College, created within the University of the Pacific in 1962. It offered a three-year fixed general education curriculum with its own residence, faculty, and calendar. It attracted a self-selected group of high achievers—and a dedicated faculty—who seemed to thrive in this intellectual milieu.[96] More typical of early initiatives was Justin Morrill College at Michigan State (1965–1980). Established as an autonomous college within the university, it had its own faculty, residence hall, and separate versions of the university's required courses. Its purpose was to provide a rigorous liberal education with an international emphasis, including a foreign

---

95   Jerry G. Gaff, *The Cluster College* (San Francisco: Jossey-Bass, 1970), 35–37.

96   For the misconceptions in these analogies, see Alex Duke, *Importing Oxbridge: English Residential Colleges and American Universities* (New Haven, CT: Yale University Press, 1996); Gaff, *Cluster Colleges*, 105–36.

language. The college offered more freedom to faculty than to students. Over time, it failed to maintain a separate identity and was gradually absorbed back into the mega-university.[97]

The most ambitious cluster college project was initiated by multiversity president Clark Kerr. One of his most important responsibilities was planning and founding three new branches of the University of California. Kerr wanted each to have a distinct personality. Himself a graduate of Swarthmore, he sought one campus that would foster the advantages of a liberal arts college—a dedication to liberal learning and undergraduate teaching—while preserving the intellectual assets of a great university. Santa Cruz was this experiment. Not only was it a liberal arts college within the UC, but it was designed to consist of separate residential colleges, each with its own faculty and distinctive focus. The first three colleges emphasized World Civilization (1965), Self and Society (i.e., social science, 1966), and Science, Culture, and Man (1967). Kerr described the plan "as a neoclassical campus with solid and cohesive academic liberal learning programs," intended to mimic colleges "similar to Swarthmore, Williams," etc. But it was soon apparent that "the period of founding successful neoclassical colleges was long past." The distinctive theme curricula were soon abandoned; faculty tired of teaching them and students resented requirements. Both early and later colleges became dominated by the counterculture and the ideal of a liberating education.[98]

In the last half of the 1960s, cluster colleges became a favored answer to the challenges of undergraduate education in the modern university. New institutions organized sub-colleges even before they became large (Oakland University, SUNY College at Old Westbury, UC San Diego). SUNY Buffalo organized nonresidential units (called colleges) that offered themed, separate curricula. The University of Michigan created its Residential College—to mention only the more prominent examples. A partial list named thirty-six such units established from 1965 to 1969.[99] Far more institutions created forms of residential instruction ("living-learning") with various designations. Only a few general conclusions can be offered about so diverse a collection of "experiments."

First, these initiatives were conditioned by the times in two respects. The widespread allegation of undergraduate neglect or anomie motivated the hopeful adoption of this potential remedy. When such colleges promised new approaches to learning, they appealed to certain kinds of students. Through a very

97 Dressel, *College to University*, 149–66. Michigan State created two more residential colleges in 1967.

98 Clark Kerr, *The Gold and the Blue: A Personal Memoir of the University of California, 1949–1967; Volume One, Academic Triumphs* (Berkeley: University of California Press, 2001), quotes pp. 280–81.

99 Gaff, *Cluster Colleges*, 16–17.

high degree of self-selection, experimental colleges attracted students with higher-than-average intelligence, awareness, aestheticism, academic orientation, and commitment to personal involvement; and who registered lower on practicality and collegiate interests.[100] Ordinarily, they would seem to be ideal candidates for a more intense learning environment, but the late sixties were not ordinary times. Cluster colleges created concentrations of such students, who were especially prone to liberating experience rather than liberal learning. And so were many of the teachers attracted to experimental settings.

More generally, cluster colleges could be moderately successful as residential units but failures as academic units. As residences, they could provide some cohesion, services, and social activities to counteract the impersonal university, but they largely failed to maintain a curricular focus or foster an intellectual identity. The greatest dysfunction occurred when separate faculties were appointed to these colleges. Faculty who were willing to leave their disciplinary moorings were likely to be idealists and/or disaffected to begin with. Many soon tired of teaching general or interdisciplinary subjects. The writer who lauded the personal interactions with students at Raymond College left after three years to join a university research institute.[101] The larger problem was the separation of faculty from their departments and disciplinary colleagues. Besides derailing individual careers, it was detrimental to the academic capabilities of the university. Rutgers was long handicapped in this way by separate faculties in its several historic colleges, and this was a problem that had to be overcome at Santa Cruz and San Diego. Among the lessons Kerr gained from the UC experience: "Departments are the supreme organizational units of the research university; do not tread on them."[102]

Thus, wherever the two dimensions of quality conflicted, academic knowledge prevailed over an idealized intellectual development of undergraduates. In fact, the two dimensions were inherently unequal. The content of academic knowledge was well defined, and the capacity of college or university faculties to master and advance this knowledge was readily gauged, as in the ACE ratings. The quality of undergraduates was measurable by inputs—grade-point averages and SAT scores—but there were few reliable measures of outputs. Judging by the large numbers continuing to graduate school, students appeared to be learning their major subjects well. And Kerr acknowledged that instruction in private colleges and universities was more conscientious and effective. However, the greatest ambiguity lay with "treatment effects"—curriculum and teaching and

---

100 Data from several studies of cluster college students is presented in ibid.
101 Ibid., xiii.
102 Kerr, *Gold and the Blue: Volume One, Academic Triumphs*, 298.

their purported effect on intellectual development. Here the thinking changed dramatically during the ten years of the Liberal Hour. At the end of the 1950s, a liberal education still implied core courses anchored in the Western tradition. By the late 1960s, experiments with different core subjects abounded, the West was passé, and liberating experience rivaled liberal education as an ideal. But these experiments proved as ephemeral as they were diverse. In comparison, the academic revolution was still ascendant, the most solid foundation for faculty careers and undergraduate instruction. For undergraduate instruction, further change lay ahead, but so did unsuspected challenges to the solid foundations of academic knowledge.

During the Liberal Hour, American higher education experienced a sweeping transformation, internally and externally. Fundamental changes occurred almost simultaneously, with the pace accelerating into the last half of the 1960s. The changes affected one another in a complex cross-pollination rather than in causal relations. The huge federal investment in civilian research touched off by Sputnik expanded expenditures but also affected the internal life of faculty and departments. The academic revolution was closely related to the growth of research, but it affected the sciences and non-sciences alike. The unprecedented expansion of knowledge inspired the perception that universities now played a central role in American society, both in the large portion of young people going to college and in the utilization of university knowledge to shape modern societies. Rapid economic growth enhanced social aspirations and affordability. The desegregation of southern *and northern* universities not only tempered (without resolving) a glaring injustice, but also advanced the notion that access to higher education was a human right in modern society. Governments at all levels poured unprecedented resources into building and transforming institutions, achieving mass higher education in more than a numerical sense, creating access for almost all populations. In the last years of the 1960s, the limits of these growth dynamics became apparent in some cases, and their desirability challenged in others. The next era would bring institutional crises and crises of confidence to higher education. However, the transformations of the Liberal Hour would endure as permanent features of American higher education.

PART III

THE UNRAVELING AND THE NEW ERA

1965–1980

★ 5 ★

THE UNRAVELING, 1965–1970

THE TUMULT OF THE LATE 1960S BROUGHT AN UNPRECEDENTED degree of social and cultural upheaval to the United States and, indeed, much of the world. Violent and nonviolent clashes and confrontations were manifestations of pervasive underlying change. While their extent and significance became more evident in retrospect, there was no mistaking their immediate challenge to prevailing institutions and beliefs—to the dominant assumptions of the American way of life.

These assumptions and conditions epitomized the conservative 1950s, but they continued to undergird developments during the Liberal Hour. Cold War fervor peaked during these years. The country was more prosperous than ever. And liberal initiatives, including the civil rights movement, promised to extend the benefits of the American way of life to all Americans. The historian James Patterson has marked 1965 as a national tipping point.[1] The first half of the year saw the culmination of President Johnson's Great Society legislative blitz—the Higher Education Act, Medicare, and the Voting Rights Act, among others—which extended federal programs into new areas. But they were accompanied by the massive escalation of the war in Vietnam and the first of the devastating urban riots in the Los Angeles district of Watts. Vietnam energized a militant antiwar movement. Watts ignited black nationalism among African Americans and weakened support for civil rights among Whites. Popular culture assumed an ominous, rebellious tone, as did student radicalism on the nation's campuses. Inherent features of the American way of life (Chapter 2) were soon challenged throughout American society, but especially on campuses.

The campus antiwar movement rejected the basic premise of the Cold War—opposition to the spread of communism. Its attacks were quickly extended to the so-called military-industrial complex and American involvement with Third World countries. The consensus in American politics around a "vital center" fractured by the late 1960s. A radical Left emerged for the first time since the 1940s, and on the Right, George Wallace won five states in the 1968 presidential election. Both the Republican and Democratic Parties were divided. The 1950s'

---

1 James T. Patterson, *The Eve of Destruction: How 1965 Transformed America* (New York: Basic Books, 2012).

norms against social deviance eased in the first half of the 1960s and dissolved in the second half. Traditional values were scorned on campuses and treated with increasing skepticism in the popular media. Even affluence could have negative repercussions, as the extraordinary prosperity of the 1960s was taken for granted by the younger generation. In the affluent society, poverty could seem intolerable.[2] Lyndon Johnson launched the War on Poverty, but students were prone to view inequality and injustice as failures of American society.

Of course, the realities that had buttressed the American way of life had not disappeared. The United States still faced a hostile nuclear power in the Soviet Union, and traditional values supporting religion, family, and patriotism were still honored widely by the American public. Richard Nixon called them the silent majority, and they elected him president—twice. Despite deepening apprehensions about the war, these Americans strongly disapproved of the demonstrations, disruptions, and riots that occurred across colleges and universities in these years. And the campus Left, in turn, strongly disapproved of them and their bourgeois values. Thus, a gulf developed in understanding and empathy between much of the American people and not only the campus radicals but also the more progressive elements among students, faculty, and administrators. By the 1970s, a new *mentalité* was emerging, especially at the leading universities, that would exert a growing influence over American higher education.

SDS AND THE GROWTH OF STUDENT RADICALISM

College students had little involvement or concern with national politics during the quiescent 1950s. Support for liberal causes was endemic at universities such as Wisconsin, Michigan, and UC Berkeley, but it was a minority taste even there. The principal issue motivating activism was a peace movement, which focused on nuclear disarmament. Toward the end of the decade, a few groups on these campuses engaged larger issues. Wisconsin nurtured a socialist presence in conservative Madison. In 1959, *Studies on the Left* appeared as a rather scholarly expression of what would become core New Left ideas. Inspired in part by the revisionist historian William Appleman Williams, *Studies* excoriated American foreign policy and the liberals it blamed for the Cold War. It coined the phrase "corporate liberalism" to attack the postwar liberal endorsement of corporate capitalism. Widely read in left circles, *Studies* fueled inchoate grievances.[3]

---

2   John Searle, *The Campus War: A Sympathetic Look at the University in Agony* (Harmondsworth, UK: Penguin Books, 1972), 145–47.

3   Matthew Levin, *Cold War University: Madison and the New Left in the Sixties* (Madison: University of Wisconsin Press, 2013), 88–95.

At Berkeley, students organized a leftist political party in 1957 to engage internal and external issues. SLATE wrested control of student government from the campus Greeks and sought to end the prohibition of political advocacy on campus. It also became involved in efforts to break the color barrier in local hiring. In May 1960 it led a disruptive demonstration against a San Francisco hearing of the House Un-American Activities Committee, which the police forcibly suppressed with mass arrests. That year brought a stirring of political consciousness, touched off in part by John F. Kennedy's call for the involvement of youth in a New Frontier. But the spark for politically sensitive students was the sit-in movement for civil rights. Liberals were galvanized in opposition to Jim Crow conditions in the South, but a few more liberal students recognized the need to confront similar conditions in the North.

At the University of Michigan, a sometime graduate student, Al Haber, organized Students for a Democratic Society, initially as the resuscitation of the student wing of the League for Industrial Democracy—an Old Left socialist party with a strong anti-communist and anti-Soviet stance. The first action of SDS was the Ann Arbor conference "Human Rights in the North" (May 1960), which positioned it as a potential leader among dispersed groups of the student Left. Haber was soon joined by Tom Hayden, editor of the *Michigan Daily* (1960–1961), who shared Haber's vision of SDS becoming the vehicle for a national student movement. In the summer of 1960, before assuming the *Daily's* editorship, Hayden had hitchhiked to Berkeley, the hearth of student activism, and acquired a tutorial on current issues and protest actions. Following graduation the next year, he became the (sole) field secretary for SDS, based in Atlanta, and liaison with the Student Nonviolent Coordinating Committee. There he experienced the brutality of diehard segregationists and came away resolved to make SDS into the SNCC for the rest of the country. Now a dedicated activist for social change, he began composing "an agenda for a generation" for an organizing convention set for June 1962 at a labor union camp outside Port Huron, Michigan.[4]

Both Haber and Hayden felt the need for a manifesto to define and unite the disparate causes of the student Left. Hayden circulated preliminary memos that became the basis for the *Port Huron Statement*, the most detailed and coherent expression of the original ideas, ideals, and aspirations of the New Left.[5] The

---

4   Tom Hayden, *Reunion: A Memoir* (New York: Random House, 1988), 25–72; Kirkpatrick Sale, *SDS* (New York: Vintage, 1973), 28–41; James Miller, *Democracy Is in the Streets: From Port Huron to the Siege of Chicago* (New York: Simon & Schuster, 1987).

5   The *Port Huron Statement* has been reprinted many times. I have used a copy downloaded from Hayden's former website: page numbers are from this edition. The iconic status of the PHS among the contemporary Left is memorialized in Howard Brick and Gregory Parker, eds., *The New Insurgency: The*

Statement provided a theoretical foundation for building a new kind of society, an indictment of the moral bankruptcy and blatant hypocrisy of American politics, and a positive guide to social action.

For theory, it posited an ideal of "participatory democracy," which was generally regarded as the most original political doctrine of the student movement. Inspired by a charismatic University of Michigan philosophy professor, Arnold Kaufmann, it sought "a democracy of individual participation" that would allow an individual to "share in those social decisions determining the quality and direction of his life." Participatory democracy was intended to bring "people out of isolation and into community" and help them "find meaning in personal life." It would transform the "economic experience," in which "the means of production should be open to democratic participation and subject to democratic social regulation."[6]

Hayden felt that a critique of "the American Way of Life ... should be the central concern of this manifesto."[7] The bulk of the *PHS* in fact described the pathology of American politics, circa 1962. No exaggeration was needed to portray the denial of basic civil rights in the South. Other paramount issues revolved around the Cold War. The *Statement* rhetorically invoked the fear of living under the threat of nuclear annihilation. Pressures for building more and more sophisticated nuclear weapons were never greater than in the early 1960s. This state of mind nourished the "military-industrial complex"—"the most spectacular and important creation of the authoritarian and oligopolistic structure of economic decision-making in America." Anti-communism further informed Cold War foreign policy by pitting the United States against the "colonial revolution."[8]

In response, the *Statement* called for the formation of a New Left. Here it echoed movement hero, the sociologist C. Wright Mills, who argued that leadership of the Left would come not from workers, the mainstay of Marxist theory, but from intellectuals. The New Left should consist of, and be oriented toward, "younger people who matured in the postwar world." Thus, it would mobilize students chiefly, but also faculty, to create "a left with real intellectual skills" capable of "action ... informed by reason." This New Left "must include liberals and socialists" and build bridges to "an awakening community of allies." However, this emphasis also made "the university the potential base and agency in a movement of social change." Hayden was of two minds toward universities. He

---

Port Huron Statement and Its Times (Ann Arbor, MI: Maize Books, 2012), which reprints Hayden's memos (24–46).

6   *Port Huron Statement*, 3, 4.
7   Tom Hayden, "RE: Manifesto," in Brick and Parker, *New Insurgency*, 42.
8   *Port Huron Statement*, 8.

severely criticized their aloof bureaucracies, the political timidity of professors, and the "radical separation of student from the material of study." Yet he envisioned "the university as an agent of change … a place of terrific controversy … where current events are fought about … where leftist intellectuals have time to engage in writing and practical politics [and] where direct influence can be generated against men in power."[9] The *PHS* concluded with words that might have been written by Clark Kerr, extolling the university as "the central institution for organizing, evaluating, and transmitting knowledge" and thus creating the "reliance by men of power on the men and storehouses of knowledge." Moreover, the university is "open to participation," "permits the political life to be an adjunct to the academic one," is distributed throughout the country, and is the obvious locus for the recruitment of young people. Implicitly, then, reshaping the university was also an objective of the New Left.[10]

The *Port Huron Statement* portrayed an array of real problems afflicting American society. If some aspirations were utopian—global disarmament, "eliminating the disparity between have and have-not nations," and much else—the direction of reform advocated was far more consistent with the ideals of American democracy than the conditions it opposed. In the years to follow, these conditions became more dire; and the prescriptions of the New Left became correspondingly more relevant and cogent, especially to students.

Thus, the *Statement* articulated sentiments that would become fundamental tenets of the student movement for the remainder of the 1960s:

- An indictment of the social, political, and economic order of the United States that incorporated the Old Left rejection of capitalism
- Adoption of the rubric of democracy as the fundamental means and mission of the student movement, contrasted with American hypocrisy
- A commitment to the civil rights movement, and more broadly the goals of racial equality and an end to discrimination
- Opposition to the pathology of the Cold War, soon magnified by the war in Vietnam
- Growing identification with the anti-colonial and leftist movements in the Third World

Universities are the only institution portrayed positively. Indeed, the SNCC, the putative model, used Historically Black Colleges and Universities (HBCUs) as

9   Ibid., 29, 5, 39.
10   Ibid., 28.

precarious bases in the campaign against Jim Crow.[11] The student movement was soon refocused on higher education by the Free Speech Movement (FSM) at the University of California, Berkeley—its first and in many ways defining triumph.

SDS was absent from this epic Berkeley confrontation and was scarcely needed among the multitude of student political organizations. The drama began at the opening of the 1964 fall semester, when the Berkeley administration withdrew the right of student political groups to man tables and distribute leaflets outside the main gate to campus. But much lay behind this arbitrary injunction.[12] Berkeley students had waged a campaign of civil disobedience to force an end to racial discrimination by San Francisco businesses that refused to hire Blacks. FSM leaders like Mario Savio had participated in the 1964 Freedom Summer in Mississippi, working for civil rights. It was long alleged that local business interests pressured the administration to suppress student civil rights activists, but no such link was ever found. Chancellor Edward Strong probably needed no external prompting: he and his top administrators convinced themselves that left-wing student groups were dominated by communists and intent on destroying the university. However, by attempting to muzzle their political activities, he created the perfect morality play—student free speech against university repression.

As events unfolded during the fall, the university attempted to uphold the untenable policy of denying "free speech" and imposing punishments on student protesters. Self-righteous students, organized as the FSM, made two significant contributions to the emerging student movement. The first was to employ the techniques of civil disobedience, which had been perfected in the civil rights movement, against the university. The initial instance was unplanned. When an FSM activist was arrested in Sproul Plaza, a crowd spontaneously surrounded the police car, prompting a legendary thirty-two-hour standoff in which the university ultimately backed down. However, a later occupation of the administration building employed well-rehearsed protest protocol, forcing the police to drag out each of the hundreds of nonresisting protesters. The spectacle was a public relations fiasco for the Berkeley administration and helped to convince the faculty to support the FSM.

11   Joy Ann Williamson, "'Quacks, Quirks, Agitators, and Communists': Private Black Colleges and the Limits of Institutional Autonomy," *History of Higher Education Annual* 23 (2004): 49–81.

12   Especially valuable for understanding the Free Speech Movement are Clark Kerr, *The Gold and the Blue: A Personal Memoir of the University of California, 1949–1967; Volume Two, Political Turmoil* (Berkeley: University of California Press, 2003); Robert Cohen, *Freedom's Orator: Mario Savio and the Radical Legacy of the 1960s* (Oxford: Oxford University Press, 2009); and Mark Kitchell, *Berkeley in the Sixties* (San Francisco: California Newsreel, 1990). A variety of perspectives are presented in Robert Cohen and Reginald E. Zelnik, eds., *The Free Speech Movement: Reflections on Berkeley in the 1960s* (Berkeley: University of California Press, 2002).

Second, in the course of the struggle students demonized the university in terms that went far beyond regulations about where students could distribute leaflets. The rhetorical assault on the University of California was inspired in part by Old Left groups on campus, particularly the Independent Socialist Club, which had been founded by a university librarian and Trotskyite, Hal Draper. The night before the Sproul Plaza affair he had given a talk, attended by FSM leaders, that characterized the university as a knowledge factory—an image repeated in the next day's speeches. Moreover, the FSM personified the message in the president of the UC System, Clark Kerr—a scholar of industrial relations whose influential characterization of the modern multiversity was noted in Chapter 3. Kerr spoke often and eloquently on the contributions of the university to the modern economy, and vice versa.[13] These views were soon pilloried in a Draper pamphlet, *The Mind of Clark Kerr* (October 1964). Draper easily distorted Kerr's nuanced arguments to claim that the university had become a knowledge factory in service to the capitalist power structure of a "monster-bureaucratic state." This diatribe was predicated on the premise that "capitalism is an outlived system ... based on a Permanent War Economy, it perpetuates poverty, unemployment, racism, and imperialism." Draper was a minor figure, but his rhetoric was readily incorporated into the FSM. Its leader, Mario Savio, who was more a moralist than an ideologue, consistently invoked the image of the university "as a factory, a knowledge factory" designed to turn its students into conforming products.[14] This was a far cry from the relatively open university depicted in the *Port Huron Statement*. In contrast, the FSM was portrayed by Savio and others as embodying the values of the New Left—individuality, freedom, and participatory democracy, exemplified by its own interminable deliberations.

In December the FSM achieved a heady victory—elimination of the restrictions on political activity on UC campuses. Rather than disband, however, it formed a loose coalition with other leftist groups to protest the growing war in Vietnam. This development paralleled a commitment by SDS to seize leadership of the inchoate antiwar movement. The Gulf of Tonkin Resolution in August 1964 had given President Johnson unlimited authority to wage war against North Vietnam and the Vietcong. The early months of 1965 brought the bombing of the North and the start of a vast escalation of U.S. military forces in the South.

---

13   Kerr offered a comprehensive theory of worldwide industrial development in Clark Kerr et al., *Industrialism and Industrial Man* (New York: Oxford University Press, 1960); Paddy Riley, "Clark Kerr: From the Industrial to the Knowledge Economy," in Nelson Lichtenstein, ed., *American Capitalism: Social Thought and Political Economy in the Twentieth Century* (Philadelphia: University of Pennsylvania Press, 2006), 72–87.

14   Hal Draper, *The Mind of Clark Kerr: His View of the University Factory and the New Slavery* (Berkeley, CA: Independent Socialist Club, October 1964); Cohen, *Freedom's Orator*.

Even before these developments, SDS had resolved to make opposition to the war its top priority and to sponsor a march on Washington in April. This was the beginning of a sustained antiwar movement, but it also brought a crystallization of New Left ideology.

Revulsion against the war was broadened to encompass the entire evil "system." SDS president Paul Potter blamed the system for "a war in Vietnam today or a murder in the South tomorrow or all the incalculable, innumerable more subtle atrocities that are worked on people all over—all the time." He asserted that the demonstrators were united with the "people of Vietnam.... All our lives, our destinies, our very hopes to live depend on our ability to overcome that system." How would they overcome the "system," sometimes dubbed "corporate liberalism"? Their answer was to "build a movement." Thus, as early as 1965, building a *movement* to oppose the *system* became the overriding objective of SDS, transcending the specific issues of war, racism, imperialism, or alleged "university complicity." These particular issues nonetheless were crucial for illustrating the iniquities of corporate liberalism (which had otherwise brought unprecedented prosperity for most Americans) and mobilizing students for the *movement*.[15] The adoption of this strategy effectively signaled the end of the intellectual phase of the New Left, in which radical notions were debated within a larger sphere of contemporary ideas. Now, events would be interpreted within the fixed categories of New Left ideology and used for their propaganda value in advancing the movement.[16]

This strategy not only met with some initial success, it refocused SDS on students and campuses. The March on Washington had a far greater impact than originally anticipated. It was followed by the influx of a new generation of SDS recruits. Less intellectual, innocent (at first) of Old Left ideological squabbles, they seemed motivated by pure alienation from the middle-class American establishment. Todd Gitlin (first-generation SDS) described them as "instinctive anarchists, principled and practiced antiauthoritarians."[17] They sported longer hair and blue work shirts, and they indulged in marijuana and antiestablishment rock and roll. Their appearance would seem to mark a significant change in the zeitgeist. Above all, the American hypocrisy that the *Port Huron Statement* had identified in 1962 resonated as glaring reality to this generation—the racial violence of die-hard segregationists, now depicted on the nightly news; the fulminations of Cold War zealots; and the escalation of the Vietnam War by the "peace"

---

15 Todd Gitlin, *The Sixties: Years of Hope, Days of Rage* (New York: Bantam Books, 1993 [1987]), 177–88.

16 For example, "complicity" joined "corporate liberalism" and the "system" in the New Left vocabulary of catch-all condemnations whose content did not require explication.

17 Gitlin, *Sixties*, 186.

candidate, President Lyndon Johnson. For every committed SDS partisan, many contemporaries shared to some degree this disillusionment and alienation. These sympathizers might participate or not in the emerging protests, but they rarely criticized the radicals, no matter how hyperbolic the rhetoric. They too suspected that there was something wrong with the *system*.

Three kindred developments soon exacerbated this state of mind: the rise of Black Power, the seductive images of Third World Revolution, and the pervasive spread and influence of the counterculture. All far transcended the universities, but they also had a powerful influence on campuses.

The civil rights movement achieved the legal emancipation of Blacks in the segregated South with passage of the Civil Rights Act of 1964 and the Voting Rights Act of 1965. Just five days after the latter act was signed into law, the black section of Watts, Los Angeles, erupted in a prolonged, destructive riot. Racially based riots ensued in inner cities across the country in the following years, especially the devastating 1967 riots in Newark and Detroit. Civil rights did little to ameliorate the oppressive conditions endured by urban Blacks outside the South.[18] The riots documented another failure of American society and, for many, underscored the Left's indictment. Nor did violence by segregationists abate in the South. There the SNCC abandoned interracial cooperation by expelling all Whites. Its new leader, Stokely Carmichael, demanded Black Power in tirades that resounded across the country.[19] In Oakland, California, the Black Panther Party for Self-Defense demonstrated its defiance by carrying unconcealed firearms and spouting simplistic communist slogans. Black Power quickly migrated to campuses, where recently recruited black students soon pressed demands for separatism and special programs (below).

The seeds of Third-World romanticism were present in the *Port Huron Statement*. Mounting frustration with the Vietnam War led to a fanciful identification with guerillas and revolution anywhere in the developing world. Prophets were readily found in the writings of Franz Fanon and Regis Debray, the revolutionary icon Ché Guevara, and Chairman Mao Zedong, then leading the Cultural Revolution. Ultimate adulation went to North Vietnam and the National Liberation Front. The New Left and Third World Revolutionaries had the same putative enemy—the government and the *system* of the United States. This identification rationalized a further turning point within SDS in 1967—toward violent resistance. Student protests soon incorporated Third World rhetoric,

18   David Steigerwald, *The Sixties and the End of Modern America* (New York: St. Martin's, 1995), 187–215.

19   Stokely Carmichael and Charles V. Hamilton, *Black Power: The Politics of Liberation in America* (New York: Vintage Books, 1967); Clayborne Carson, *In Struggle: SNCC and the Black Awakening of the 1960s* (Cambridge, MA: Harvard University Press, 1981).

sometimes in conjunction with Black Power and other times calling for Third World Studies.

The counterculture became all pervasive on campuses by the end of the 1960s.[20] Students expressed their rejection of bourgeois America with long hair, working-class clothing (or not much clothing at all), obscene language, anti-establishment rock and roll, widespread use of marijuana and occasionally LSD, and sexual license. A visceral abhorrence of all forms of hierarchy and authority prevailed, including the authority of universities. Anti-intellectualism was inherent in the emphasis on feelings—enhanced by sex, drugs, and rock and roll. Countercultural rejection of American society mirrored New Left condemnation of the *system*.[21] Although many hippies sought personal emancipation by dropping out, they generally supported demonstrations or protests that opposed straight society, whether for Black Power, Third World revolution, opposition to the war, or transformation of the university.

By the summer of 1966, the leadership of SDS was frustrated; its membership was growing, but tactics such as draft resistance were ineffectual. Nationally, the antiwar movement was a singular issue that was making no headway; and civil rights had been eclipsed by Black Power. The leadership (most of whom were no longer students) resolved to shift its organizational energies to universities and students. It specifically sought to exploit local issues on individual campuses. Its explicit goal was not to achieve academic reform or greater student power, but rather to transform students into a generation of committed radicals, agents for changing the political and social structure of the country.[22] This fundamental strategy of the SDS National Office was key to understanding the escalation of the number and severity of campus protests in the following years. Issues were chosen chiefly to manipulate—they would say "mobilize"—students for this larger purpose. Efforts to block armed forces recruiters from campus aimed to expose university complicity in the war and American imperialism; protests against university rules were meant to reveal the authoritarian nature of establishment institutions.

For the next academic year, SDS organizers from the national office and local chapters sought to invent or inflate campus grievances into confrontations that

---

20 Popular usage of the term is attributed to Theodore Roszak's account of the ideas employed to rationalize this phenomenon: *The Making of a Counter Culture: Reflections on the Technocratic Society and Its Youthful Opposition* (New York: Doubleday, 1969; first published in the *Nation*, March–April 1968). The phenomenon was well established and even commercialized by that late date. For example, the "Human Be-In" of January 1967, was the high point of the Bay Area counterculture. See Peter Braunstein and Michael William Doyle, *Image Nation: The American Counterculture of the 1960s and 1970s* (New York: Routledge, 2002), 5–14.

21 The linkage between the counterculture and the New Left is described in Gitlin, *Sixties*, 195–221.

22 Sales, *SDS*, 295–96.

would gain recruits and demonstrate university complicity with corporate liberalism. Most major universities experienced protests over administrative authority, parietal rules, or required curricula. On some campuses, radical students gained control of student government and made far-reaching demands. SDS was responsible for staging protests against armed forces recruiters and corporate symbols, especially Dow Chemical, the manufacturer of napalm. Berkeley led the way in raising the intensity of protest when students blocked access to a Navy recruiter. Complaining self-righteously that the university had allowed the Navy to use space reserved for students, militants were able to escalate this confrontation into a five-day strike. Harvard's SDS achieved notoriety by temporarily blockading Secretary of Defense Robert McNamara. By the spring of 1967, protests had increased in frequency and intensity; the aim of SDS was to utilize these protests to generate "revolutionary consciousness": "We need to move from protest to resistance; to dig in for the long haul; to become full time, radical, sustained, relevant. In short, we need to make a revolution."[23]

The organization now dedicated to fomenting an American revolution consisted of a national office with about a dozen full-time workers, eight "regional travelers" who spread the gospel to campuses, and a national membership of 6,400. More impressive were SDS chapters on 250 campuses with a total membership near 30,000. One survey found almost two-thirds to be students—40 percent undergraduate and 25 percent graduate. Of others with known status, 20 percent were nonstudents and 10 percent were in high school. Internally, all shades of leftist ideologies were represented, including varieties of communism, socialism, and anarchism. A contingent from the Maoist Progressive Labor Party was a growing (and unwelcome) presence. However, all except Maoists were pretty much united in opposition to the war, support for Black Power, infatuation with Third World revolution, and condemnation of university complicity. In these positions they could count on the sympathies of thousands more inside and outside of universities. Despite the existence of numerous antiwar groups or mobilization committees, SDS was the largest and best organized student group. The leadership characterized its members as 85–90 percent shock troops— mostly young students "completely turned off by the American system ... anti-intellectual ... morally outraged." Intellectuals made up perhaps 5–10 percent, mostly graduate students who theorized and strategized but made fairly tepid protesters. Just 5 percent were "organizers," who kept the chapters running, actively recruited members, and attended regional and national meetings. In this loose structure, the linkage between the national office and the chapters was

23   Ibid., 336. The theoretical rationalizations for embracing violence, or "resistance," drawn from Franz Fanon, Herbert Marcuse, and others, are traced in Steigerwald, *Sixties*, 137–40.

tenuous. Protest activities on individual campuses depended on the strength and radicalism of SDS chapters, their allies, and the receptivity of the local environment.[24] The national office and the national officers lived in an ideological cocoon in which revolution seemed a realistic possibility. But then so had Lenin. However, in 1917 Lenin inherited a true revolution, while SDS sought to foment an academic Armageddon.

ACADEMIC ARMAGEDDON:
THE 1968 ERA, 1967–1970

Confrontations in fall 1967 far exceeded all previous protests. By one count, sixty large campus protests took place, two-thirds against recruiters, half of whom were from Dow Chemical. SDS turned Dow into a symbol of corporate-university complicity, and the company reported that one-third of their campus visits (113 of 339) experienced harassment. Nearly half of the recruitment demonstrations involved violence, and universities called in police in at least twenty of them. A particularly "successful" confrontation was orchestrated at the University of Wisconsin. Hundreds of students blockaded a Dow recruiter and, in the new spirit of resistance, refused to disperse. The university brought in reinforcements from the Madison police, and a bloody melee spilled out of the building and onto the campus in a confused mixture of tear gas and rock throwing. Campus outrage against the police assault was expressed in a mass rally the next day and in a five-day strike. The strategy of resistance had succeeded in banishing the Dow recruiter, closing the university, provoking alleged police brutality, and, perhaps for some, raising revolutionary consciousness.[25]

The same week at Berkeley a coalition of radical groups that now included SDS tried to shut down the draft induction center in Oakland. Violently repulsed on Tuesday, they returned in greater force on Friday to stage a destructive riot that succeeded in preventing the center from operating that day.[26] These violent clashes set an unfortunate precedent for both sides: radicals imagined that resistance was succeeding, that they could impose their will through physical confrontation; and the authorities concluded that decisive physical force was imperative to prevent that from happening.

---

24   Sales, *SDS*, 271, 351–55.

25   Ibid., 369–83; Tom Bates, *Rads: The 1970 Bombing of the Army Math Center at the University of Wisconsin and Its Aftermath* (New York: Harper Collins, 1992), 81–92. For every confrontation, parallel accounts allege police brutality and student violence against police; student "strikes" were only partially honored.

26   Kitchell, *Berkeley in the Sixties*.

The escalating protests in fall 1967 set the stage for the most prolonged, violent, and destructive confrontations, from spring 1968 to spring 1970: the 1968 Era. The following accounts describe the protests that received most media attention, most affected public opinion, and inflicted the greatest disruption on their respective institutions.[27] Each of these episodes was a discrete event, unique in terms of actors, issues, and outcomes, but all were conducted as if there were well-understood rules for student class warfare.[28]

COLUMBIA UNIVERSITY: APRIL 23–30, 1968. Columbia University in 1968 was a loose collection of sixteen schools and three affiliates—Barnard College (for women), Teachers College, and Union Theological Seminary. Just 6,000 of its 20,000 students were undergraduates, nearly half enrolled in Columbia College.[29] The SDS historian Kirkpatrick Sale likened the development of the Columbia chapter to "the history of many SDS chapters of the time, writ larger ... but in essentials the same."[30] Formed in 1965, it began staging aggressive confrontations over university complicity the next year but also suffered from periodic lapses of energy. By 1968 it consisted of perhaps fifty core members and one hundred earnest hangers-on. Columbia had begun recruiting black students seriously in 1964, and the following year they formed the Society of Afro-American Students (SAS), largely for social support. Radical activists were a minority among Columbia undergraduates, and substantial numbers of students, later organized into the "majority coalition," opposed the disruptions.

SDS was divided between an older faction focused on education and base-building and an "action faction," led by Mark Rudd, that advocated direct struggle. In March 1968 Rudd established his reputation by throwing a pie in the face of a Selective Service System colonel. He was promptly elected chapter chairman on the promise "to Get the SDS Moving Again and Screw the University." Increasingly audacious confrontations, in violation of university prohibitions,

27 The most notorious confrontation of the 1968 Era was the protests at the Democratic Convention in Chicago. Occurring before the fall 1968 semester, the Chicago protests glorified the SDS doctrine of resistance. After the 1968 riots in Chicago protesting the Democratic National Convention, the SDS added at least 100 new chapters and many new members.

28 Awareness of actions on different campuses was widespread through the many underground publications, including the SDS's *New Left Notes* and SDS "travelers," who circulated among campuses.

29 For a succinct and balanced account, see Robert A. McCaughey, *Stand Columbia: A History of Columbia University in the City of New York, 1754–2004* (New York: Columbia University Press, 2004), 423–89; the official account: *Crisis at Columbia: Report of the Fact-Finding Commission Appointed to Investigate the Disturbances at Columbia University in April and May 1968* (New York: Random House, 1968).

30 Sale, *SDS*, 430.

were overlooked by the administration in the hope of avoiding negative publicity. Meanwhile, SDS sought to mobilize students by exploiting two university issues. First, for some eight years Columbia had pursued a dubious project to build a gymnasium in adjoining Morningside Park. The facility would supposedly be used by Columbia College students and, separately, residents of neighboring Harlem. By 1968 both city officials and the black community had soured on the project, but the university broke ground nonetheless to prevent its permits from expiring. The alleged perfidy of this project purportedly illustrated the university's inherent racism. The second issue aimed to dramatize Columbia's complicity in the war by focusing on its membership in the Institute for Defense Analysis (IDA). The institute was a think tank that provided the Defense Department with access to university expertise, scarcely a malevolent activity; but the SDS national office had targeted such university affiliations as symbolic of participation in the war effort. Rudd would later brag, "we manufactured the issues," as events soon revealed.[31]

On April 23, SDS and SAS joined for yet another rally to protest these iniquities. After stoking their indignation, a crowd of about 200 set out to vent their anger at a suitable symbol of authority. Unable to enter the administration building, the mob proceeded to the inactive Morningside construction site. Finding it guarded by police, they returned to campus and entered Hamilton Hall, the seat of Columbia College, and continued the demonstration. They remained in the building at the end of the day, turning the rally into a building occupation and the college dean into a hostage. At midnight, the SAS caucused and, in the spirit of Black Power, resolved to expel the white demonstrators. SDS complied but asked what their role should now be: "Get your own building," someone suggested. Rudd led his followers to the main administration building and occupied the president's office, fully expecting to be forcefully removed. When that did not happen, another building was taken over, and soon two more. At this point, and for the following days, the occupations themselves became the only issue that mattered.

The administration contemplated forcefully removing the occupiers but was fearful of provoking the Blacks in Hamilton Hall and imagined sympathizers in nearby Harlem. Any decisive university action was then paralyzed by the attempts of concerned faculty to mediate. They wished, above all, to prevent bringing the police onto the campus. They proposed terms that would have met

---

31 McCaughey, *Stand Columbia*, 485. In his memoir, Mark Rudd appeared oblivious to any serious consideration of political issues and chiefly concerned with action, as well as what was then called an ego trip: *Underground: My Life with SDS and the Weathermen* (New York: Harper-Collins, 2009).

almost all radical demands—ending the Morningside project, withdrawal from IDA, and most important, virtual amnesty for demonstrators. But Rudd summarily rejected the terms and negotiations, galvanizing the occupiers to remain until forcefully removed. The rejected terms were tantamount to capitulation and enraged the majority coalition of students and unsympathetic professors. The faculty's fruitless measures occupied most of five days and, for faculty and administration, caused enormous anguish. Finally, after eight days, the inevitable police bust took place—fully covered by the New York media. The Blacks in Hamilton Hall exited peacefully into police vans, and the most radical pockets of SDS resisted. Charges of police brutality abounded, but no serious injuries occurred. The administration, however, was discredited; the university community divided and demoralized. Mark Rudd had won the battle, if not the war.

The accounts in newspapers and journals were devastating. Conservatives decried Columbia's actions as pusillanimous; liberals sympathized with the ostensible goals and alleged sufferings of the demonstrators. An ensuing strike was preempted only by suspending classes. President Grayson Kirk resigned within three months, and his provost and heir apparent was passed over for the succession. Criminal charges against the protesters were dropped, and university discipline brought only letters of admonition. IDA was abandoned, and Columbia took further steps to forbid classified research and scrutinize relations with outside agencies. The highly regarded Naval Reserve Officers Training Corps was scuttled, and the ill-starred Morningside Park project was terminated as well. The SAS dissociated from SDS and presented its own list of demands to enhance the black presence at Columbia. Although typically extravagant, their specific objectives were largely granted in subsequent negotiations. The number of students of color in the next year's class almost doubled.

SDS and Mark Rudd clearly overreached with a second occupation of Hamilton Hall in May. Forcibly ejected that evening with accustomed violence and vandalism, this time they received no sympathy from the former coalition. The university remained badly divided over different approaches for rebuilding. A faculty executive committee was formed and became the de facto voice of the university. Over the next twelve months, it laid the basis for restructuring the administration and beginning the rebuilding process. Just one year after the crisis, the university voted overwhelmingly to create a university senate that would set policy on university-wide matters. The lasting damage to the university was nevertheless severe. Some of the most illustrious professors departed; others withdrew from active roles. Promising younger faculty also left for more congenial settings. Columbia's tenuous financial condition further deteriorated. The university's difficulties were not all caused by the crisis of April 1968. But the crisis exposed inherent weaknesses in its governance and structure, and it would be another decade before the university "bottomed out," in the judgment of the university historian.[32] The unique strength of Columbia—its august stature in American intellectual life—was more difficult to reclaim.

STATE UNIVERSITY OF NEW YORK AT BUFFALO: AUGUST 1968–JUNE 1970. The SUNY Buffalo experiment, as seen in Chapter 4, juxtaposed an aggressive academic expansion and a conservative upstate industrial locale. President Martin Meyerson's charm, enthusiasm, and ambitions for academic excellence lured top academics to this work in progress. He emphasized building the almost nonexistent liberal arts, hiring an especially distinguished (and left-leaning) group of writers and critics for the English department. Excellent students were attracted as well. The number in the top 10 percent of their graduating classes rose from 10 to 80 percent (1958–1968). The City of Buffalo's population, in contrast, was heavily ethnic and strongly Catholic, with a history of racial clashes and latent anti-Semitism—a community with little sympathy for the new academia of the 1960s or the New Left.[33]

The Buffalo chapter of SDS was formed in 1965 and immediately began antiwar protests. They were opposed, often physically, by conservative pro-war citizens, the Buffalo police, and an active FBI unit. Frustrated, the antiwar movement became more radical in 1966 and joined forces with the Marxist-Maoist Youth Against War and Fascism. Meyerson inherited a fractured campus. Conservative faculty in engineering and medicine demanded and were given permission to conduct research for the Defense Department, despite his reservations; and a student referendum actually supported cooperation with the Selective Service. Escalating antiwar protests intensified the polarization—between liberal arts and the conservative faculties, and between the university and the city. Meyerson became increasingly unpopular with Buffalonians, especially after he froze construction on the new campus over racial discrimination in union hiring, but he was soon reviled equally by radicals.

The confrontations at Buffalo turned violent after August 1968. Draft resisters took refuge in a local Unitarian church, supported by more than 200 demonstrative sympathizers. After several days, a police bust produced nine arrests. Henceforth celebrated as the Buffalo Nine, their trials provided further occasions for agitation. From this point on, a virtual state of war existed between

---

32 McCaughey, *Stand Columbia*, 528–31.

33 Kenneth J. Heineman, *Campus Wars: The Peace Movement at American State Universities in the Vietnam Era* (New York: New York University Press, 1993); Warren Bennis, *The Leaning Ivory Tower* (San Francisco: Jossey-Bass, 1973), 126.

campus radicals and the community. For the next two years, the confrontations became more prolonged and destructive. SDS claimed 500 members and issued far-fetched, nonnegotiable demands. Physical attacks were launched against the construction site for a defense project and the offices of Air Force ROTC. SDS effectively took over the student government by mobbing its meetings. Meyerson's decentralized design had created a parallel system of academically autonomous subunits called colleges, three of which were dominated by radical/counterculture students and faculty. They offered "experimental" courses taught by nonfaculty that were a pretext for activism and allowed students to grade themselves.[34]

All this was the prelude to two weeks of a campus-police riot and student-faculty strike in February–March 1970. Crowds of more than one thousand rampaged against the usual targets and directly battled equally infuriated police. The campus suffered more than $200,000 in damages; 125 students, faculty, and police were hospitalized; and in the denouement 45 faculty were arrested for an illegal sit-in.

When passions finally cooled, the dreams of an academic Berkeley of the East were a distant memory. Meyerson had taken leave in fall 1969 and gladly accepted the presidency of the University of Pennsylvania. His successor, Robert Ketter, represented the old University of Buffalo. The star faculty recruited by Meyerson soon departed, and those who remained were swept into the SUNY faculty union. Ketter imposed more traditional academic standards but chafed against the SUNY bureaucracy. He sought to mend relations with the Buffalo community, but enrollments declined nonetheless. SUNY Buffalo survived and eventually moved to its new campus with only memories of the scars and the promise of the 1968 Era.[35]

SAN FRANCISCO STATE COLLEGE: NOVEMBER 1968–MARCH 1969. San Francisco State became part of the California State College system when it was reorganized under the Master Plan in 1961. Formerly known for a heterogeneous mixture of unorthodox and mature students, the faculty soon resented the yoke of the system bureaucracy. In liberal San Francisco, the college was early in endorsing civil rights and opposition to the war, but relations with the black

---

34 The unique system of colleges at SUNY Buffalo is analyzed in Arthur Levine, *Why Innovation Fails* (Albany: SUNY Press, 1980).

35 Patricia A. Malony, "Presidential Leadership, Change, and Community: SUNY Buffalo from 1966 to 1981," in John B. Clark, W. Bruce Leslie, and Kenneth P. O'Brien, eds., *SUNY at Sixty: The Promise of the State University of New York* (Albany: SUNY Press, 2010), 144–58; Roger L. Geiger, "Better Late Than Never: Intentions, Timing, and Results in Creating SUNY Research Universities," in Clark et al., *SUNY at Sixty*, 171–83.

community were poor, and the small black enrollment in decline. The Black Student Union (BSU) was organized in 1963, and it assumed a posture of black nationalism after an SNCC organizer arrived in 1966. Other students of color organized the parallel Third World Liberation Front. Their chief objective was a black studies program, toward which the college was sympathetic but slow to act. San Francisco State was permissive toward its students. Disciplinary action, if any, was determined by a student board; students controlled invitations to campus speakers; and the Experimental College was created for student-organized courses. Black students used the latter to establish a black studies curriculum, emphasizing black nationalism and adopting the Black Panthers' logo.[36]

The white-run student newspaper became loudly critical of what it called black racism. The resulting conflict intensified until a group of Blacks invaded the paper offices and assaulted the editor in November 1967. Several attackers were subsequently arrested, including George Murray, a tutor in black studies and a Black Panther. In the next months, several buildings were occupied to protest disciplinary actions against the black students. Murray nonetheless continued as a student and tutor, but he also inflamed the situation. He traveled to Cuba (about the same time as Mark Rudd) and attacked the U.S. in a fiery antiwar speech that was reported in national media. Back home, he advocated that students carry guns to protect themselves against racist administrators. Outrage against the retention of Murray as an instructor and the continuing turmoil on campus finally led the chancellor of the state system to demand Murray's suspension. The BSU countered that suspension would trigger a strike. On November 1, the president succumbed to the pressure and suspended Murray, and five days later the campus was engulfed in a strike that included students and faculty.[37]

The BSU issued ten "nonnegotiable" demands that included the creation of a black studies department under their control with twenty full-time faculty positions; the admission of all black students who wished to attend; and the retention of Murray. The Third World Liberation Front added demands for a school of ethnic studies with fifty faculty slots. The Third World Strike soon forced the closing of the campus. When the president and faculty suggested university-wide discussions to achieve (hopefully) a peaceful resolution, the president was fired.

36 Fabio Rojas, *From Black Power to Black Studies* (Baltimore: Johns Hopkins University Press, 2003), 45–92; Algo D. Henderson, "San Francisco State College: A Tale of Mismanagement and Disruption," in David Riesman and Verne Stadtman, eds., *Academic Transformation* (New York: McGraw-Hill, 1973), 287–302; Alden Dunham, *Colleges of the Forgotten Americans* (New York: McGraw-Hill, 1969), 147–50.

37 The faculty strike involved a minority of American Federation of Teachers members who sought the right to organize and strike. The strikes and violence included large numbers of nonstudents: Henderson, "San Francisco State."

The linguistics professor S. I. Hayakawa became the college's third president of that year, though opposed by the faculty as representing the state system. A hard-liner toward student protest, his awkward but earnest efforts at times disarmed the strikers. Still, with all sides enraged, clashes continued into the spring, on one day causing 454 arrests (252 students). The college was willing to establish a black studies department but not to reinstate Murray. When Murray was arrested and jailed on weapons charges, that issue became moot. San Francisco State reopened on March 21 after the longest college disruption of the 1968 Era. The BSU achieved a black studies department under its control, which now meant under the influence of the Black Panthers. Its extremist teaching almost cost the college its accreditation. The conflict launched the career of S. I. Hayakawa as an icon of resistance to student radicalism. It also prompted legislation giving universities greater powers over obstreperous students, though institutions were scarcely willing to use them.

CORNELL UNIVERSITY: APRIL 1969. The crisis at Cornell also drew inspiration from Black Power but raised deeper issues of university integrity. Cornell president James Perkins (1963–1969) epitomized the enlightened liberalism of the early 1960s. Much like his good friend Clark Kerr, he envisioned a university committed to addressing and ameliorating challenges facing American society. He was early to implement aggressive recruitment and special programs for dis-advantaged black students, raising their numbers from 8 to 250 by 1968. The Afro-American Society (AAS) was formed in 1966 and soon became increasingly militant under the influence of Black Power. By no means did all black students support the militants, but moderate Blacks were threatened for not doing so. An active SDS chapter played a secondary role, assisting the AAS and supporting their demands.[38]

Racial animosity passed a threshold in spring 1968, when the AAS accused an economics professor of racism and demanded his dismissal, then occupied the economics department. Terminating even a visiting professor on the basis of an AAS interpretation of his teaching would have been an egregious violation of academic freedom. This demand was rationalized by invoking the Black Power concept of "institutional racism." According to this new theory, historically white institutions unconsciously committed subtle forms of racism. In effect, anything that gave offense to black students could be viewed as evidence of institutional

---

38 Donald Alexander Downs, *Cornell '69: Liberalism and the Crisis of the American University* (Ithaca, NY: Cornell University Press, 1999): an exemplary study of the failure of liberalism; Glenn C. Altschuler and Isaac Kramnick, *Cornell: A History, 1940–2015* (Ithaca, NY: Cornell University Press, 2014), 155–90.

racism. Given the prevalence of liberal guilt, exacerbated by a handful of actual (or possibly staged) anti-black incidents, many faculty, administrators, and President Perkins sympathized with this view, at least in part. They acknowledged the responsibility to modify their speech and behavior to avoid giving offense. In this atmosphere, academic freedom and the enforcement of campus laws and regulations, let alone civil behavior, were subordinated to the appeasement of black sensibilities—as defined by the AAS. As the administration largely ignored increasing provocations, black militants became more paranoid in identifying ubiquitous institutional racism and more strident in their demands.

The centerpiece of those demands was creation of a black studies program. After relenting on an original demand for a separate college, the chief point of disagreement became the extent of student control. After prolonged negotiations an agreement was reached in early April, largely on the president's insistence, that accorded black students an unprecedented role in determining curricula and selecting faculty. Militant Blacks were nonetheless frustrated by the lengthy process and had begun to acquire rifles for "self-defense," like the Black Panthers. The crisis was precipitated by the decision of the judicial board to reprimand three AAS activists for previous disruptive acts. The AAS responded by occupying a campus building, Willard Straight Hall. Feeling threatened, they smuggled rifles into the building. The next day, facing armed students and a potential catastrophe, university negotiators capitulated to all the AAS demands, including nullification of the student reprimands. The occupiers then marched out of the building brandishing their rifles and giving the Black Power salute for the national news media and all the world to see. Still, the university's humiliation was not finished.

The next day the faculty repudiated the administration agreement as a capitulation to force and an abandonment of academic integrity. SDS then joined in by organizing a huge demonstration, accompanied by explicit threats of violence from the AAS. Under great pressure, the faculty acceded to this intimidation and reversed its vote, approving the administration's agreement. However, the reaction to this surrender was also intense. Several professors resigned immediately, including the (black) economics professor Thomas Sowell, who charged that black students were not being held to the same standards.[39] Others formally protested the abdication of academic freedom at Cornell. President Perkins was soon gone, and the Cornell Africana Studies Center became one of the most po-

---

39   Downs, *Cornell '69*, 273. Allan Bloom, almost two decades later, articulated his disgust with Cornell '69: *The Closing of the American Mind: How Higher Education Has Failed Democracy and Impoverished the Souls of Today's Students* (New York: Simon & Schuster, 1987), 313–55. See Chapter 7.

liticized units of this type.[40] At Cornell, well-meaning liberal efforts to rectify racial inequality resulted instead in compromising fundamental university values of academic freedom and integrity.

STANFORD, HARVARD, AND BERKELEY: APRIL–MAY 1969. Besides Cornell and San Francisco State, at least eighty-three other colleges and universities experienced black protests in 1968 and 1969.[41] But other issues also animated activists in the manic spring of 1969. At Stanford University growing opposition to classified research came to a head in April, when antiwar activists occupied the Applied Electronics Laboratory for nine days, eventually leaving peacefully under threat of expulsion. Protesters had two targets. Electronics research had helped raise Stanford to the top ranks of American research universities, but much of this work was done for the Pentagon and much of that classified. The university also sponsored the Stanford Research Institute (SRI), a nonprofit institution originally founded to perform research for local industry. By the 1960s SRI had become largely a contractor for the Defense Department. Classified military research received little sympathy from Stanford's liberal faculty and students, although it was the livelihood of more than 1,000 employees. The occupiers were generally applauded on campus, increasing pressure on the university. The faculty senate voted to end all classified research on campus, and the trustees soon followed by cutting ties with SRI, making it an independent nonprofit research institute. No classified research was terminated, but it no longer was performed under the Stanford aegis. With this issue removed, support for disruptive actions by the core of radical students gradually waned.

Harvard had one of the largest chapters of SDS, and its chief focus was opposition to the war.[42] As elsewhere, it adopted more confrontational tactics from 1967 onward, as frustration with the war grew among students and faculty. In 1968–1969, the existence of the Reserve Officers' Training Corps (ROTC) was the issue chosen to exemplify university complicity. The administration effectively eviscerated the program, but SDS used the lack of immediate cessation as a pretext to occupy the administration building. Harvard '69 was in some ways a reprise of Columbia '68. Student revolutionaries cared little for the ostensible issues. Once in control of University Hall, the occupation itself became the chief

---

40   Altschuler and Kramnick, *Cornell*, 192–203.

41   Downs, *Cornell '69*, 65.

42   In early 1967 the SDS was disappointed by an inconclusive debate on the war with the UN Ambassador Arthur Goldberg and rejected "mere correctness or rationality" if they do not advance "political effectiveness": Morton Keller and Phyllis Keller, *Making Harvard Modern: The Rise of America's University* (New York: Oxford University Press, 2001), 308.

issue—and the resort to a police bust two days later, the principal source of subsequent controversy. Liberal faculty could show their antiwar bona fides by criticizing the use of police, and moderates who blamed the students found themselves on the defensive. Harvard, however, was a far stronger university and community than Columbia, and neither the occupation nor the bust caused irreparable damage. Two years later, law school dean Derek Bok—a critic of the bust—replaced the beleaguered Nathan Pusey as the new president of Harvard and would prove to be an exemplar for the management of student dissent.[43]

At Berkeley, the battle of People's Park became the reductio ad absurdum of student protest. Confrontations between dedicated radicals and authorities escalated during 1968–1969. The regents' refusal to allow the Black Panther Eldridge Cleaver to teach a course led to a building takeover, vandalism, and a violent bust. In the spring, the Third World Liberation Front attempted to close the campus with a strike. In May, in an effort to mobilize the large, local counterculture population, activists attempted to turn an unused piece of university property into a "people's park." An eclectic collection of hippies, radicals, students, and others fashioned a park of sorts. This strangely constructive effort struck the fancy of the community. A student referendum favored the park by six to one. However, the park had no legal standing and was adamantly opposed by the regents and Governor Ronald Reagan. They ordered the park to be fenced off, but to do this against local opposition required state police protection. Supporters stoked their indignation at a large rally, then marched on the park, setting off a full-scale riot. Protesters actively fought with the police, who fired shotguns seemingly indiscriminately at rioters, killing one (an unconnected riot tourist). The National Guard had to be mobilized to restore order and occupy the park. Ironically, the battle of People's Park and its aftermath tended to unite hippies, radicals, and the Berkeley community against the police and the governor, but in fact it signaled the demise of large-scale student protest at the university.[44]

KENT STATE UNIVERSITY: MAY 1–4, 1970. President Nixon's invasion of Cambodia (April 30, 1970) provoked exasperation, frustration, and rage at campuses across the country.[45] Kent State had a fairly small radical community. Protests the previous year had been dealt with harshly, with the jailing of demonstra-

43   Roger L. Geiger, *Research and Relevant Knowledge: American Research Universities since World War II* (New York: Oxford University Press, 1993), 254–56.

44   Kitchell, *Berkeley in the Sixties*; W. J. Rorabaugh, *Berkeley at War: The 1960s* (New York: Oxford University Press, 1989).

45   Nixon had promised to end the war and began ineffective peace talks in 1969 while increasing military pressure. The invasion of Cambodia was consistent with this devious policy but was interpreted as an escalation of the war and hence a betrayal of peace efforts.

tors and banning of the SDS. Cambodia provoked an angry but peaceful rally on Friday, May 1. That night, crowds in the downtown bars turned ugly, starting a riot, defying local police, and vandalizing businesses. The town declared a state of emergency and requested the National Guard. The next night a protest rally turned into a defiant mob that set fire to the ROTC building and celebrated as it burned. From this point, the National Guard and its mission to restore and enforce order became the chief source of resentment. The situation deteriorated until the morning of May 4, when an unplanned gathering of students confronted the assembled soldiers. At least some students behaved badly, hurling stones and epithets at the guard, but presenting no physical threat. For reasons that have never been determined, the guard opened fire—sixty-one rounds that randomly killed four and wounded nine students.[46]

AFTER ARMAGEDDON. After the killings at Kent State, the era of violent student protest effectively ended.[47] The tragedy at Kent State, followed by the killing of two students by police at Jackson State, climaxed the most disruptive year in the history of American higher education: "9,408 incidents of protest, 731 of them involving the police and arrests, 410 involving damage to property, [and] 230 involving violence to persons."[48] After Cambodia, universities acknowledged that events were spinning out of control by suspending classes and terminating the spring semester. When students returned in the fall 1970, their politics were no different, but the illusion that direct action would have any effect was replaced by sullen resignation and pervasive cynicism. Moreover, the most radical leaders, advocates of resistance who had been responsible for the most damaging confrontations of the 1968 Era, were largely missing—dropped out, suspended, or gone underground.[49] Shell-shocked universities, for their part, were prepared to appease any remotely feasible student demand in order to avoid confrontation. What then were the direct consequences of these and the other confrontations?

Considering the extreme demands and revolutionary objectives of protesters, there was never any chance for fulfillment. However, in other respects, the

46 *Report of the President's Commission on Campus Unrest* (Washington, DC: GPO, 1970).

47 Heineman, *Campus Wars*, 257–66: Antiwar protests persisted through 1972, often using civil disobedience but generally eschewing the violence advocated by 1968-Era extremists.

48 Gitlin, *Sixties*, 409.

49 Sympathizers have blamed the demise of the student movement on repression led by the federal government, especially the FBI's COINTELPRO, which included agents provocateurs, and the fragmenting effect of the women's liberation movement, which diverted women to their own special cause: Caroline Rolland-Diamond, *Chicago: le moment 68: Territoires de la contestation étudiantes et repression politique* (Paris: Éditions Syllepse, 2011), 331–36; Seth Rosenfeld, *Subversives: The FBI's War on Student Radicals, and Reagan's Rise to Power* (New York: Farrar, Straus, and Giroux, 2012), describes COINTELPRO at Berkeley as insidious but ineffectual: 414–15.

protesters achieved some degree of success. Insofar as Mark Rudd was determined to "screw the university," he delivered. Blacks at Cornell took down a liberal president in ignominious fashion. And Harvard radicals had the satisfaction of forcing the university into the embarrassment of calling in the police and alienating its largely liberal constituency. Whatever short-term gratification these triumphs may have brought, they appear hollow in a longer perspective.

Campaigns against defense research and ROTC obtained some results. Columbia was willing to concede on these issues. Stanford curtailed defense research and divested SRI. MIT likewise moved its huge weapons R&D operations into a separate organization, the Draper Labs. Weapons research thus continued in the same buildings by the same people, only now under new, nonuniversity management.

Black students obtained many of their objectives in terms of recruitment of students and faculty, special living arrangements, and black studies programs largely under their control. Universities had been willing to grant most of these demands as commitments to racial equality in higher education. Confrontations orchestrated by militant black students burnished the ideology of Black Power and succeeded in obtaining more far-reaching measures than universities considered prudent or academically legitimate.[50] These concessions were often achieved at some cost to their respective institutions. Harvard was acutely embarrassed by ceding control of its black studies program to students, but it soon rectified this anomaly. The capitulation at Cornell was a stain on the reputation of the university for years to come, as black students continued to defend their gains with the same belligerent tactics.[51] And San Francisco State's surrender to the BSU for a time undermined the academic credibility of the entire university.

Elsewhere, the direct results of the confrontations of the 1968 Era were largely negative. SUNY Buffalo perhaps suffered the greatest long-term damage. While it seems unlikely that it could have become the Berkeley of the East within the confines of the SUNY System, the destructiveness of the demonstrators and adversaries doomed its once promising bid for academic distinction, or even academic leadership within SUNY. At Berkeley, and Madison too, the academic core largely weathered the turmoil of these years. At Berkeley, much violence was

50   E.g., Joy Ann Williamson, *Black Power on Campus: The University of Illinois, 1965–1975* (Urbana: University of Illinois Press, 2003). Some writers praise these confrontations in terms of results achieved rather than the means employed: Martha Biondi, *The Black Revolution on Campus* (Berkeley: University of California Press, 2012); Ian Wilhelm, "Ripples from a Protest Past: In 1969, an Armed Occupation by Black Students Roiled Cornell's Campus. Here's Why It Still Matters Today," *Chronicle of Higher Education* (April 17, 2016).

51   Altschuler and Kramnick, *Cornell*, 290–96.

deflected off campus, although that was not true for Madison, where the August 1970 bombing of the Army Math Center by antiwar terrorists killed one victim and caused extensive damage. Some of these scars would heal, but the student rebellion brought permanent changes to American higher education.

AFTERMATH AND BEGINNING OF A NEW ERA

The events of the 1968 Era had a traumatic impact on universities that was scrutinized in an avalanche of publications detailing the confrontations at major universities, the worldwide student rebellion, and the apparent failings of university governance and practice.[52] Written so close to events, this literature reflected the themes and superficial analyses of the period. Youth, or students, were discovered to have inherent tendencies to rebel against the authority of the preceding generation, a finding that was documented back to medieval Oxford and Cambridge, even to Oedipus. Student charges against universities were given credence, though no such grievances had been evident short years before. Universities were now viewed and judged through a different cultural lens.

During the Liberal Hour, universities had been celebrated for producing new knowledge and training knowledge workers for the emerging postindustrial society. The ideology of basic research was ascendant, and society rewarded universities with appropriations, buildings, and research funds to pursue the activities they valued most highly. All this fueled the academic revolution, whose benefits extended far beyond the faculty and doctoral students. The 1960s achieved a high point in the intellectual tone and accomplishments of undergraduates, evidenced by the flourishing of liberal arts to the heights noted in Chapter 3. The unprecedented number of graduates who proceeded to doctoral studies was also testimony to the seriousness and stimulation of undergraduate studies. Even while the New Left devolved into nihilism, far more students found intellectual growth and commitment in their (supposedly irrelevant) studies. Far from neglecting students, the youngest and best-trained faculty in the history of higher education inspired 1960s students to pursue academic studies. The academic revolution, at least at the stronger colleges and universities, brought college education closer then ever to the academic ideal. The tragedy of the 1968 Era was that revolutionary rhetoric, counterculture affectations, and persistent disruption obscured the high level of academic achievement. The momentum of the academic

52 The President's Commission on Campus Unrest with a staff of hundreds produced an overview of events and issues by September 1970: *The Report of the President's Commission on Campus Unrest* (Washington, DC: GPO, 1970).

revolution would persist in disciplines, departments, and laboratories, but the zeitgeist affecting higher education, students, and the public changed at the end of the decade.

Writing at the end of this period, Jencks and Riesman expressed underlying skepticism even while depicting the ethos of the academic revolution. But in retrospect, Lewis Mayhew captured the essence of the transformation: "Between 1968 and 1970 profound changes ... were sharply at variance with [those] ideals, values, and practices.... Rationality and intellectuality, meritocracy, selectivity, collegiality and shared authority, campus autonomy, professional expertise and training, and the primacy of professors in instruction and evaluation—all were called into question." In short, academic authority was undermined, and universities found themselves defending their fundamental purposes against unsympathetic and hostile critics, external and internal.[53]

Clark Kerr observed in 1970 that authority in universities was a zero-sum situation, and that events of what he called the "climacteric" had produced gainers and losers.[54] The influence of governments over higher education had clearly advanced. The federal government now provided one-quarter of all funds for higher education, and the expansion of federal regulation under the Great Society had only begun (Chapter 6). States had become more intrusive, not only in response to campus anarchy but also to gain some control over growth and expenditures. The latter was a longer-term trend, as states consolidated campuses into systems and established coordinating bodies.[55] More immediately, state politicians were emboldened to propose legislation to punish student dissidents or curtail university funding, but enactment of such vindictive legislation was nearly always avoided. The California legislature, however, expressed its displeasure in 1970 by denying a 5 percent cost-of-living raise to only the faculty at the state university and colleges. The sacrosanct autonomy of public universities was lost in these years, and governments no longer had any compunction against intervening in the areas Mayhew named.

Kerr regarded governing boards and presidents as net losers. Governing boards saw their sphere of authority erode from the aggrandizement of governments. The governance of American colleges and universities had traditionally been based upon a strong president. Among the less academically distinguished institutions,

53   Lewis B. Mayhew, *Legacy of the Seventies: Experiment, Economy, Equality, and Expediency in American Higher Education* (San Francisco: Jossey Bass, 1977), 2; Geiger, *Research and Relevant Knowledge*, 252–54.

54   Clark Kerr, "Changing Loci of Power—Governance and Functions [1970]," in Kerr, *The Great Transformation of Higher Education, 1960–1980* (Albany: SUNY Press, 1991), 207–16.

55   Joseph W. Garbarino, *Faculty Bargaining: Change and Conflict* (New York: McGraw-Hill, 1975), 3–9; Robert O. Berdahl, *Statewide Coordination of Higher Education* (Washington, DC: ACE, 1971).

long-serving presidents often were regarded as benevolent autocrats. New faculty in the 1960s tended to challenge the status quo; new or strengthened faculty senates supported a growing faculty voice. A president's broad administrative authority became useless in political crises on polarized campuses. In such situations, presidents lacked supporting constituencies. The prevailing liberal cast of campuses was one reason. John Searle exaggerated only slightly in observing that "liberals are not primarily loyal to men (or even to institutions) but to principles.... Campus crises are nothing if not issues of principle—and the liberal's loyalties are to his principles and not to his superiors." In such situations, a double standard existed in which administrative defenses were assumed to be self-serving and disingenuous, but radical denunciations were given credence.[56] When administrations lost credibility, they lost control. But presidents were sometimes betrayed by their past actions and inability to comprehend their adversaries. Such manifest failures of Presidents Kirk, Perkins, and Pusey made their positions untenable and their departures inevitable.

Students appeared to be the great new force, "challenging the inner sanctum of the campus where faculty and administration have ruled supreme."[57] However, their most conspicuous gains came in abolishing the panoply of rules that had upheld order and decorum in student life. The legal basis for the doctrine of in loco parentis was undermined by a 1961 court decision that accorded students the right to due process. With the former basis for student discipline compromised, the arbitrary codes of conduct, dress, and student hours unraveled in the late 1960s and were largely abandoned by 1970. Student bodies now set standards, if any. Residence halls came under the control of their inhabitants, who accepted no constraints over living arrangements or behaviors like smoking pot. Curriculum was the second area in which students made gains. The establishment of black studies departments was a signal achievement. Although administrations were willing to form such units, confrontation won far-reaching concessions. Elsewhere, student advocacy brought pass-fail grading and provisions for experimental courses. Such measures were achieved with the support of sympathetic faculty who shared the prevailing permissiveness. Such attitudes tended to undermine some fundamental academic processes. When faculty adopted the manner and dress of students and conducted egalitarian classrooms, they generally eschewed rigorous grading as well. It was no coincidence that these years witnessed the greatest grade inflation in history. In general, student influence was not resisted. Student representatives were added to departmental, college, and university governing bodies, largely in the hope that having an official voice

56   Kerr, "Changing Loci," 212–13; Searle, *Campus War*, 93–102.
57   Kerr, "Changing Loci," 210.

might domesticate their demands, or perhaps because their attending such meet-ings was a perverse form of revenge.

Generalizing about "students" is at best inexact. Undergraduates in American higher education could be likened to Heraclitus's river, which is never the same at different points in time. A survey of students in 1969, at the height of the re-bellion, found students located across the political spectrum, with just 45 percent left of center. At leading universities that figure was closer to two-thirds, and they were three times more likely to identify as Far Left (15 percent). Southern students were more centrist, though they too sometimes engaged in protests, and students were comparatively more moderate across less distinguished col-leges and universities. But students everywhere endorsed the conventional veri-ties of the era with near unanimity (>90 percent): higher education should be available to all who want it; faculty should be free to present any ideas in class; coursework should be relevant to contemporary life; and teaching should be the primary criterion for faculty promotion.[58] Such convictions formed a founda-tion for what John Searle calls "dramatic categories," by which students inter-preted campus events through images that were impervious to counterarguments or evidence. Such categories as "black oppression" and "university complicity" undergirded the quasi-religious fanaticism of the confrontations described in the previous section. The portion of students identifying as "radical or far Left" rose from 4 percent in spring 1968 to 11 percent in spring 1970.[59] The politics would persist even as the fanaticism faded.

Student demonstrations continued through 1971 and 1972, but with decreas-ing frequency, intensity, and publicity. The student river flowed on. Whereas entering students in 1968 and 1969 arrived eager to protest, subsequent cohorts gradually turned more practical, materialistic, and resistant to manipulation—but not necessarily less liberal. Harvard students, for example, were more leftist in 1972 and 1974 than they had been in 1969, but instead of lumping all griev-ances together and blaming an evil system, they tended to react to individual issues separately.[60] Leftist students turned their energy from national and in-ternational enormities to efforts to affect local conditions. To withdraw from

58   Martin Trow, ed., *Teachers and Students: Aspects of American Higher Education* (New York: McGraw-Hill, 1975), 18–29; Jeffrey Turner, "From the Sit-ins to Vietnam: The Evolution of Student Activ-ism on Southern College Campuses, 1960–1970," *History of Higher Education Annual* 21 (2001): 103–36.

59   Searle, *Campus War*, 72–7; Gitlin, *Sixties*, 409.

60   Marshall W. Meyer, "After the Bust: Student Politics at Harvard, 1969–1972," in Riesman and Stadtman, *Academic Transformation*, 127–53; Seymour Martin Lipset and David Riesman, *Education and Politics at Harvard* (New York: McGraw-Hill, 1975), 252–56. By the second half of the 1970s, students were considerably more moderate: Arthur Levine, *When Dreams and Heroes Died* (San Francisco: Jossey-Bass, 1980).

the capitalist economy, they organized food co-ops, tenant organizations, and student-run book stores. Resistance was discredited; counterculture peace and love (and pot) were still honored. In politics, the student Left now sought to enlist the university to support an agenda of egalitarianism and social justice. Politically active students in the 1970s worked within the system to advance student interests through lobbying organizations and Public Interest Research Groups.[61] Protests were still a viable mode of advocacy, but these milder manifestations were often all that was needed to spur responses from administrations desperate to avoid confrontations. Appeasement was the rule.[62] This was especially the case with women's groups, the most effective advocacy coalitions on campus (Chapter 6). The student Left, diminished in size, found new causes as it became a permanent campus presence.

FACULTY. Faculty sometimes assert that they *are* the university,[63] since they embody its knowledge core. The academic revolution empowered faculty as never before, by privileging their contributions to the advancement of knowledge. By the late 1960s, faculty involvement in the governance and function of universities was also expanding, largely as a consequence of politicization and confrontation. College and university faculty were the most liberal identifiable group in America. Seven of nine voted for Lyndon Johnson in 1964. But there were four distinct gradients within that population; the highest proportion of liberals were found (1) at the most academically eminent institutions; (2) among high achievers in their fields; (3) in humanities and social sciences; and (4) among the younger faculty.[64] With the rise of the New Left, the preponderance of liberal faculty were supportive of student demands and increasingly opposed to the Vietnam War, but by 1968 they had divided into more moderate and more radical factions. The two defining issues were support or criticism of student disruptions, and advocacy or opposition for attempts to force universities and professional organizations to officially endorse antiwar and other leftist declarations. Faculty played a decisive role in some campus crises. When radical faculty supported protesters, as they did at Buffalo and San Francisco State, administrations

61   Philip G. Altbach and Robert Cohen, "American Student Activism: The Post-Sixties Transformation," *Journal of Higher Education* 61, 1 (1990): 32–49; Levine, *When Dreams and Heroes Died*, 39–54.

62   Geiger, *Research and Relevant Knowledge*, 254–56.

63   E.g., Richard Hofstadter, "Columbia University Commencement Address, 1968," in Wilson Smith and Thomas Bender, eds., *American Higher Education Transformed, 1940–2005: Documenting the National Discourse* (Baltimore: Johns Hopkins University Press, 2008), 383–86.

64   Everett Carll Ladd, Jr., and Seymour Martin Lipset, *Academics, Politics, and the 1972 Election* (Washington, DC: American Enterprise Institute, 1973).

lost control. Moderate faculty, on the other hand, failed to control events at Columbia and Cornell. The political divisions of faculty affected their disciplines as well.

The conflicts among faculty were most intense in the professional disciplinary associations. These were weak, membership organizations devoted to advancing their fields and recognizing meritorious contributions through meetings and publications. Annual meetings drew the most active and interested members, and attendees at the business sessions in which resolutions were voted were ordinarily even more narrowly self-selected. Radical caucuses organized in all the humanities and social science associations, and "professional meetings by the late 1960s came to resemble a war zone."[65] These were largely generational wars, with young insurgents seeking to wrest control of the association from its patriarchs and commit it to New Left positions. Antiwar resolutions were carried in the Modern Language Association and the associations for anthropology, political science, and sociology. In 1969, moderates in the American Historical Association outorganized the radicals to quash an antiwar resolution and block the presidential candidacy of New Left media star, Staughton Lynd. (An antiwar resolution was passed a few years later.) But these were surface manifestations of deeper struggles that pervaded these fields. All were rent by bitter internecine struggles over ideology, methodology, and tactics. Insurgent literary scholars trashed the New Criticism, sociologists belittled structural-functionalism, political scientists touted alternatives to behavioralism, and historians rejected objectivity. All fields debated whether the university was a repressive institution, as the New Left maintained, or a sanctuary of intellectual freedom; and whether scholarship should aim to advance the class struggle or respect the value-free ideal. But the battle lines were not always obvious. At the 1969 AHA meeting, the radical insurgents were vehemently opposed by the Marxists of an older generation who defended the university. Marxism presented an ideological challenge in all these fields.[66] The Marxist Literary Group was established at this time and soon became the largest group affiliated with the MLA, and the ASA later established a section on Marxist sociology. All these differences were also contested on home campuses.

When it came to departmental and university politics, the liberal majority might divide in a variety of ways, but those further to the left were likely to pri-

---

65   Ira Katznelson, "From the Street to the Lecture Halls: The 1960s," in Thomas Bender and Carl E. Schorske, eds., *American Academic Culture in Transformation: Fifty Years, Four Disciplines* (Princeton: Princeton University Press, 1997), 331–52, quote p. 342.

66   Peter Novick, *That Noble Dream: The "Objectivity Question" and the American Historical Profession* (New York: Cambridge University Press, 1988), 417–38. For the 1969 generational clash at the MLA, see Margery Sabin, "Evolution and Revolution: Change in the Literary Humanities, 1968–1995," in Alvin Kernan, ed., *What's Happened to the Humanities?* (Princeton: Princeton University Press, 1997), 84–103.

oritize social goals, and the moderates to support academic standards. The more liberal factions on many campuses organized into parties or caucuses, which magnified their influence beyond mere numbers. By anticipating issues and participating in meetings, they were often able to shape agendas and affect voting. Active participation was itself an advantage, since colleagues more committed to academic work tended to avoid such drudgery. Unlike the war zones of professional meetings, faculty meetings were more likely to consider mundane local issues. Moderate liberals tended to be tolerant and progressive and particularly respectful of due process. They generally accepted liberal changes that broadened curriculum or enhanced social inclusiveness. When more divisive issues arose, the academic Left could count on the backing of student activists. Thus, after the crises of the 1968 Era, the academic Left continued to have a strong presence, especially at the more distinguished institutions.[67]

The tolerance for extreme leftist behaviors seemed to reach a limit at Stanford. H. Bruce Franklin was a tenured English professor and a zealous communist, dedicated to what he was convinced would be an imminent revolution. He proclaimed this certitude to all listeners and worked toward this end in his teaching and by leading student protests. He propounded "revolutionary truth" and condemned the university as a bourgeois institution. In short, he actively opposed everything that Stanford University stood for while exploiting its protection as a tenured faculty member. In February 1971 President Richard Lyman suspended him for leading an occupation of the computer center, urging protesters to ignore police orders to disperse, and inciting violence and the destruction of university property. An advisory board of seven eminent faculty listened to a million words of public testimony before recommending five to two for dismissal.[68] The Franklin case paralyzed the university for most of a year and provoked a national debate over the limits of academic freedom. In retrospect, one of his colleagues marveled that faculty who disapproved of Franklin's antics were reluctant to criticize him publicly or sanction his removal.[69] Despite the grueling exercise of due process, some faculty still criticized the university, as did many

---

67   Searle, *Campus War*, 116–41. Judging by votes for McGovern in 1972 vs. Humphrey in 1968, older faculty and those outside the humanities and social sciences had become less liberal, but their counterparts remained just as liberal: Ladd and Lipset, *Academics*, 78.

68   Franklin joined Maoist movements for a short time and edited *The Essential Stalin* (1972), then returned to teaching with temporary appointments at Wesleyan and Yale followed by a tenured appointment at Rutgers-Newark (1975). Subsequently, he was widely celebrated in leftist academic circles for contributions to American Studies, no longer Maoist but always critical of the United States, as was common in that field.

69   In turn, he called them "ignorant self-deceived parasites": William M. Chace, *100 Semesters* (Princeton: Princeton University Press, 2006), 143–52.

throughout the country.[70] After 1970, university administrations elsewhere felt emboldened to begin rolling back the excesses of extremists among the faculty, which was invariably a prolonged process against considerable faculty resistance.[71]

During these same years, faculty altered their role in university governance in a most orderly and bureaucratic way—by unionizing. The unionization movement was launched during the 1968 Era and accelerated through the early 1970s. By 1974, 14 percent of faculty at four-year institutions were organized in most of the states where it was legal. At the outset, unionization seemed to be linked with the liberal inclinations that faculty demonstrated in other matters. A 1969 survey found the majority of faculty in elite universities to be favorable, but five years later none of those institutions had named a bargaining agent. Active scholars, it seemed, valued professionalism over solidarity.[72] Instead, unionization was affected by diverse and unrelated factors. Most important initially were state laws permitting collective bargaining by public employees. Once that threshold had been crossed, outcomes depended upon the different institutional sectors, determination of the composition of bargaining units, and competition between the more professionally oriented American Association of University Professors and the more trade-union-oriented American Federation of Teachers (AFT) and National Education Association (NEA).[73]

New York's 1967 Taylor Act inaugurated the unionization movement. The City University of New York, where salaries were already pegged to the city's unionized teachers, quickly voted the next year to organize its twenty campuses. The voting revealed a pattern of support for unionization that would hold throughout the country:

70   Ibid., 143–52; Donald Kennedy, *Academic Duty* (Cambridge, MA: Harvard University Press, 1997), 131–34. Franklin's views are reprinted in Smith and Bender, *American Higher Education Transformed*, 362–69. The chair of the advisory board who voted against dismissal, Donald Kennedy, was appointed the next president. Academic freedom at Stanford was defined with the new Statement on Faculty Discipline (1972).

71   For the process of asserting administrative control over the radical colleges at SUNY Buffalo, see Levine, *Why Innovation Fails*, 85–151.

72   Garbarino, *Faculty Bargaining*, 52–54; Everett Carll Ladd, Jr., and Seymour Martin Lipset, *Professors, Unions, and American Higher Education* (Berkeley, CA: Carnegie Commission on Higher Education, 1973).

73   The National Education Association predominated in K-12 education and was consequently favored by community colleges. The American Federation of Teachers was associated with trade unionism and considered more militant, and it tended to be either shunned or embraced for that reason. The American Association of University Professors had traditionally defended the values of the academic profession: Philo A. Hutcheson, *A Professional Professoriate: Unionization, Bureaucratization, and the AAUP* (Nashville, TN: Vanderbilt University Press, 2000).

The lower the tier of academe, in terms of security, income, prestige, and involvement in the graduate scholarly-research culture, the stronger the vote for unionization ... ; the higher the level, the greater the likelihood of votes for "no representation," or for the least "union-like" faculty organization on the ballot."[74]

The CUNY union was decidedly egalitarian, equalizing salaries across junior and senior colleges and negotiating more generous raises for the lower echelons. By 1974, two CUNY campuses had the highest-paid faculties in the country.

Unionization of the unified Hawaiian system of higher education exemplified the same pattern of preferences. The run-off election pitted the AFT, a classically egalitarian trade union, against an AAUP unit that promised to preserve quality and academic competitiveness at the University of Hawaii. The majority of university faculty favored the AAUP, but they were swamped by AFT supporters at the community colleges. Michigan's public colleges and universities duplicated this pattern while acting independently. The University of Michigan had no interest in unions (though the teaching assistants did organize), but at Michigan State a protracted process ended with a decisive vote of "no agent." Wayne State and Oakland Universities voted to unionize with the more professional AAUP; regional and community colleges voted for the NEA or AFT.[75]

The majority of unionized campuses and faculty members were in state systems, which included doctoral universities in only a few cases, like Hawaii.[76] The SUNY university centers and medical schools attempted to fend off unionization by favoring the academic senate as a bargaining agent but were included in a joint NEA-AFT union voted by the entire system. Rutgers organized with the AAUP out of fear of being swept into the AFT union that organized the eight New Jersey state colleges. By 1974, state systems of regional colleges had opted to unionize in Pennsylvania, Nebraska (NEA), Vermont, and Massachusetts (AFT)—joining CUNY, SUNY, Hawaii, and New Jersey. The disgruntled faculty of the huge California State system would unionize when allowed to at the end of the decade. These faculties had many reasons to trade the vision of academic meritocracy for the tangible rewards, both psychological and monetary, of collective security. Remote state system bureaucracies allowed little autonomy

---

74   Ladd and Lipset, *Professors*, 49.

75   Ibid., 50–54.

76   The National Labor Relations Act (1970) covered most private schools and permitted them to unionize, but few chose to do so. Unions were voted down almost as often as accepted, usually with the AAUP. At St John's University a bitter dispute between faculty and administration provoked unionization. Garbarino, *Faculty Bargaining*, 57–60, 87, 103.

for individual campuses and hence little scope for shared governance. The shortage of faculty ended with the 1960s, leaving them with little market power. And a widespread mood of relative deprivation, exacerbated by inflation, encouraged expectations of salary gains. Collective bargaining largely delivered the expected benefits. The lower ranks of faculty and professionals enjoyed the greatest relative gains, but everyone received job security, ease of promotion and tenure, higher salaries, and a voice in governance.[77]

THE NEW EGALITARIAN AGE. The acceptance of trade unionism by faculty was symptomatic of a public disenchantment with American higher education. The ethos of the academic revolution was now replaced by widespread allegations that colleges and universities had failed as institutions and that the system required far-reaching change. This new consensus was expressed in quasi-official documents, two reports to the secretary of the U.S. Department of Health, Education, and Welfare (HEW) by task forces led by Frank Newman, and a report by leading scholars and university presidents—the academic establishment—who formed the Assembly on University Goals and Governance. Newman pronounced in his second report that American higher education had evolved from a period of meritocratic values to a new "egalitarian" age in which "increasingly, the American public has assumed that everyone should have a chance at a college education." The assembly's eighty-five "theses" included a highly qualified defense of academic merit, but they also endorsed the major changes recommended in the Newman reports.[78]

Traditional patterns of undergraduate and graduate education were labeled as dysfunctional. The Newman Report attacked the "academic lockstep" of students proceeding directly from high school to college to graduate school. In calling for education that was less academic and more integrated with experience, it urged students to delay entering college, to stop out, or to attend part time. This advice was coupled with animadversions toward the power of university credentials in hiring and careers. To compensate, recognition and equivalent status should be given to vocational and technical education, including that offered by proprietary schools. The domination of the curriculum by theoretical academic specialties (i.e., disciplines) was roundly criticized. Relevance to experience and

---

77 Ladd and Lipset, *Professors*; Garbarino, *Faculty Bargaining*, 87 et passim.

78 Frank Newman et al., *Report on Higher Education, March, 1971* (Washington, DC: GPO, 1971); Frank Newman et al., *The Second Newman Report: National Policy and Higher Education* (Cambridge, MA: MIT Press, 1973), 2; Martin Meyerson et al., "A First Report of the Assembly on University Goals and Governance," *Chronicle of Higher Education* (January 18, 1971), reprinted as "The Assembly on University Goals and Governance," *American Higher Education: Toward an Uncertain Future, volume II: Daedalus* 104, 1 (Winter 1975): 322–46.

curricular experiments were encouraged, along with the usual bromides about placing greater value on teaching.[79] Graduate education was denigrated as "excessively specialized and unreasonably time-consuming." The "near monopoly" of the PhD for academic appointments was "challenged," with a recommendation that more professors be hired on the basis of practical accomplishments. More surprising, especially for the assembly, was the restrictive position taken toward academic research. Their report disdained large-scale sponsored research and advocated instead that university research be tied to educational purposes and supported with internal rather than federal funds.[80] Seemingly vanished was the erstwhile belief that university research was vital to national needs, could contribute to alleviating social problems, and played a central role in a knowledge-based society.

As the traumatic events of the crisis years receded, a consensus emerged over the problems facing higher education and the directions it ought to take to meet the challenges of the new era. This consensus was articulated by the Carnegie Commission on Higher Education. Under Clark Kerr's direction, it sponsored and published eighty research projects and twenty-one policy reports (1967–1973), which composed the broadest and most competent examination of American higher education ever conducted. Its mandate was to examine "where American higher education is now headed, where it should be headed, and how it is going to get there."[81] Thus, the reports offered specific policy recommendations that were based on the research projects but also reflected the cultural values of egalitarianism and social justice that characterized the new era. In this sense, the commission's views mirrored the consensus of the higher education establishment in the aftermath of the student rebellion.

Universal higher education was presented as inevitable and desirable. All high school graduates should have a right to two years of postsecondary education. The commission looked to the states to provide community colleges, which would be open to all eighteen-year-old-and-over aspirants and within commuting distance of all citizens. More flexible degrees and certificates should be devised, and continuing education should be made available to adults throughout their lives. "Postsecondary education" should encompass proprietary schools, and

79   Newman, *Report on Higher Education*, 4–19; "The Assembly on University Goals and Governance," 327–30, 332–33.

80   Newman, *Report on Higher Education*, 33–43, 76–78, 82–86; "The Assembly on University Goals and Governance," 331, 337–38.

81   Research projects are summarized in *Sponsored Research of the Carnegie Commission on Higher Education* (New York: McGraw-Hill, 1975), quote p. 3; policy reports are in *A Digest of Reports of the Carnegie Commission on Higher Education: With an Index of Recommendations and Suggested Assignments of Responsibility for Action* (New York: McGraw-Hill, 1974).

their students be made eligible for public student financial aid (a source of much future grief).[82] Universal higher education implied a heavy vocational component, and both private and regional public colleges were urged to devise more career-oriented programs and seek transfer students from the two-year sector. For the more effective recruitment of disadvantaged students, the commission proposed regional coordination. For Blacks, the commission advocated public programs to upgrade and modernize the HBCUs. For women, it recommended measures to ensure equality of educational opportunity and affirmative action to boost faculty hiring, thus endorsing the growing momentum of the women's movement (Chapter 6). The commission looked to the federal government to accomplish many of its goals. It proposed a national foundation for the development of higher education, which would have multiple responsibilities for planning and funding a variety of institutional programs. New forms of federal student financial aid were outlined, along with several types of institutional aid. Specific federal programs were proposed for virtually all worthy purposes: educational technology, urban universities, developing institutions, community colleges, HBCUs, libraries, and international studies. The states too were advised to spend more for new and existing forms of support. The commission proposed spending metrics to measure state effort, or lack thereof. Additionally, specific funding should aid the health and competitiveness of the private sector and provide additional aid to community colleges and urban universities. In sum, the main thrust of the commission's recommendations sought to expand nontraditional forms of higher education in order to increase the participation of underserved populations. It reflected the mentality of the new era that higher education was a human right, that achieving greater participation by underrepresented groups advanced social justice, and that accomplishing this was the responsibility of government.

Traditional higher education and the ethos of the academic revolution were now tainted by association with the student rebellion. In an egalitarian era, they connoted hierarchy, meritocracy, and inequality. Largely neglected by the commission, the coverage traditional colleges and universities did receive reflected this general disfavor. Liberal education was no longer honored as an ideal: "The liberal university, which transmitted a culture in which knowledge and a moral conception of its use were joined, is dying." Liberal arts colleges were enjoined to expand and diversify their enrollments, "undertake substantial change of internal government and management," and become more efficient by simplifying curricula. Smaller private colleges might be worthy of public support if "awarded in such a way as to preclude the ... college's aping its elitist confreres." Remarks

---

82   See Chapter 8.

on graduate education focused on government responsibilities to block new PhD programs and roll back some existing ones. As a substitute, it advocated the Doctor of Arts as a new, non-research degree for postsecondary teachers. The commission would limit federal support for scientific research to a fixed percentage of the GNP but increase research spending for social science, humanities, creative arts, instructional technology, and the academically disadvantaged.[83]

Out of favor or not, traditional higher education would continue to serve the majority of college, graduate, and professional students; however, it labored, underappreciated and underfunded, against several of the major trends of the 1970s. The Carnegie Commission was correct about the general thrust favoring nontraditional forms and clienteles, but it was overly optimistic about many policy recommendations and short-sighted about others. Governments moved aggressively to intervene in higher education, but they fell short in funding most programs envisioned by the commission. Nontraditional students proved less eager to take advantage of the opportunities for postsecondary education than higher education reformers had supposed. Disadvantaged minorities made significant gains in the early 1970s that proved difficult to sustain near term. None gained more than not-so-disadvantaged women. And undergraduates voted with their majors against the liberal arts and in favor of business—a career destination not considered by the commission. The 1970s proved to be difficult times for American higher education, which was buffeted by economic and cultural trends largely beyond its control.[84]

83   *Sponsored Research*, 72, 86–87, 91. The commission strongly advocated the expansion and strengthening of training and research in health care.

84   For an overview, see Mayhew, *Legacy of the Seventies*.

★ 6 ★

SURVIVING THE SEVENTIES

N THE FIRST HALF OF THE 1970S, THE FEDERAL GOVERNMENT attempted to reshape fundamental aspects of American higher education through legislation and through regulation. In the second half of the decade, market forces played a larger role in shaping the behavior of colleges and universities, as evolving student preferences and financial pressures affected the institutional order that had emerged from the 1960s. Unlike that decade, when the actions of governments and markets had created a golden age for colleges and universities, at least until the turmoil of the final years, the developments of the 1970s acted against the grain, requiring continual adaptation to challenging conditions.

THE FEDERAL GOVERNMENT AND HIGHER EDUCATION

President Richard M. Nixon's first term saw the most liberal legislation since the heyday of Lyndon Johnson's Great Society. A Democratic Congress aggressively addressed the nation's shortcomings, and the president took little direct interest in domestic affairs. Legislation established the Environmental Protection Agency, the Occupational Safety and Health Administration, Supplemental Security Income, and greater spending on poverty programs. The Nixon administration also transformed the enforcement of civil rights with affirmative action.[1] And Congress formulated federal policy toward higher education with the Education Amendments of 1972.

The Education Amendments, so-called because they incorporated previous legislation on higher education as well as new measures, were the most consequential federal intervention in higher education since the Morrill Land-Grant Act of 1862. The provisions they established for student financial aid would, forty years later, be the largest source of funds for higher education.[2] The prohibition in Title IX of discrimination against women would spawn an entire

---

1 James T. Patterson, *Grand Expectations: The United States, 1945–1971* (New York: Oxford University Press, 1996), 718–29.
2 See Chapter 8.

217

industry of women's intercollegiate athletics as well as forcing a recalibration of cultural assumptions about gender. The law was prompted by a widespread conviction that higher education faced a financial crisis that could be remedied only by the federal fisc. A consensus also existed that the nation fell well short of equal educational opportunity and that a federal effort was needed to advance toward that goal. Further, the disturbances of the late 1960s seemed evidence of grave failures in higher education.

The need for such legislation may appear puzzling in retrospect. The nation's colleges and universities had absorbed the demographic Tidal Wave, increasing from 3.4 million students in 1959 to 7.5 million in 1969 (+122 percent); and educational expenditures in that decade had grown from $4.5 billion to $15.8 billion (+250 percent). However, the goal of equal educational opportunity was rooted in the Liberal Hour, and the additional financial needs reflected the aspirations of that era. The 1965 Higher Education Act created the first federal scholarships based solely on financial need, a long-standing goal of reformers first proposed by the President's Commission on Higher Education. Educational Opportunity Grants were intended primarily for students "of exceptional financial need." They were supplemented by the College Work-Study Program, enacted the previous year in the Office of Economic Opportunity, and by federal insurance for student loans. Funding for these three campus-based programs expanded rapidly to more than $400 million in 1970 but was still insufficient to produce more than a minor impact on opportunity. Administered by institutions, they were available only to already-enrolled students. Another program, Strengthening Developing Institutions, namely HBCUs, provided $28 million. Congress regarded the Higher Education Act as a work in progress, amending it in 1966 and 1968, and considered the goal of equalizing educational opportunity as unfinished business.[3]

Participation in higher education has always been stratified by socioeconomic status (Chapters 2 and 4). In the 1960s, individuals from the top economic quartile were three times more likely than those from the bottom quartile to attend and graduate from a four-year institution. The growth of mass higher education in the decade brought substantial increases in first-generation attendees from middle- and lower-middle class families but little progress among those at the bottom of the economic pyramid. However, a study specifically aimed at extending access by identifying "new students" observed: "For men, at least, low academic ability is keeping more students from continuing their education than is

3   Lawrence E. Gladieux and Thomas R. Wolanin, *Congress and the Colleges: The National Politics of Higher Education* (Lexington, MA: Lexington Books, 1976), 11–13.

the barrier of lack of financial resources."[4] An article of liberal faith nonetheless held that social justice would be served by providing the financial means for more poor students to attend college.[5] This belief was powerfully reinforced, if not motivated, by the racial crisis. The historic underrepresentation of Blacks was being gradually ameliorated by the actions of individual institutions, as already seen; but for Blacks overall, aspirations to higher education exceeded attainments.[6] And the plight of Blacks raised awareness of the scarcity of Hispanics and Native Americans in college. For liberals, higher education was part of the "rights revolution"; in fact, an early proposal was entitled "The Higher Education Bill of Rights."[7] Thus, enlargement of federal student aid for needy students was certain to be addressed in the impending legislation.

Urgency was heightened by a perceived financial crisis. Between 1968 and 1973, fourteen separate studies documented varying degrees of financial distress at all types of institutions. Most publicized was a Carnegie Commission study by Earl Cheit with a self-explanatory title, *The New Depression in Higher Education*.[8] Conducted in 1970, the study found that half of public institutions and three-quarters of private ones were "in financial difficulty" or "headed for financial trouble." The basic cause, first apparent around 1967, was expenditures increasing more rapidly than revenues. Expenditures were forecast to rise by 6–7 percent, even with some belt-tightening, and income by 4.4–4.8 percent. However, the problem stemmed from the 1960s, when the academic and enrollment expansion already described caused core spending to rise by an average of 8 percent per year. This spending momentum persisted after 1967, when adverse trends affected both income and costs. Rising inflation pushed all costs higher, but particularly those tied to academic upgrading and competition. The new social agenda increased commitments to student aid. At the same time, federal research funds leveled off, as did state appropriations and private giving for many

4 K. Patricia Cross, *Beyond the Open Door* (San Francisco: Jossey-Bass, 1971), 10–11.

5 Little sociological evidence suggested an unmet demand for higher education among low-income high school graduates. On surveys, 15–30 percent of nonattenders indicated financial limitations, but low-income individuals faced myriad additional obstacles: 60 percent of students from the lowest quartile were in the lowest two ability quintiles: Robert H. Berls, "Higher Education Opportunity and Achievement in the United States," in *Economics and Financing of Higher Education in the United States* (Joint Economic Committee, 91st Congress: GPO, 1969), 145–206.

6 Cross, *Beyond the Open Door*, 114–30.

7 Samuel Walker, *The Rights Revolution: Rights and Community in Modern America* (New York: Oxford University Press, 1998); Patterson, *Grand Expectations*, 568, 638; Gladieux and Wolanin, *Congress*, 92.

8 National Commission on the Financing of Postsecondary Education, *Financing Postsecondary Education in the United States* (Washington, DC: GPO, 1973), 415–19; Earl F. Cheit, *The New Depression in Higher Education: A Study of Financial Conditions at 41 Colleges and Universities* (New York: McGraw-Hill, 1971).

institutions. Financial shortfalls appeared across the institutional spectrum. In the *New Depression* sample, Stanford and UC Berkeley were "in financial difficulty"; Harvard, Chicago, Michigan, and Minnesota were "headed" that way. Private institutions were more vulnerable. First-year matriculates in the private sector declined after 1965, and the growing tuition gap with public institutions was a source of increasing concern. Adjusting from an era of supercharged growth and ambition was painful for most all institutions, but now they looked to the federal government for relief.[9]

In 1970, Congress began seriously considering higher education legislation with two potential mandates: financial aid for colleges and universities was the top priority for institutions and the higher education associations representing them, while broadening educational opportunity was an almost sacrosanct liberal value. The Carnegie Commission, with Clark Kerr as spokesman, played an influential role. Espousing "quality and equality," it advocated federal aid for low-income students as well as public support for the other measures noted in Chapter 5. An internal report by Alice Rivlin made equality of educational opportunity the touchstone and ominously argued that aid for institutions would do nothing to advance it. The 1971 Newman Report criticized existing colleges and universities, arguing that they needed change, not more money to preserve the status quo. These basic views were sifted, sorted, attacked, and defended by senators and representatives for more than a year before they produced the Education Amendments in mid-1972.[10] In the end, education opportunity was favored over institutional balance sheets, and nontraditional postsecondary education received a federal imprimatur.

The amendments established a charter for need-based federal student aid. The centerpiece was Basic Education Opportunity Grants (BEOGs; later called Pell Grants after the senator who steered the bill's passage). These promised up to $1,400 in annual support, depending on family income, intended to cover 50 percent of the cost of attendance at a postsecondary institution, including proprietary vocational schools. The campus-based programs, which tended to benefit moderate-income students and the private sector, continued to receive Congressional backing; in fact, these programs had to be fully funded before funds could be appropriated to the BEOGs. The student loan system was given needed liquidity by creating the Student Loan Marketing Association. And matching

---

9 A follow-up study by Cheit two years later found institutions adapting: "Whatever the validity of the charge that neither exhortations, rebellion, or new outside world can make colleges and universities change, it is now clear that a shortage of money can": Earl F. Cheit, *The New Depression in Higher Education—Two Years Later* (Berkeley, CA: Carnegie Commission on Higher Education, 1973), 15. The oil shock of 1973 and the resulting recession soon brought even more difficult conditions.

10 The legislative process is recounted in detail in Gladieux and Wolanin, *Congress*.

federal funds for State Student Incentive Grants encouraged states to provide supplemental student aid programs. The tilt toward nontraditional forms was symbolized in the substitution of "postsecondary" for "higher education" in government-speak. The Office of Education was instructed to form new bureaus for occupational and adult education and community colleges. The Carnegie hope for the National Foundation for the Development of Higher Education was whittled down to the small Fund for the Improvement of Postsecondary Education (FIPSE), whose suggested focus on innovations for alternative forms of career education largely reflected the thrust of the Newman Report.

The amendments included Title IX, stating: "No person in the United States shall, on the basis of sex, be excluded from participation in, denied the benefits of, or be subjected to discrimination under any education program or activity receiving Federal financial assistance." The first attempt to include such language was rejected in the Senate as "non-germane." It was included in the House version by Rep. Edith Green (D, Oregon), a women's rights advocate who was the law's chief backer. The Senate then accepted it without objection. Sex discrimination in hiring had been outlawed by Title VII of the 1964 Civil Rights Act, but that provision did not apply to educational institutions until amended in 1972. Congress the same year overwhelmingly passed the Equal Rights Amendment (1972) and other legislation with clauses prohibiting sex discrimination. Title IX appeared to be a natural extension of the rights revolution and was accepted by both political parties. And for good reason. Professional schools, for example, typically used quotas to limit the admission of women. More generally, traditional gender roles, now increasingly contested, slighted women in numerous ways, which was demonstrated in "massive" statistical evidence of unequal treatment.[11] Passed almost unnoticed in 1972, Title IX soon raised a storm of controversy when applied to the unique circumstances of male and female intercollegiate athletics (below).

Title IX was but one example of a new relationship between universities and the federal government: the imposition of federal mandates, based on abstract conceptions of the social good (rights), that substantially affected established practices. Hitherto, universities were considered agents for the common good and were accorded autonomy to manage their own affairs for research, learning, and teaching. In the 1970s, that mystique evaporated, undermined by the student rebellion, perceptions of mismanagement, and the critique of traditional institutions. As one commentator explicitly stated: "Higher education, like business and the professions, cannot be trusted to serve the public interest on its own

---

11 John D. Skrentny, *The Minority Rights Revolution* (Cambridge, MA: Harvard University Press, 2002), 230–49.

initiative."[12] Government intervention was enlarged and emboldened by the rights revolution and by the expansion of governmental responsibilities that began with the Great Society. These factors subjected universities to two kinds of regulation. Universities were included under laws governing other employers. Thus, private colleges were made subject to the National Labor Relations Board and hence open to unionization. The voluminous regulations of the Occupational Safety and Health Administration applied to higher education too. Other regulations were imposed specifically on higher education.[13] Those not only disregarded the previous deference to autonomy, but they were imposed without hearings or serious consideration of their larger impacts. Edith Green deliberately discouraged discussion of the implications of Title IX, especially for athletics.[14] The Educational Amendments also ordered the states to create bodies (termed 1202 Commissions) to coordinate state higher education. Research was not spared. Regulations were proposed that would have stifled experiments with recombinant DNA, but complaints from scientists brought relief in this case. However, HEW established cumbersome bureaucratic procedures for all research involving human subjects, a solution that far exceeded the problem. The Buckley Amendment, which opened confidential files to students, was enacted on an impulse without any attempt to determine if a problem existed or if it should be a federal concern. In an appalling piece of special interest legislation, the Health Professions Education Assistance Act of 1976 required medical schools to admit transfer students who had studied abroad after failing to gain admission to an American school. In the single successful example of principled opposition, several universities risked their federal funds by refusing to accede, and the most coercive features of the law were repealed.[15]

AFFIRMATIVE ACTION. The federal imposition with the greatest impact, affirmative action, was both a general policy and unique in its application to higher education. Implemented by the first Nixon administration, affirmative action was chiefly designed like all civil rights legislation to address the unique situation

---

12   Roger L. Geiger, *Research and Relevant Knowledge: American Research Universities Since World War II* (New York: Oxford University Press, 1993), 260; Walter C. Hobbs, ed., *Government Regulation of Higher Education* (Cambridge: Ballinger, 1978), quote p. 29.

13   Various studies estimated regulatory costs as 1–8 percent of institutional budgets: Hugh Davis Graham and Nancy Diamond, *The Rise of American Research Universities: Elites and Challengers in the Postwar Era* (Baltimore: Johns Hopkins University Press, 1997), 96–99.

14   Skrentny, *Minority Rights Revolution*, 247–49. The amendments generated intense controversy over an antibusing provision, which pleased neither side and overshadowed other issues.

15   Geiger, *Research and Relevant Knowledge*, 257–60; Graham and Diamond, *Rise of American Research Universities*, 98.

of African Americans.[16] Other groups were included without any specific prompting. The 1964 Civil Rights Act defined minorities to include Spanish-heritage groups, Native Americans, and Asians, and this definition was used for all subsequent laws and regulations. Women had been included in Title VII (hiring) but only gradually assumed the status of an official minority. By 1969 the racial crisis created acute concern that Title VII should be extended beyond the limited mission of forbidding job discrimination against individuals, so that real employment gains for Blacks could be achieved. The 1969 Philadelphia Plan ordered the building trades of that city to establish hiring goals for minorities based on local supply and timetables for achieving them. The key was linking enforcement to Federal Contract Compliance: no affirmative action plan, no federal contract.[17]

Civil rights laws provided the legal backing for affirmative action, but the policy was created by executive orders, implemented by the federal bureaucracy in the Departments of Labor and HEW, and enforced through the Office of Civil Rights (OCR) and the Equal Employment Opportunity Commission. In higher education, the impetus for imposing affirmative action came from women's groups on and off campus. The basic requirements for affirmative action were decreed in executive orders (1970–1972). According to the 1972 HEW *Guidelines*:

> *Affirmative action* requires the contractor to do more than ensure employment neutrality with regard to race, color, religion, sex, and national origin.… Affirmative action requires the employer to make additional efforts to recruit, employ and promote qualified members of groups formerly excluded, even if that exclusion cannot be traced to particular discriminatory actions.

These efforts included "the required compilation of available data on women and minorities" and setting "goals to overcome" underrepresentation "within a reasonable time."[18] The government was adamant that such goals were not quotas, which were illegal. For the regulated, however, unmet goals could mean difficult negotiations or lawsuits, while meeting these non-quotas was a safe harbor. Moreover, a single complaint triggered investigation of the entire institution.

---

16 Skrentny, *Minority Rights Revolution*: Title IX basically extended the discrimination prohibition of Title VI of the Civil Rights Act to women in education.

17 John D. Skrentny, *The Ironies of Affirmative Action: Politics, Culture, and Justice in America* (Chicago: University of Chicago Press, 1996), 133–39.

18 *Higher Education Guidelines, Executive Order 11246* (HEW, October 1972), quoted in Carnegie Council, *Making Affirmative Action Work in Higher Education* (San Francisco: Jossey-Bass, 1975), 115–17; the Department of Labor "Revised Order No. 4" (December 4, 1971) was more draconian: ibid., 97–100, 115–29.

In 1968 Bernice Sandler organized the Women's Equity Action League (WEAL), which advanced its cause in Washington and on campuses.[19] WEAL sent letters to campus groups across the country apprising them of executive orders requiring nondiscrimination language. In 1970 Sandler filed a class-action antidiscrimination suit against all colleges and universities with federal contracts and then helped organize specific complaints against more than 250 universities. WEAL had to overcome initial resistance at Labor and HEW, where the bureaucracy was committed to attacking discrimination against minorities, not women. Leading research universities resisted too, but not for long. Harvard initially refused to release personnel records, but 1,400 students and employees signed a petition for an affirmative action plan, and the university learned that language in its federal contracts required such disclosure. At the University of Michigan, administrators were at first dismissive, but women volunteers compiled statistics on underrepresentation that prompted creation of a Commission for Women and, ultimately, reorganization of the personnel system, including equity pay upgrades. In Washington, WEAL lobbied with others to obtain for women equal inclusion in affirmative action regulations for minorities, which was achieved in 1971.[20] Administrators and the preponderance of the higher education community soon supported the social goals of affirmative action. Many universities had promised to hire minority faculty in response to 1968-Era protests, and they could scarcely object when women were added to the mix. Administrators had further reasons to endorse these objectives, since virtually every campus had a militant constituency demanding these ends. During these years, the Women's Movement formed the largest and most organized proponents (below). Affirmative action, along with Title IX, made women the chief beneficiaries of the rights revolution in higher education. In fact, higher education became a principal arena for affirmative action in the 1970s, propelled by legions of highly educated women activists.

Affirmative action requirements were particularly awkward for higher education, where institutions sought to hire the most qualified candidate for single, highly specialized faculty positions. Nathan Glazer called it "adversarial regula-

19 Bernice Sandler was remarkably effective as a Washington insider and promoting women's organizations in universities. She had a long career as a women's rights advocate and was dubbed "the godmother of Title IX" by the *New York Times*, but the effectiveness of WEAL was due to exploiting executive orders and affirmative action: Bernice Sandler, "A Little Help from Our Government: WEAL and Contract Compliance," in Alice S. Rossi and Ann Calderwood, eds., *Academic Women on the Move* (New York: Russell Sage Foundation, 1973), 439–62.

20 Ibid.; Skrentny, *Minority Rights Revolution*, 132–41: Revised Order No. 4 (n. 13) accorded women the same affirmative action status as minorities. Howard H. Peckham, *The Making of the University of Michigan, 1817–1992*, edited and updated by Margaret L. Steneck and Nicholas H. Steneck (Ann Arbor, University of Michigan, 1994), 310–12.

tion," which hints of special pleading by an industry unaccustomed to being regarded as an adversary. [21] In fact, affirmative action was consciously intended social engineering. Unlike regulations intended to bring a few violators in line, *every* university was guilty of underrepresentation. Patterns of employment, promotion, and compensation formed by everyday practices over past decades were no longer acceptable or legal under the new standards. Unsurprising, transition to this Brave New World was for a time chaotic. Neither institutions nor HEW knew just what standards were to be enforced, and the zeal of inexperienced bureaucrats became a driving force. HEW tripled the number of contract compliance investigators in 1972. Unfamiliar with the higher education "industry" and committed to literal interpretations of equality, they imposed affirmative action without regard for academic procedures. The Secretary of Labor—the former Harvard economist John Dunlap—admitted that any attempt to mollify the regulations would outrage his own bureaucracy, and HEW secretary Caspar Weinberger likewise felt impotent to impede this juggernaut. By 1975 almost all universities had developed elaborate affirmative action plans. However, when calculations of relevant labor pools were made, projections required relatively few new hires. These plans proved less onerous than feared. When submitted to the swamped OCR, only 16 percent had received any form of approval by that year. [22] Affirmative action affected universities less through government enforcement than through internal advocacy.

Despite the zeal of bureaucrats, universities were able to fend off extreme interpretations of affirmative action. When HEW ordered that Harvard's next Chinese historian must be a woman, a call from President Derek Bok to Caspar Weinberger rectified the diktat. UC Berkeley created a model by calculating the available labor pools for each separate department, based on past numbers of PhDs awarded. Since the pools for minorities were quite small, and those for women limited as well, most "deficiencies" were fractions of persons and did not require the setting of goals. [23] At Princeton, however, shortfalls of 0.5 persons were used to set a hiring goal, and at Duke even smaller fractions justified hiring. Going beyond affirmative action requirements became a badge of social commitment. Available labor pools in the sciences were so small that these fields were

21   Carnegie Council, *Making Affirmative Action Work*, 56–62; Nathan Glazer, "Regulating Business and Regulating Universities: One Problem or Two?," in Paul Seabury, ed., *Bureaucrats and Brainpower: Government Regulation of Universities* (San Francisco: Institute for Contemporary Studies, 1979), 113–40. Of course, regulation of the Philadelphia building trades was "adversarial" as well.

22   Geiger, *Research and Relevant Knowledge*, 258–60; Caspar W. Weinberger, "Regulating the Universities," in Seabury, *Bureaucrats*, 47–70; Carnegie Council, *Making Affirmative Action Work*, 61–69.

23   At Berkeley, thirty-one of seventy-five departments established goals for women, one for Blacks, two for Asians, and none for Chicanos or Native Americans: Carnegie Council, *Making Affirmative Action Work*, 137–42, 209–13; Weinberger, "Regulating Universities."

originally little affected. But faculty recruitment was transformed in other ways. Job openings now had to be advertised widely, minority candidates sought, and search-committee protocols scrupulously observed. The eagerness of universities and many departments to hire minorities and women produced a pervasive "tilt" in job searches and various subterfuges. Given the competition for promising women and minorities, the leading universities tended to have first pick of highly qualified affirmative action candidates. They frequently hired promising doctoral candidates before they finished their dissertations, which could be a handicap in launching an academic career. Some universities felt compelled to adopt more aggressive strategies. Naming black or women's subjects in job descriptions circumscribed the applicant pool. Many universities set aside funds available to any department solely for affirmative action hires. Affirmative action forced universities to move faster and more deliberately to achieve ends that administrators and much of the academic community considered desirable and socially responsible in any case. This combination of coercion and willingness quickly produced results. In 1973, more female than male new PhDs were hired at stronger universities and colleges, despite recent male PhDs being five times more numerous.[24]

More recently, affirmative action has been associated with admissions, but this was a different situation involving federal courts rather than affirmative action enforcement. Prior to affirmative action regulations, colleges and universities had established affirmative admissions programs on their own initiative, as seen in Chapter 4. This was positive discrimination.[25] Although special admissions programs were originally intended to recruit Blacks, they incorporated the federal definition of official minorities. The combination of affirmative admissions and increased availability of urban and two-year institutions raised black enrollments to over 1 million by 1976, almost four times the total for 1967. Blacks composed 10 percent of students, compared to a 12 percent share of the population. Roughly 45 percent of black high school graduates were continuing in higher education, just five percentage points less than Whites. But fewer Blacks finished: they were only 6.4 percent of college graduates. Professional schools followed their undergraduate colleges in establishing affirmative admissions for minorities. By the mid-seventies, 85 percent of medical schools and 93 percent of law schools had voluntarily established such programs for Blacks, and most included

24   Carnegie Council, *Making Affirmative Action Work,* 196–97: based on the top three of five categories of universities and colleges. Males earned 56,661 doctorates in 1971–1973 vs. 11,479 degrees for females.

25   The 1970 decision in *Adams v. Richardson* ordered nineteen states to develop long-range desegregation plans for higher education, which aimed chiefly at the protection and qualitative improvement of HBCUs.

other minorities.[26] Professional schools, with fixed class sizes and well-defined admissions criteria, constituted zero-sum situations in which it was possible to demonstrate reverse discrimination against white applicants.

Alan Bakke was such an applicant. Despite a superior academic record, he was twice denied admission to the UC Davis medical school, which reserved 16 of 100 places for supposedly "disadvantaged" minorities. Bakke sued, citing violations of equal protection under the Fourteenth Amendment and Title VI prohibition of discrimination. The case was appealed to the Supreme Court, where four justices found the racial quota acceptable and four considered it unconstitutional. In a "famously tortured opinion," Justice Powell found the quota unconstitutional, but that race was permissible as one factor in an admissions decision. As the first significant test of racial preferences, the *Bakke* case left a good deal of ambiguity (Bakke at least was admitted). It was notable for the introduction of "diversity" into the issue. Amicus briefs from elite private universities argued that diversity made a positive contribution to the educational process. This claim had not been raised previously as a justification for civil rights and preferences for official minorities, but now Justice Powell invoked it to assert that racial or ethnic background could be an acceptable "plus factor" in admissions. Diversity thus became a new and convenient rationale for affirmative action without recourse to disadvantage or social discrimination.[27]

No internal history of higher education can account for the transformation that occurred from the late 1960s to the mid-1970s. The federal government changed the rules, and the way colleges and universities operated changed as well. These changes have been described here and will be noted further below, but one must look beyond campuses to explain why they occurred. They were the product of a fundamental shift in national cultural values regarding individual rights and societal responsibilities, refracted through the legislative, administrative, and judicial branches of the federal government. After 1965, wrote the public-policy historian Hugh Davis Graham, "the civil rights era moved from Phase I, when anti-discrimination policy was enacted into federal law, to Phase II, when problems and politics of implementation produced a shift of administrative and judicial enforcement from a goal of equal treatment to one of equal results." Further, "the 1965–1975 period was a minority rights revolution," noted

26 National Council for Education Statistics (NCES), *Digest of Education Statistics: 2016* (Washington, DC: US Department of Education, 2018): 22 percent of black students enrolled in HBCUs (1976). This compares with 267,000 black students in 1967, 45 percent in HBCUs (Chapter 4). Skrentny, *Minority Rights Revolution*, 170.

27 Skrentny, *Minority Rights Revolution*, 173–78. "Disadvantaged" was never defined at Davis or elsewhere.

the sociologist John Skrentny, "led by the Establishment. It was a bipartisan project, including ... Presidents, the Congress, bureaucracies and the courts."[28] Both scholars marvel at how the most consequential features of this transformation were adopted casually without consideration of rationales or implications: the assumption that the official minorities and women (and later, people with disabilities)—but not other groups—deserved the same preferential treatment as African-Americans; or, the progressive abandonment of concern for discrimination and enhancing social opportunity in favor of the employment of minorities in numbers equal to their proportion in the population (a quixotic standard found nowhere for other groups in the American workplace).[29] Such developments were built upon deep cultural frames (Skrentny calls them "meanings") that accorded sacrosanct status to human rights and equal opportunity, joined with the government's hopeful efforts to rectify inequality through social engineering. In this sense, the Education Amendments and affirmative action were cultural siblings, one seeking to provide any person the opportunity, hence the right, to postsecondary education, and the other, through preferences to disadvantaged groups, asserting a right for them to attain statistically equivalent outcomes.

Both policies were in their infant stage in the early 1970s. Congress was slow to authorize funding for the BEOG Program, and support for low-income students expanded slowly during the decade. After 1975 the political consensus behind the minority rights revolution began to fray. Public opinion grew increasingly skeptical of preferences but remained solidly opposed to discrimination and approving of the growing visible attainments of Blacks and women. Both policies were destined for the long haul. Federal student financial aid would grow relentlessly until it dominated higher education finance. Changing the racial and gender composition of higher education was a long-term project with its own relentless momentum. However, within a decade of the passage of Title IX, it was already apparent that the standing of women in higher education had significantly advanced and that minority rights on campuses was a permanent revolution.

THE RISE OF WOMEN

The years 1969–1973 witnessed an abrupt cultural transformation in higher education. Previously, the idea that women deserved equal treatment with men was considered unnatural and unrealistic; afterward it became not only legitimate

28   Hugh Davis Graham, *The Civil Rights Era: Origins and Development of a National Policy* (New York: Oxford University Press, 1990), 456; Skrentny, *Minority Rights Revolution*, 2.

29   Skrentny emphasizes that "affirmative action had almost no organized support *or* opposition," and public opinion was consistently "rather solidly against it." It was constructed by the executive branch to fulfill expectations raised by the civil rights legislation: *Ironies of Affirmative Action*, 2–6.

but, officially at least, the prevailing view. Although women in the 1960s had full access to undergraduate education, they were assumed to put home and family ahead of profession or career. They were regarded as less likely to complete advanced degree programs, less dedicated to professional careers, and less inclined to attain positions of leadership. Christopher Jencks and David Riesman, although attempting a sympathetic portrait in the late 1960s, were typically patronizing: "The typical woman is unlikely ever to be as career-oriented as the average man," they wrote. "A world in which women were established as fully equal to men" they regarded as fanciful.[30] Five years after *The Academic Revolution*, the equality of women in careers and education was the law of the land, as just seen, enforced by the authority of the federal bureaucracy and judiciary. More significant, it had become for growing cohorts of women a personal conviction and political cause, especially on American campuses. What accounted for this abrupt change?

The women's movement of the 1960s questioned the complacent gender stereotypes of the American way of life but made little substantive progress until the end of the decade. Then, two separate channels of the women's movement converged in higher education. Betty Friedan was an outspoken crusader following *The Feminine Mystique* (1963), but frustration with meager results prompted her to spearhead the founding of the National Organization of Women in 1966. NOW carried the banner for women's rights, including the Equal Rights Amendment, but its unstable coalition fragmented in 1968. One offshoot, WEAL, at this point championed the cause of women's rights in higher education and brought that movement to campuses. NOW emerged in 1970 as the national voice for women's rights, while WEAL spearheaded legalistic challenges at colleges and universities, as seen in the previous section.

The second channel developed out of and in reaction to 1960s civil rights and New Left movements. Women had contributed significantly to SDS and SNCC in the early years, but the inherent sexism of both organizations became more arrogant after mid-decade. Women who sought to register their specific grievances against American society were ignored or treated with condescension. The official SDS ideology held that capitalism was the source of oppression, not male supremacy. Beginning in 1967, groups of women formed to express their own protest. Originally identifying as "radical women," they disassociated from SDS and became known as radical feminists, or more popularly, women's liberation. Their distinctive cause was total opposition to all manifestations of male

30   Saul D. Feldman, *Escape from the Doll's House: Women in Graduate and Professional Education* (New York: McGraw-Hill, 1974), 1–20; Christopher Jencks and David Riesman, *The Academic Revolution* (Chicago: University of Chicago Press, 1968), 298–99.

dominance, or "patriarchy." The original groups, such as the Women's International Terrorist Conspiracy from Hell (WITCH) or the lesbian collective the Furies, celebrated defiance and staged outrageous protests. However, these fringe groups had two traits that were readily transmissible: they excluded all men from their meetings, and they indulged in intense discussions of personal frustrations with male dominance, or consciousness-raising.[31] Women's liberation migrated spontaneously to campuses as gatherings—chiefly of faculty, faculty wives, and graduate students—met together, raised consciousness, and began to organize against the male predominance, now labeled sexism, that surrounded them.

The rise of women in higher education united these two channels in these transitional years. The push for women's rights was the force behind a developing organizational network concerned with these issues. However, the key was the tremendous élan that was generated chiefly from consciousness raising. Conversion to feminism was akin to a religious experience. When women raised their consciousness by sharing their experiences, they elevated their awareness beyond male dominance of society and intellectual life to how these things circumscribed and inhibited their lives at work and at home. Viewing the world through a feminist lens, the realities and consequences of patriarchy became apparent in myriad phenomena. In addition to becoming angry, women were liberated from a "false consciousness" and energized to act upon this newfound creed.[32]

There was no lack of evidence for the feminist indictment. Society in the United States—and every other country—maintained differentiated gender roles and separate conventions of behavior and treatment for men and women. The feminists' most compelling argument applied to the workplace, where separate treatment was clearly discriminatory and had financial consequences. Opportunities for women in higher education had been stagnant for most of the century. Women received 11 percent of doctorates in 1910 and the same portion in 1957. Several postwar trends worked against them. Early marriage and childbearing interdicted career possibilities even for those who sought to transcend 1950s stereotypes. The GI Bill boosted the number of males in faculty careers, and the heightened competitiveness of the academic revolution favored men. Highly educated women were frequently in the position of "trailing spouse," accepting lesser teaching positions, seldom publishing, and shouldering housekeeping

31   Todd Gitlin, *The Sixties: Years of Hope, Days of Rage* (New York: Bantam Books, 1993 [1987], 362–76; Alice Echols, *Daring to Be Bad: Radical Feminism in America, 1967–1975* (Minneapolis: University of Minnesota Press, 1989).

32   Ruth Rosen, *The World Split Open: How the Modern Women's Movement Changed the World* (New York: Viking, 2000), 196–201: Rosen's terms are "euphoria" and "intoxication"; comparable "to the experience of religious or intellectual conversion" (199).

duties.[33] In 1970, women comprised 24 percent of faculty in higher education, but they were clustered at undergraduate teaching institutions. Societal expectations condoned these realities, but evidence of discriminatory treatment was overwhelming. Florence Howe, who directed the Modern Language Association Commission on the Status of Women, stated: "My feminism … formed itself not on ideology but on statistical data. I was … an empirical feminist."[34]

Radical feminists extended the critique much further with a growing literature that tended to reinforce the élan, and the anger. One prominent work was Kate Millett's *Sexual Politics* (1970). Through cultural and literary criticism (her PhD thesis at Columbia), she decried how the subordination of women permeated society, including "patriarchal monogamous marriage." She first shared these revelations in campus talks and was soon on the cover of *Time* (August 31, 1970). By that juncture, women's liberation had become the focus of copious media attention, although often somewhat patronizing or bemused. Women's lib acquired national publicity, if not followers. But in higher education, it formed an insurgency with specific, attainable goals that had already inspired a remarkable proliferation of women's organizations.[35]

By 1971, 125 campuses had compiled reports on the conditions of women, and 50 women's groups had formally organized in academic associations.[36] At institutions, agitation by informal women's groups led to the appointment of a commission, committee, or task force on the status of women. A counting of heads quickly documented the underrepresentation and underemployment of women and, as at Michigan, provided a compelling case for action. Given affirmative action and Title IX, universities had little recourse but to create plans to address these issues. Women's commissions usually advocated additional measures to accommodate women's needs. It was assumed, with some validity c. 1970, that female faculty and graduate students would be married, often with children. Hence, ubiquitous recommendations for day-care facilities. Greater flexibility for part-time study was a perceived need for presumably nontraditional students. Suggestions for special administrators for counseling women or overseeing women's programs were generally adopted in some form. Women's commissions often

---

33   In the humanities and social sciences, first-generation feminists earned PhDs after marriage and children; in the sciences, fully credentialed women faced pervasive discrimination: Margaret W. Rossiter, *Women Scientists in America: Before Affirmative Action, 1940–1972* (Baltimore: Johns Hopkins University Press, 1995).

34   Florence Howe, *A Life in Motion* (New York: Feminist Press, 2011), 246.

35   Kate Millett, *Sexual Politics* (Garden City, NY: Doubleday, 1970), 23; Rosen, *World Split Open*, 296–302.

36   Lora H. Robinson, "Institutional Variation in the Status of Academic Women," in Rossi and Calderwood, *Academic Women on the Move*, 199–238; Kay Klotzburger, "Political Action by Academic Women," in ibid., 359–91.

became permanent bodies, providing an official voice for the interests of the feminist community.[37]

Women also sought greater academic recognition by organizing caucuses within the professional associations. Most associations incorporated these groups as formal commissions or committees, but some caucuses persisted as independent, often more militant, bodies. They were particularly motivated to promote new scholarly areas relevant to women. The leadership of disciplinary associations was based upon seniority and past scholarly attainment and hence were decidedly male. Women's caucuses became the means to challenge these conditions. With such backing, Florence Howe, an assistant professor without a PhD at a women's college, was elected by write-in votes president of the Modern Language Association (1971). Her campaign argued that social activism was more important than scholarship. Inside the MLA, Howe's tenure was in her words "useless," but the presidency provided a bully pulpit for women's studies and academic feminism.[38]

The signature achievement of the women's movement in higher education was women's studies. The first program was organized at San Diego State in 1969; Cornell followed the next year. For a higher education innovation, it spread with astonishing rapidity. By 1976, 270 programs had been organized, and 15,000 courses were being offered at 1,500 institutions. Women's studies stemmed from the women's liberation tradition and as such was truly a grassroots phenomenon. In the early years, most courses were pioneered by informal groups of feminists who felt a pressing need to advance the cause through the curriculum. Their initial efforts produced idiosyncratic courses but with a singular purpose. First courses were usually team-taught by pioneers from several departments, and hence were often multidisciplinary, but these were soon elaborated into consistent patterns, assisted by the wide dissemination of syllabi. "Programs" were created when sufficient courses were recognized by their institutions for certificates, minors, or major fields, according to local conventions. Unlike American or black studies, which tended to be staffed by new hires, virtually all women's studies programs were first assembled by on-campus personnel, another indication of its voluntary foundations and the energy generated by feminist élan.[39]

---

37 Carnegie Commission on Higher Education, *Opportunities for Women in Higher Education: Their Current Participation, Prospects for the Future, and Recommendations for Action* (New York: McGraw-Hill, 1973).

38 Howe, *Life in Motion*, 254–59.

39 Florence Howe, *Seven Years Later: Women's Studies Programs in 1976*, Report of the National Advisory Council on Women's Educational Programs (Washington, DC: National Advisory Council on Women's Educational Programs, June 1977); Florence Howe and Carol Ahlum, "Women's Studies and Social Change," in Rossi and Calderwood, *Academic Women*, 393–423. Many of the 15,000 courses were

The central goals of women's studies were consistent from the outset: first, "to raise the consciousness of students and faculty ... about the subordinate status of women today as well as in the past"; second, to correct the omission and distortion of women in the curriculum and to build a body of research that would "reenvision the lost history and culture of women and the construction of gender"; third, "to work actively for social change."[40] This basic orientation combined two missions: promoting scholarship on and about women and a political agenda to bring about personal conversion and social change. These two missions were essentially joined during the early years of women's studies and tended to energize each other.

Scholarship on women opened a vast terrain of possibilities, enriched by feminist perspectives. Historically, social institutions and intellectual traditions revealed a patriarchal bias when viewed from such perspectives. Other studies resurrected the neglected contributions of women writers and historical figures. The unequal treatment of women, past and present, could be readily demonstrated, but many feminist scholars sought to explore and illuminate distinctive female differences. Female experience, accordingly, gave rise to separate women's cultures that produced their own literary and intellectual traditions.[41]

In terms of scholarship and curricula, the women's movement soon evolved from grass roots to formal sponsorship. Mariam K. Chamberlain, a program officer for higher education at the Ford Foundation, convened a meeting of movement leaders in late 1971 that inspired the Women in Higher Education Program. During its first years, the program provided fellowships for faculty and doctoral students in women's studies. This was followed, beginning in 1974, by support for some fifteen university centers for research on women. These major efforts substantially enhanced the recognition and intellectual resources of the field. They also favored academic scholarship, since proposals for research projects or centers had to conform to academic norms. Additionally, the Ford program provided ready funding, often in small grants, for various initiatives to further the study of women, including conferences, backing for the Feminist Press, and attempts to integrate women's subjects into liberal arts curricula. A small grant in 1975 launched *Signs: The Journal of Women in Culture and Society*.[42]

---

cross-listed and thus not women's studies per se, but still endorsed it. Berkeley was frowned on for hiring away prominent women faculty from other institutions.

40 Howe wrote: "And perhaps a hundred times a year for the next two decades I explained ... [the] goals of women's studies programs": *Life in Motion*, 252.

41 Rosalind Rosenberg, "Women in the Humanities: Taking Their Place," in David A. Hollinger, ed., *The Humanities and the Dynamics of Inclusion since World War II* (Baltimore: Johns Hopkins University Press, 2006), 247–72.

42 Mariam K. Chamberlain, "There Were Godmothers, Too," in Florence Howe, ed., *The Politics of Women's Studies: Testimony from the 30 Founding Mothers* (New York: Feminist Press, 2000), 353–62;

The political mission of women's studies assumed was inherently adversarial. Radical feminism and women's liberation were born by transposing the New Left critique of America into sexual terms. Patricia Gumport's study of feminist scholars found "an overall tension ... between feminism and scholarship." For some, political commitments remained predominant over academic ones, and they gravitated toward women's studies. Historians appeared less affected by this dichotomy, given history's strongly empirical basis. But feminists continually wrestled with epistemological justifications for discounting academic knowledge in favor of ideology. Specifically, Gumport concluded, "logical positivism and empiricism, which dominated the sciences and mainstream social sciences ... have notions about human nature, reality, the bases of human knowledge, and social change that run directly counter to feminist scholarly premises that are grounded in a social constructivist framework."[43] In other words, academic feminism was inherently subjective and had a limited purview in the realm of science and empirical scholarship.

Subjectivity was rationalized with the same facile argument used by leftist academics and proponents of black studies; namely, that existing scholarship was inherently political in upholding capitalism or white supremacy or male dominance, and consequently Marxist or black or women's scholarship was justified in forwarding its own political bias. "Scholarship is politics" was the seductive rhetoric. This dichotomy between academic scholarship and a political agenda would become more overt after 1980. When Harvard finally approved a women's studies program in 1986, it felt the need for a disclaimer: the program was not intended to "foster a 'dogmatic' or 'ideological' approach.... Women's studies is a critical discipline—but one which must not confuse criticism with dogma."[44] This was a problematic distinction for the National Women's Studies Association.

Forming a national association is the hopeful destiny of every academic specialty, but the first gathering of the NWSA in 1979 revealed aspirations beyond advancing scholarship. The association unabashedly embraced the activist pole of the profession. Refusing "to accept sterile divisions between the academy and community ... Women's Studies, then, is equipping women to transform the world to one that will be free of all oppression ... [and be] a force which furthers the realization of feminist aims." Although it did not exclude scholarship, activism steadfastly served as its animating principle. However, the new association itself

---

Rosa Proietto, "The Ford Foundation and Women's Studies in American Higher Education," in Ellen Condliffe Lagemann, ed., *Philanthropic Foundations: New Scholarship, New Possibilities* (Bloomington: Indiana University Press, 1999), 271–86.

43   Patricia Gumport, *Academic Pathfinders: Knowledge Creation and Feminist Scholarship* (Westport, CT: Greenwood Press, 2002), 85, 101–9, 46.

44   Ibid., 41–42.

was not free of allegations of oppression. The women's movement in higher education from its outset had been characterized by extraordinary camaraderie as participants sympathetically validated experiences shared in consciousness-raising and cooperated in launching grass-roots voluntary initiatives. Now, however, ideological fault lines arose over differences among women. Black feminists disparaged what they called white women's studies, identifying themselves with black studies and raising the flag of racism. Conflict over heterosexual orientation ("sleeping with the enemy") and degrees of lesbianism that had wracked radical feminism earlier in the decade now became a prominent feature of the women's studies movement. Where one existed on the sexual-preference continuum became a defining identity.[45] Class was a third fault line, as issues of privilege became salient. These were not academic topics that might be resolved by further study. Race, class, and gender formed matters of identity that defined individuals and affected the theory, pedagogy, and activism of academic feminism. Professional associations typically define themselves in their early years, often through confrontation. Such was the case with the NWSA, whose immersion in identity politics and ideology would deepen over time.[46]

Two additional aspects of the rise of women in the 1970s lie outside of the women's movement. The admission of women to the male cloisters of Harvard, Yale, and Princeton—as well as other all-male schools—occurred for reasons peculiar to the culture of that sector of higher education, with little outside influence. The inclusion of women in intercollegiate athletics was linked to the women's movement through Title IX and feminist support. However, unlike the developments just described, it faced determined resistance and advanced with a logic all its own.

COEDUCATION. In fall 1969, Harvard, Yale, and Princeton admitted women to the undergraduate college for the first time. Harvard's full acceptance of the women from Radcliffe, its coordinate college, was a major step psychologically, even though the two organizations had been dismantling barriers throughout the decade. Princeton's decision was momentous, however, the culmination of a painstaking inquiry into all possible ramifications of coeducation. President Kingman Brewster vainly sought to avoid admitting women to Yale College by

---

45   Rosen, *World Split Open*, 164–75; Daphne Patai and Noretta Koertge, *Professing Feminism: Education and Indoctrination in Women's Studies* (New York: Lexington, 2003), 44–80.

46   With "an all but overwhelming commitment to diversity and radicalism," "the NWSA ... serves to sustain the activist mission of women's studies." "The women's studies professoriate ... who produce the new scholarship on women present their work elsewhere.": Marilyn Jacoby Boxer, *When Women Ask the Questions: Creating Women's Studies in America* (Baltimore: Johns Hopkins University Press, 1998), 179–85.

establishing a coordinate women's college, but when Princeton's conversion became evident, he quickly capitulated.[47] The actions at Yale and Princeton were most significant for the sector, and they were determined by both background and foreground developments. Attitudes toward women changed markedly at both schools. As late as 1965, the prospect of admitting women provoked general hostility, but attitudes toward women were evolving nationally, and in 1969 coeducation was met with overwhelming approval internally, if not among alumni. Increasingly liberal public opinion was an intangible factor, but one that influenced the presidents to conclude that coeducation was inevitable—and also that it would be beneficial. More immediately, shifting preferences among prospective students were causing admissions alarms at both schools. More of the students they sought expressed preferences for coeducational campuses. Most alarming, their competitive position with respect to semi-coed Harvard was deteriorating. Both Yale and Princeton were now seeking to broaden their recruitment, and this meant tapping populations unfamiliar with and unattracted by single-sex education.

Princeton's comprehensive report on coeducation by the economist Gardner Patterson concluded unequivocally, "The admission of women will make Princeton a better University." It also included an unexpected finding—coeducation would cost much less than had been feared. The expansion of graduate education, research, and departmental faculty during the academic revolution had created what amounted to excess capacity that could be utilized to expand undergraduate instruction. In addition, more tuitions would help to pay for that capacity. Thus, at Princeton and elsewhere, admission of women forced consideration of an institution's academic and financial structure. A crucial issue was always, how many women? Every institution sought to introduce coeducation without diminishing the number of places for men, perhaps the most sensitive point for alumni. Yale aimed to enroll up to 1,500 women, versus 4,000 men, and Princeton 1,000, to join its 3,000 men. Once women were admitted, pressures inexorably pushed those numbers higher. The quality of more highly selected female applicants resulted in superior female candidates being rejected in favor of less qualified males. Moreover, quotas raised the stigma of discrimination and were attacked from the outset. Yale and Princeton, and other formerly all-male schools, soon eliminated quotas and committed to admit men and women on equal terms.[48] This last development was testimony to the unequivocal success of coed-

---

47 The following draws on the definitive account: Nancy Weiss Malkiel, *"Keep the Damned Women Out": The Struggle for Coeducation* (Princeton: Princeton University Press, 2016).

48 Jerome Karabel, *The Chosen: The Hidden History of Admission and Exclusion at Harvard, Yale, and Princeton* (Boston: Houghton-Mifflin, 2005), 412–48.

ucation. Princeton and Yale had considered admitting women largely in terms of the impact it would have on the men. As an afterthought, they asked what they might offer women. A great deal, it turned out. Drawn from the top of the talent pool, "coeds" outperformed the men academically and quickly assumed leadership roles in campus activities. Everywhere, testimony held that the campuses became happier and healthier places, except perhaps Dartmouth (coed in 1972), where men continued to honor and practice crude male chauvinism.[49] Institutions also achieved their goals. Top institutions like Princeton and Yale received more applications from more talented candidates, male and female.

Coeducation after 1969 accelerated from a trend to a stampede. From 1969 to 1972, women were admitted to the elite Northeastern men's colleges, the research universities Caltech and Johns Hopkins, Duke and the University of Virginia in the South, and major Catholic universities—with additional stragglers in following years (Amherst in 1975). The precedent set by Princeton and Yale no doubt made these decisions easier; in fact, several schools drew guidance from Princeton's Patterson Report. In these cases too, the same forces tilted decisions in favor of coeducation—the egalitarian zeitgeist, financial considerations, and admissions competition. Many of these schools foresaw financial difficulties that could be assuaged by expansion and economies of scale. They too faced a waning attraction of single-sex campuses among their most sought-after recruits and that women would be academically stronger than additional students drawn from the limited pool of males. These schools too embraced coeducation out of institutional self-interest, not the contribution they might make to women's education.[50] In the event, that contribution proved enormous. Coeducation at elite colleges and universities was a major advance for women's education and careers. Previously, high-achieving women might attend a limited menu of pinnacle institutions—Stanford, Cornell, Northwestern, the University of Chicago, and Swarthmore—or they could choose the insular cultures of the Seven Sisters. Now they could also attend the Ivy League, the best New England liberal arts colleges, or top universities previously off limits. However, this signal achievement in the rise of women posed a dire threat for women's colleges.

Selective women's colleges faced the same financial and admissions challenges as men's institutions, often in more severe form. The admission of women by the prestigious schools mentioned above clearly diminished their pool of prospective students, especially the most academically able. Admitting men could increase the admissions pool but not raise its quality. Nonetheless, many women's

49   Malkiel, *"Keep the Damned Women Out,"* 464–88.

50   Ibid., 595; Elizabeth A. Duffy and Idana Goldberg, *Crafting a Class: College Admissions and Financial Aid, 1955–1994* (Princeton: Princeton University Press, 1998), 109–16.

colleges felt compelled to take this plunge, including Vassar, Connecticut, Bennington, and Sarah Lawrence in 1969. After the 1960s, however, the growing influence of feminism caused a reconsideration of this step. Smith in 1969 seemed destined to join the coeducation trend, which was favored by two-thirds in a student vote. The requisite in-depth study of the issue produced a less-than-ringing endorsement of coeducation as "desirable" and "feasible," but the welling women's movement prompted misgivings. A rousing 1971 commencement address by Gloria Steinem may have been a catalyst, challenging Smith to take the lead in the larger transformation of women's consciousness. Other factors played a role in rejecting coeducation, but the zeitgeist had shifted. Two-thirds of Smith students now favored remaining a women's college. Wellesley followed a similar course. A lengthy study of the issue from 1969 to 1971 recommended coeducation, but the president turned against it and then so did the trustees.[51] Neither embracing nor rejecting coeducation resolved the inherent difficulties facing these colleges. Amid a general decline in college credentials, these colleges fared somewhat worse than average. Smith and Wellesley saw SAT scores decline by more than 100 points during the 1970s, but at Vassar the drop was almost 200 points. In fact, all selective private institutions, in implicit or explicit competition for top students, were negatively affected by the expansion and attractiveness of the leading, formerly men's colleges.[52]

TITLE IX AND WOMEN'S ATHLETICS. If coeducation largely occurred at the front end of the women's movement, the application of Title IX to women's athletics was a trailing consequence. Although women's participation in athletics was growing from the mid-sixties in secondary and higher education, traditional sex roles tended to predominate. Female athletes, conscious of transgressing gender roles, more often emphasized femininity than feminism. Women's athletics was controlled by separate women's physical education departments, which championed a women's model based on health, recreational, and educational values. They sought to enhance virtues of cooperation and sportsmanship, while deploring the commercialism and competitiveness of men's sports. The Association for Intercollegiate Athletics for Women (AIAW), formed in 1971, represented those entrenched interests. The association, for example, forbade recruitment and athletic scholarships until forced to relent. Title IX contradicted this ethos of intentional inequality, but the implications were initially unclear. As HEW began to formulate guidelines in 1974, the NCAA sought to preclude any steps that might make claims on the honey pot of revenue-producing sports (namely football).

51   Malkiel, *"Keep the Damned Women Out,"* 351–437.
52   Ibid., 346; Duffy and Goldberg, *Crafting a Class*, 84–91.

But this effort provoked a reaction that brought the attention of the women's movement to athletics along with the emergence of a more resolute group of women's athletics administrators. The regulations issued by HEW in 1975 were a transitional compromise that recognized the interests of male revenue sports but created guidelines for equitable treatment for women; however, the regulations also allowed a three-year grace period, during which most universities did little. When the grace period ended, HEW was in the process of writing new, more comprehensive regulations, which were promulgated in 1979. The last half of the 1970s saw a deluge of complaints, but enforcement was sporadic by an HEW more concerned with higher civil rights priorities than women's athletics. The Reagan administration that followed had no interest in enforcing Title IX. After an initial surge, women's sports had to develop under its own momentum.[53]

Howard Bowen's famous law holds that universities raise all the money they can, and spend all the money they raise. Athletic departments spend all the money they raise—and then some. Women faced a long difficult road in wresting equitable funding from athletic department budgets that spared few funds for nonrevenue sports. In the 1970s, women's teams received a small fraction of male-team budgets even for the items identified for equalization in the 1975 regulations—equipment, travel, facilities, salaries, etc. But women's athletics managed to grow on shoestring budgets. The number of athletes doubled in the five years after Title IX, and by the end of the decade, a number of dedicated coaches produced nationally reputable teams. Title IX forced a transition to the male model of competitive intercollegiate athletics. When the NCAA sponsored national championships in several women's sports in 1980, it marked the death knell for the AIAW. Women's athletics would continue to grow during the 1980s, despite pressure on budgets and a lacuna in enforcement, and they would take off when conditions improved in the next decade.[54] The internal dynamism of women's athletics was largely made possible by Title IX. Its passage initially induced universities to hire the coaches and to begin upgrading teams from the era of women's physical education. The mandate for equality and the regulations, even given lax federal enforcement, gave women considerable leverage within their institutions to press their cause. Support for women's programs came not at

53   Kelly Belanger, *Invisible Seasons: Title IX and the Fight for Equity in College Sports* (Syracuse: Syracuse University Press, 2016), 27–78; Welch Suggs, *A Place on the Team: The Triumph and Tragedy of Title IX* (Princeton: Princeton University Press, 2006), 66–96.

54   The Civil Rights Restoration Act of 1988 reestablished a basis for enforcement of Title IX, and subsequent court decisions gave greater leverage to sue. In 1993 OCR issued new regulations that further strengthened enforcement. Budgets for women's athletics soared—but so did budgets for the men: James L. Shulman and William G. Bowen, *The Game of Life: College Sports and Educational Values* (Princeton: Princeton University Press, 2001), 121–24.

the expense of the men but rather was eked out of the growing revenues of commercial intercollegiate sport.[55] However, the mushroom growth of women's intercollegiate athletics was driven above all by the enthusiasm and dedication of female athletes to develop their skills and compete at the highest levels.

The sports historian Ronald Smith called the transformation of women's sports "the greatest reform in American intercollegiate athletics." It also marked another milestone in the rise of women as they secured athletic opportunities that would become equal to men's.[56] Thus, both the opening of all top colleges and universities and the elevation of women's athletics represent significant achievements of gender equality for American women. In academics, the women's movement and affirmative action produced a similar achievement, although one that fell short of feminist aspirations. Refusing to acknowledge that opportunities for study and academic careers were now tilted in their favor, a portion of the women's movement still felt oppressed by the persistence of patriarchy and made that the basis for identity politics. But the new cohorts of women who entered higher education after the 1970s by and large preferred to take advantage of the newfound opportunities rather than to assume the identity of victims.

THE INVERSION OF THE SEVENTIES: STUDENTS

Beginning around 1968, American higher education experienced a gradual transformation of its clientele in terms of who attended colleges and universities, where they attended, and why. During the golden-age conditions of the Liberal Hour, students flocked to traditional colleges and universities, raising admissions standards; but by the mid-seventies a majority of new students chose to enter community colleges. Those who did matriculate at four-year institutions had, on average, less academic aptitude and fewer academic interests. The proportion of liberal arts graduates declined from its zenith in the late 1960s as business became the most popular major. Before 1968 the American economy had a seemingly insatiable demand for college graduates of all stripes, but afterward, graduates exceeded the openings for college jobs, and the relative earnings of all graduates declined. Student idealism atrophied as well, and the primary motivation for attending college became financial. As the attraction of college diminished, for men in particular, fewer attended, and by the end of the decade women

---

55 For developments at Michigan State, see Belanger, *Invisible Seasons*; Suggs, *Place on the Team*, passim. Men's athletics did suffer after 1992, when teams in minor sports were dropped to create more equal male-female proportions.

56 Ronald A. Smith, *Pay for Play: A History of Big-Time College Athletic Reform* (Urbana: University of Illinois Press, 2011), 150; Shulman and Bowen, *Game of Life*, 126–56.

composed the majority. The colleges, accustomed to selecting their students from an abundance of eager applicants, now sought to attract applicants by offering what the "consumers" of higher education desired.

The enormous demographic expansion of higher education in the 1960s enlarged the participation of all social groups and enrollments in all types of institutions, but by the end of the decade it appeared that some traditional patterns of attendance had reached a limit, while other pathways were still expanding. This picture is oversimplified, but it provides a starting point for isolating and explaining the changing demographics of the 1970s. First to top out were private colleges and universities, whose core clientele was traditional students from traditional college-going groups. Their intake of freshmen peaked in 1965 at almost 400,000.[57] In the following years the entering classes fluctuated slightly below that level and did not rise much above it for more than two decades. Overall, private enrollments grew modestly from incremental increases in graduate and professional students, but the dearth of undergraduates posed difficulties for private colleges, as will be seen in the next section.

Freshman enrollments in public, four-year institutions peaked a decade later, in 1975; but during the intervening years the number of new students entering community colleges and/or studying part time grew much faster. These developments ultimately depressed the productivity of undergraduate education. In 1967, 20 percent of the age cohort earned a bachelor's degree; in 1974, when the decade's largest number of bachelor's degrees was awarded, graduates reached the equivalent of 26 percent; but by 1980 this figure fell to 22 percent.[58] The age-equivalent figure for associate degrees rose from 6 percent in 1970, to 10 percent in 1974, and to 11 percent in 1980. After 1975, American higher education had for the first time in its history ceased to grow. Incremental increases at the end of the decade were confined to community colleges, underlining the relative unattractiveness of traditional colleges and universities. However, when men and women are viewed separately, two different stories emerge.

From 1961 to 1969, the enrollment of women roughly doubled and so did that of men. Over the next decade, female enrollments grew at ten times the rate for males (56 vs. 5.5 percent). Women became a majority of students in higher education at the end of the 1970s, and their advantage continued to increase thereafter. They earned the most associate degrees beginning in 1976, bachelor's in 1982, master's in 1987, and doctoral degrees in 2006. Their predominance in

---

57   Enrollment data are from NCES, *Digest of Education Statistics*, multiple years.

58   These figures are bachelor's degrees per twenty-three-year-olds (author's calculation), not actual graduation rates of individuals.

undergraduate education appeared to stabilize in the twenty-first century with women earning four of seven bachelor's degrees.[59] This phenomenon was soon replicated in the higher education systems of almost all developed countries, a core cultural feature of the worldwide institutionalization of education. This was part of the rights revolution, which became a global phenomenon, spearheaded by higher education.[60] Still, it occurred first in the United States in the 1970s under the singular conditions of that era.

Underlying the changing behavior of women was the transformation of social norms. In 1967, 43 percent of high school females felt that married women should not be employed; six years later that figure had dropped to 17 percent. During this critical period, women received abundant signals that they should expect the same rights and opportunities as men—coeducation at Princeton and Yale; widespread media coverage of women's liberation; and congressional passage of the (unratified) Equal Rights Amendment, among other federal actions. Women responded by adopting more ambitious educational strategies, beginning in high school. One factor boosting college attendance was better preparation, helped by taking more advanced math and science courses, with the greatest gains occurring in the transitional years, 1972–1982. In college, women entered formerly male fields, like business, where their share of degrees increased from 9 percent in 1971 to 45 percent in 1985. Women had ample economic incentives for such actions. The college wage premium for women was always high, largely due to the low wages of noncollege women; but lifetime earnings were depressed by intermittent employment. Now women became committed to careers; the proportion planning to be employed shot from 30 percent in 1968 to 80 percent in 1979. Not only did women have access to higher-paying careers, but their lifetime employment patterns began to resemble those of men. These educational advances were led initially by higher-SES women, but perhaps the most remarkable inversion occurred among lower-SES families. The latter families had always favored educating sons over daughters, and male-female discrepancies were greatest in these social strata (Chapter 2). But this pattern was completely reversed by the 1980s, as the female proportional advantage in college attendance became greatest among children of the lower half of SES families, where male and female participation moved in opposite directions.[61]

59   "For Every 100 Girls . . . ," *Postsecondary Education Opportunity* 271 (January 2015).

60   John W. Meyer and Francisco O. Ramirez, "The World Institutionalization of Education," in Georg Krücken and Gili S. Drori, eds., *World Society: The Writings of John W. Meyer* (New York: Oxford University Press, 2009), 206–21.

61   Claudia Goldin, Lawrence F. Katz, and Ilyana Kuziemko, "The Homecoming of American College Women: The Reversal of the College Gender Gap," *Journal of Economic Perspectives* 20 (Fall 2006): 133–56.

Compared with the rise of women, explaining the decline of men is more conjectural. The Vietnam War is sometimes invoked as causing an "over-enrollment" of males, estimated at 4–6 percent.[62] The enrollment rate of eighteen- to nineteen-year-old white males fell from 44 percent in 1971 to 35 percent in 1974. An economic rationale can be found in the decline of the college wage premium throughout the 1970s. This was accompanied as early as 1969 by copious publicity on the scarcity of college-level jobs (below). The greatest decrease in enrollment occurred among lower-middle-class males, who were likely most sensitive to the job market, but decline was evident across the income spectrum.[63] However, the momentum of college expansion and hype had brought increasing proportions of students, mostly male, with marginal preparedness, intellectual ability, and/or motivation to succeed in college. Male high school students on average did less homework and received lower grades than their female counterparts. Yet 200,000 more men than women entered as full-time freshmen in 1970; 120,000 more in 1975. In 1974, male bachelor's degrees exceeded women's by 110,000; by 33,000 in 1979. For the first time, women became more likely to complete college than men. In 1972, 39 percent of male freshmen entering four-year colleges had less than a B average, versus 22 percent of women. Weakly prepared (or motivated) males were less likely to persist, making economic returns poor if not negative. Lack of persistence to graduation was also a problem for minority students, who received strong inducements to go to college in spite of generally weak high school preparation. Their college continuation rates rose to equal that of white students in the mid-1970s, but those rates were not sustained, falling to a five-point deficit in the 1980s.

Academic achievement was largely discounted or ignored in egalitarian rhetoric. A 1970 ACE conference at the height of expansionist fever advised, "Higher education in the United States must make a long overdue effort to redefine 'the college student.'" But more sober economists wrote in 1975: "Further progress in increasing equality of educational opportunity at the level of higher education probably requires an increase in academic achievement at the primary and secondary levels."[64] This did not happen. Academic achievement and the quality of schooling were in fact deteriorating in the 1970s.

62   David Card and Thomas Lemieux, "Going to College to Avoid the Draft: The Unintended Legacy of the Vietnam War," *American Economic Review* 91 (May 2001): 97–102.

63   Roger L. Geiger, "The Case of the Missing Students," *Change* (December 1978–January 1979): 64–65; Richard B. Freeman, *The Over-Educated American* (New York: Academic Press, 1976), 34–37.

64   W. Todd Furniss, *Higher Education for Everybody? Issues and Implications* (Washington, DC: ACE, 1971); Roy Radner and Leonard S. Miller, *Demand and Supply of U.S. Higher Education* (New York: McGraw-Hill, 1975), 8.

The official advisory panel that investigated falling SAT scores found that after 1970 academic achievement declined across all levels. They attributed this to conditions in both schools and society. The steepest falloff, in 1972–1974, was preceded by both a loss of authority in schools and "distracting" developments in American society. In schools, curricula had fragmented, placing less emphasis on reading and writing, and student motivation was perceptibly lower. The panel further surmised that family environments had become less supportive of learning, with excessive television watching hypothesized as a negative influence. Other indicators of student learning registered a similar decline, precisely in the same years of the early 1970s.[65] While the causation may have been speculative, the effects of falling academic achievement were fully evident: fewer high scores, even among valedictorians; a decline of intellectual aspirations; the eclipse of the liberal arts in favor of vocational majors; a majority of freshmen entering community colleges; and, for men, "a virtual collapse in the long-run trend in educational attainment."[66]

Academic achievement was high for the front edge of the baby boomers, who entered college from 1964 to 1968. In 1970 a shift in behavior first became perceptible, and in 1975 a full-fledged tipping point was evident. From 1972 to 1985, when this trend bottomed out, bachelor's degrees in business rose by 92 percent, or 112,000—slightly more than the number lost in education. English degrees fell by 54 percent, history by 63 percent, and leading the decline in social science, sociology by 61 percent. Psychology was mixed, with 7,000 male defectors and 10,000 additional female grads. The intellectual retreat was signaled by the attitudes of entering freshmen. In 1969, 82 percent felt it "very important" to "develop a meaningful philosophy of life," but in 1985 only 43 percent felt this way. Instead, those aspiring to be "very well off financially" rose from 40 percent to 71 percent. Similarly, in the late 1960s, 2.1 percent of men and 1.5 percent of women aimed to become college teachers, but in 1985 those figures were 0.3 percent and 0.2 percent. Students not only deserted the liberal arts, but even top students became alienated from academe, most decidedly from 1970 to 1975.[67]

65   *On Further Examination: Report of the Advisory Panel on the Scholastic Aptitude Test Score Decline* (New York: College Entrance Examination Board, 1977); Arthur Levine, *When Dreams and Heroes Died* (San Francisco: Jossey-Bass, 1980), 73–75.

66   David Card and Thomas Lenieux, "Dropout and Enrollment Trends in the Postwar Period: What Went Wrong in the 1970s?," in Jonathan Gruber, ed., *Risky Behavior among Youths: An Economic Analysis* (Chicago: University of Chicago Press, 2001), 483–522. By the 1980s, young men on average would receive less education than their fathers for the first time ever.

67   *The American Freshman: National Norms for Fall, 1969, 1972, 1980, 1985* (ACE and Higher Education Research Institute, UCLA); Roger L. Geiger, "Demography and Curriculum: The Humanities in American Higher Education from the 1950s through the 1980s," in Hollinger, ed., *Humanities and the Dynamics of Inclusion*, 50–72.

These changes in student behaviors corresponded to decisive changes in the American economy—for the worse. The economist Robert J. Gordon has identified the half century from 1920 to 1970 as the "One Big Wave" of productivity growth, in which annual increases averaged 2.82 per cent. After 1970, however, productivity growth fell to 1.62 percent, as the technological, social, and demographic factors that had driven the Big Wave were either exhausted or diminished. These changes had enormous long-term effects, depressing improvement in the standard of living and increasing economic inequality.[68] For contemporaries, palpable effects were experienced as recessions in 1969–1970, 1973–1975, and 1980–1982, and the highest decadal inflation rate in American history. These were the conditions facing the country's largest cohorts of college graduates.

The job market for college graduates began to turn down in 1969, when a weakening economy was accompanied by a surge in the number of graduates. The impact of the baby-boom generation on employment was somewhat delayed because a large percentage of the initial cohorts pursued graduate studies, not work. But college graduates increased by 50 percent from 1968 to 1974—300,000 additional graduates. And colleges and universities continued to award more than 900,000 bachelor's degrees for the rest of the decade. In 1975, an economic nadir, 16 percent of recent humanities and social science graduates were unemployed. For graduates fortunate enough to find work, starting salaries were lower in real terms than in 1960. The college wage premium, which had expanded strongly in the 1960s, surrendered all those gains by the end of the 1970s. Student behavior was consistent with these economic forces: continuation rates fell, at least for white males; vocational majors eclipsed the liberal arts; and students reduced their financial investment in higher education by enrolling in community colleges. The economist Richard B. Freeman, who analyzed these trends in mid-decade, predicted "the period of severe 'overeducation' [was] likely to last for about a decade," followed by a new equilibrium "at a lower plateau. In contrast to the past, higher education will be a 'marginal' investment, not a sure 'guarantee' to relatively high salaries and occupational standing."[69]

EDUCATION EXPANSION AND THE NEW-MODEL SOCIETY. Freeman's dour diagnosis of overeducation was echoed by many contemporary observers, but it contradicted the prevailing faith in educational expansion. This was a case of reality confronting ideology. The expansionist ideology transcended the United States. As depicted by John Meyer and associates, it was a global "model

---

68   Robert J. Gordon, *The Rise and Fall of American Growth: The U.S. Standard of Living since the Civil War* (Princeton: Princeton University Press, 2016), 14–16, 605–40.

69   Freeman, *Over-Educated American*, 188.

of a more liberal, participatory, and developing society in which much future progress could be built on education expansion."

> Liberal dominance created a whole new world political order, filled with governmental and nongovernmental associations ... infused with all sorts of doctrines about the virtues of indefinitely expanded education.

This new model "undercut the older closed model of education and society, with fears of over-education and anomie."[70]

The foregoing depiction of the development of American higher education has illustrated at numerous points how those "governmental and nongovernmental associations," implicitly or explicitly, promoted this new model, first through the expansion of traditional colleges and universities and, after 1970, with visions of education for all. State governments were largely responsible for increasing the supply of undergraduate education, as the federal government was for graduate education. The Education Amendments of 1972 then underwrote financing (in theory) for all who wished to attend. A panoply of nongovernmental organizations provided ideological support. The American Association of Junior Colleges, with backing from foundations, relentlessly advocated expansion (Chapter 4). The American Council on Education was consistently expansionist, sponsoring the 1971 conference "Higher Education for Everybody? Issues and Implementation." The Commission on Non-Traditional Study published three promotional reports (1972–1974). Perhaps most influential was the Carnegie Commission. In addition to the expansionist positions described in Chapter 5, it sponsored studies that envisioned specific continuation rates of 80 percent (1971) and 90 percent (1975).[71] The expansionist ideology rationalized the growing imbalance between college graduates and appropriate employment. Frank Newman's Task Force on Higher Education actually encouraged high school graduates to delay going to college or to pursue other forms of schooling, while simultaneously advocating institutional experiments to bring new programs to new students. To this end, the Carnegie Commission recommended a more adaptable degree structure and lifelong learning.[72] Despite the variety of arguments and recommendations, all supported the expansionist ideology of the new-model society. The consensus in the early 1970s held that the momentum of expansion in

70 Meyer and Ramirez, "World Institutionalization of Education," 363–64.

71 Furniss, *Higher Education for Everybody?*; Cross, *Beyond the Open Door*; Radner and Miller, *Demand and Supply*.

72 Frank Newman et al., *Report on Higher Education, March 1971* (Washington, DC: GPO, 1971); Carnegie Commission on Higher Education, *Less Time, More Options: Education beyond the High School* (New York: McGraw-Hill, 1971).

postsecondary education could be maintained through nontraditional students and nontraditional institutions.

The nontraditional movement brought together three ideologically kindred phenomena.[73] It drew inspiration and rhetoric from the critique of traditional academic practices that was amplified in the late 1960s. Dissatisfaction among students and reformers inspired abundant initiatives and experiments to displace or reconfigure courses, lectures, degree credits, examinations, and grades—all intended to liberate the learning experience. These efforts largely sought to restructure education within traditional colleges and universities, or subunits created for this purpose, but such innovations and their animating spirit contributed to the idealistic goals of the growing nontraditional movement. The movement was also centrally concerned with reaching "new" students, those largely absent from traditional higher education. For the last half of the 1960s, these efforts were focused intensively on African Americans, with lip-service paid to other low-income populations. One goal was to assist their enrollment in traditional colleges and universities, but it was also recognized that special programs and institutions were also needed to meet these ends. Finally, by 1970, the mission of serving new students was generalized to the entire population through the emphasis on adult and part-time students. The nontraditional movement was envisioned as meeting the educational needs of all citizens at all points of their lives.

The nontraditional movement distinguished itself from established higher education by embracing several ideals. It honored "the goal of assuring to each individual the amount and type of education needed to develop his or her potential as a person." This aspiration mirrored the cultural ideal of individual agency and human rights, a central tenet of the global, new-model society. Such a goal was utopian, but as a cultural ideal it stood beyond argument for the nontraditional faithful. A more practical ideal was that nontraditional education must be flexible to reach diverse populations: "Teaching and learning should take place whenever it is convenient for students." Institutions readily obliged. Most state universities already sponsored extension divisions, which could be (and were) easily and cheaply expanded. More surprising, many hard-pressed private colleges established extension units or external degrees in largely vocational subjects. Wayne State (and others) established a unit that taught all courses on weekends for working students; and a Long Island university attempted to reach commuters by offering instruction on their trains. The movement also favored extricating education from formal educational institutions. The chief manifestation of this

---

73 Lewis B. Mayhew, *Legacy of the Seventies: Experiment, Economy, Equality, and Expediency in American Higher Education* (San Francisco: Jossey Bass, 1977), 41–68.

impulse was the awarding of college credit for life or work experience. This seductive notion faced grave difficulties of measurement and accreditation, so that it tended to be favored by new institutions with greater flexibility.[74] Finally, in keeping with the first ideal, nontraditional institutions attempted to individualize educational programs, most notably with learning contracts.

Many of these ideas had been tried previously in American higher education, but the early 1970s was their time to shine.[75] Every major state established a new institution to offer external degrees for these purposes. In 1971, SUNY chancellor Ernest Boyer launched Empire State College to provide student-centered adult education where students could determine their educational needs, purposes, and level of effort. Working with faculty mentors, students would design study plans consisting of courses, independent study, residencies, and credit for prior learning from work and life experience. Backed by the financial resources of SUNY, it became a resource for thousands of degree-seeking adults. With more meager backing, Minnesota established Metropolitan State University (1971) as an upper-division institution to provide degrees for nontraditional students incorporating credit for previous academic work and life experience. Founded through the efforts of a higher education entrepreneur despite the absence of ostensible need, it operated in the 1970s in rented space with largely adjunct faculty. Its distinctive feature was a competency-based curriculum based on individually determined degree plans.[76]

The devices generally employed to accommodate "new" students included "shortening the time required to earn a degree; granting credit for life experience; making use of considerable, relatively unsupervised, independent study; [and] taking programs to students rather than requiring them to come to campus."[77] These practices were inherent to competency-based education and degree plans or contracts. Conscientiously employed by highly qualified faculty or mentors, such approaches might accomplish some of the goals of nontraditional advocates. Employed otherwise, they left considerable scope for shortchanging learning and cheapening degrees. Institutions could count on federal support for

---

74 Ibid., quotes p. 42.

75 For perspective, see Joseph F. Kett, *The Pursuit of Knowledge under Difficulties: From Self-Improvement to Adult Education in America, 1750–1990* (Stanford, CA: Stanford University Press, 1994), 428–30 et passim.

76 David Riesman, *On Higher Education: The Academic Enterprise in an Era of Rising Student Consumerism* (San Francisco: Jossey-Bass, 1980), 116–17; Arthur Levine, *Handbook on Undergraduate Curriculum* (San Francisco: Jossey-Bass, 1988), 405–9. The British Open University, which was launched in 1969, was an inspiration for nonresidential state institutions for adult higher education. In the UK, the restrictive nature of universities created a huge potential market for external degrees. The Open University was well financed and had relatively rigorous academic standards.

77 Mayhew, *Legacy of the Seventies*, 93–94.

developing such efforts. The Fund for the Improvement of Postsecondary Education backed initiatives to "deliver" such education. In 1974, FIPSE inaugurated a special program to promote competency-based education for regular as well as nontraditional students. Competency curricula were explicitly intended to challenge and hopefully displace the dominance of the academic disciplines. However, they fared poorly in regular colleges and universities.[78]

These same techniques also appealed to colleges seeking to accommodate more unconventional, "old" (college-age) students; namely, students from upper- or upper-middle-class families who could not tolerate structured, traditional college programs but instead sought the freedom to express their own identities. Practices that accommodated such orientations included individualized curricula, experiential learning, and self-generated quasi-educational projects. A few institutions organized their curricula around such practices, but many institutions established subunits to provide for such nonconformists. These experiments were rooted in the late-sixties critique of academic practices and the quest for liberating education, but they melded with the nontraditional zeitgeist of the early 1970s. They have been uncharitably labeled "havens for the upper-class counterculture."[79] At the other extreme of the social spectrum, the University Without Walls was opened at Morgan State (1971) to reach low-income minorities, women, prisoners, and veterans through open admissions, performance criteria, and learning contracts.[80]

The nontraditional movement was essentially a supply-driven phenomenon. Proponents were motivated by the conviction that postsecondary education ought to be available to all Americans. Institutions like those identified above were created for this purpose, with little knowledge of demand or heed of long-standing adult education programs found in urban universities or distance education. The Commission on Non-Traditional Study conducted a sample survey that assured educators that 79 million Americans, ages eighteen to sixty, desired some kind of formal education.[81] Given the ill-defined nature of nontraditional students, it is scarcely possible to determine their numbers, but the contours of American higher education changed in the 1970s. The traditional college constituency—

---

78 Thomas Ewens, "Analyzing the Impact of Competency-Based Approaches on Liberal Education"; David Riesman, "Encountering Difficulties in Trying to Raise Academic Standards: Florida State University"; Zelda Gamson, "Understanding the Difficulties of Implementing a Competence-Based Curriculum;" all in Gerald Grant et al., *On Competence: A Critical Analysis of Competency-Based Reforms in Higher Education* (San Francisco: Jossey-Bass, 1979), 160–98, 363–409, 224–58.

79 Examples include Hampshire College, Fairhaven College of Western Washington, Evergreen State, and the three institutions named New College, in California, Florida, and Alabama.

80 Argentine S. Craig, "Contracting in a University without Walls Program," *New Directions for Higher Education* 10 (1975): 41–52.

81 Mayhew, *Legacy of the Seventies*, 56.

full-time students aged eighteen–twenty-four—declined from 60 to 50 percent of enrollments. Part-time students accounted for 64 percent of growth in the decade, and 71 percent of those additional students were women. The proportion of female part-time students older than twenty-four grew from 58 to 70 percent during the decade, an increase of 1,246,000 versus 460,000 additional adult men. By any measure, in the 1970s American higher education acquired an additional dimension of new institutions and new units of existing institutions intended to serve adult and part-time students. Whether or not this met the idealistic vision of the nontraditional movement is another matter.

An inherent vulnerability of the nontraditional movement stemmed from the rejection or incomprehension of the nature of academic knowledge. Realizing that it could not achieve its goals playing by the rules of academe, it denigrated traditional higher education and sought to redefine the college student and academic learning.[82] But academic knowledge is not easily displaced. Ideally, it rests upon objective evidence, aims to be universal in nature, and is dynamic in its openness to continual advancement and interpretation. Immersion in academic knowledge is assumed to develop high levels of ability in reading, writing, numeracy, and thinking. This centuries-old foundation of the Western academic tradition was castigated from many perspectives in the 1970s, but the tradition persisted as the core intellectual practice of universities. The nontraditional movement sought to validate other forms of learning based on subjective experience, particularistic accomplishments, and acquisition of information. Such learning might have considerable value, but many doubted that it deserved to be counted for college credit. The American system of higher education has been exceedingly tolerant of large gradients of quality in academic degrees and probably became more so in the 1970s. But awareness of the relative quality of different academic degrees still prevailed among the educated public.

The hopeful premise underlying degree plans or contracts was that students were capable of defining their learning goals. This was a demanding task for a neophyte, even with the assiduous guidance of a mentor (who was often more of an auditor). When these students were surveyed, roughly two-thirds expressed a desire for academic credit toward a degree or credential.[83] In other words, most

---

82   E.g., "Traditional education ... is based on a mechanistic model of man which defines the human as a passive, robot [sic], reactive organism which is inherently at rest.... Nontraditional study, on the other hand, has sprung from an organismic [sic] model of man which defines the human being as an inherently and spontaneously active, growing, developing, self-actualizing organism": quoted in Noel F. McGinn, "Adult Higher Education for Social Change," *New Directions for Higher Education* 14 (1976): 83–106, quote pp. 94–95.

83   Mayhew, *Legacy of the 1970s*, 62–63; Kett, *Pursuit of Knowledge*, 431–37.

nontraditional students wanted traditional degrees. Since retention of nontraditional students was tenuous, learning contracts were intended to expedite the process by finding life or work experience, or other expedients, worthy of credits. This was obviously a lenient process or it would have defeated the purpose of shortening the course. But the corollary was a cheapened degree. Degree holders from such nontraditional institutions thus were perceived as falling at the lower end of the broad American spectrum of college graduates. This did not negate the value of their education. Validating a student's personal experiences as college-level learning could enhance an individual's morale and self-esteem. And, by checking the "college graduate" box on a job application, a bachelor's degree could open some gates in the American workforce regardless of its provenance.

Nontraditional higher education was not new in the 1970s, but it emerged as a powerful, self-conscious movement at the beginning of the decade. As such, it initiated a new dimension of American higher education that not only persisted but would discover enormous commercial potential in the twenty-first century.

THE INVERSION OF THE SEVENTIES: INSTITUTIONS

American colleges and universities in the 1970s experienced a reversal of the trends that had dominated during the Golden Age of the 1960s. The nature of higher education is notorious for resistance to change, as the decade's earnest reformers learned; but institutions now confronted countervailing forces, from the markets and the culture, that compelled adaptations in ongoing operations and future aspirations: fiscal budgets, student clienteles, curricular dislocations, and the research mission all were affected. Financially, retrenchment was the watchword from the beginning of the decade. Resources that had flowed to higher education since the 1950s ceased to grow at the end of the 1960s, while rising inflation created different kinds of pressure on expenditures. Appropriations for public institutions in many states were curtailed in real terms, and voluntary support contracted in the private sector. The postwar era of continuous expansion was over, with few exceptions, and institutions at different times and to different degrees faced the painful necessity of reducing spending and commitments—retrenchment. At the same time, the widespread disparagement of academic values was the backdrop for other pressures. Changing student demand required institutions to offer new subjects like women's studies and to expand curricula like business. Enthusiasm for the mission of advancing knowledge waned in the 1970s, along with external funding. Support for graduate education was sharply reduced. Institutions from private liberal arts colleges to public research universities were affected by different facets of these trends, but the general effects were similar: instead of striving to fulfill aspirations as they had in the 1960s, institutions were compelled to lower expectations and modify behaviors in often painful ways.

The fiscal tourniquet on colleges and universities during the "long seventies" (1969–1981) is difficult to grasp from dollar figures alone. Current fund revenues for all higher education grew from $21.5 billion in 1969 to $72.2 billion in 1981. In constant dollars, this increase was about 50 percent, but enrollments grew by slightly more than that. Real revenues per student over those dozen years fell by 3 percent. Inflation was the obvious culprit, but inflation affected different categories of revenues and expenditures in different ways.

As a labor-intensive industry, higher education had difficulty matching gains in the general price level driven by productivity growth in the economy.[84] High rates of inflation worsened the problem. Faculty salaries had lagged woefully behind the rapid rise in prices after the war but then recovered admirably during the prosperous years of the Liberal Hour, only to fall behind again during the 1970s. Compensation for faculty and staff could not keep pace with the rising cost of living, but pressure to try was intense. Salary increases were imperative to retain faculty and maintain morale, and on many campuses unions applied additional pressure. The youthful faculties of the 1960s were now due for promotions, and the cost of employee benefits rose markedly as well. Average faculty salaries, not including these last two items, declined in real terms by 17 percent from 1972 to 1980.[85] A second spending imperative is what economists call factor costs—all the things institutions must purchase in open markets. Here inflation was most cruel when the 1973 Oil Shock multiplied prices for heating oil and electricity. All institutions faced the rising costs of employee compensation, benefits, and factor prices, but their capacity to deal with them depended on their sources of income.

Yale exemplified the predicament of even wealthy private research universities. Despite having the second largest endowment, retrenchment was a necessity during these years as the university struggled with recurring deficits. The endowment fluctuated in value but was the same in 1976 as it had been in 1967 (current dollars). Income from gifts was flat as well during these years. Their combined contribution to Yale's income declined from 33 to 22 percent. This was only partially offset by student charges, which rose by an annual average of 9 percent,

84   William G. Bowen, *The Economics of Major Private Universities* (New York: Carnegie Commission on Higher Education, 1968). Writing at the end of the Golden Age, Bowen calculated that private universities needed to increase expenditures by 7.5 percent per year (given 2 percent inflation) to match the increase in the general wage levels and cover other rising costs.

85   "The ratio of tenured faculty to total faculty was 47 percent in 1969 and 65 percent in 1973, resulting in a kind of 'tenure blockage'": Graham and Diamond, *Rise of American Research Universities*, 87;

versus a 6 percent increase in the consumer price index. Yale's total income grew by 8 percent annually, with a good part coming from the medical school, but even this seeming revenue growth was consumed by growing expenditures. The quality of the faculty was no doubt Yale's highest priority, but maintaining the status quo was a struggle. Faculty numbers remained the same, but more senior ranks raised the salary bill. The faculty still ceded 2 percent of its share of the university budget. Yale tried to economize on purchases, deferred maintenance, and staff salaries, but two strikes by unionized staff captured the 2 percent of budget lost by the faculty. Utilities and benefits claimed almost 5 percent more of the university budget, while relative spending for books and student aid declined. In sum, fiscal necessity warped Yale spending toward noneducational spending (staff, benefits, and utilities) and away from its educational priorities (faculty, books, and student aid).[86] However, the university also took steps to deal proactively with these conditions.[87]

Kingman Brewster (1963–1976) is credited with bringing Yale into the modern academic world, enhancing its quality in both students and faculty and opening Yale College to a broader population, including minorities.[88] However, budget shortfalls in the early 1970s forced spending cutbacks that caused "real qualitative losses," Brewster admitted in 1973. In response, he resolved that year to launch a major fund-raising campaign. This was a highly controversial step, given the president's unpopularity with "Old Blue" alumni over Yale's modernization, coeducation, reductions in the admission of alumni children, and Brewster's alleged sympathy with student radicals.[89] Brewster knew he had to accommodate his critics. To gain approval from the Yale Corporation, he announced that he would retire when the campaign had assured "Yale's capital requirements." He further promised that "every effort be made to admit, and to gain acceptance of every qualified alumni son and daughter"; and further, "to give positive weight to athletic distinction if an applicant is otherwise qualified." Brewster thus re-

Linda A. Bell, "Ups and Downs: Academic Salaries Since the 1970s," *Academe* 85, 2 (March 1999): 12–20.

86   Yale University, "Achieving Financial Equilibrium at Yale: A Report on the Budget" (New Haven, CT: December 1977).

87   In 1974 the Yale faculty approved establishing a summer session in hopes of educating more students without hiring more faculty. The expected extra revenues were deemed worth compromising a long-standing principle that a Yale education consisted of a four-year residential experience. The summer session was never popular, and it proved costly in terms of faculty who, by combining summer teaching and sabbaticals, could be absent from campus for extended periods of time. It was soon dropped.

88   Geoffrey M. Kabaservice, "Kingman Brewster and the Rise and Fall of the Progressive Establishment," PhD Diss., Yale University, 1999.

89   Geiger, *Research and Relevant Knowledge*, 246–48; John Perry Miller, *Creating Academic Settings: High Craft and Low Cunning* (New Haven, CT: J. Simeon Press, 1991), 211–26. Brewster may have prevented an impending riot at Yale by famously saying that he was "skeptical of the ability of black revolutionaries to achieve a fair trial anywhere in the United States": Kabaservice, *Kingman Brewster*, 478–546.

versed the policy of his first decade in office, which emphasized diversity and merit in admissions. Alumni legacies increased by 56 percent and attained the same odds of admission in 1974 as they had pre-reform in 1964.[90] But wealthy old grads were far from mollified. The Campaign for Yale was launched in 1974 with a goal of raising $370 million in three years—the largest university campaign to date, although still inadequate for Yale's projected qualitative needs. In the face of rising inflation, falling stock prices, and smoldering alumni resentment, the campaign struggled. After Brewster resigned in 1976 to become ambassador to the Court of St. James, the campaign was reorganized and declared victory in 1979, two years after the target date. Although the campaign goal was officially met, the university had already dialed back the original expectations for meeting Yale's needs. When the Yale budget incurred a $6.6 million deficit in 1976–1977, a thoroughgoing financial review imposed spending restrictions to achieve "financial equilibrium." The university accepted that it would "not restore Yale to the affluent days of the 1960s, [but rather] ensure continued excellence in a period of economic uncertainty."[91] Yale muddled through the 1970s, but at a cost to its own perception of academic quality.

LIBERAL ARTS COLLEGES. Private liberal arts colleges faced the same financial pressures as Yale, but with additional complications. Most experienced decreases in the size and qualifications of their applicant pools as well as defections from the liberal arts mission. The trends of the era all ran against them. Declining scholastic aptitudes shrunk the number of well-prepared students these institutions sought. Moreover, new coeducational opportunities provided more opportunities for high achievers at highly competitive universities. Tuition differentials became more problematic. The difference between average tuition at a private versus public university was $1,261 in 1968 and $3,360 in 1980 (and even more at selective residential colleges).[92] The percentage increases in public and private tuition were comparable, but for families of prospective students the dollar amount mattered. Finally, the mission of these colleges to offer liberal arts, preparation for graduate/professional school, and a collegiate experience all lost favor in the 1970s. For liberal arts colleges, adaptation to these realities was imperative.

90   Miller, *Creating Academic Settings*, 216–17; Karabel, *Chosen*, 449–67.
91   Yale, "Achieving Financial Equilibrium," 78. Deficits of this magnitude were intolerable and potentially embarrassing: 94 percent of the Yale endowment was restricted, so that $6.6 million represented 20 percent of working capital.
92   Average tuition at a public university in 1980 was $915 versus $4,275 for privates (NCES); average total cost at a private university in 1976 was $4,715 compared to $6,425 at Yale.

This adaptation had to be led by the college administration. The colleges had always been loosely run organizations, with long tenures for congenial presidents and continuity of traditional practices. Retrenchment required unpopular decisions that were implemented in both quotidian spending and major budgetary reorganizations. As presidencies turned over, boards of trustees sought managers who could balance budgets rather than peacemakers to appease protesting students. Like Yale in 1977, virtually every college experienced one or more concerted efforts to economize in the decade, usually prefaced by a lengthy study and report. The overall effect was a general enhancement of managerial control by college administrations. Federal mandates for reporting, health, and safety regulations required more administrators. Relative salaries posed a contentious issue as all classes of employees fell behind the galloping consumer price index. And downsizing, whether of academic departments or administrative offices, sparked controversy no matter how strategically justified and financially necessary it was. One result was a growing estrangement between administrations and faculty. The number of administrators tended to increase over the decade, and faculty did not. Some faculty worked with the administration on the numerous commissions that sought to cope with the decade's challenges, but a faction always harbored latent hostility toward administrative efforts. Faculty morale was depressed for good reason. The trends of the 1970s offended prevailing liberal sensibilities. Austerity frustrated former expectations of continued academic development. The collapse of the faculty market left individuals frozen in place, and budgetary pressures meant tenure and promotions were less generously awarded. Discontented faculty seldom viewed the college's predicament realistically. At Franklin and Marshall, for example, extensive deliberations in 1971 over ways to cut $500,000 from the base operating budget produced a plan for reducing faculty and administrative positions. A group of faculty then offered a counterproposal that would cut only administrative staff in admissions, alumni and public relations, and development, with those tasks assumed by the faculty as extra duties.[93] Wisely rejected, the faculty plan was shortsighted, to say the least: Addressing the college's difficulties more than ever required professional expertise in those critical offices.

Enrollments and income were the central concerns, and for colleges heavily dependent on tuition, they were the same thing. A detailed study of admissions at sixteen selective liberal arts colleges in Ohio and the Northeast revealed the impact of the changing student market from 1965 to 1980. In those years, the median combined SAT score of high school graduates declined by 77 points

93   Sally F. Griffith, *Liberalizing the Mind: Two Centuries of Liberal Education at Franklin & Marshall College* (University Park: Pennsylvania State University Press, 2010), 361–63.

nationally. These colleges all experienced declines, some exceeding 200 points. However, "the colleges with the highest mean SAT scores in 1965 tended to lose the least ground between 1965 and 1980, whereas the colleges with the lowest scores in 1965 experienced the largest SAT drops."[94] Other admissions benchmarks followed this same pattern—increases in acceptance rates, declines in yields, and fewer students from the top quintiles of high school classes. The results for the less selective colleges in the study sample are more representative of the Liberal Arts 1 colleges of the Carnegie Classification.[95] This development continued the "resorting of American higher education" described by Caroline Hoxby (Chapter 2), whereby increasingly mobile top students gravitated toward higher-quality institutions. However, a distinctive feature of the 1970s was that fewer students followed this strategy of maximizing academic quality (most freshmen were enrolling in community colleges). But given the pressures on enrollments, these colleges greatly expanded efforts to recruit those students who did seek a quality liberal education. In 1970 the College Board began offering the Student Search Service, through which colleges could purchase names, addresses, and SAT scores of test takers. Direct mail to prospective students quickly became the staple of every selective institution's admissions office. High school students suddenly found well-known institutions that they had never considered begging them to apply. Due in part to aggressive recruitment, liberal arts colleges with largely regional clienteles suffered the poaching of their natural clientele by more prestigious institutions, and they naturally responded by undertaking their own poaching.[96]

The experiences of liberal arts colleges in these years was diverse, with crises and recoveries occurring at different intervals at different institutions. In general, conditions improved near the end of the decade, and some institutions emerged stronger. The economy between the 1975 and 1979 recessions provided some respite, but institutions mainly learned to adapt. Longer term, private colleges could control admissions, payrolls, and fund raising, and the long-range studies they conducted led to realistic plans. Recruitment efforts by admissions offices were not only vastly expanded but also refined to become more effective. Most colleges also maintained various low-profile units that offered part-time, evening,

---

94   Duffy and Goldberg, *Crafting a Class*, 85.

95   Carnegie Foundation for the Advancement of Teaching, *A Classification of Institutions of Higher Education* (Princeton: CFAT, 1987): LA 1 colleges were highly selective, primarily undergraduate colleges that award more than half of bachelor's degrees in the arts and sciences. The number of private LA 1 colleges decreased from 144 in 1970 to 123 in 1976, no doubt due to declining selectivity; average size remained ca. 1,250.

96   Caroline M. Hoxby, "The Changing Selectivity of American Colleges," NBER Working Paper No. 15446 (October 2009); Duffy and Goldberg, *Crafting a Class,* 54–57.

or extension courses, and these could be expanded to bring additional tuition from nontraditional students. Fund-raising in the 1970s was difficult, but such efforts still brought in badly needed funds. But as these colleges contemplated fiscal measures, they reexamined their missions as well. Almost unanimously, they concluded that above all they would remain committed to quality—that preserving their market required protecting and hopefully enhancing reputations. Some colleges limited or reduced enrollments to uphold student quality. A concern for faculty quality was reflected in more circumspect hiring and promotions. Additional capital spending became a necessity both for academic facilities and campus amenities, like student centers, for purposes of recruitment. And widespread reexaminations of curricula took place to fashion a more appealing core and electives. Such measures were tantamount to acts of faith in the 1970s, but they proved prescient for the next decade when liberal arts returned to favor.

The strategies adopted by LA 1 colleges in the 1970s proved long lasting, as did those of less selective private colleges. The Carnegie Classification of Liberal Arts 2 colleges contained a heterogeneous grouping of small, less wealthy institutions, most with present or past religious affiliation. Although they accepted most applicants, they tended to attract students with average or better test scores in the 1960s, but scores sank below the average thereafter.[97] To maintain enrollments, most offered a variety of vocationally oriented courses of study. Business majors were offered everywhere, despite the difficulty of hiring instructors with appropriate credentials. They also created programs to tap niche markets in the health fields (dental hygiene, physical therapy, medical technology) and education (athletic trainer, recreation). A decade later, when David Breneman assessed the condition of liberal arts colleges, he dismissed 330 of 540 LA 2 institutions that awarded more than 60 percent of degrees in professional subjects. He called them "essentially small professional schools with few liberal arts majors, but usually with a liberal arts core and tradition."[98] Lacking the resources to adopt the quality strategies of LA 1 colleges, they nonetheless remained viable by adapting to a challenging environment.[99]

PUBLIC REGIONAL COLLEGES AND UNIVERSITIES. In the public sector, regional colleges and universities ("Comprehensive" in the Carnegie Classification) faced challenges of adaptation under different conditions. The mushroom

---

97 Hoxby, "Changing Selectivity," Figure 1.

98 David Breneman, *Liberal Arts Colleges: Thriving, Surviving, or Endangered?* (Washington, DC: Brookings Institution, 1994), 12–13.

99 James W. Logue found their relative prosperity in the 1990s largely due to fund raising: "An Analysis of the Survival Ability of Private Colleges and Universities in Pennsylvania," PhD diss., Pennsylvania State University, 2003.

growth of this sector stalled in the early 1970s and then stagnated for decades. Student qualifications at these largely open institutions declined along with national averages, but retention rates, if anything, improved—although these schools typically graduated less than half of their students. State support of public higher education grew by more than 10 percent annually during the decade. The vicissitudes of state budgets and distribution among different sectors created a complicated picture. Cutbacks and retrenchment were more prevalent in states that had formerly led in higher education funding, chiefly in the Midwest, while laggards, particularly in the Sunbelt, increased relative spending (below). However, for the decade overall, states contributed more than $3.00 for the operations of public colleges and universities for every dollar of student tuition—a public commitment to affordable, quality higher education that the country was unlikely to ever see again.

Among public institutions, the regional colleges faced the difficult task of changing mission—again. In the 1960s, the arts and sciences university had overgrown the teachers college, but in the 1970s students' preferences shifted to professional programs. The nature of these institutions impeded adaptation. Most were part of state systems or were treated as such by state legislatures. In Pennsylvania, for example, the fourteen state colleges received orders for a hiring freeze in 1975, followed by mandatory layoffs. All colleges were treated alike, regardless of enrollments or programs. In addition, most systems adopted collective bargaining in the 1970s, introducing further rigidity. These institutions were expected to offer the full range of programs demanded by local students. Thus, the kind of long-range planning that guided private colleges through difficult times was scarcely possible for state colleges.[100]

Some of these difficulties were exemplified by Ball State University in Muncie, Indiana, a regionally focused former teachers college that had ballooned to over 17,000 students in 1970 but still operated "in comparative isolation from mainstream academic currents."[101] Ball State's predicament can be summarized in one statistic: in 1964, 84 percent of graduates earned degrees in education; in 1981, just 11 percent did. In the 1960s it had advanced academically toward becoming a comprehensive university. For example, the Department of Social Studies in the education school was divided into the standard disciplines of anthropology, economics, political science, and sociology. But by the end of the 1970s, 35 percent of entering students wanted to major in business. Building a

---

100   Riesman, *On Higher Education*, 199; Eda Bessie Edwards, *Profile of the Past, a Living Legacy: Bloomsburg State College, 1839–1979* (Bloomsburg, PA: Bloomsburg College Alumni Association, 1982), 211–12.

101   Anthony O. Edmonds and E. Bruce Geelhoed, *Ball State University: An Interpretive History* (Bloomington: Indiana University Press, 2001), 187–246, quote p. 189.

business school under steady-state conditions was more difficult than expanding the arts and sciences had been. Accreditation by the American Association of Collegiate Schools of Business was critical, but Ball State was denied it in 1976 for having too few faculty with PhDs. The expense of hiring additional instructors for business at one point antagonized the campus by causing the cancellation of class sections in other units. However, the largest stumbling block was an antiquated salary structure based on seniority, a relic of the egalitarian teachers-college days. To hire qualified faculty the administration attempted to implement compensation based on "market" (salaries comparable to those in similar institutions and fields) and "merit" (individual accomplishments). Most faculty were in less competitive subjects and published little—hence, they were unlikely to benefit and adamantly opposed the plan. Two presidents resigned under pressure (1978 and 1981) in large part over this issue. But "mainstream academic currents" ultimately prevailed. Ball State's business school won accreditation by the AACSB and became the largest in Indiana.

CITY UNIVERSITY OF NEW YORK. The country's third-largest university system, the City University of New York, was a world unto itself, but in the 1970s it experienced extremes of both inclusionary expansion and fiscal retrenchment.[102] Intended to serve graduates of the city's public schools, its nine senior colleges and six community colleges charged no tuition. Led by the renowned City College, the senior colleges were about as selective as state flagship research universities. Their students were drawn predominantly from white Jewish and ethnic communities. Blacks and Puerto Ricans, who were now a large portion of the city's population, fared poorly in the city's high schools and composed only 9 percent of 1969 freshmen. The system's chancellor, Albert Bowker, who was hired in 1963 to develop graduate programs, saw the necessity of incorporating minorities into CUNY. He envisioned phasing in a graded but inclusive system of admissions by 1975, but events forced the issue. In 1969, amid a national racial crisis and student protests, minority students demanding open admissions occupied part of City College and effectively closed the campus. Unlike the confrontations described in Chapter 5, this occupation transcended the university, touching off a citywide political conflict that embroiled the different ethnic populations. Given these warring factions, the only feasible resolution became, "let them all in"—open admission to CUNY for all NYC high school graduates. Students

---

102   These developments are analyzed in David E. Lavin, Richard D. Alba, and Richard A. Silberstein, *Right versus Privilege: The Open-Admissions Experiment at the City University of New York* (New York: Free Press, 1981), and David E. Lavin and David Hyllegard, *Changing the Odds: Open Admission and the Life Chances of the Disadvantaged* (New Haven, CT: Yale University Press, 1996).

could qualify for senior colleges with either a strong high school average (as always) or by placing in the top half of their graduating class, thus accommodating minorities. Anyone else could enter a community college.

New York City thus instituted "higher education for all" in an abrupt and radical manner, the single largest expansion of minority enrollments of the era. In fall 1970, 35,000 freshmen enrolled—an increase of 75 percent. Black entrants increased threefold, Hispanics more than doubled, and minorities composed almost one-quarter of the class. In fact, a larger number of white students took advantage of the open path. However, CUNY's open admissions experiment had a short life, at least in this form. By 1975, the city's impossible finances could no longer be sustained. Budgetary cuts fell especially hard on CUNY. Subsequent conditions only worsened as the city budget, including CUNY, passed into the hands of the Emergency Financial Control Board. The city's fiscal crisis became a university crisis. In May 1976, with the year's budget spent, CUNY defaulted on payments and the university was closed. The price of state relief, to allow the school year to be completed, was the imposition of tuition equal to that charged by SUNY and a tightening of admission criteria. In fall 1976, 11,000 fewer freshmen enrolled. CUNY admissions remained essentially "open," but now two-thirds of students entered community colleges (up from 43 percent).

The battle for CUNY invoked incompatible principles. Opponents predicted that open admissions would lower academic standards and undermine the value of CUNY degrees. Proponents held that the right to higher education required compensating for the handicaps of class, race, and inferior education in minority-majority schools. They later complained that the restrictions imposed in 1976 compromised these efforts.[103] The key actions, both establishing open admissions and curtailing it, were political decisions made under crisis conditions. The original political objectives were achieved in terms of enrollments and, to some extent, results. Among the early cohorts of open-admissions entrants to senior colleges, a remarkable 56 percent were estimated to have graduated by 1984.[104] Analysis of these results revealed, on balance, that those who succeeded had relatively better high school grades and academic preparation, which suggested that comparable results might have been achieved under the more prudent Bowker plan. CUNY pre-1970 was clearly too socially restrictive considering its mission as a municipal university, but post-1970 it was too "open" in terms

---

103   "Open admissions was based on a new premise: college education is a right, just [like] grammar school and high school education," Lavin et al., *Right versus Privilege*, 307.

104   Lavin and Hyllegard, *Changing the Odds*, 46. An earlier analysis found that one-quarter of the first cohort of open-admission entrants to senior colleges obtained a bachelor's degree in five years (Lavin et al., *Right versus Privilege*, 129). A characteristic of CUNY students was irregular attendance and extended time-to-degree.

of unsustainable cost and the burden of instructing ill-prepared students. At the end of the decade, CUNY still fulfilled something like its historic mission, offering unique opportunities to the city's diverse commuting students: City College was still rated "very competitive"; minorities composed a majority of students; and, as in the past, CUNY offered the opportunity for upward mobility to the children of the city's many immigrants.

RESEARCH UNIVERSITIES. Research universities too were forced to retrench in the early 1970s. Given the many undertakings of these multiversities, they endured cutbacks to numerous programs, with graduate education particularly vulnerable. But these institutions also possessed extensive resources and multiple sources of income, the better to absorb selective downsizing. The general disparagement of academic values and research was disheartening and also had tangible repercussions. Congress reduced federal funds for academic research, and many state legislatures tilted state funding away from flagship universities. On campuses, the research role faced greater competition from more fashionable activities, principally undergraduate education. However, the mission of advancing knowledge was essential and implacable. As academic and scientific knowledge inexorably grew, research universities had not merely to keep abreast but also to participate in that process. How much and how well they did this was predicated on developments on several levels. In the research economy, the funds supplied for supporting research influenced the amount of it that universities conducted and the health of different fields. Within institutions, the performance of research was conditioned by the resources each university commanded and how it allocated them among its multiple activities. Finally, research and scholarship were decentralized activities, emanating from the work of individuals or teams in academic departments and research units. Here resided the independent spirit of curiosity and inquiry that might be furthered or retarded by external grants or university priorities, but it was sustained by its own inherent momentum.

In the research economy, the shrinkage of federal science funding occasioned the largest adjustments and the loudest complaints. Federal funds supported 73 percent of university research in 1967. Over the next decade, it declined slightly in real terms, but the failure to grow ended two decades of astronomical increases and inflated expectations. The changing nature of this support made adaptation all the more trying. In retrospect, there was some fluff in federal science budgets by the end of the "golden" post-Sputnik decade. Funds for science development, graduate training, and R&D infrastructure were scaled back or eliminated, thus depriving universities of extra revenues that had facilitated and encouraged the research enterprise. The National Science Foundation, in particular, sacrificed such activities to focus its budget on research per se. In constant dollars, NSF support for academic science was essentially flat for the decade, while funding for defense and space research was sharply curtailed. The exception was the National Institutes of Health, which doubled its support for academic research during the decade. Congress's disillusionment with the basic research ideology of the 1960s was manifested in attempts to promote practical applications, including health care. NSF was tasked with the Research Applied to National Needs Program in 1971, but this government approach to connecting research with applications was deemed a failure and was terminated in 1977. President Nixon's War on Cancer fared better, not necessarily in its putative objective but in augmenting NIH's contribution to advancing the revolution in biotechnology. Federal support for academic research turned up in the Carter administration and, selectively, in President Reagan's first term. Support for the social sciences remained depressed, but engineering and computer sciences joined biomedicine as favored fields, more than doubling from the mid-seventies to the mid-eighties. This pattern also continued the federal emphasis on potential applications (Chapter 7).[105]

In the academic departments of research universities, a rather different picture emerged even during the retrenchment of the early 1970s. There the dominant tone was set by the long tail of the academic revolution. The number of doctorates awarded doubled from the 1964 to 1969 academic years, exceeding 29,000. In the next three years, they rose to a peak of 34,000 and remained only slightly below that level for the rest of the decade. These were the best-trained scholars and scientists in U.S. history, emerging from the intense academic atmosphere of the 1960s and steeped in the latest theories and methods of rapidly advancing disciplines. The best of them were readily absorbed by research universities. From 1969 to 1974, the average public Research 1 university added 250 regular faculty (18 percent), and the private ones added 400 (55 percent). And scholarly activity expanded even more rapidly. The average number of scientific publications by those public universities doubled; the private ones increased by 121 percent.[106] Except for a handful of institutions, academic development was not sacrificed to financial hardship. But for each university, the constraints and opportunities were mixed.

Universities possessed unique combinations of academic strengths, financial resources, and discretion in allocating spending. Yet all belonged to an organiza-

---

105   Data from National Science Foundation; Graham and Diamond, *Rise of American Research Universities*, 84–107; Geiger, *Research and Relevant Knowledge*, 245–73.

106   Graham and Diamond, *Rise of American Research Universities*, 102, 107.

tional field—research universities—with well-defined norms and values. Hence, universities made realistic assessments of their relative position and the possibilities for preservation or improvement. After the mid-seventies, when research activity began to revive, these perennial processes altered the configuration of research universities. Separately budgeted research expenditures are the most general indication of research performance, but in an era of high inflation, the best relative measure is each institution's share of total academic R&D. For financial strength, the most relevant measure is the change over time in a university's instructional budget (as Cartter found), which consisted largely of faculty salaries. A thorough study that compared universities on these two measures from the mid-seventies to the mid-eighties revealed the impact of the developments just discussed on the system of research universities.[107]

Among top fifty universities that increased research share and had above-average growth in instructional budgets, nine of eleven were in Sunbelt states (Arizona, Georgia Tech, Louisiana State, North Carolina State, Virginia Tech, Texas and Texas A&M, Stanford, and Southern California). The first five universities were comparatively new entrants to the ranks of large research performers, and they were joined by fifteen more neophytes having smaller but rising research shares. Most of those institutions benefited from the Sunbelt states belatedly joining the academic revolution.[108] State investments in public universities increased after 1970 in the Southeast, as well as in Oklahoma, New Mexico, and Arizona. As these universities expanded, they enjoyed a buyer's market for academic talent, which was soon reflected in rising research shares.

The opposite quadrant—institutions with declining research share and below average instructional spending—contained all the Big Ten universities, save Iowa and private Northwestern, as well as smaller state universities across the Midwest. The former group had been among the chief benefactors of the academic revolution, building some of the largest faculties, graduate programs, and research budgets. Their challenge was to preserve these myriad commitments in the retrenchment of the 1970s and the erosion of state support that followed.

In 1982, the first comprehensive *Assessment of Research-Doctoral Programs* since 1969 reflected these changes. The same eight Big Ten schools with declining research shares all dropped in their overall quality rating. Michigan and Wisconsin remained in the top dozen, but Michigan State and Ohio State dropped

107   The following draws on Jennifer R. Krohn, "Advancing Research Universities: A Study of Institutional Development, 1976–1986," PhD diss., Pennsylvania State University, 1992.

108   For a prospective view of the challenges facing southern research universities, see Allan M. Cartter, "Qualitative Aspects of Southern University Education," *Southern Economic Journal* 32 (July 1965): 39–69; Geiger, *Research and Relevant Knowledge*, 283–86.

out of the top twenty-five. The Sunbelt public universities advancing in that elite group were North Carolina, Texas, UCLA and UC San Diego, as well as private Caltech and Stanford. UC Berkeley remained no. 1.

The ten leading private universities present a different profile. Most lost a portion of research share (exceptions: Caltech and Stanford). Already having the highest salary scales, growth in instructional costs was average, and they added few faculty. They tended to be less concerned with research volume per se and more concerned with what Yale earlier called "continued excellence." In that sense, their high salaries allowed them to benefit from the buyer's market for faculty talent, especially the ability to raid public universities. But they were reluctant to pursue research opportunities with high marginal costs—new buildings or infrastructure.[109] Hence, research shares drifted lower. However, they succeeded in the goal of continued excellence: five rose substantially in the 1982 *Assessment*, and four remained in the same high rank in the top fourteen. Only Harvard declined! From second to a tie for third, its august faculty were apparently becoming somewhat superannuated.[110]

The hierarchy of research universities at the beginning of the 1980s showed both stability and change. Stability existed at the top, where the sixteen leading institutions were no different from those identified by Cartter in 1964, and Keniston before him.[111] However, in the next twenty-five places, at least ten universities were new entrants to the research university club. Four were literally new: the additions to the University of California at Irvine, San Diego, and Santa Barbara, and SUNY's campus at Stony Brook. Four others had been transformed from largely teaching institutions: Arizona, Georgia Tech, Maryland, and Carnegie-Mellon. Virginia and Southern California also raised their academic profile.[112] These developments add a significant dimension to any interpretation of American research universities or higher education's dismal decade. Despite a difficult fiscal environment, governmental disfavor, and cultural disdain

109   This distinction did not apply to medical research, where NIH assumed most costs and paid overhead; hence, the more research grants the better, for public and private universities.

110   Lyle V. Jones et al., *An Assessment of Research-Doctoral Programs in the United States* (Washington, DC: National Academy Press, 1982); David S. Webster, "America's Highest Ranked Graduate Schools, 1925–1982," *Change* (May–June 1983), 14–24; Krohn, "Advancing Research Universities"; Morton Keller and Phyllis Keller, *Making Harvard Modern: The Rise of America's University* (New York: Oxford University Press, 2001), 383–431.

111   These sixteen universities had average departmental ratings from 3.67 to 4.78: Geiger, *Research and Relevant Knowledge*, 135–46. Except for Johns Hopkins (out), and UCLA (in), these are the same prewar institutions identified as research universities in Roger L. Geiger, *To Advance Knowledge: The Growth of American Research Universities, 1900–1940* (New York: Oxford University Press, 1986).

112   These institutions had average ratings of 2.9 to 3.6 and were rated lower or not at all by Magoun ("Cartter Report," 1966; see Chapter 3): Geiger, *Research and Relevant Knowledge*, 208–9: Arizona and Georgia Tech are analyzed on pp. 273–95.

for academic values, the most academically eminent universities managed to pre-serve and augment their academic distinction. Further, given the momentum of the academic revolution, ambitious universities advanced both in academic quality and research performance.[113] This dynamism would become even more pronounced when conditions favored research universities, as they did in the next decade.

113   The study by Hugh Davis Graham and Nancy Diamond focused on rising research universities and, using per capita faculty data, demonstrated the growing productivity of academic scientists: *Rise of American Research Universities*, passim.

PART IV

THE CURRENT ERA IN AMERICAN HIGHER EDUCATION

THE DAWN OF THE CURRENT ERA, 1980–2000

THE ELECTION OF RONALD REAGAN TO THE PRESIDENCY IN 1980 was hailed as a new "Morning for America." This juncture marked the dawn of a new era for American higher education as well. No events directly linked these two developments. However, the new directions that emerged in higher education mirrored the conservative tone enveloping much of the country.

For higher education, the 1970s were a dismal decade. The frustration of the lofty expectations of the academic revolution set the tone, exacerbated by financial retrenchment and the declining academic preparation and interests of students. But the policies adopted in the decade sought more egalitarian participation by all groups in American society and the provision of institutions to accommodate them. This was largely accomplished. The plateauing of enrollments and participation rates in the last half of the decade indicated that the demand for higher education was being met. These years marked a high point in affordable higher education of reasonable quality, taught by the abundant graduates of doctoral programs in recently expanded institutions. Of course, sentiment in the higher education community envisioned measures to further extend educational opportunity, but the national mood no longer favored that course. After three decades of public exertions by state and federal governments to erect the world's most comprehensive and competent system of higher education, the tide was turning toward privatization.[1]

Two triggers, both prior to the 1980 election, marked turning points. Important in their respective spheres, they also portended larger shifts in public attitudes. In 1978, Congress passed the Middle Income Student Assistance Act, which eliminated income restrictions on federal Guaranteed Student Loans. A sop to middle-class voters, it was the first step toward opening a new source of income for colleges and universities—the future earnings of students. Longer

---

1   The pervasive drift toward market coordination—privatization—in higher education is analyzed in Roger L. Geiger, *Knowledge and Money: Research Universities and the Paradox of the Marketplace* (Stanford, CA: Stanford University Press, 2004).

term, student loans would transform the funding of higher education. In 1980 the Bayh-Dole Act allowed universities to patent discoveries made with federal funds and instructed them to commercialize such innovations. Intended to aid the competitiveness of American industry, it invoked economic development as a new and compelling rationale for university research. Both developments were central threads in the transformations that shaped American higher education to the end of the twentieth century.[2]

UNIVERSITIES AND ECONOMIC RELEVANCE: REVIVAL OF THE RESEARCH MISSION

The rapprochement between industrial and academic science made little progress through most of the 1970s.[3] Despite previous admonitions from President Johnson in the 1960s and programs initiated under President Nixon, the respective cultures of industrial and academic science remained largely incompatible. University scientists were wedded to the ideology of basic research and had become accustomed to feeding from the federal trough. Industrial investments in technological innovation had stagnated since the early 1960s, as had relations with university science. Interactions persisted among technologically oriented institutions and in fields like chemistry, engineering, and agriculture, where collaboration was long-standing. Still, the early 1970s was the nadir for industry sponsorship of university research. Conditions began to change near the end of the decade with public and private initiatives to foster greater cooperation and with the manifold impacts of biotechnology.

The biotechnology revolution and the rise of university patenting were intrinsically linked, but this linkage resulted from the conjuncture of separate developments. First, basic scientific discovery was fundamental. In 1973, twenty years after James Watson and Francis Crick deciphered the structure of DNA, Herbert Boyer of UC San Francisco and Stanley Cohen at Stanford discovered a technique for inserting genetic material into different organisms. The discovery constituted one of the major scientific revolutions of the twentieth century, the foundation for limitless further advances in genomics and molecular biology. It also established the basis for genetic engineering—biotechnology. Boyer, for one, sought applications for this discovery. In 1976 he joined with a venture cap-

---

2   Roger L. Geiger, "Postmortem for the Current Era: Change in American Higher Education, 1980–2010," *Higher Education Forum* 10 (March 2013): 1–22.

3   Elizabeth Popp Berman, *Creating the Market University: How Academic Science Became an Economic Engine* (Princeton: Princeton University Press, 2012); Roger L. Geiger, *Research and Relevant Knowledge: American Research Universities Since World War II* (New York: Oxford University Press, 1993), 296–301.

italist to form Genentech. In just two years, the firm's researchers succeeded in synthesizing the human gene for insulin.[4]

By that date, the notions that the lack of innovation was responsible for the malaise of American industry and that stimulating innovation was a potential remedy were finding increasing public favor. An editorial in *Science* observed, "Industrial innovation has become a buzzword in bureaucratic circles." In political circles, innovation could be invoked to justify any number of policies. But Elizabeth Popp Berman has noted that the "innovation frame" was decisive in overcoming prevailing attitudes hindering scientific development. Safety concerns, for example, had motivated Congress to seriously consider measures to restrict research on recombinant DNA, but these efforts were dropped when the emphasis shifted to the danger of obstructing an innovative industry. Similarly, NIH had taken steps to make patenting more difficult for federally funded discoveries, but instead, arguments invoking innovation helped to achieve the opposite in the Bayh-Dole Act. The innovation frame at the end of the 1970s began to supersede the decade's reservations toward university research, and government policies in 1980 overcame them entirely.[5]

The events of 1980 not only validated the innovation frame, they altered the culture of university research. In June, a 5:4 Supreme Court decision in *Diamond v. Chakrabarty* ruled that living organisms could be patented. In October, Genentech stock was offered to the public and doubled in its first day of trading. In December, Stanford and UC San Francisco were issued the Cohen-Boyer patent on the technique for producing recombinant DNA. And the same month, the University and Small Business Patent Procedures Act was passed, sponsored by Senators Birch Bayh and Robert Dole. The Chakrabarty decision cleared the path for patenting the fruits of biotechnology, and Bayh-Dole ensured that universities could own these and other patents. The Cohen-Boyer patent, which ultimately yielded more than $250 million in university royalties, and Genentech's debut revealed the enormous financial potential of biotechnology. A frenzy of activity followed, but in a new context. Biotechnology, like atomic energy before, restored the faith that the most basic scientific research could produce discoveries of incalculable value and significance. But unlike previous discoveries, it inserted academic science into the commercial economy. Advancing human health through patents and biotech start-ups had financial potential that universities could neither ignore nor resist. Universities, and molecular biologists, were

4   Geiger, *Research and Relevant Knowledge*, 301–9.
5   David C. Mowery et al., *Ivory Tower and Industrial Innovation: University-Industry Technology Transfer before and after the Bayh-Dole Act in the United States* (Stanford, CA: Stanford University Press, 2004), quote p. 90; Berman, *Creating the Market University*, 54–56, 70–72, 102–5.

in a position of doing well by doing good. They emphasized the latter, while critics focused on the former.

Harvard president Derek Bok candidly admitted that the millions that might be gained from Wall Street "stir the blood of every harried administrator struggling to balance an unruly budget."[6] Indeed, Harvard succumbed to this temptation in 1980 by attempting to participate in a biotech start-up based on the research of a faculty biologist. The plan was dropped after it was attacked by faculty, alumni, and major newspapers for raising inherent conflicts of interest. Molecular biologists in the forefront of biotech research were the critical scarce input for potential discoveries, and they were avidly recruited for commercial ventures. They were also extremely talented and valuable members of university faculties. Some 200 biotech firms were founded between 1980 and 1984, most created by venture capitalists seeking to capitalize on the expertise of these scientists. Universities were challenged on the one hand to find acceptable ways to tap the value of discoveries being made in their laboratories, and on the other to deal with inherent issues of secrecy, conflict of interest, and faculty responsibilities. These issues rose to national prominence, provoking Congressional hearings in which representatives posed as defenders of academic values against the alleged perils of commercialization. In an attempt to form some consensus—and avert a crisis—Stanford president Donald Kennedy in 1981 summoned the presidents of Harvard, MIT, Caltech, and the University of California to a confidential summit on university-industry relations. After a frank exchange of views, they could agree only on the need to formulate policies that would protect academic values and reassure the public. Specific measures for contract disclosures, patent licensing, or conflict of interest were left to the circumstances and practices of each university.[7]

In fact, after the tumult of the biotech revolution, university policies toward commercial ties gradually assumed the similarity, or isomorphism, that could be expected of a well-integrated organizational field. Universities (including Harvard) devised ways to have indirect or arms-length investments in start-up firms, although few of these brought very large returns. In 1981–1983, at least eleven multiyear, multimillion-dollar research contracts were concluded between universities and chemical and pharmaceutical corporations, but such arrangements

6   Derek Bok, *Beyond the Ivory Tower: Social Responsibilities of the Modern University* (Cambridge, MA: Harvard University Press, 1982), 141. Bok would later find it "unhealthy for universities to have their integrity questioned repeatedly by reports of excessive secrecy, conflicts of interest, and corporate efforts to manipulate and suppress research": Derek Bok, *Universities in the Marketplace: The Commercialization of Higher Education* (Princeton: Princeton University Press, 2003), 78.

7   Geiger, *Research and Relevant Knowledge*, 303–7.

proved to be few and temporary.[8] Instead, the greatest leverage of universities in the commercial economy existed in the patenting and licensing of faculty discoveries.

Universities had long patented the occasional faculty invention, although this was a controversial practice, especially when human health was concerned. Few universities did this themselves, instead consigning inventions to the Research Corporation, a nonprofit patent-management organization.[9] Universities produced about 100 patents annually prior to 1970. During that decade, several universities established their own intellectual property offices, including Stanford (1970) and Harvard (1977). By 1980, twenty-three universities had such units, and universities were awarded 350 patents. The biotech revolution changed perceptions and practices. In the 1980s, sixty-three more universities established intellectual property offices, and soon every research university would have one. In twenty years, university patents increased tenfold. Intellectual property offices had three functions. They provided a service to faculty who wished to see their findings put to practical use, and perhaps profit from them as well. They embodied the new university mission of technology transfer—translating university research into innovations for economic development. And they were expected to make money. Patents have no value unless licensed to users. The professional expertise of technology transfer officers was needed to evaluate the potential value of invention disclosures, guide the patenting process, and devise marketing strategies that would yield license income for inventors, universities, and support for their own offices.[10]

University commitment to patenting was driven by biotechnology, which produced one-half of university patents and 87 percent of licensing income. Without biotech, most universities would have lacked the incentive and the financial base to justify intellectual property offices. Initially, relatively few universities actually conducted advanced research in molecular biology, but they all quickly committed substantial investments. For purely scientific reasons, universities needed to participate in these pathbreaking fields, but "big hits"—multimillion-dollar patents, almost all in biotechnology—were an inescapable lure. Universities could scarcely resist the inducements to control homegrown intellectual property, but once they had done so, an additional dynamic operated.

8   Geiger, *Research and Relevant Knowledge*, 319, 304; Berman, *Creating the Market University*, 152–53.

9   Mowery, *Ivory Tower*, 35–84; Roger L. Geiger and Creso M. Sá, *Tapping the Riches of Science: Universities and the Promise of Economic Growth* (Cambridge, MA: Harvard University Press, 2008), 32–34.

10   Berman, *Creating the Market University*, 111–18; Geiger and Sá, *Tapping the Riches of Science*, 34–8, 117–55.

Technology transfer offices embraced the ideology of Bayh-Dole—the mission of translating university discoveries into contributions to the public good. They also were expected to support themselves through the income they generated. Both these imperatives, the idealistic and the pecuniary, motivated them to promote technology transfer within the university. This meant encouraging scientists to disclose inventions and undertake the considerable effort required to commercialize discoveries. These efforts assured an increasing volume of university patents and, hopefully, licensing revenues. The adoption of technology transfer as a university mission spawned a new bureaucracy and activities that extended well beyond the intellectual property office.

An additional, if less dramatic dimension of technology transfer developed alongside the biotech phenomenon. The impetus for university-industry collaboration came from neither partner but rather from public and private officials inspired by the innovation logic. In 1978, NSF devised a formula for industry-university research centers (IURCs).[11] Although previous efforts had floundered, NSF sponsorship and funding now provided stability for their persistence and development. Only four centers were created in the first two years, but their success caused the Carter administration to propose a substantial enlargement. This was squelched by a skeptical Reagan administration, but Republicans soon came around to supporting and enlarging IURCs.[12] Even sooner, states embraced this model to stimulate innovation and growth in local industries. By 1984 thirty-three states had established such programs in some form. Arrangements varied, but they included million-dollar commitments to economic development initiatives in Arizona, California, North Carolina, and Pennsylvania. The NSF in 1984 launched a much larger and costlier program of Engineering Research Centers (ERCs). Indeed, NSF was the chief locus for these federal efforts. IBM's research director, Erich Bloch, became the first NSF director appointed from private industry (1984–1990). He not only launched the ERCs but also gave engineering equal billing with science at the agency. By 1988, when President Reagan endorsed the new Science and Technology Centers Program, a broad consensus backed this approach. An NSF study in 1983 estimated that 250 IURCs were operating, but a survey in 1990 found four times that number (1,056 IURCs) with federal, state, or institutional sponsorship. Industrial affiliate programs, usually established with a department or center, also proliferated after 1980. Univer-

---

11 Officially called Industry/University Cooperative Research Centers, they were devised to deflect a Congressional initiative to allow private firms to compete for NSF research grants: Berman, *Creating the Market University*, 132–35.

12 George Keyworth, Reagan's science advisor, became a proponent of university-industry collaborations as key to economic development.

sity research parks were another strategy to foster collaboration through propinquity. Nearly 100 were added during the decade to the 24 existing in 1980.[13] All these developments represented a cultural change. In the 1970s universities and industry had little interest in working together, but in the 1980s, with strong external encouragement, they forged mutually beneficial relationships.

The two channels of university-industry interaction correspond with the two different paths of innovation in industry. In the first, most industrial innovation was developed in the research laboratories of large corporations. There, intellectual property was zealously guarded. These laboratories looked to academic science for generic expertise to complement and enhance their investigations as they developed their own products and patents. In the second, innovation that sprang directly from inventions tended to be the province of smaller companies, particularly start-ups. University inventions usually required considerable further development to become commercial products, which was typically accomplished through venture capital, start-up firms, or university-sponsored business incubators.

Corporations largely invested in relationships with academic scientists— through IURCs, affiliate programs, or individual consultants—that would complement their internal laboratories.[14] Thus, university ties with corporate labs were responsible for most industrial support for university research. These relationships corresponded with the growth of research in industry as well as universities. From 1975 to 1990, industry spending on basic and applied research doubled in real terms, as did the percentage of industry funding for academic research. Although the latter was just 7 percent, a good deal more was linked with the subsidized forms of university-industry interaction developed in the 1980s.

Industry funding was only one aspect of the revival of academic research in the 1980s. Real expenditures rose by 70 percent in the decade, enlarging its small share of GDP by one-quarter.[15] Federal funding grew by 47 percent but provided less than half of the increase. One-quarter of additional funding came from academic institutions themselves. Like industrial funding, most funding growth in the decade was intended for potential applications. The areas of greatest growth were medicine (+104 percent) and engineering (with computer science, +113

13   Berman, *Creating the Market University*, 135–43, 151; Geiger, *Research and Relevant Knowledge*, 298, 308–9; Geiger, *Knowledge and Money*, 205–6.

14   Geiger and Sá, *Tapping the Riches of Science*, 28–70; Roger L. Geiger, "University Supply and Corporate Demand for Academic Research," *Journal of Technology Transfer* 37 (2012):175–91.

15   Hugh Davis Graham and Nancy Diamond, *The Rise of American Research Universities: Elites and Challengers in the Postwar Era* (Baltimore: Johns Hopkins University Press, 1997), 117–43; Geiger, *Knowledge and Money*, 132–79.

percent). Medical research accelerated the growth momentum of the 1970s with a huge contribution from clinical fields. In addition to the stimulus of biotechnology, medical schools reaped a windfall from ballooning federal reimbursements for clinical procedures. Some of this income was recycled for research, which helped to account for a rising proportion of research support from university funds. This phenomenon accounted for the emergence of pure medical universities as major performers of academic research, such as UC San Francisco, Baylor College of Medicine in Houston, and the University of Texas Southwestern Medical Center.[16] Engineering benefited from the expansion of defense research and from industrial support. Now, however, the Defense Department tailored its research investments rather narrowly to weapons systems. Even the social sciences had an applied bent. Funding for psychology and sociology came primarily from the Department of Health and Human Services, and the largest patron of economics was the Department of Agriculture.[17]

In the 1980s, American society seemingly endorsed its research universities once again, this time for their inherent usefulness. But this progress was not matched, as during the academic revolution, by public approbation. By the end of the decade, universities faced a growing chorus of detractors.[18] Publicity on biotech and university patenting was almost invariably negative, and enthusiasm for university-industry collaborations tended to wane along with government support. IURCs were virtually invisible to the public. Each was unique, often limited in duration, and difficult to replicate. NSF established twenty-nine ERCs by 1990, but none for the next five years. Research parks were launched with inflated expectations that were often disappointed, at least in the short term. The recession of 1990–1991 and a slow recovery depressed the growth of academic research, accompanied by negative sentiment toward universities.

From the end of the 1980s, a succession of books attacked universities and higher education. Written by professors but addressed to the general public, these diatribes charged that most university research was worthless and that performing it caused academics to neglect their teaching and their students.[19] It is difficult to say if such broadsides were exploiting or fanning a general distrust toward the more privileged sector of higher education. But the image of universities was further damaged in 1991, when Stanford was discovered gouging on indirect-cost recovery on federal grants. Additional investigations and charges against other universities found little wrongdoing but prolonged the negative publicity. The

16 Respectively, ranked 15, 40, and 56 in research expenditures, 1997: National Science Foundation, *Science and Engineering Indicators 2000*, vol. 2, Table 6-4.

17 Graham and Diamond, *Rise of American Research Universities*, 122–38.

18 Geiger and Sá, *Tapping the Riches of Science*, 15–21.

19 See below, note 102.

Harris Poll registered a stunning 40 percent drop in public confidence in colleges and universities from 1990 to 1991. Real federal support for academic research, which had grown by 50 percent from 1982 to 1989, increased by half that much over the next seven years.[20]

Pessimism pervaded the academic research community in the early 1990s. A report by Leon M. Lederman, a Nobel laureate and president-elect of the American Association for the Advancement of Science, gloomily echoed Vannevar Bush forty-five years before: *Science: The End of the Frontier?* His central contention was that inadequate federal support was failing to match the expansion of science, cramping the prospects of junior faculty and graduate students, neglecting to provide necessary infrastructure, and squeezing research budgets at federal agencies. Three other national reports alleged an "overcapacity" in academic research and warned institutions not to emulate the research university model. University leaders foresaw no prospect that federal policies would improve.[21] These critics, however, were reflecting changes in the academic research system as much as its shortcomings. Intensely concerned with maintaining the vitality of American science, they looked to the federal government to fulfill that role as it had in the past. But the federal share of academic research support had declined from 67 to 59 percent in the 1980s—it was still a substantial amount, but one that was now parceled among additional objectives. The goal of economic development claimed a portion of federal funding, leaving less for basic science in the traditional disciplines. Moreover, to take advantage of growing fields required special provisions, whether for client-oriented units or laboratories to accommodate biotechnology, microelectronics, materials science, and other emerging fields. The number of centers and institutes at research universities grew by 30 percent in just the first half of the 1980s, and the number of nonfaculty researchers doubled in the decade. Creating such units imposed additional costs on universities that were not fully covered by research grants; hence, the complaints of universities that revenues could not keep pace with increasing responsibilities or, as Derek Bok lamented, that the research university had become an "overextended organization."[22] But science had not reached the end of the frontier. Academic research in 1990 attained its largest-ever share of GDP, and by the end of that decade the new research regime would regain momentum.

20 *Harris Poll*, March 7, 1994.

21 Leon M. Lederman, "Science: The End of the Frontier?," a supplement to *Science* (January 1991); Geiger, *Research and Relevant Knowledge*, 323–27; Graham and Diamond, *Rise of American Research Universities*, 141–42; *The American Research University: Daedalus* 122, 4 (Fall 1993).

22 Derek Bok, *President's Report, 1989–1990* (Harvard University, 1991), 6; Geiger, *Research and Relevant Knowledge*, 326–27.

Institutional patterns of research reflected this new regime. The twenty highest-rated universities on the 1982 NRC Assessment of Doctoral Programs lost more than 4 percent of their share of research funds in that decade. The next tier of fifty institutions with "good" to "strong" departments on average, plus some stand-alone medical universities, gained an equivalent amount. The leading universities appeared less able or less willing to adapt to the new conditions. They had large cadres of senior professors—the source of their academic prestige—and their capacity for research was near optimal or ceiling levels. They were most attuned to the traditional federal research economy, in which they possessed a competitive advantage, and hence most vocal in complaining about its tightening. Universities gaining shares, in contrast, had room to grow. They extended their research capacity in growth areas linked with economic development. Engineering schools, such as Texas A&M, Penn State, and Georgia Tech did well in the 1980s. Southern schools continued to develop as research universities, particularly Maryland, Virginia Tech, and North Carolina State among the public institutions, Duke and Emory among the private ones. While all universities increased their performance of research in the 1980s, a study by Hugh Davis Graham and Nancy Diamond identified a set of smaller universities with growing participation in the research economy.[23]

The 1995 ratings of *Research-Doctorate Programs* revealed a pervasive rise in departmental quality since the 1982 ratings, with improvement evident among both highly rated and "good" departments.[24] This was due in part to an abundance of well-trained scientists graduating from American doctoral programs. But it was also owed to a growing number of universities committed to upgrading faculty and research. The late 1990s experienced a renaissance of the research spirit. These were the years of the dot-com boom on Wall Street and a celebration of new technologies. "Innovation" was the new mantra (again), both in industry and in policy circles.[25] The economic rationale for research investment morphed from generic research that might be shared with industry to "research-based technologies"—basic scientific research that promised future technological

23 Roger L. Geiger and Irwin Feller, "The Dispersion of Academic Research in the 1980s," *Journal of Higher Education* 66 (1995): 336–60; Graham and Diamond, *Rise of American Research Universities*, 144–98.

24 Marvin L. Goldberger, Brendan A. Maher, and Pamela Ebert Flatau, eds., *Research-Doctorate Programs in the United States: Continuity and Change* (Washington, DC: National Academy Press, 1995); Geiger, *Knowledge and Money*, 149–52.

25 Geiger and Sá, *Tapping the Riches of Science*, 25–27 et passim.; Thomas L. Friedman, *The World Is Flat: A Brief History of the Twenty-First Century* (New York: Farrar, Straus and Giroux, 2005); William J. Baumol, *The Free-Market Innovation Machine: Analyzing the Growth Miracle of Capitalism* (Princeton: Princeton University Press, 2002); Jan Fagerberg, David C. Mowery, and Richard R. Nelson, eds., *The Oxford Handbook of Innovation* (New York: Oxford University Press, 2005).

breakthroughs. Biotechnology had shown the way, and now information technologies were transforming industries and individual lives. The seminal contributions of research universities were once again appreciated in the media, government, and in university administrations.[26]

How universities reacted depended on individual circumstance. Until the end of the decade, public universities had to cope with shrinking state appropriations (below). The University of California lost 20 percent of its state appropriation (1990–1993), causing the reduction of 10,000 employees, including 2,000 faculty. But appropriations began to be restored in 1995, permitting a rejuvenation of faculties with new hires and new initiatives, making the UC campuses stronger than ever.[27] Michigan countered declining state funding with aggressive privatization—tuition revenues and private fund-raising. It stimulated research by establishing some eighty new research units in the decade. Major public research universities that suffered prolonged erosion of their fiscal base— Illinois (Urbana), Minnesota, Texas, and Wisconsin—all formulated plans to strengthen research by the decade's end. Private universities, in contrast, flourished throughout the 1990s. The chief source of their prosperity was the rising income from undergraduate tuition and later the booming stock market. They consequently devoted much of their growing resources to the "selectivity sweepstakes"— attracting and nurturing talented undergraduates (discussed below). However, academic distinction was an essential component of their prestige, and it too required investment. Through the 1980s and 1990s, private universities grew wealthier, increasing their faculties by 20 percent and research dollars by more than 100 percent. Public universities struggled financially, enlarging faculties by 10 percent and research dollars by 140 percent (constant dollars).[28]

The research profiles of public and private universities tended to diverge in these years with respect to the academic core, centers and institutes, and university health centers. Core academic departments jointly produced teaching and research and were funded by the general-funds budget. The vitality of faculty scholarship and research was consequently affected by the fortunes of general funds, that is, adversely for public universities for much of the 1990s and positively for private ones. Private universities enjoyed a growing salary advantage

---

26   Representative contributions are described by Jonathan Cole, *The Great American Research University* (New York: Public Affairs, 2009), 207–342.

27   Reductions were made through early retirement buyouts, and many retired faculty remained on campus, even teaching part time. Thus, when younger (cheaper) replacement faculty were hired, UC was academically stronger than ever: C. Judson King, *The University of California: Creating, Nurturing, and Maintaining Academic Quality in a Public University Setting* (Berkeley, CA: Center for Studies in Higher Education, 2018).

28   Geiger, *Knowledge and Money*, 147–65. Tuition increases accounted for revenue growth at public universities: see below.

and higher academic ratings. The average 1995 departmental ratings for the leading private universities was 4.25; for leading public ones, 3.91.[29] Private universities emphasized quality over quantity in the academic core, but health centers could afford to augment both. Biomedical research in university health centers operated in a separate research economy dominated by the NIH. In this respect, private universities were no different from public ones. But many private universities with moderate-sized liberal arts colleges and faculties deliberately expanded research in medical centers. Among the largest such gainers of medical research in the 1990s were Duke, Emory, Vanderbilt, and Washington University, all with prominent liberal arts colleges. Public universities struggled to sustain academic units that covered more numerous and diverse subjects. These difficulties as well as the nature of the new research regime favored the use of centers and institutes to leverage faculty research. Conditions encouraged three types of organized research units: interdisciplinary centers to address new or complex subjects, which also attracted patrons; scientific institutes required to house sophisticated research technologies and instruments; and consumer-oriented centers, such as those intended for collaboration with industry. Graduate education was linked—in fact, enriched—by these activities, but the teaching of undergraduates receded from the purview of research-active faculty.[30]

By the end of the twentieth century, universities had emerged from three tumultuous decades with their research mission more secure than at any time since the academic revolution. In 1998, Congress committed to doubling the $11 billion NIH budget, which it accomplished in the next five years. In 2000, $1 billion of annual funding was promised to the National Nanotechnology Initiative—another emerging science-based technology. And the nexus between research and economic development was endorsed by a Republican president, George W. Bush, who announced the intention of doubling federal spending for the physical sciences as part of the American Competitiveness Initiative (unfulfilled).

Universities fully embraced this mandate, some beginning in the 1990s, but the dispersion of academic research to lower-ranking institutions diminished. As universities of all types placed greater emphasis on the research mission, the research system became even more competitive, and the quality margin of traditional leaders worked to their advantage. By the late 1990s, ten of the twenty leading universities had outperformed the averages for quality, quantity, and

---

29   Geiger, *Knowledge and Money,* 154, 160; Graham and Diamond, *Rise of American Research Universities,* 203–8.

30   One countertrend: The provision of opportunities for undergraduates to engage in research has become ubiquitous. The Council for Undergraduate Research was founded in 1979 and gained momentum for two decades before taking off after 2000. Most members are undergraduate teaching institutions, but research universities have all adopted formal programs: https://members.cur.org.

impact of their research. The same was true for twenty of the next thirty universities. The hierarchy of research universities resumed a stability in which the academic leaders asserted their competitive advantage.[31]

If the research mission remained robust, it also became increasingly self-contained, set apart from other university activities and preoccupations. An autonomous research role had emerged with postwar federal research support, but conditions in the 1980s and 1990s favored still further separation. With one-third of federal funds awarded to medical research, another portion designated for economic development, and a substantial portion absorbed by centers and institutes, the research activities of major universities increasingly acquired a life of their own.

PRIVATIZATION: PUBLIC AND PRIVATE HIGHER EDUCATION AND THE SELECTIVITY SWEEPSTAKES

The years around 1980 saw the beginning of a far-reaching transformation in the ways Americans paid for higher education and in the financing of public and private institutions. Like the increasing commercial ties of university research, these too constituted a form of privatization: for students, a greater financial burden increasingly imposed through loans; for public institutions, increasing dependence on tuition; and for the private sector, often depicted as endangered in the 1970s, the emergence of conditions that now worked to their advantage, particularly for wealthier institutions. These trends developed in stages for two decades and then strengthened after the turn of the century.

FEDERAL STUDENT FINANCIAL AID. The system of federal student financial aid incorporated in the Education Amendments of 1972 aimed to make college affordable for lower-income students through four kinds of grants: Basic Educational Opportunity Grants (later called Pell Grants) for low-income students, a supplemental grant program for students attending more expensive (private) institutions, College Work-Study, and federally subsidized State Student Incentive Grants (Chapter 6). Federally guaranteed student loans were intended as a backstop for those with additional needs. In 1978, loans began to assume

---

31 Calculations of relative values for academic ratings, research expenditures, and citations for mid-1990s vs. mid-1980s were made by the author, Nancy Diamond, and Dmitry Suspitsin, Pennsylvania State University (2000); Steven Brint and Cynthia Carr, "The Scientific Research Output of U.S. Research Universities, 1980–2010," *Minerva*, doi: 10.1007/s11024-017-9330-4. Derek Bok has doubted the ability of middling universities to rise in the rankings: "the price is too high and the advantage of well-established competitors too great to overcome": *Higher Education in America* (Princeton: Princeton University Press, 2013), 336–37.

greater prominence, eventually fostering a loan culture in which many students became routinely dependent on loans to meet a portion of their educational expenses, and institutions became dependent on those monies for tuition. From that juncture, federal loans and the loan culture advanced relentlessly, growing incrementally in normal years and making quantum leaps when new forms and terms were introduced. By 2010 the majority of undergraduate students were borrowers, and federal loans had increased more than tenfold since 1979 (constant dollars). How and why this occurred has more to do with politics and markets than with higher education per se.[32]

The financial aid provisions of 1972 reflected the egalitarian spirit of that era. Making higher education affordable for lower-income students was regarded as promoting a more just and equal society and implied that financial aid should be based solely on financial need.[33] This need-based rationale was superseded later in the decade when Congress reacted to a "middle-class revolt" that demanded federal financial-aid provisions be extended to families with larger incomes. A concerted effort to establish tuition tax credits (a giveback to parents of existing students that would not promote greater access) was averted. Instead, the Middle Income Student Assistance Act (MISAA, 1978) relaxed criteria for basic (Pell) grants to make more middle-class families eligible and removed all income restrictions for Guaranteed Student Loans. Loan volume roughly doubled in the next two years; however, the folly of lending to any and all at 7 percent when inflation was near 20 percent quickly became apparent. In 1981, income caps were restored, but loans did not decrease. They continued to edge higher for the rest of the decade.

The MISAA challenged the principle of need-based financial aid for the benefit of special interests, namely middle-class voters and the banking industry, for whom guaranteed loans were guaranteed profits. Going forward, the combination of interests and politics caused student financial policy aid to "drift."[34] The Reagan administration, philosophically opposed to social spending, annually proposed budgets that would eliminate some grant programs and cut funding for others. In Congress, supporters of the educational equity agenda, backed by the higher education industry, managed to restore most funding, although bud-

32   Suzanne Mettler, *Degrees of Inequality: How the Politics of Higher Education Sabotaged the American Dream* (New York: Basic Books, 2014).

33   James C. Hearn, "The Paradox of Growth in Federal Aid for College Students, 1965–1990," *Higher Education: Handbook of Theory and Research* IX (1993): 94–153; Edward P. St. John, *Refinancing the College Dream: Access, Equal Opportunity, and Justice for Taxpayers* (Baltimore: Johns Hopkins University Press, 2003).

34   Hearn, "Paradox of Growth," 116–23; St. John, *Refinancing the College Dream*, 100–127.

get constraints limited such efforts. As loan policy drifted, basic (Pell) and other grants lost purchasing power, but loans were an entitlement and continued to grow. Loans disproportionately benefited the middle class, and Congress appreciated their popularity.

Federal student aid policies were intended to facilitate growth in enrollments, but whether or how much they did was far from clear. The demand for higher education was influenced by numerous factors: principally, the economic return to college graduation, assiduously charted by economists as the wage premium; academic preparation for college study; and affordability, which was the target of federal aid. Probably most influential was the growth and culture of the middle class, which reflected the close association of college-going with parental education and income. From 1945 through the 1960s, family incomes steadily rose and so did enrollment rates in higher education. In the 1970s, family income stagnated and, after a slight lag, so did enrollment rates. Other factors were negative as well. The wage premium plummeted, although expanding opportunities for women still made college attractive. And academic preparation by all measures was depressed as well. The single positive factor was increased federal financial aid, which did not seem to have a discernable effect.

From 1980 until the early 1990s, the number of high school graduates plunged by 25 percent, but enrollments remained stable as more graduates chose to go to college. After 1983, family incomes rose in a strong economy. The college wage premium began a prolonged rise, and academic preparation appeared to strengthen. Only grant aid shrunk as Congress appropriated fewer real dollars for more students. Overall, conditions favored traditional higher education—full-time students in four-year colleges and universities. Enrollment rates rose first for white students, while attendance by African Americans, following the recruitment blitz of the 1970s, sunk to a temporary nadir. Participation rates for high school graduates in all income quartiles rose in parallel fashion, but total enrollments for the lowest quartile were still depressed by low high school graduation rates.[35] Given rising tuition prices, affordability may have been an issue for families below the median income. Loans, on the other hand, were most likely to be utilized by middle-class students, especially at private institutions.

The 1990s began with a prolonged economic slowdown but concluded with robust economic expansion. The trends of the 1980s persisted after 1990 in spite of the recession, including rising enrollment rates. These received little help from Pell Grants, which barely kept pace with inflation. The Clinton administration

---

35   National Council for Education Statistics (NCES) data; *Postsecondary Education Opportunity* 277 (November 2015); 278 (December 2015).

and Congress instead pandered to the middle class, providing tax deductions for tuition and additional kinds of student loans.[36] Student borrowing doubled in the decade, with 3 million more borrowers (+67 percent) in 2000 obtaining loans averaging an additional $1,000 (+36 percent). Participation rates of African Americans recovered and continued to increase in the 1990s. More important, their share of college graduates rose from a low of 6.2 percent in 1990 to 9.2 percent in 2000. At the end of the twentieth century, American higher education was once again on a strong growth path. Federal student financial aid of $48 billion undoubtedly played some role in this, but additional enrollments of un-aided students were comparable to those of aided students. Forty percentage points separated the continuation rates of high school graduates in the top and bottom quartiles in 1980 and again in 2000.[37] Other factors shaped who went to college and where.

PRIVATE HIGHER EDUCATION. For private colleges and universities that had weathered the dismal 1970s, prospects for the 1980s appeared dire. Besides raging inflation, the impending 25 percent drop in college-age cohorts threatened disaster. They continued to face a pricing disadvantage vis-à-vis public universities, and interest in their signature liberal arts programs showed no sign of renewal. They faced fierce competition to recruit enough paying customers, let alone the high-ability students they traditionally sought. But compete fiercely they did, in marketing, offerings, and—by manipulating financial aid—pricing.

Private colleges in the 1980s redoubled recruitment efforts and adopted more sophisticated marketing. One typical college increased direct mail from 35,000 to 110,000 (for a class of 800). Larger admissions staffs and alumni volunteers made more direct contacts with prospective applicants. Most colleges adopted business practices by conducting market research to devise recruitment strategies. They hired consulting firms to analyze characteristics of accepted applicants who did or did not enroll. Colleges established offices of institutional research, which were keenly focused on probing and refining such strategies. Directors of admission became key figures, responsible for the lifeblood of their institutions. They were elevated to high administrative rank and designated "enrollment managers." The latter position united marketing with the evaluation of applications, acceptances, and offers of financial aid. Enrollment management was responsible for optimizing enrollments, institutional reputation, and revenues. The admis-

---

36   Mettler, *Degrees of Inequality*.

37   *Chronicle of Higher Education, Almanac Issue* 38, 1 (August 28, 1991): 11; Ibid., 48, 1 (August 31, 2001): 18; *Postsecondary Education Opportunity*, 278 (December 2015): 11.

sions process by itself became a growing expense, often consuming 10–20 percent of an incoming class's tuition.[38]

Given their higher cost, the attraction of private colleges and universities rested heavily upon reputation. Here, Oberlin spoke for the sector when it concluded that while making "cost more attractive does have a positive effect on yield, turning attention to academic reputation and social life provides a larger return."[39] Private institutions preferred to compete on the basis of quality. Academic quality in this case did not reflect research, in which flagship public universities excelled, but rather strong teaching, successful graduates, and a faculty distinguished by less specialized accomplishments. However, social life was also a vital selling point. The glossy viewbooks distributed by direct mail portrayed attractive students and charismatic teachers in idyllic campus settings. Both academics and social life were affected by the talents and abilities of fellow students (considered below). Hence, qualitative competition encouraged increasing expenditures—for campus facilities, faculty salaries, low student-teacher ratios and small classes, amenities and social life, and the recruitment of top students. Private colleges and universities succumbed to the relentless pressure to increase expenditures by raising prices.[40]

In the 1970s, private institutions had been reluctant to raise relative prices in the face of weak student demand. In 1978, Harvard challenged this mentality by increasing tuition by 18 percent, to $5,265 from $4,450, while also increasing student financial aid with internal funds. Experiencing no falloff in applications, Harvard raised tuition by an average $840 for each of the next ten years, and its high-priced peers followed its example. The key to raising tuition so aggressively was institutional financial aid. Previously, private institutions had provided such aid from a dedicated, and hence fixed, budget. Now they provided aid by simply discounting tuition.[41] In addition, federal loans were available for those with additional need. Tuition discounts and student loans combined to form a system of *high-tuition/high-aid* for the private sector. By using the standardized "expected

---

38 Elizabeth A. Duffy and Idana Goldberg, *Crafting a Class: College Admissions and Financial Aid, 1955–1994* (Princeton: Princeton University Press, 1998), 60–65; Charles T. Clotfelter, *Unequal Colleges in the Age of Disparity* (Cambridge, MA: Harvard University Press, 2017), 147–56: in 1983, 1.4 million students took the SAT examination and the College Board sold 30 million names to colleges (p. 153).

39 Duffy and Goldberg, *Crafting a Class*, 64.

40 Ronald G. Ehrenberg, *Tuition Rising: Why College Costs So Much* (Cambridge, MA: Harvard University Press, 2000).

41 Michael S. McPherson and Morton Owen Schapiro, *The Student Aid Game: Meeting Need and Rewarding Talent in American Higher Education* (Princeton: Princeton University Press, 1998), 15–22. Self-funded student aid in the private sector had long been stable at under 20 percent of tuition income. From 18 percent in 1980 it rose to 29 percent in 1988.

family contribution" plus any eligible grants or loans, colleges determined the maximum amount a student could afford to pay. Tuition discounts could then cover the difference to meet the list price. Colleges thus avoided price resistance in the form of reduced demand: they were free to raise tuition for those who could afford it while providing an appropriate tuition discount for those who could not.[42]

High-tuition/high-aid spread throughout the private sector in the 1980s, refined and promoted by marketing consultants. It was chiefly adopted for its effectiveness. Average per-student expenditures in the 1980s rose by 40 percent in private colleges and more than 60 percent for private research universities (constant dollars). These gains accelerated further in the last half of the 1990s. For private research universities, net tuition rose by 138 percent, and total spending by 142 percent (1980–2000). By all indications, increased spending enhanced academic quality. Private institutions had a minor building boom in the 1980s. They hired more and better faculty and paid them more.[43] The prosperity of the private sector was an astonishing reversal of 1970s anxieties, but several features of the high-tuition/high-aid regime were worrisome.

The escalation of list tuition was both breathtaking and disturbing. Top tuitions rose from $4,000 in 1976 to $24,000 in 2000 in current dollars (150 percent in real terms), a seemingly outrageous jump to contemporaries. Average list private tuitions rose from about 20 percent of median family income in 1980 to 40 percent in 2000. The system was most advantageous for the wealthier and more prestigious institutions, which had a more affluent clientele and larger applicant pools. They were able to charge higher tuitions and achieve greater increases in net revenues. Under high-tuition/high-aid, the rich got richer, while the poor became solvent. The inexorable rise in tuitions caused the discount rate to rise as well. It averaged 25 percent in 1990 for moderately selective colleges and 30 percent in 2000.[44] At the latter rate, institutions had to raise tuition by $1,000 to obtain $700 of additional revenue—thus generating a need for even higher tuition. Tuition discounts were thus a slippery slope with no apparent exit. Finally, most selective schools paid lip service to a policy of "need-blind, full-need"

42 Geiger, *Knowledge and Money*, 36–42.

43 Geiger, *Knowledge and Money*, 50–62; David W. Breneman, *Liberal Arts Colleges: Thriving, Surviving, or Endangered?* (Washington, DC: Brookings Institution, 1994), 102–5; Charles T. Clotfelter, *Buying the Best: Cost Escalation in Elite Higher Education* (Princeton: Princeton University Press, 1996); Robert A. McCaughey, *Scholars and Teachers: The Faculties of Select Liberal Arts Colleges and Their Place in American Higher Learning* (New York: Barnard College, Columbia University, 2004).

44 Claudia Goldin and Lawrence F. Katz, *The Race between Education and Technology* (Cambridge, MA: Harvard University Press, 2008), 276–78; Clotfelter, *Unequal Colleges*, 160; Breneman, *Liberal Arts Colleges*, 51–89; Geiger, *Knowledge and Money*. The tuition discount rate for all private colleges was 36 percent in 2010 and 44 percent in 2016. Tuition discounts are "front-loaded"; for incoming freshman in 2016 it was 49 percent: Leslie McBain, "Unfamiliar Territory," *Business Officer* (June 2017): 33–37.

admission, but by the 1990s all but the wealthiest had sacrificed this principle to institutional budgets. It proved irresistible for institutions to manipulate the relative weights of institutional aid (discounts) and loans to favor the most sought-after applicants. Through "preferential packaging," colleges offered more generous aid to students with high ability or other desirable talents; they also provided inducements to applicants who could pay full tuition. The student-aid practices of private schools, which were originally intended to accommodate students with financial need, evolved toward awarding more of their aid on the basis of merit to students with little or no need.[45] The financial health of the private sector, however gratifying, brought further subjection to the forces of a competitive market—the selectivity sweepstakes.[46]

THE SELECTIVITY SWEEPSTAKES. The market for freshman places in higher education changed appreciably in the 1980s. Some practices had historical roots. The Ivy League universities were the first to expand the geographical scope of their recruitment in the 1930s, and in the 1950s selective private colleges did the same (Chapter 2). Improvements in travel and communication inexorably widened the purview of selective institutions, allowing them to recruit from larger populations. Information was a second factor in making markets. SAT scores and National Merit tests provided information for consumers and producers in the 1950s, and guidebooks distributed such information widely in the 1960s. Marketing through direct mail provided another source of consumer information in the 1970s, and these efforts were more than redoubled in the 1980s. Pricing, a third market factor, especially for private schools, was in theory intended to be neutralized by need-blind, full-need policies, as formalized in the high-tuition/high-aid system just described. But competitive price discrimination using preferential packaging and merit aid quickly appeared. Finally, consumer preferences may have played the largest role. In the egalitarian 1970s, antibusiness sentiments gradually dissipated, along with economizing educational strategies. After 1980 the popularity and validation of worldly success made it (once again) a laudable objective. One conspicuous symptom was the Yuppie phenomenon—well-publicized examples of young, upwardly mobile professionals obsessed with money and consumption and reputedly disdainful of the social concerns that had dominated the previous decade. The caricature of the Yuppie was reviled in academic circles but clearly appealed to many young people, who increasingly

45 McPherson and Schapiro, *Student Aid Game*, 91–103. The College Scholarship Service was formed in 1954 to determine how much families could be expected to pay for higher education. Institutions associated with it pledged to admit students on a need-blind basis and award financial aid only on the basis of need. Later public forms of financial aid were predicated on these principles (pp. 6–9).

46 Geiger, *Knowledge and Money*, 77–83, 234–38, 244–49.

sought a path to professional success by attending the best colleges that would have them.

In 1983, *U.S. News and World Report* captured the emerging spirit of the times perfectly by publishing a ranking of colleges and universities that was based on a reputational survey. Expanded with quantitative measures in 1987, it has been published separately since 1990 as *America's Best Colleges*. Besides the reputational survey, the rankings incorporated several measures of admissions selectivity and institutional resources, and they were tweaked every year to yield slightly different results. Overall, they largely measured selectivity and wealth—which were highly correlated. Like the witch's mirror on the wall, the *U.S. News* rankings reflected the selectivity sweepstakes, declaring the most selective colleges and universities to be the fairest of them all.[47]

The *U.S. News* rankings added a new dimension to the higher education market, provoking an intensification of the competition among selective institutions. Instead of facing traditional rivals or regional competitors, institutions were compared with and ranked against the entire set of national colleges or universities. Originally an artifact of the market, the rankings soon defined the market. A 1999 study confirmed what administrators no doubt already knew: slippage in the rankings for top colleges lowered the number and quality of applications the following year, depressing SAT scores and requiring more financial aid.[48] Some institutions attempted to game the system by manipulating measured variables, and a few resorted to fraudulent reporting. But relative wealth and selectivity were facts of institutional life that were not easily disguised, if at all. Heightened competition caused intense pressures on high aid and high tuition. At less affluent institutions, net spending per student was often less than the list tuition, so that full payers subsidized their classmates. Financial aid expenditures at private colleges and universities composed 8.2 percent of expenditures in 1990 and 11.4 percent in 2000.[49] While most private colleges and universities faced an annual scramble to meet their enrollment targets, the selectivity sweepstakes chiefly affected the selective sector.

The selective sector is a hypothetical construct reflecting student characteristics and institutional aspirations and behavior. A practical definition would be the *U.S. News* top fifty "national universities" and "national liberal arts colleges," which in 1999 had roughly 145,000 freshman places: 64,000 in sixteen public

47 Clotfelter, *Unequal Colleges*, 102–7; Geiger, *Knowledge and Money*, 80–83.

48 James Monks and Ronald G. Ehrenberg, "The Impact of *U.S. News and World Report* College Rankings on Admissions Outcomes and Pricing Policies at Selective Private Institutions," Working Paper 7227, National Bureau of Economic Research (July 1999).

49 *Chronicle of Higher Education* 38 (1991): 35; ibid., 48 (2001): 30. For accounting purposes, tuition discounts are recorded as student aid expenditures.

universities; 56,000 in thirty-four private universities; and 25,000 in fifty colleges. They constituted 8 percent of first-year students at four-year public universities and 17 percent at private ones. For most of these institutions, at least half of the freshman class scored in the top 10–15 percent of test takers.[50] Enrolling such students was essential for the rankings and for institutional prestige. A reputation for high quality translated into higher revenues from more full payers and lower discounts. Less selective institutions had correspondingly fewer full payers and larger tuition discounts. Prestige also encouraged alumni gifts, which soared in the 1990s, again favoring the already wealthy. But those institutions became much wealthier chiefly through the growth of endowments during a twenty-year bull market in equities, especially in the last years of the 1990s. Such returns made the rich that much richer. Harvard, Yale, and Princeton doubled their real educational expenditures in the 1990s, while the median private research university (still relatively affluent) raised spending by 37 percent.[51] And wealth engendered greater selectivity. By the late 1990s, economic theory was advanced to explain this phenomenon.

The key concept was peer effects—situations in which consumers of an entity also serve as inputs to the value of that entity.[52] Such was the case with higher education, where students play an important role in educating one another. For this reason, Caroline Hoxby argued, top students were motivated to cluster together. They also favored the highest-quality schools, those investing the largest amounts in their education. Institutions that provided superior (costlier) education thus not only attracted better students, but those students through peer effects supplied a kind of multiplier, enhancing the educational outcomes further. Hoxby demonstrated that the historical integration of a national market for higher education, referred to above, revealed the cumulative working of this process over time.[53] Another economist, Gordon Winston, focused the Williams Project on the Economics of Higher Education on peer effects and institutional wealth. He described the effects of qualitative competition as a "positional

---

50   Alternatively, *Barron's Profiles of American Colleges* (1985) classifying solely on selectivity rated thirty-two institutions as "Most Competitive," and sixty as "Highly Competitive." There is no sharp cut-off point for the selective sector, since many institutions consider themselves as belonging.

51   Geiger, *Knowledge and Money*, 84–86, Appendix A; Roger L. Geiger, "The Ivy League," in David Palfreyman and Ted Tapper, eds., *Structuring Mass Higher Education: The Role of Elite* Institutions (New York: Routledge, 2009), 281–302; Clotfelter documents how these trends accelerated to 2013: *Unequal Colleges*, 127–46.

52   Michael Rothschild and Lawrence J. White, "The Analytics of the Pricing of Higher Education and Other Services in Which the Customers Are Inputs," *Journal of Political Economy* 10, 3 (1995): 573–86.

53   Caroline M. Hoxby, "How the Changing Market Structure of U.S. Higher Education Explains College Tuition," Working Paper 6323, National Bureau of Economic Research (December 1997); Geiger, *Knowledge and Money*, 81–83.

market," in which institutions compete for relative prestige or position. Positional markers were selectivity, expenditures, and *U.S. News* rank—all highly correlated. The extent to which hierarchical position depended on spending came to be called the "arms race." Winston noted, "Hierarchy based on donative resources becomes highly skewed," and any attempt to opt out of the arms race would be "fiduciary irresponsibility": "in a positional market there is never too much of a good thing ... and in the hierarchy, wealth is fundamentally a good thing."[54] Economic theory thus provided a powerful endorsement for the qualitative competition of the selectivity sweepstakes and pronounced the limitless pursuit of institutional wealth to be an inherently good thing.

Hoxby compiled extensive data to show that the evolution of the higher education market matched this economic model. Her 1997 paper documented the growing concentration of high-ability students at institutions with high expenditures from 1966 to 1991. At the same time, the academic abilities of students at less selective colleges declined. The differences in average student ability (as measured by ACT and SAT tests) between more and less selective schools grew larger, while the range of abilities within individual institutions became smaller. These patterns were more pronounced for private institutions but also evident among public ones. Other studies documented this same phenomenon.[55] The concentration of high-ability students was most evident among the most selective 10 percent of institutions, and the decline in average ability was largest at and below the median. In a 2009 paper, Hoxby related this pattern directly to institutional resources. These data showed a steadily rising trendline of increasing resources for all institutions, but the magnitudes of spending increased greatly with selectivity. After 1996, the expenditures of institutions in the 96–98th percentile of selectivity rose steeply, to $48,000 per student in 2006; and those in the 99th percentile shot up geometrically, to over $90,000. Hoxby maintained, somewhat implausibly, that these enormous expenditures were chiefly for instructional purposes and assumed that they would be justified when "higher aptitude students can earn the market rate of return on a larger human capital investment." Further, since "their returns are greater in absolute terms ... their donations as alumni will be larger and will buy more resources for the next generation of students."[56] Like Winston, Hoxby believed that there could never be too much of a "good thing." But good fortune also brought perplexing issues.

---

54 Gordon Winston, "Subsidies, Hierarchies, and Peers: The Awkward Economics of Higher Education," *Journal of Economic Perspectives* 13 (Winter 1999): 13–36, quotes pp. 27, 31.

55 Hoxby, "Changing Market Structures"; Clotfelter, *Unequal Colleges,* 207–27.

56 Caroline M. Hoxby, "The Changing Selectivity of American Colleges," *Journal of Economic Perspectives* 23, 4 (Fall 2009): 95–118, quote p. 110. It seems implausible that students could increase their

First, there was what might be called admissions gridlock. Selective schools had always considered criteria other than academic merit in admissions. Ironically, as the surfeit of qualified applicants grew, admissions decisions increasingly depended on nonacademic criteria. Shaping an incoming class was a political challenge to appease internal and external special interests. Alumni were the most powerful of these interests; minorities had to be apportioned a given share; traditional feeder schools demanded consideration; coaches needed players; engineers needed gearheads. As one admissions officer explained, these constituencies lobby "against each other for a set number of places.... Even a slight dip in one year brings a kind of pressure that pushes up that measurable item the next year at the probable expense of some other variable." In the 1980s, for example, Asian American students mobilized to protest discrimination in admission to Harvard, since their academic credentials far exceeded those of preferred groups. Their lawsuit, although unsuccessful, elevated the standing of Asians as a special interest. It also bared the workings of this secretive process, to the embarrassment of Harvard and its ilk, opening them to criticism for favoring legacies, athletes, or minorities.[57] The nuanced process of selection has proven highly effective in identifying students likely to achieve subsequent success, but it was difficult to defend against singular grievances—hence, the gridlock in which sacrosanct categories were preserved with only minor adjustments.

Second, there was the perpetuation of inequality. It was estimated in 2000 that only the top 6 percent of families had incomes sufficient to afford the $30–35,000 price of a year at one of these colleges. At Ivy League and similar institutions, more than half of students were from that strata and received no aid. Remarkably, this pattern had prevailed throughout much of the twentieth century. In 1961, Yale's admissions dean Arthur Howe estimated that for financial viability Ivy League institutions needed to recruit 60 percent of their students from the wealthiest 5 percent of families; and the sociologist Joseph Soares has shown that Yale, and no doubt its peers, consistently upheld these metrics in both pricing and recruitment. Indeed, this was the case for highly selective colleges at the end

---

human capital at rates commensurate with the geometric rise in expenditures or that "the vast increase in expenditures is due primarily to increases in instructional spending" (p. 110).

57   Jerome Karabel, *The Chosen: The Hidden History of Admissions and Exclusion at Harvard, Yale, and Princeton* (Boston: Houghton Mifflin, 2005), 499–513, quoted on p. 545. In a reprise of the discrimination charge, a 2014 suit on behalf of Asian American applicants was tried in 2018, again exposing Harvard's secretive admissions process. Asian American applicants had the highest ratings for academic credentials and the lowest for subjective personal qualities. Admitting only 4.6 percent of highly qualified applicants is an inherently discriminatory process. The plaintiffs' goal was to abolish affirmative admissions (see "The Culture Wars," below).

of the twentieth century.[58] At the same time, the social composition of these highly selective schools had undergone a far-reaching transformation. As academic standards rose, the proportion of old elites decreased, largely replaced by new elites from professional families, including many children of academics. In addition, the diversity of the small contingent of nonwealthy students greatly increased.[59] However, the high-tuition/high-aid system required large numbers of students whose parents could pay all or most of the high tuitions. And in the United States, high academic ability was associated, not accidentally, with high incomes (Chapter 8). Hence, wealthy, selective institutions were locked into this pattern: lower tuition would merely subsidize their wealthy clientele, and class-based affirmative action for lower SES students would unacceptably disrupt admissions gridlock.

Third, there was the issue of elite education and earnings. The implacably growing applications to the most selective institutions attested to the conviction that their degrees were worth the expense and effort. Scholars have nonetheless found this issue compelling, especially the question of why—whether or how much such earnings are due to initial aptitudes, peer effects, institutional expenditures, or the acuity of the selection process. Soares emphasized the latter: "At Yale and in the top tier, we have a student body drawn from a self-selected wealthy and academically proficient applicant pool, people who are uncommonly capable of personal performance."[60] With the development of the selectivity sweepstakes in the last two decades of the twentieth century, the benefits of an elite education were no longer taken for granted but had become a preoccupation of both proponents and critics (discussed in Chapter 8).

PUBLIC HIGHER EDUCATION. The privatization of public higher education is well known and widely lamented. It has chiefly meant the transfer of funding for public colleges and universities from state tax revenues to students, parents, and their loans. These institutions have also sought whatever other private sector funds they might obtain, but only tuition can replace shrinking state appropriations. Student tuition revenues in 1980 averaged one-quarter of state appropriations; by 2002, tuitions were two-thirds of appropriations; and after 2010, tuition revenues exceeded the states' contributions. Dependence on tuition has varied by state—net tuition provided 25 percent of expenditures in the most

---

58   Joseph A. Soares, *The Power of Privilege: Yale and America's Elite Colleges* (Stanford, CA: Stanford University Press, 2007), 55–67, 162–67; Roger L. Geiger, "High Tuition–High Aid: A Road Paved with Good Intentions," (paper presented to the Association for the Study of Higher Education, Sacramento, CA, November 2002).

59   Karabel, *Chosen*, 510–13, 521–22; Soares, *Power of Privilege*, 172–90.

60   Soares, *Power of Privilege*, 129–35, quote p. 135.

supportive decile of states and 75 percent in the least. This seemingly inexorable trend developed in stages.

David Breneman observed that "in the final analysis, the well-being of higher education is so closely tied to the well-being of the economy that planners can virtually ignore other conditions."[61] After 1980 this became less true for the private sector and increasingly so for the public. The "double-dip" recessions of the early 1980s resulted in four years in which real, per-student state appropriations fell below the 1980 level. In the decade's ensuing prosperous years, this figure rose to roughly 15 percent above that of 1980. The mild recession of 1990 was followed by a slow recovery and weak state revenues. State appropriations fell back to the mid-1980s level, and they did not exceed the 1980s levels until the boom years that ended the decade. State funding for higher education was cut back severely following the recession of 2001, and a partial recovery was reversed by the Great Recession, which brought even more draconian reductions. Each cycle of the funding roller coaster became less favorable for public higher education. Like an actual roller coaster, the overall direction was down.

In the 1980s, public universities initially raised tuitions to compensate for reduced appropriations. They then continued to increase tuition by 7–8 percent as appropriations were more than restored. These additional funds were badly needed. Appropriations and tuition income stagnated in the 1970s and suffered in the economic turmoil of the early 1980s. Now institutions needed to raise salaries to catch up with inflation, cover a host of rising costs, and adapt to changing demands. Such needs persisted through the 1990s, and again budget increases were largely funded with rising tuition. However, the propensity of states to support their institutions of higher education declined steadily. A detailed analysis of both decades by Michael Rizzo found that higher education's share of state educational spending declined precipitously—from 22 percent to 16 percent. In part, perhaps, due to crowding-out, but the willingness of legislators to support state colleges and universities clearly waned. Some additional state monies were directed to students instead. Moreover, Rizzo also found that greater availability of student financial aid encouraged institutions to raise tuition, which in turn provided an additional rationale for states to cut appropriations.[62] These trends accelerated after 2000.

---

61 Breneman, *Liberal Arts Colleges*, 31.

62 Michael J. Rizzo, "A (Less Than) Zero-Sum Game? State Funding for Education: How Higher Education Institutions Have Lost," PhD. diss., Cornell University, 2004: Cornell Higher Education Research Institute, Working Paper 52 (August 2004). Unlike their actions, the motives of state legislators are obscure: whether they act from purely budgetary constraints or react to university variables like high tuition, financial aid, or nonresident students; or if they comprehend social vs. private returns to higher education.

Described in such macro terms, the modern plight of the public sector appeared dire—and was described as such, or worse, in numerous publications.[63] More generally, the resort to high tuition to compensate for stagnant public support posed a trade-off: greater tuition revenues were needed to sustain or advance the quality of education, but tuition growth far exceeding that of family incomes served to diminish affordability and hence access. The circumstances of individual institutions and the various states, and their adaptations to these forces, naturally varied over these decades. In general, public research universities were most concerned to uphold quality, and the mass-serving regional universities and community colleges struggled to preserve affordability and access. Within this national pattern, every state had its own story, but California, Michigan, and Georgia exemplify major trends.

Perhaps the situation was starkest, and most disheartening, in California, the first state to achieve universal access to higher education under the 1960 Master Plan. That social promise, according to Simon Marginson, "was honored in full for the first two decades ... enabling California to achieve a major increase in participation and educational attainment. It was honored intermittently in good budget years for the next two decades." Since 2000, "for all practical purposes, the 1960 promise was dead." As of 2000, UC maintained a high level of quality by educating a limited proportion of public sector students, drawn from the top 12 percent. The California State University (regional colleges) enrolled 50 percent more students, but with a woeful graduation rate of 45 percent. Community colleges enrolled about 70 percent of public students, but their implicit transfer function deteriorated. All sectors have at times reduced the admission of qualified students—"California's stock response to financial difficulty." California fell to the lowest third of states for the percentage of bachelor's degrees, an output judged inadequate to meet the state's requirements for college-educated workers. The state essentially forfeited its capacity to deal constructively with these challenges. Public education, once the strongest in the nation, sank to the bottom in spending and achievement. It appeared to be a root cause of troubling regional, social, and ethnic disparities in educational attainment. Financial mandates created by voter propositions left higher education to compete for a narrow slice of the state's boom-or-bust budgets.[64] A stock-taking analysis in 2018

63   Christopher Newfield, *Unmaking the Public University: The Forty-Year Assault on the Middle Class* (Cambridge, MA: Harvard University Press, 2008); Newfield, *The Great Mistake: How We Wrecked Public Universities and How We Can Fix Them* (Baltimore: Johns Hopkins University Press, 2016); St. John, *Refinancing the College Dream.*

64   Simon Marginson, *The Dream Is Over: The Crisis of Clark Kerr's California Idea of Higher Education* (Berkeley: University of California Press, 2016); Patrick M. Callen, "The Perils of Success: Clark Kerr and the Master Plan for Higher Education," in Sheldon Rothblatt, ed. *Clark Kerr's World of Higher*

reported that since 2000 the UC had lost one-half of its core state funding and recouped slightly more than half that sum through tuition. But the resilience of a premier research university was evident. The UC increased enrollment by 40 percent, with no loss in quality. Undergraduate applications doubled in these years, and graduation rates rose to 89 percent. Federal research support also grew at an above-average rate. Austerity had its costs in terms of larger classes and greater use of non-tenure-track faculty, but the multiversity campuses of the UC fared better than California regional and community colleges.[65]

Harold Shapiro assumed the presidency of the University of Michigan in 1980, just as the economic downturn signaled a severe and prolonged drop in state appropriations. Austerity measures were unavoidable, but he also resolved on a five-year plan to make the university "smaller but better." After difficult internal discussions, Michigan significantly reduced expenditures for the Colleges of Art, Education, and Natural Resources and eliminated nonacademic units as well as the Department of Geography (despite strong protests). Shapiro redeployed initial savings to the professional schools—Business, Engineering, and Law. They not only needed strengthening but could raise assets on their own. With the help of the state, the university rebuilt its antiquated medical campus. Michigan's long-range planning was a rarity for a public university and put it in the forefront of privatization. It benefited from national trends: the revitalization of professional education, cooperation with industry for economic development, and growing research funding for medicine and engineering. Appealing to the private sector, it conducted a successful capital campaign. Above all, Michigan looked to tuition for revenue growth. The university raised tuition for nonresident students to near private levels and enlarged their enrollments from 18 to 30 percent. Tuition revenues rose from $50 million in 1977 to $200 million in 1987. When Shapiro departed that year to become president of Princeton, Michigan was one of the most privatized public universities.[66]

Education Reaches the 21st Century (Dordecht: Springer, 2012), 61–84; Gerald R. Kissler and Ellen Switkes, "The Effects of a Changing Financial Context on the University of California," in Ronald G. Ehrenberg, ed., *What's Happening to Public Higher Education? The Shifting Financial Burden* (Westport, CT: Praeger, 2007), 85–106.

65 John Aubrey Douglas and Zachary Bleemer, *Approaching the Tipping Point? A History and Prospectus for Funding for the University of California*, SERU Report, Center for Studies in Higher Education, UC Berkeley (August 20, 2018). For the unique measures for upholding quality at the University of California, see King, *University of California*, 417–82.

66 Howard H. Peckham, *The Making of the University of Michigan, 1817–1992*, edited and updated by Margaret L. Steneck and Nicholas H. Steneck (Ann Arbor: University of Michigan, 1994), 325–43; Keith H. Brodie and Leslie Banner, *The Research University Presidency in the Late Twentieth Century: A Life Cycle/Case History Approach* (Westport, CT: Praeger, 2005), 155–67.

Privatization allowed the University of Michigan to prosper despite adverse state policies. In the 1990s, regressive policies cut local property taxes, effectively diverting state funds to K-12 education to the detriment of higher education (as happened in California). In 2000 the state adopted merit aid, which far outstripped a meager program of need-based student aid. A 2004 commission that investigated the causes of Michigan's below-average graduation rate recommended measures to improve preparation and transfer but did not address the fiscal tourniquet afflicting higher education.[67]

In 1993, Georgia instituted merit aid by combining two socially regressive policies. HOPE Scholarships provided tuition grants for all state high school graduates with a B average or better, and a state lottery was created to fund the program. Thus, predominantly lower-income lottery players subsidized predominantly upper-income academic achievers. Both policies nonetheless succeeded. Lottery revenues exceeded expectations and allowed the state to expand the provisions of the HOPE program. Merit aid succeeded as well. In the age of the selectivity sweepstakes, HOPE Scholarships retained significant numbers of high achievers in the state. SAT scores increased most at Georgia Tech and the University of Georgia, as did their *U.S. News* rankings. Attendance, retention, and graduation all rose appreciably, no doubt in part due to HOPE.[68] However, these benefits came at a high cost in terms of the funding available for public higher education. With the state paying a large portion of tuition, it was reluctant to raise tuition. By the end of the decade, the state appropriations began to turn down as well, especially on a per-student basis. The state thus tended to revert toward the national funding pattern, albeit with relatively low tuition.[69] However, by this juncture Georgia's HOPE Scholarships were widely admired and emulated. Thirteen states enacted versions of merit aid. In fact, the states paralleled the federal initiatives that directed non-need-based aid to middle-class students through tax deductions and loan programs.

Public research universities that could draw upon strong professional schools, loyal alumni, and research prowess in strategic fields were able to advance academically in the 1980s and 1990s despite the relative shrinkage of state support. Average per-student real expenditures grew by $4,000 in the 1980s, with states providing $3 for every $2 from students. In the 1990s, these expenditures grew by

---

67 Stephen L. DesJardins et al., "Michigan Public Higher Education: Recent Trends and Policy Considerations for the Coming Decade," in Ehrenberg, *What's Happening?*, 159–205.

68 Susan Dynarski, "The New Merit Aid," in Caroline M. Hoxby, ed., *College Choices: The Economics of Where to Go, When to Go, and How to Pay for It* (Chicago: University of Chicago Press, 2004), 63–100: Arkansas was the first state to adopt "new merit aid" in 1991.

69 Christopher Cornwall and David B. Mustard, "Assessing Public Higher Education in Georgia at the Start of the Twenty-first Century," in Ehrenberg, *What's Happening?*, 107–34.

$3,000, but states provided one incremental dollar for every $3 from students. The principal research universities registered improvement in ratings of academic programs during the 1980s, with notable gains among the relative newcomers (Arizona, Florida, Georgia Tech, Penn State, Texas A&M, UC Davis, and UC San Diego). In the 1990s, the leading public research universities bolstered their standing in the selectivity sweepstakes. The competitive situation there differed from that described for private colleges. These universities often enrolled as many top students as highly selective private schools, but in incoming classes of 3,000 to 6,000. They also achieved peer effects through internal, or horizontal, differentiation, as such students clustered in honors colleges and demanding science majors. They had prominent brand names and impressive intellectual and physical facilities. Average SAT scores for the leading public research universities increased markedly in these decades, and matriculation of top students increased toward the end of this period. These universities had the market power to raise tuitions and attract students in a national market.[70]

The regional and urban universities in the "open," or nonselective, sector had few of the attributes that allowed research universities to cope with privatization. They were far more dependent on state appropriations and had few alternatives for substituting tuition increases for shortfalls in state support. They also served a nonaffluent clientele. For the least selective half of public four-year institutions (1990) 25 percent of students were lower-income and 40 percent, middle-middle class.[71] Empirical research has shown that such students were particularly ill-served by the rising tuition and institutional austerity caused by shrinking appropriations. In nonselective state systems, 51 percent of students graduated, but only one-half of them did so in four years. These results reflected low per-student spending. As one study found: "Expenditures per student are important to graduation rates. State governments that ignore this fact and call for higher graduation rates and do not increase funding (but rather cut funding) will not have success."[72] Other studies indicated why this might be the case. Students in larger classes achieved lower grades, and more part-time faculty were associated with

70   Geiger, *Knowledge and Money*, 42–50, 83–93; Roger L. Geiger, "Expert and Elite: The Incongruous Missions of Public Research Universities," in Roger Geiger, Carol Kolbeck, and Roger L. Williams, eds. *The Future of the American Public Research University* (Rotterdam: Sense Publishers, 2007), 15–34. "Elite public research universities" identified here were (in descending order of average 2003 SAT scores): Georgia Tech, Virginia, UC Berkeley, UNC, Maryland, UCLA, UC San Diego, Michigan, Florida, Illinois, Wisconsin, Texas, and Penn State.

71   Clotfelter, *Unequal Colleges*, 237.

72   William G. Bowen, Matthew M. Chingos, and Michael S. McPherson, *Crossing the Finish Line: Completing College at America's Public Universities* (Princeton: Princeton University Press, 2009); Gary L. Blose, John D. Porter, and Edward C. Kokkelenberg, "The Effects of Institutional Funding Cuts on Baccalaureate Graduation Rates," in Ehrenberg, *What's Happening?*, 71–82, quote p. 77; John Bound, Michael

lower rates of completion.[73] Finally, high tuition in itself posed an impediment to enrollment, persistence, and graduation. Part-time or full-time work negatively affected academic progress, and lower-income students were averse to loans, perhaps wisely considering the poor odds of graduating.

For the majority of public-sector students in nonselective institutions, the contraction of public support in the 1980s and 1990s eroded quality education. Rizzo summarized the consequences: declining state support for public institutions would result in "continued tuition increases, movement away from full-time tenure-track faculty ... increases in student-faculty ratios, an erosion of liberal arts and humanities programs ... increases in time to degree and dropout rates, a decline in public service expenditures, an increase in loan burden on students ... a limitation of program offerings, and a multitude of additional factors."[74] Indeed, after 2001 such was the case.

In the last two decades of the twentieth century, American higher education embarked on a new course that was shaped by federal and state policies and the unleashing of market forces. Federal legislation first made the emergence of the loan culture possible and then funded its hypertrophy. The availability of student loans was a major factor in the escalation of tuition in both the public and private sectors at rates far exceeding family incomes or consumer prices. Thus, the basic funding of higher education was transformed. Private institutions benefited most, as they maintained enrollments and increased revenues largely through student loans and price discrimination using tuition discounts. For public colleges and universities, rising tuition undergirded by student financial aid at best compensated for the relative shrinkage of state appropriations, their principal source of support in the twentieth century. Privatization not only made public institutions more dependent on student revenues, including loans, but also affected their behavior in fund-raising, working with industry, and competing in the market for able students. The competition for high-ability and/or high-paying students—the selectivity sweepstakes—was the development that perhaps best characterized the era. Given the connection of selectivity and high expenditures, the competition spurred increases in tuition and strongly favored the

Lovenheim, and Sarah E. Turner, "Why Have College Completion Rates Declined? An Analysis of Changing Student Preparation and College Resources," NBER Working Paper No. 15566 (2009).

73   Edward Kokkelenberg, Michael Dillon, and Sean M. Christy, "The Effects of Class Size on Student Grades at a Public University," CHERI Working Paper No. 88 (February 2006); Ronald G. Ehrenberg and Liang Zhang, "Do Tenured and Tenure-Track Faculty Matter?" CHERI Working Paper No. 53 (December 2004); John Bound, Michael Lovenheim, and Sarah Turner, *Understanding the Decrease in College Completion Rates and the Increased Time to the Baccalaureate Degree*, Population Studies Center, University of Michigan, Report 07–626 (Ann Arbor, MI: Institute for Social Research, November 2007).

74   Michael J. Rizzo, "State Preferences for Higher Education Spending: A Panel Data Analysis, 1977–2001," in Ehrenberg, *What's Happening?*, 3–35, quote pp. 29–30.

wealthiest institutions. The result was an exaggeration of inequality among institutions, with the wealthiest achieving undreamt of affluence. High prices in addition limited who could purchase higher education and what kind. Need-based financial aid and the educational equity agenda were constant preoccupations throughout this era, and indeed were vital for the access achieved by lower- and middle-income students at all levels of the system. But the dynamics of the system promoted inequality, both in public policies and institutional incentives. The federal government gave the middle class tuition tax deductions, and several states favored merit aid over need-based aid. Private colleges provided as much need-based aid as they could afford but directed most aid toward recruiting the meritorious. Instructional spending became far more skewed across high- and low-cost institutions. After 1980, American higher education became increasingly bifurcated between selective institutions—with their higher prices, expenditures, student qualifications, and graduation rates—and open institutions of mass education—with their lower levels of resources, SAT scores, and graduation rates.

THE CULTURE WARS

Andrew Hartman's *History of the Culture Wars* identified its origins in the 1960s revolt against the traditional norms of American society and sympathy toward previously marginalized groups. However, the antagonism it spawned long festered before erupting in the publicized confrontations of the 1980s and 1990s.[75] Universities were one arena among many for the culture wars, but they played a central role by both generating and absorbing ordnance for these struggles. The persistence of these polarities into the twenty-first century, and their apparent irreconcilability, belie the fervency of convictions. Basic orientations to reality stem from deep cultural ones that provide the frameworks for ideologies, beliefs, and politics. Three of these cultural frames seem to have emerged in the 1960s and undergirded widespread challenges to the existing order.

First was a disidentification with the United States and American society. For many, revulsion from the Vietnam War was generalized to a rejection of what the country ostensibly stood for. Taken to an extreme, the New Left regarded the enormity of the American *system* as justification for revolution. However, a more pervasive repudiation of national identity and disdain for citizenship persisted widely, especially among the highly educated. Disidentification was particularly hostile to the customs and values associated with the American way of life.

---

75   Andrew Hartman, *A War for the Soul of America: A History of the Culture Wars* (Chicago: University of Chicago Press, 2015), 9–37.

Second, was an apotheosis of the individual. The psychologist Herbert Maslow gave scientific credibility to "self-actualization." The novelist Tom Wolfe called the 1970s the "me-decade." Consumerism reigned in higher education. Underlying this ubiquitous emphasis was what the sociologist John Meyer termed "personhood" and human agency—pervasive belief in the right of all individuals for more-or-less unrestrained self-fulfillment. Thus, in the public sphere, cultural individualism translated to an expansive interpretation of human rights.[76]

Third, a fundamentally changed model of society acquired global influence and impact: as Meyer noted, "It was a model of a more liberal, participatory, and developing society ... built upon educational expansion." This was a central element of "world society" in which the ideal of equitable treatment of all groups in relation to government, politics, education, or human services became a cultural creed. This model, which approximated liberalism in the U.S., in fact diffused worldwide, largely through the actions of governmental and nongovernmental organizations, especially universities.[77]

These three frames interpenetrated one another. While disidentification was inherently American, the values of world society elsewhere juxtaposed traditional national identities against liberal ideals, especially in developing countries. Equitable treatment of all groups in society was expressed and promoted as a human right. Educational expansion was universally advocated as a means for individual self-fulfillment as well as national progress. These cultural frames, then, underlay multiple interpretations of reality, but given such deep foundations, conflicting interpretations resulted in neither compromise nor resolution. They produced the culture wars.

In the history of the American culture wars, higher education constituted a single distinctive battlefield.[78] Hostilities erupted in the late 1980s when conservatives attacked manifestations of the academic Left. The rise of the academic Left to dominate several fields was a significant development of the 1970s and 1980s. The term was employed loosely by both practitioners and detractors, but it applied meaningfully to groups espousing a set of doctrines related to postmodern thought. The several strands of postmodernism were in fact critiques of modernity, specifically the heritage of the Enlightenment. Poststructuralist interpretations of language were employed to deny the possibility of objective truth and discredit the academic dominion of reason. The progress of Western civili-

---

76   David Frank and John W. Meyer, "The Contemporary Identity Explosion: Individualizing Society in the Postwar Period," *Sociological Theory* 20, 1 (March 2002): 86–105.

77   Georg Krücken and Gili S. Drori, *World Society: The Writings of John W. Meyer* (New York: Oxford University Press, 2009), quote p. 363.

78   Hartman devotes one of nine chapters to higher education: "The Battle for the American Mind," *War for the Soul*, 222–52.

zation was inverted by emphasizing the oppression of much of humankind and the hegemony of the privileged through capitalism and liberal democracy.[79]

Todd Gitlin located the origins of the academic Left in the identity politics that emerged at the end of the 1960s. Blacks led this movement when they endorsed an "Afro-American" identity and rejected the ideal of assimilation. This separatism fractured the assumption of a single society that had been axiomatic for liberals as well as the Old and the New Left. It posited a fundamental disidentification that abandoned any hope or wish for reforming American society through existing channels. Feminism underwent a similar transformation, displacing the earlier focus on equal pay and equal rights within existing society with more radical notions of a separate feminist identity. Other groups responded to these cues. Those with Spanish-speaking heritage coalesced around a Chicano (later Hispanic) identity; gays and Asian Americans also asserted distinctive identities. Identity politics characterized a second generation of the Left, according to Gitlin, not the veterans of the 1960s New Left. They assumed faculty positions in the 1970s and formed the academic Left. As their numbers increased, "academic cultures of separation began to harden into fortified enclaves," most notably in culture studies.[80] Each group articulated its grievances against American society. Each claimed to be oppressed. Hence, for each the status of victim became an inherent part of its identity, invoked both to claim a status separate from American society and to appeal for recognition and special treatment.

The attack on objectivity was fundamental to the academic Left and pursued with a diverse arsenal of concepts. The social constructivist framework on which feminist scholarship was grounded was noted in Chapter 6. A major inspiration came from literary studies, in which "deconstruction" denied any singular meanings of texts. By calling into question the nature of language, these doctrines provided a rationale for casting doubt on the foundations of Western culture. The emergence of structuralism and post-structuralism further supported this inherent relativism by interpreting phenomena as entirely shaped by culture. These postmodern perspectives were employed to support disidentification by relativizing and hence undermining the Western Enlightenment tradition. The contributions of Michel Foucault, who achieved a wide following in the U.S. in the 1970s, further buttressed the critique of the academic Left. His writings depicted culture as forms of domination. Behind institutions, practices and language are all interpreted in terms of the interests that are served. He thus stressed

79 George Fallis, *Multiversities, Ideas, and Democracy* (Toronto: University of Toronto Press, 2007), 222–59.

80 Todd Gitlin, *The Twilight of Common Dreams: Why America Is Wracked by Culture Wars* (New York: Metropolitan Books, 1995), 126–65, quote p. 145. Many New Left veterans eventually became faculty, but this group often clung to universal visions rather than atomized individualism.

the ubiquity of power in all social relations. This notion of power galvanized the academic Left. They ascribed Foucault's animus against his image of bourgeois society to the social and cultural realities they opposed—to the power of the dominant, privileged, white male culture. Considered self-evident, such claims were advanced with illustrative examples, eschewing analysis.[81]

The academic Left was on particularly weak ground in challenging objectivity in science. For Paul Gross and Norman Levitt, who sought to defend science against efforts to undermine its validity, the academic Left was characterized by "perspectivism." This viewpoint sought to discredit Western modes of thought and particularly regarded the notion of objectivity as reflecting only the perspective of privileged, white, European males. They claimed equal or superior validity for interpretations from the perspectives of Blacks, women, or Third World revolutionaries. For Gross and Levitt, these views "assumed that the oppressed are endowed with uniquely privileged insights, and that the intellectual, as well as moral authority of the victim is beyond question."[82] Subjective perspectivism could raise interesting historical questions about the social and institutional contexts of doing science. But empirical scientific findings were impervious to such speculation.

This summary conveys the ideological tone rather than the substance of the several literatures that were reference points of the academic Left. How they came to dominate culture and literary studies, as well as have a preponderant influence over the fields of history, education, and the nonquantitative social sciences, is more problematic. The theories alluded to represented novel contributions to the intellectual discourse of their respective academic fields. They were extended and modified by legions of scholars, only some of whom stressed the ideology indicated above. The political implications of these doctrines stemmed from the intrinsic disidentification of identity groups. Scholars holding these views were recruited to faculty positions in the 1970s in part to further demographic inclusion, but chiefly because they represented and expounded these new fields, the latest theoretical perspectives in their disciplines. By the 1980s they constituted a majority in many departments and recruited like-minded associates pursuing similar theoretical interests. There was no evident resistance to these developments by senior faculty. They shared much of the same worldview. Most of them heartily backed the advance of underrepresented groups and the disapproval of past social practices that this underrepresentation implied.

---

81   Daniel T. Rodgers, *The Age of Fracture* (Cambridge, MA: Harvard University Press, 2011), 102–7; Roger Scruton, *Fools, Frauds, and Firebrands: Thinkers of the New Left* (London: Bloomsbury, 2015), 99–113.

82   Paul R. Gross and Norman Levitt, *Higher Superstition: The Academic Left and Its Quarrels with Science* (Baltimore: Johns Hopkins University Press, 1994), 34–41, quote p. 40.

They also welcomed the bearers of the latest theoretical approaches and shared the reigning subjective individualism. Thus, there was no resistance—actually eager acceptance—of the doctrines that embodied the gradual politicization of the humanities and social sciences.[83] When resistance appeared in the 1980s, it came from outside the academy.

William J. Bennett, director of the National Endowment for the Humanities, organized a blue-ribbon study group in 1984 that issued *To Reclaim a Legacy: A Report on the Humanities in Higher Education*. The report sought to draw public attention to "the erosion in the place of the humanities in the undergraduate curriculum and in the coherence of the curriculum generally." It deplored the precipitous decline in humanities majors, and even more so the abandonment of course requirements for core subjects. It only alluded to politicization: the displacement of intellectual authority by "intellectual relativism," literature used as a "handmaiden of ideology," and subordination "to a certain social stance." Perhaps worse, they felt, were professors like Stanley Fish who allegedly maintained the humanities had "no inherent meaning because all meaning is subjective and relative to one's own perspective." But uppermost in the report was Bennett's conviction that "the core of the American college curriculum—its heart and soul—should be the civilization of the West." With this mission Bennett sought to revive a curricular corpse that had expired in the 1960s.[84] This effort was a provocation for identity partisans, who dubbed Bennett's core the "Western canon," a symbolic enemy and rallying point.

The battle over the canon acquired national notoriety when Stanford University terminated a required course on Western Culture, which had only been established in 1980 to provide some coherence and commonality to the curriculum. In 1986, identity groups charged that the reading list of great books was racist, sexist, and hurtful to them. The faculty committee formed to rectify this injustice rejected merely adding women and minority authors and instead substituted a new course, Culture, Ideas, and Values, or CIV. Debate over this fairly minor curricular adjustment drew national attention. Rev. Jesse Jackson led a march of Stanford students chanting, "Hey, hey, ho, ho, Western Culture's got to go." William Bennett, now secretary of education, came to campus to argue that

---

83   The National Association of Scholars, founded in 1987, might be regarded as an internal opponent of "the rise of political correctness" (https://www.nas.org/about/history). Vilified by the academic Left, it generally practices the toleration and civility it advocates and has had little influence. The Association of Literary Scholars, Critics, and Writers (founded 1994), based at Boston University, has sought to counter postmodernism in the humanities.

84   William J. Bennett, *To Reclaim a Legacy: A Report on the Humanities in Higher Education* (Washington, DC: National Endowment for the Humanities, 1984), 16, 30. In another context Roger Scruton observed: "Culture becomes an object of conservation only when it has already been lost": *Conservatism: An Invitation to the Great Tradition* (London: All Points, 2018).

"the West is the culture in which we live." Major newspapers resuscitated this recondite issue with impassioned editorials. CIV retained most of the great books among reading options but essentially bowed to the multiculturalists. All CIV courses had to include "works by women, minorities, and persons of color" and at least one reading that addressed issues of race, sex, or class. The reading possibilities included a 1960s New Left favorite, *The Wretched of the Earth*, Franz Fanon's anti-colonial paean to violence. The facile logic is revealed in a comment made by the assistant dean for undergraduate studies: that Fanon might be more relevant to social justice than John Locke. Traditionalists received no sympathy from university administrators. Stanford downplayed the significance of the change. President Donald Kennedy assured Stanford loyalists that "the primary voices for change have been the faculty." Quite right—they shared much the same worldview as the protesters and had no interest in teaching Homer, Plato, Augustine, etc.[85]

The Stanford melodrama unfolded at a time when Allan Bloom's *Closing of the American Mind* was on the *New York Times* best-seller list. Selling over a million copies, this idiosyncratic contribution to the culture wars provided a disarming depiction of American higher education that was incongruously highlighted with analogies from classical literature. A classicist on the Chicago Committee on Social Thought, Bloom advanced several arguments. At the core was a lofty ideal of liberal education as the untrammeled pursuit of truth. This was best pursued through the Western classics, but not in the existing historicist treatments. Rather, this literature should be read and taught to convey how these authors had struggled to discover truth. But American higher education had been thoroughly imbued with relativism, a legacy of German philosophy that led inevitably to nihilism. Hence, students had become inherently relativist and largely unreceptive to a liberal search for truth. Nor were humanities professors, with the prevailing nihilistic denial of meaning, capable of offering liberal education.[86]

Formerly a professor at Cornell, Bloom had experienced the 1969 fiasco, and he blamed the "unmitigated disaster" of the late 1960s for the subsequent prevalence of nihilism, especially in the humanities. But components of the university were affected differently. The professional schools "went home and closed the shutters…. The natural scientists were above the battle, an island unto them-

---

85 Hartman, *War for the Soul*, 227–30; Roger Kimball, *Tenured Radicals: How Politics Has Corrupted Our Higher Education* (New York: Harper & Row, 1990), 27–32; Dinesh D'Souza, *Illiberal Education: The Politics of Race and Sex on Campus* (New York: Free Press, 1991), 59–93. Other universities at this time established mandatory courses in Third World and non-Western cultures or ethnic studies; Stanford in 1990 established a new required course in diversity (D'Souza, *Illiberal Education*, 68, 92).

86 Allan Bloom, *The Closing of the American Mind: How Higher Education Has Failed Democracy and Impoverished the Souls of Today's Students* (New York: Simon & Schuster, 1987); Hartman, *War for the*

selves, and did not feel threatened." The social sciences became a battleground for everyone "who might care about prosperity, peace or war, equality, racial or sexual discrimination," but they also "had a certain scientific conscience and integrity about reporting" on these issues. In the humanities, "passion and commitment ... found their home.... But they worked to their own undoing, for it is the humanities that have suffered the most as a result of the sixties." Bloom mixed polemic with qualifications and distinctions to present a credible depiction of higher education for at least some of his many readers. No one seems to have been moved by his impossible ideal for seeking truth in great books, but the decadence of contemporary liberal education was more apparent.[87]

The critiques of Bennett and Bloom were countered with ever bolder assertions from the higher education community. The Commission on Minority Participation in Education and American Life, chaired by Cornell president Frank Rhodes and sponsored by ACE, issued a report pleading that "the full participation of minority citizens is vital for our survival as a free and prosperous nation." A worthy and important goal, but as the rhetoric suggested, this was an ideological rather than an intellectual exposition. Without considering the social basis for minority underperformance, nor the effects of existing policies, it simply called for a steeper tilt to existing preferences: commitments from each institution of higher education to "recruit minority students more aggressively at every level.... [And] place special emphasis on inspiring and recruiting minority candidates for faculty and administrative positions."[88] Such efforts might advance minority individuals already within the higher education system, but they did not address the causes of underrepresentation. Moreover, a decade after the *Bakke* decision, the higher education establishment was oblivious to reverse discrimination.

Humanists organized a riposte to their critics under the auspices of the American Council of Learned Societies. Addressing the critics' charges directly, their report denied allegations of decline and regarded current *theory* as reflecting intellectual vitality, which perhaps was true from their perspective. It defended specialized research, concluding that "the humanities are better conceived as fields of exploration and critique rather than materials for transmission." So much for teaching a humanities core. Their rejection of the "positivist ideal" was uncompromising: "'objectivity' and 'disinterest' are often the means by which the equation of truth and ideological positions can be disguised." But humanists were aware how these ideologies could "delude us into promoting as universal

Soul, 230–37.

87 Bloom, *Closing*, 320, 347, 351–54.

88 *One-Third of a Nation: A Report of the Commission on Minority Participation in Education and American Life* (Washington, DC: ACE, 1988), 21–22.

values that in fact belong to one nation, one social class, one sect." In contrast, the humanities could "advance awareness of cultural difference by promoting the notion of American culture as an arena of competing, marginalized, suppressed interests, situations, traditions, rather than as a common possession." What the critics' alleged to be failures of the current humanities were in fact virtues and vital correctives to the prejudice and obtuseness of traditional American society.[89]

The strident defenses of multiculturalism and identity politics elicited further attacks from conservatives outside of higher education. The pretentions of the literary Left were pilloried by the conservative critic Roger Kimball in *Tenured Radicals*. He attended symposia at which these authors were unrestrained in expressing these views, and he quoted them extensively to document their "ideologically motivated assaults on the intellectual and moral substance of our culture." His title rhetorically linked the politicization of literary studies with student radicalism of the 1960s.[90] Dinesh D'Souza, a young journalist with conservative sponsorship, skewered multiculturalism in *Illiberal Education: The Politics of Race and Sex on Campus*. Based on extensive interviews across a range of American campuses, he portrayed the "victim's revolution" in seemingly neutral language. Also a best seller and widely covered in the media, his account conveyed the impression that colleges and universities were afflicted by a shallow and hypocritical attachment to multiculturalism and largely disengaged from American society.[91] This impression, or at least the atmosphere generated by the culture wars, led to several reactions: an attempt from the political center to sort out and depolarize these issues; concerns with multiculturalism and "political correctness"; and a political reaction to affirmative action.

For some moderate liberals, the extreme claims of identity politics threatened to undermine reasonable efforts to work toward racial and ethnic comity while also inflaming right-wing resistance to any kind of reform.[92] Representative of that view was Arthur M. Schlesinger, Jr., who had attempted to articulate a "vital center" of American politics more than four decades earlier. *The Disuniting of America: Reflections on a Multicultural Society* sought to define a middle, liberal course between militant multiculturalists on the left and bigoted monoculturalists on the right. The former would Balkanize American society further, while the latter sought to "sanitize the past and install their own patriotic set of heroes and

---

89   George Levine et al., *Speaking for the Humanities*, ACLS Occasional Paper No. 7 (1989).

90   Kimball, *Tenured Radicals*, xviii. Kimball elaborated this last point in *The Long March: How the Cultural Revolution of the 1960s Changed America* (San Francisco: Encounter, 2000).

91   D'Souza, *Illiberal Education*.

92   Among the moderate, liberal critics: David Bromwich, *Politics by Other Means: Higher Education and Group Thinking* (New Haven, CT: Yale University Press, 1992); Gitlin, *Twilight of Common Dreams*, 177.

myths." Todd Gitlin too belonged with these writers. He condemned identity politics precisely because it undermined the sense of national unity and purpose that a reformist politics required. Gitlin also criticized the media counteroffensive against the Left that popularized the notion of "political correctness."[93]

Political correctness on campuses and PC depicted in the media were rather different phenomena. PC on campuses was a tangible reality, embodied in compulsory diversity courses, speech codes, and diversity workshops, which one attendee likened to water torture. By 1991, required diversity courses had been established on half of American campuses, and mandated diversity content on two-thirds. These institutional efforts to promote multiculturalism may have been counterproductive. An extensive survey of college students in the late 1990s found that "America's colleges are *deeply* divided." In contrast to two decades previous, students now defined themselves largely in terms of identity groups. Moreover, each group harbored resentment that in some ways it was treated unfairly, creating a pervasive sense of victimization. Group members largely associated with each other, so that campuses had become increasingly segregated. The authors concluded: "Tolerance is becoming a scarce commodity.... Multiculturalism remains the most unresolved issue on campus today [1998]."[94]

Speech codes punishing alleged "hate speech" raised alarms in the general population. The courts ruled some codes to be unconstitutional suppression of free speech; they were attacked by President George H. W. Bush in a University of Michigan commencement address; and legislation was introduced in Congress (but not enacted) to withhold federal funds from offending institutions. More insidious, the monopoly of PC views precluded frank discussion or critical research on germane scholarly topics involving race or gender. Indications of skepticism or disbelief by faculty or graduate students, at least in departments of humanities or social science, risked ostracism. PC domination of campuses was first featured in the popular media in response to descriptions of campus intolerance, like those offered by D'Souza. Conservative commentators seized upon examples of PC excesses to discredit the Left and universities in general. The Right thus used allegations of PC to uphold the outdated views that fit the stereotypes of the academic Left, but which had long since been transcended by

93   Arthur M. Schlesinger, Jr., *The Disuniting of America: Reflections on a Multicultural Society* (New York: Norton, 1992); Gitlin, *Twilight of Common Dreams*, 166–77. Gitlin dates the media concern with political correctness from the Winter of 1990–1991; "political correctness," or PC, was second in voting for the "word of the year 1990."

94   Arthur Levine, "Worlds Apart: Disconnect between Students and Their Colleges," in Richard H. Hersh and John Merrow, eds. *Declining by Degrees: Higher Education at Risk* (New York: Palgrave Macmillan, 2005), 155–69, quote p. 163; Arthur Levine and Jeanette S. Cureton, *When Hope and Fear Collide: A Portrait of Today's College Student* (San Francisco: Jossey-Bass, 1998), 71–91, quote p. 91.

most academics and most Americans.[95] Still, the conditions that gave rise to political correctness on campuses endured.[96]

The backlash against identity policies had its most tangible impact in the repudiation of affirmative action at the University of California. In July 1995 the university regents voted to remove considerations of race, ethnicity, and gender from employment, contracting, and university admissions. This action largely resulted from the determined campaign by one regent, the black businessman Ward Connerly. Partly through his efforts, affirmative action became a political issue in California, where Governor Pete Wilson sought to exploit it for a possible presidential bid, and nationally, where President Clinton defended it. However, its fatal liability was the prevailing ideology of multiculturalism within the university. It was widely recognized that affirmative action had created a bifurcated student body. D'Souza had reported that Berkeley had "two sets of admission standards: one for certified minorities, and one for everybody else." Official statistics showed that 58 percent of minorities graduated, compared with 84 percent of everybody else.[97] Still, affirmative admissions were strongly supported in the university administration and largely among students as well.

The UC system was officially committed to a student body that approximated the ethnic proportions of the California population.[98] But it was also bound under the Master Plan to a high academic standard. Together, mission impossible. Each campus and professional school controlled its own admissions. Berkeley, for example, devised a plan by which 50 percent of undergraduates would be admitted solely on academic merit, and the rest according to multiple criteria, of which affirmative action comprised one-half. When Ward Connerly challenged the university administration on affirmative action in 1994, it strongly defended the principle but scarcely knew how it was implemented. Admission was largely in the hands of zealous, mid-level administrators. The usual practice was to create a separate applicant pool for minorities, and some campuses simply admitted all of them. Racial numbers took precedence over the goal of expanding social opportunity. Many of the affirmative action admits came from professional or upper-middle-class families, while the Asian American applicants whom they

95   Geiger, *Research and Relevant Knowledge*, 327–31; Gitlin, *Twilight of Common Dreams*, 170–72.

96   Neil Gross and Solon Simmons, eds., *Professors and Their Politics* (Baltimore: Johns Hopkins University Press, 2014); Robert Maranto, Richard E. Redding, and Frederick M. Hess, eds., *The Politically Correct University: Problems, Scope, and Reforms* (Washington, DC: AEI Press, 2008).

97   D'Souza, *Illiberal Education*, 25–58, quote p. 50; John Aubrey Douglass, *The Conditions for Admission: Access, Equity, and the Social Contract of Public Universities* (Stanford, CA: Stanford University Press, 2007), 159. The following draws on the Douglass study, *Conditions for Admission*, 151–83.

98   A 1974 legislative resolution specified: "Each segment of California public higher education shall strive to approximate the ethnic, sexual, and economic composition of recent high school graduates": King, *University of California*, 533.

statistically displaced often had lower SES backgrounds. The partisans on both sides of this struggle operated from inflexible political convictions, but the university's vulnerability stemmed from an inability to reconcile rationales and principles with practices. The historian John Douglass concluded: "Institutions such as the University of California lost their bearings in their ardent effort to become more inclusive of underrepresented racial and ethnic groups; their advocacy inadvertently diminished the viability of affirmative action within the political culture."[99]

By the late 1990s, affirmative action had axiomatic backing within higher education but was losing the battle for public support.[100] California voters passed Proposition 209 in 1996 by 54 percent, outlawing all racial preferences by the state. Similar measures were later enacted in Washington, Michigan, and Florida. However, it was left to the courts—again—to reconcile the contradictions between racial preferences and equal protection of the law. In 1995 the Supreme Court narrowed the purview of affirmative action, ruling it justified only when "strict scrutiny" indicated past discrimination and remedies were "narrowly tailored" to apply to the affected groups. Lower courts ruled against affirmative admissions in some cases, while the Supreme Court avoided the issue. However, in 2003 two admissions cases from the University of Michigan forced the issue. In the case involving undergraduate admissions (*Gratz v. Bollinger*), the court found that automatically awarding affirmative action applicants a substantial number of points toward acceptance was an unconstitutional favoring of race. But in law school admissions (*Grutter v. Bollinger*), it held that the university's compelling interest in diversity justified considering race and ethnicity as one factor in a *holistic* evaluation of applicants. The *Grutter* decision allowed universities considerable leeway if they evaluated each applicant individually. This was the practice for undergraduate admissions at selective private institutions, and it was immediately adopted by major public universities like Michigan, despite the additional time and expense this entailed. The UC had already adopted Comprehensive Review in 2001 as a stratagem to admit more minorities. It then adopted holistic review to restore (perhaps more moderate) preferences. Under *Grutter* it became possible for institutions to attain diversity goals while treating applicants as fairly as could be expected in a process based on assessing incommensurate qualities.[101]

99   Douglass, *Conditions for Admissions*, 181.

100   Affirmative action probably never had majority support: John David Skrentny, *The Ironies of Affirmative Action: Politics, Culture, and Justice in America* (Chicago: University of Chicago Press, 1996); and Chapter 6.

101   Douglas, *Conditions of Admission*, 238–39. The UC Comprehensive Review used fourteen criteria: Judson, *University of California*, 551–52. Problems remained in states like Texas that replaced affirmative

The culture war in higher education was an unbalanced conflict. The critics, above all, launched their attacks in the public sphere, with little expectation of affecting colleges and universities directly. Their diatribes and aspersions changed nothing in higher education but made the political proclivities of the academy more or less a fixture in polarized political narratives. Whether part cause or part effect, the culture wars coincided with a decided loss of confidence in American higher education.

The literature just discussed represented the more intellectually coherent criticism of higher education, but it was joined in these years by a host of more scurrilous attacks: *Profscam: Professors and the Demise of Higher Education* (1988); *Imposters in the Temple: American Intellectuals Are Destroying Our Universities and Cheating Our Students of Their Future* (1992); and *Killing the Spirit: Higher Education in America* (1990).[102] Among other grievances, these books invariably invoked concern for students, who allegedly failed to receive the education they deserved and paid dearly for, and contempt for their teachers. A second, related theme was hostility toward academic research. They dismissed the idea that the mission of universities was to advance as well as disseminate knowledge. The sociologist Neil Gross sought to explain why this campaign attained prominence at this juncture, despite conservative complaints against the liberal professoriate going back to William F. Buckley's *God and Man at Yale*. By the 1980s, "Conservative advocacy organizations that took on the liberal professoriate arose" largely through the efforts of "midlevel moral entrepreneurs" (e.g., D'Souza). Their message "had already become a well-established part of the conservative repertoire," and it found ready moral and financial support from political organizations.[103] The conservative critique of colleges and universities thus became an omnipresent feature of American political culture.

The culture wars, conservative diatribes, and the alleged polarity of teaching and research—all contributed to a negative climate for higher education through the first half of the 1990s. And in a negative climate, negative things happen. Federal research support slowed, and the academic research complex feared far worse. State appropriations for public higher education lost ground, actually falling for two of those years. Tuition increased, and students were compelled to rely

---

action with automatic admission of the top 10 percent of high school classes; and Michigan passed legislation barring racial preferences following the *Gratz* decision.

102　Charles J. Sykes, *Profscam: Professors and the Demise of Higher Education* (New York: Simon & Schuster, 1988); Martin Anderson, *Imposters in the Temple: American Intellectuals Are Destroying Our Universities and Cheating Our Students of Their Future* (New York: Simon & Schuster, 1992); Page Smith, *Killing the Spirit: Higher Education in America* (New York: Viking, 1990). Three of many such attacks.

103　Neil Gross, *Why Are Professors Liberal and Why Do Conservatives Care?* (Cambridge, MA: Harvard University Press, 2013), 289–91.

more heavily on loans. Ward Connerly succeeded in an improbable crusade against affirmative action at the University of California. Research universities were subjected to hostile audits of indirect-cost reimbursements. And the president and Congress attacked universities for abridging freedom of speech. Yet American higher education emerged from these years somewhat tarnished, but whole. And prospects soon brightened.

Enrollments continued to grow during the early 1990s, as did the prosperity of the private sector. But in the second half of the decade, economic growth brought a new sense of optimism to American higher education. State funding of public higher education compensated for some of the shortfalls of the previous years. Private colleges and universities experienced growing revenues from tuition and endowments, as well as healthy student demand. The selective sector especially prospered as students increasingly sought quality. Congress recognized the essential contribution of academic research to national needs with increased financial support. Research universities responded to critics with concrete measures to bolster undergraduate teaching. American higher education returned to its historic path of intrinsic growth in participation, in academic quality, and in the advancement of knowledge. The twentieth may have been the American Century, as Henry Luce once observed, but it was also the century of the American university.[104]

104   Geiger, *Research and Relevant Knowledge*, 98–100, 261–68.

★ 8 ★

AMERICAN HIGHER EDUCATION IN THE TWENTY-FIRST CENTURY

ISTORIANS SHOULD APPROACH THE PRESENT WITH TREPIDATION. Few of the materials used for historical analysis are available. What is available—in overabundance—provides information about events in the near past and what seems to be occurring currently. More problematic is why things happened, and even more conjectural is what their significance might be. This history will follow the story of American higher education into the twenty-first century fully aware of these limitations but hopeful that a historical perspective can bring some insight. In higher education, the developments of the twenty-first century in large measure extended and often accentuated the major trends of the preceding two decades. No new initiatives by state or federal governments significantly altered the momentum of these developments. Rather, market forces continued to shape American higher education and define its relation to American society.

Higher education in the twenty-first century became larger and more inclusive, more expensive and more stratified. It became more intertwined with society beyond the campus and more oriented toward relations with the commercial economy. It became more driven by markets and less by governments. More dependent on private-sector resources, it became increasingly responsive to consumers. American universities continued to lead the global knowledge system, even as the weaknesses of undergraduate learning became increasingly apparent. An industry that educated 20 million students in more than 4,000 establishments is beyond complex—it is multiform and multidimensional. Yet, it served, as it always had, to exercise three basic functions. As a source of culture and status, higher education was instrumental in sorting individuals into the social roles they would fulfill. As a provider of knowledge and skills—human capital—it prepared individuals for productive contributions to society and remuneration for themselves. And as the chief repository of advanced knowledge, universities created, preserved, processed, purveyed, and reproduced a large share of the intellectual resources of our civilization. Culture, careers, and knowledge have been the foci of American colleges and universities since their colonial beginnings.[1] More consequential than ever, and hence more contested, these functions of higher education continued to evolve in the twenty-first century.

THE $1,000,000,000,000 DEBT

From 2000 to 2016, enrollments in higher education grew from 15 million to 20 million and exhibited a number of positive trends. The college-going rate of high school graduates grew from 63 to nearly 70 percent. This included an estimated increase from roughly 48 to 52 percent for students from the lowest quintile of families. Enrollment rates for Blacks inched up from just under to just over 60 percent, while college-going by Hispanics grew by 20 percentage points to equal that of Whites at 69 percent. The over-achievement of Asian American students widened. More students attended four-year institutions, and more attended full time. Especially positive, bachelor's degrees grew by 50 percent as more students completed college.[2]

On the negative side, until the end of the twentieth century, the United States had the highest proportion of young people graduating from higher education, but by 2010 the U.S. had been surpassed by ten other countries. Bare enrollment figures obscure the persistence of inequality in access and outcomes. The wealthier a student, the more likely she would attend a four-year college; and conversely, the less wealthy a student, the more likely she would enter a community college. Among four-year institutions, the more selective an institution, the higher the average family incomes of its students. These differences resulted in graduation rates that were far more socially skewed than participation rates.[3] Financially, privatization accelerated in the twenty-first century. Tuition, room, and board at a high-priced public university (90th percentile) increased from $12,000 to $26,000 (2000–2015); at the same percentile private university, from $33,000 to $63,000. Median increases in constant dollars for tuition alone were 83 percent in public institutions and 52 percent in private ones, from a higher

1 Roger L. Geiger, *The History of American Higher Education: Learning and Culture from the Founding to World War II* (Princeton: Princeton University Press, 2015), 275–76; Mitchell L. Stevens, Elizabeth A. Armstrong, and Richard Arum, "Sieve, Incubator, Temple, Hub: Empirical and Theoretical Advances in the Sociology of Higher Education," *Annual Review of Sociology* 34 (2008): 127–51.

2 National Center for Education Statistics (NCES), *Digest of Education Statistics: 2017*, Table 302.20. Some values are averaged from survey data and hence approximate. The participation rates for all eighteen-year-olds is lower than the continuation rates of high school graduates.

3 Charles T. Clotfelter, *Unequal Colleges in the Age of Disparity* (Cambridge, MA: Harvard University Press, 2017); Martha J. Bailey and Susan M. Dynarski, "Inequality in Postsecondary Education," in Greg Duncan and Richard Murnane, eds., *Whither Opportunity? Rising Inequality, Schools, and Children's Life Chances* (New York: Russell Sage Foundation Press, 2011), 117–32.

base. These increases far outstripped family resources, causing a massive growth in student loans. Student debt grew from $250 billion in 2003 to $1,250 billion in 2016—a trillion-dollar wager on the future financial credit of student borrowers. Finally, 20 percent of additional students enrolled in for-profit corporate universities, many for dubious programs. This sector grew from 450,000 students in 2000 to more than 2 million in 2010, before falling back to 1.35 million in 2015.[4]

After witnessing enrollment rates in California higher education exceed 50 percent by 1970, Martin Trow offered a typology for how social relations changed as systems transitioned from elite to mass to universal higher education. In the universal stage, barriers between higher education and society gave way as lifelong learning assumed multiple forms with multiple providers. For children of the middle and upper classes, it became an obligation to maintain social status. In the twenty-first century, Simon Marginson drew upon examples of nations that had crossed the universal threshold to elaborate a model of "high participation systems." Such systems tended to bifurcate into elite and open sectors. Governments capped potentially runaway expenditures in the burgeoning open sector and concentrated spending on institutions having the greatest value to society, or to them. Notions of higher education as a public good lost credence. Greater reliance on private resources favored elite institutions. Thus, achieving high rates of participation in higher education, in the United States and elsewhere, may have provided social benefits but also increased inequality and stratification.[5]

The bifurcating tendencies in American higher education have been remarked upon several times. The dynamics of the "re-sorting" process analyzed by Caroline Hoxby tended to create growing institutional disparities in student abilities and educational expenditures.[6] Viewed historically, the difference between the top and the bottom college ranks was probably never greater than in 1900, when William Rainey Harper appraised the dismal *Prospects of the Small College* from the Olympian perspective of the University of Chicago.[7] The expansion and upgrading of public colleges and universities to accommodate the Tidal Wave may have made the educational capabilities of institutions more comparable in

---

4   NCES, *Digest of Education Statistics: 2017*, Tables 303.10, 303.20. Enrollment at Title IV-eligible for-profits were 2.4 million in 2010 (13 percent) when nondegree students are included.

5   Michael Burrage, ed., *Martin Trow: Twentieth-Century Higher Education, Elite to Mass to Universal* (Baltimore: Johns Hopkins University Press, 2010), esp. 558–59; Simon Marginson, "Universal Higher Education in the Global Era" (paper presented at The Dynamics of High Participation Systems—An International Seminar, Moscow, September 26, 2013).

6   Caroline M. Hoxby, "How the Changing Market Structure of U.S. Higher Education Explains College Tuition," NBER Working Paper No. 6323 (December 1997); Hoxby, "The Changing Selectivity of American Colleges," *Journal of Economic Perspectives* 23, 4 (Fall 2009): 95–118.

7   Geiger, *History of American Higher Education*, 275–76.

the 1970s than before or since, at least among four-year institutions. After 1980, the American system evolved toward greater inequality—bifurcation—through public disinvestment and the selectivity sweepstakes.

But first, the expansion of the 1970s constituted growth from the bottom. The college-for-all ideology flourished in the first part of the decade (Chapter 6), when there was little potential for growth among traditional students. From 1966 to 1980, 80 percent of the increase in first-year enrollments occurred in community colleges. For total enrollments in the 1970s, two of every three additional students were part-time, reflecting the growth of nontraditional programs. These sectors and their clienteles became established features of the higher education system.

In the 1980s, social inclusion was gradually reemphasized. An objective ever since the civil rights movement and affirmative action, it now advanced under the banner of diversity. That term had received a judicial seal of approval in the *Bakke* decision and henceforth became the official rationale for the recruitment and special treatment of Blacks, Hispanics, and soon gay and lesbian students. Diversity also received unequivocal backing from the foundations and associations that composed the higher education establishment. The American Association of Colleges and Universities, in particular, altered its advocacy from liberal arts to diversity. It thus became an obligatory goal across the institutional spectrum. When Steven Brint analyzed university strategic plans after 2000, "the *only* theme each one shared in common was a stated and seemingly heartfelt commitment to diversity."[8]

The substantial resources and efforts poured into furthering diversity succeeded in narrowing or closing the enrollment gaps with Whites (variously measured), but this progress had less impact on the large discrepancies in social class. College continuation rates (of high school graduates), although rising, remained skewed by socioeconomic status, and families below median incomes made little progress on college graduation.[9] By 2010, alarm over the declining international rank of the U.S., as well as concern for social justice, prompted greater public focus on overall educational attainment (with no less regard for diversity). President Barack Obama, wishing to restore international leadership in college attainment, set goals for every child to attain at least one year of postsecondary education by 2020, and for an additional 8 million college graduates. For the Bill

---

8   Steven Brint, *Two Cheers for Higher Education: Why American Universities Are Stronger Than Ever—And How to Meet the Challenges They Face* (Princeton: Princeton University Press, 2018), 134.

9   William G. Bowen, Matthew M. Chingos, and Michael S. McPherson, *Crossing the Finish Line: Completing College at America's Public* Universities (Princeton: Princeton University Press, 2009); Bailey and Dynarski, "Inequality in Postsecondary Education"; *Postsecondary Education Opportunity* 256 (October 2013).

and Melinda Gates Foundation and the Lumina Foundation, the goal to lessen inequality and bolster the American economy was to double the proportion of young people earning higher education credentials by 2025. The Gates Foundation alone spent more than $300 million to promote the completion agenda through technology and competency-based programs.[10] The gains for such lofty goals would have to come from the lower half of family incomes and particularly lower-income Whites, who had been left out of the social-inclusion agenda. A concern for "first-generation" students became a new preoccupation of the industry.[11] Forty years after the Carnegie Commission reports, "college for all" was again a featured goal for American higher education.

Despite the zeal for educational expansion, educational attainment stagnated in the 2010s, just as it had in the 1970s. The intervening decades saw college continuation rates rise from one-half to two-thirds and overall participation increase by 60 percent.[12] But expansion faced formidable headwinds in deficiencies in academic readiness, the rising cost of college, and public disinvestment. In the crucial area of reading, 37 percent of twelfth-grade students rated "proficient" or better in 2015, meaning they were at least moderately prepared for college-level work. About the same proportion rated as "basic" in reading skills. The proficiency figure had risen modestly during the 1980s but declined after 2000 and registered no improvement to 2015. The College Board estimated that 43 percent of SAT examinees were academically prepared for college-level work, and the ACT put that figure at 40 percent.[13] Thus, roughly one-half of high school graduates who continue to college lacked the requisite academic skills.[14] The proportion of academically prepared students entering college roughly equaled the 36 percent of twenty-five- to twenty-nine-year-olds who attained a bachelor's degree (2016). Lack of college preparedness was a formidable obstacle to the college-for-all agenda. The multiple efforts to address this problem through federal policies, foundation initiatives, and campus programs are beyond the scope of this

10 Marc Perry, Kelly Field, and Beckie Supiano, "The Gates Effect," *Chronicle of Higher Education* (July 14, 2013).

11 Brint, *Two Cheers*, 136–37.

12 NCES, *Digest of Education Statistics: 2017*, Table 302.60. Enrollments as a percentage of eighteen to twenty-four-year-olds grew from 25 percent in the 1970s to 40 percent ca. 2010.

13 National Assessment of Educational Progress, Department of Education; Dennis A. Ahlburg, "Is Higher Education a Good Investment for All Students?" (Trinity University, 2016).

14 A long-standing problem: James E. Rosenbaum charged that high schools instilled an expectation of college in students but did not provide the requisite preparation: *Beyond College for All: Career Paths for the Forgotten Half* (New York: Russell Sage, 2001), chap. 3. Also, Sarah E. Turner, "Going to College and Finishing College: Explaining Different Educational Outcomes," in Caroline M. Hoxby, ed., *College Choices: The Economics of Where to Go, When to Go, and How to Pay for It* (Chicago: University of Chicago Press, 2004), 13–61, esp. 39–41.

history. They may well have contributed to the gains in graduation noted above, but expansion faced additional obstacles in the economics of higher education.

The two recessions of the 2000s produced substantial reductions in state funding and substantial hikes in tuition. These trade-offs were more direct and of larger magnitudes than in the 1980s and 1990s, as states abandoned their former resistance to tuition increases. Previously, real annual tuition growth had been nearly 3 percent, far more than the growth in median family incomes or consumer prices; but it had occurred from a low base. The increases of the 2000s were much larger in terms of dollars, making tuition income comparable to state appropriations in most states, and far more in some. Public colleges and universities became increasingly dependent on tuition for their operations. Tuition revenues equaled 73 percent of instructional costs in 2009, and 83 percent in 2014.[15]

Going to college in the 2010s for most students meant engaging with the financial aid system. Five principal sources of aid helped students meet the escalating costs of college attendance.[16] No single figure can be placed on this aid, since each of the components has multiple forms for many types of recipients.

- The largest number of beneficiaries—13 million—took advantage of tuition credits to deduct an average of $1,400 from federal income taxes. A middle-class benefit from the outset, this program was expanded in 2009 to include households with incomes of $100,000–180,000. Since this costly program was a delayed rebate for families of enrolled students, it had no effect on access. However, it apparently created an incentive for states to raise community college tuitions, which would be offset with federal tax deductions.[17]
- In 2016–2017, more than 7 million students received Pell Grants averaging $3,740. Over half of Pell recipients were independent students, and nearly half were adults twenty-five or older. Just 2.4 million recipients were dependent undergraduates from households with incomes under $40,000, the recipients for whom the program was initially intended. From 1995 to 2015, tuition at public colleges and universities rose by $5,000, and private tuition by $14,000, in constant dollars; the maximum Pell Grant increased by $1,700, even after a hefty boost in 2009, and covered less than 60 percent of public tuition.

15   NCES, *Digest of Education Statistics: 2017*, Tables 333.10, 334.10. In 2017, tuition revenues exceeded state appropriations in the majority of states.

16   College Board, *Trends in Student Aid, 2017* (New York: College Board, 2017). This discussion omits College Work-Study, veteran benefits, and private grants.

17   Bridget Terry Long, "The Impact of Federal Tax Credits for Higher Education Expenses," in Hoxby, *College Choices*, 101–65.

- State grants averaged $790 per undergraduate recipient but ranged from $2,100 in South Carolina to zero in New Hampshire. About one-quarter of state aid was merit based, a proportion that held steady from the late 1990s. Only fifteen states awarded more than half of aid on merit, including Georgia at 100 percent, but most of those states awarded the largest amounts.

- Tuition discounts were classified as institutional grants and as such were the fastest growing form of student aid—rising 60 percent in private doctoral universities and 100 percent in public ones (2005–2015). The overall tuition discount rate in the private nonprofit sector rose from 35 to 45 percent (2007–2017), but since the Great Recession, these policies produced miniscule gains in net tuition.[18] The adoption of tuition-discounting as a regular practice among public research universities (53 percent of undergrads) would seem to reflect their increasing dependence on high tuition.

- Finally, loans, mostly federal, composed $106 billion of $180 billion in total student aid in 2016–2017 (excluding tuition discounts). This sum, in constant dollars, was about where it was ten years previously. In the interim, the fleeting boom in for-profit higher education caused a spike to $127 billion in 2011 and a subsequent tapering (below). The $106 billion of borrowed funds were vital for the funding of American higher education; they represented three-quarters of total tuition revenues. The burden to students and their families was highly variable. The average borrower in the public sector graduated with a debt of $27,000 in 2016; in the private nonprofit sector $32,000. All three sectors contributed to the mushrooming student loan debt (public, 46 percent; nonprofit, 37 percent; and for-profit, 17 percent). One-eighth of high borrowers (>$60,000) owed one-half of the total, much of it for graduate/professional degrees. The government reduced by half the amount of subsidized loans in 2012, thus raising borrowing costs; but additional payment options were offered that might have reduced borrowers' repayment obligations.

Tax-based support for American higher education, including state appropriations, totaled close to $220 billion in 2016, with loans providing nearly one-half. This sum represented a substantial portion of the educational expenditures of American colleges and universities. With state funding basically flat in the twenty-first century—and declining on a per-student basis—the balance of funding

18 Lesley McBain, "Unfamiliar Territory," *Business Officer* (June 2017), 32–37.

shifted to the federal government. However, federal student aid support comprised an incoherent collection of targeted programs, periodically adjusted according to narrow considerations of their several purposes.[19] In contrast, Australia, Canada, and the United Kingdom have loan programs with uniform terms that provide income-contingent repayment linked with the income tax system for a limited number of years.[20] An American student is blindly assigned the requisite loans by an institutional financial aid office through an incomprehensible process, so that most students have little idea how much they will owe and what repayment terms might be.[21] In 2017, 53 percent of the $1.3 trillion debt was being repaid, and another 13 percent of borrowers were still in school; one-third of the debt was in default or not being repaid. But the federal government officially expected to profit from its portfolio of student loans. The absence of consensus over the rationale for federal support for higher education has made a coherent policy impossible. It has also made federal programs vulnerable to corruption.

In 2000–2010, more than 25 percent of the increase in degree-granting higher education occurred in the for-profit sector, which grew from 3 to 10 percent of enrollment. This was expansion from the bottom, although it had little relation to the college-for-all ideology or social inclusion. Rather, private actors exploited the system of federal student aid to reap extravagant profits.

For-profit trade schools that offered nondegree vocational courses were made eligible for Title IV student aid by the 1972 Education Amendments. For the next two decades, this sector harbored reputable, long-standing providers as well as fraudulent operators. Congress periodically attempted to limit abuses by the latter. Legislation in 1992 stipulated that no more than 85 percent of revenues could come from Title IV funds; recruiter compensation could not be based on sales incentives; and no more than 50 percent of instruction could be off-site (then, correspondence courses). Perhaps in response, the for-profit schools organized a powerful association to lobby Congress and channel significant campaign

19 From 2007 to 2017, veteran's grants increased by 300 percent, tuition tax deductions, 102 percent, Pell grants, 75 percent, subsidized loans, 27 percent, College Work-Study, 14 percent: College Board, *Trends in Student Aid*, 9.

20 Simon Marginson, *The Dream Is Over: The Crisis of Clark Kerr's California Idea of Higher Education* (Berkeley: University of California Press, 2016), 196–98. These loan schemes cost the government 25–40 percent of the principal—the government subsidy of higher education. In the U.S., nonpayment of student loans may cost a similar amount, but Congress never accepted the idea that student loans should subsidize the education of students.

21 By one count, the Department of Education offered six student loan programs, nine repayment plans, eight forgiveness programs, and thirty-two deferment options (2018): *Wall Street Journal* (May 17, 2018), A19. A study of financial award letters by the New America Foundation found that most used obscure terminology, omitted vital information, presented deliberately deceptive financial calculations, and made it difficult for students to compare colleges: *Wall Street Journal* (June 14, 2018), A21.

contributions to candidates. Republicans in Congress, who had opposed waste, abuse, and student aid, now embraced free enterprise in higher education; Democrats supported these schools for serving minority and lower-income populations. In 1998 the reauthorization of the Higher Education Act raised the limit on federal revenues to 90 percent. As the climate in Washington warmed, for-profit schools began offering associate and bachelor's degrees. They were also inspired by the huge growth of the Apollo Corporation's University of Phoenix, which originally catered to working adults who were mostly funded by their employers. Under the George W. Bush administration, the climate became even more hospitable. A for-profit-sector lobbyist was placed in charge of the higher education division of the Department of Education, and she gutted the restrictions on recruiters (2002). In 2006, Congress granted the sector's fondest wish by eliminating the 50 percent on-site rule, opening the gates for online universities. The gold rush was on, only in this case the treasure was Pell Grants and federal student loans, available for whoever could be signed up.[22]

Complaints abounded against for-profit institutions for substandard teaching, worthless degrees, misrepresentation, and high-pressure recruitment, but the dimensions of this fiasco were not fully exposed until 2012, when a Senate committee under Thomas Harkin published the results of a two-year investigation.[23] The industry largely consisted of thirty companies: fifteen publicly traded and fifteen privately held. The largest were recently transformed from earlier education companies (Apollo, DeVry, Kaplan, Strayer) or created by Wall Street through mergers and acquisitions. All operated in the lucrative market for selling education to federally funded students. All set annual tuition near the $13,000 available from maximum Pell Grants and loans. Almost all students were low-income and independent, thus qualifying for Pells; 96 percent took loans. In fact, a crucial selling point of recruiters was "no out-of-pocket expenses." The chief objective of these firms was growth, which brought soaring stock valuations and executive compensation. This put the onus on recruitment, which absorbed 22.4 percent of income. Profits took 19.4 percent and instruction just 17.7 percent. Recruiters operated in a boiler-room atmosphere where they were under intense pressure to meet quotas—for extra compensation or to retain their jobs. They preyed on unsuccessful and dispirited young adults, often found in welfare and unemployment offices and public housing. Members of the armed forces were

---

22 Suzanne Mettler, *Degrees of Inequality: How the Politics of Higher Education Sabotaged the American Dream* (New York: Basic Books, 2014); A. J. Angulo, *Diploma Mills: How For-Profit Colleges Stiffed Students, Taxpayers, and the American Dream* (Baltimore: Johns Hopkins University Press, 2016).

23 The Harkin Report: U.S. Senate, Health, Education, Labor and Pensions Committee, *For-Profit Higher Education: The Failure to Safeguard the Federal Investment and Ensure Student Success* (July 30, 2012).

choice prospects, especially valuable because veteran benefits did not count against the 90 percent federal limit.

These "nontraditional" students, recruited with mendacious sales pitches, stood little chance of academic success. Some 54 percent withdrew within two years. Recruiters at some institutions had to replace the equivalent of the entire student body each year. Teaching by part-time instructors was rudimentary or worse, and student services were almost nonexistent. For these programs, for-profit institutions collected 25 percent of federal student aid by 2010, and even more of veteran benefits. One in five starting students defaulted on her loans within three years; the overall default rate was 46 percent. Students who persisted to graduation—with an average $33,000 debt—were often disappointed. Although all these institutions were accredited—a requirement for receiving Title IV funds—many of their programs were not. Graduates frequently found they could not qualify for work in their chosen fields and could not transfer credits to other colleges and universities.

Periodic efforts to curb these practices were ineffective. California and New York successfully prosecuted firms for fraud in obtaining state student aid, but the settlements were pinpricks to the industry. The Obama administration made a concerted attempt at reform, which was fiercely resisted by the industry in Congress and the courts. A weak reform bill passed in 2011 but was overturned by a federal judge. A second bill in 2015 succeeded in establishing a standard for "gainful employment" of graduates for eligibility for Title IV funds. This was the industry's most vulnerable point, since few courses provided the promised preparation for employment. Federal enforcement pressured the entire industry. Corinthian Colleges, which had 132,000 students in 2010, declared bankruptcy in 2015 after being denied Title IV funding. Most companies were able to adapt, with difficulty. Profits fell precipitously along with share prices. The sector lost one-third of its enrollments (2010–2015) but continued to garner two times its enrollment share in federal student aid funds.

The creation and boom of for-profit higher education presented two stories— one financial and one educational. Financially, it was a familiar case of crony capitalism and regulatory capture—essentially paying (bribing) politicians to maintain conditions for loosely regulated access to lucrative government grants and loans. This was a failure of government—both the inability to devise and implement fair and effective policies and the cupidity of elected representatives. There was nothing inherently abominable about for-profit education. Wherever vouchers provide funds for educational services, free markets attract for-profit providers. Considerations of consumer costs and relative value then should de-termine the market shares of different providers. In this case, the subsidy far exceeded the cost of providing minimal educational services; consumers were asked to pay no out-of-pocket costs, and value (if any) was concealed and misrepresented. Hence, there was no relationship between product and price—a situation guaranteed to entice investors solely seeking short-term gains. What was abominable was the damage inflicted on gullible individuals who became the means for turning federal student aid into investor profits.

In the twenty-first century, the for-profit sector became a much larger part of American higher education. It provided another pathway for nontraditional students—an extension of universal higher education's interpenetration with society. Some for-profit universities, not all, offered respectable courses that provided value to students. This was particularly true for graduate programs, in which convenience was often paramount, customers were less gullible, and something like market competition prevailed.[24] A good portion of the sector engaged in online higher education, which these firms in some ways pioneered in the 2000s. There they faced a competitive market in which large public and nonprofit providers had an edge in quality, brand names, and usually pricing. The largest providers, after the University of Phoenix, were specialized nonprofit universities—Western Governor's, Southern New Hampshire, and Liberty Universities.[25] There are many niches in this market, including nondegree educational services that traditional institutions seldom offer.

Unlike public and nonprofit institutions, corporate universities were capable of rapid adaptation. They reacted to tightened federal regulations by shuttering offending programs and campuses (nearly one-half of offerings) while marginally improving quality and services. No longer able to flout the rules, they took steps necessary to conform. But federal regulatory pressure and deteriorating market conditions forced a wholesale reorganization of the sector. Several firms converted all or in part to nonprofit status. Profits were not forsaken, however, since the for-profit remainders reserved substantial management fees for themselves. Apollo and DeVry were purchased by private equity investors, and Kaplan was acquired by Purdue University. The boom in fraudulent programs ended not in a "bust" but in the restructuring of for-profit higher education.[26]

24   Paul Fain and Doug Lederman, "Boom, Regulate, Cleanse, Repeat: For-Profit Colleges' Slow but Inevitable Drive Toward Acceptability," in Michael W. Krist and Mitchell L. Stevens, eds., *Remaking Colleges: The Changing Ecology of Higher Education* (Stanford, CA: Stanford University Press, 2015), 61–83.

25   Julie E. Seaman, I. Elaine Allen, and Jeff Seaman, *Grade Increase: Tracking Distance Education in the United States* (Wellesley, MA: Babson Survey Research Group, 2018), 29.

26   Dan Bauman and Goldie Blumenstyk, "How For-Profit Higher Education Has Shifted," *Chronicle of Higher Education* (March 14, 2018); Paul Fain, "Ashford Seeks to Become a Non-Profit," *Inside Higher Education* (March 14, 2018).

BIFURCATION REVISITED

Writings on the structure of American higher education, including my own, have emphasized a growing disparity between the selective and open sectors of undergraduate education. The depiction of the selectivity sweepstakes in Chapter 7 summarized how high-ability students and high levels of spending were increasingly concentrated among the wealthiest private colleges and universities. Marginson's argument that incremental resources in high-participation systems would be invested in institutions valued most by society was borne out in the United States, where federal research dollars upheld overall academic quality in research universities, and private patronage steeply favored elite institutions. Charles Clotfelter's data in *Unequal Colleges* reaffirmed the concentration of high academic credentials and resources in the top 10 percent of private institutions. Caroline Hoxby documented a geometric rise in resources at the very top of the hierarchy. However, Clotfelter's top 10th percentile of private colleges and universities composed just 5 percent of undergraduates, and 0.6 percent (49,000) attended the 99+ percentile charted by both Hoxby and Clotfelter.[27] Viewed from this pinnacle, higher education indeed became more unequal. However, such a view reveals little of developments across the broad and varied spectrum of undergraduate education in the twenty-first century. A mixture of trends affected institutional inequality, which has always been an inherent feature of American higher education.

An overview of selectivity may be had from *Barron's Profiles of American Colleges*, which has classified four-year colleges since the 1960s employing a consistent methodology. Its five levels of selectivity are "most competitive," "highly competitive," "very competitive," "competitive," and "less competitive."[28] About half of colleges are found in the "competitive" category. In 1983, students at these schools had average to slightly above mean test scores, which would be consistent with Hoxby's data. And 30 percent of schools were less competitive, in that their incoming students tested below SAT/ACT mean scores. In 1997, 23 percent of schools were rated less competitive; and in 2016, 13.5 percent. In other words, the "bottom" of American four-year colleges was shrinking—not sinking as Hoxby's data seemed to show (at least to 1991). At the top in these same years, the number of institutions in the most competitive class rose from 33 to 54 to 106—a stark reflection of the selectivity sweepstakes. But the number of institu-

27 Hoxby, "Changing Market Structure"; Marginson, "High Participation Societies"; Clotfelter, *Unequal Colleges*, Appendix. The 99+ percentile category could only contain five or six institutions.

28 *Barron's Profiles of American Colleges*, 1985, 1999, and 2018 editions. The smaller categories of "nonselective" and "special" are not relevant.

tions above the competitive-category average rose from 250 to 400 in 1997 and remained at that level to 2016—a plateau possibly indicating the finite limits to selectivity. What did change was the number of public research universities in the top two categories: from 6 to 11 to 28. Their rise adds a qualification to Hoxby's prediction that public institutions could not compete at the higher levels of selectivity because of lower per-student expenditures.

The rise of the bottom was by no means general. The less competitive category, and many marginally stronger competitive institutions, consisted of a wide variety of small private colleges, separately listed branch campuses, and a portion of regional universities in state systems. For the latter two, this status reflected their role of providing local or regional, broadly accessible, publicly subsidized higher education. Their students reflected those local conditions. As a sector, they were heavily dependent on state appropriations and suffered accordingly from disinvestment. It is scarcely possible to judge the quality of their instruction, but superficial characteristics provide some indication of their performance. Selectivity reflects the academic preparedness of students, and graduation rates vary according to selectivity.[29] With large proportions of working and commuting students, often a majority of graduates took six years. The choice of majors indicated a vocational rather than academic orientation. Still, the overall picture was not one of decline. Clotfelter's per-student data for the lower half of public institutions showed a decline in state funding and subsidies but rising tuition produced an overall increase in educational spending (1990–2009). Student qualifications, although below average, improved slightly over these years.[30]

Systems of regional universities developed differently across states.[31] In 1983, eight of the eleven campuses of the University of Wisconsin System were rated less competitive. They required neither SATs nor ACTs for admission and typically graduated 30–40 percent of students. By 2016 they were substantially improved: two had risen to very competitive, none were in the lowest category, and most graduated more than 50 percent of a class. The California State universities developed in the opposite direction despite a fixed mission defined in the Master Plan. In 1983, three were rated very competitive and none were less competitive; but in 2016, eight had sunk to less competitive. These campuses had low four-year graduation rates but often graduated over 50 percent in six years. The decline in competitiveness probably reflected falling academic achievement in California schools, while the extended time to graduation might be attributable in

29   NCES, *Digest of Education Statistics: 2017*, Table 326.50; Bowen et al., *Crossing the Finish Line*, passim.

30   Constant dollar, per-student expenditures: Clotfelter, *Unequal Colleges*, 141, 143, 223.

31   The following draws upon the profiles of a sample of regional colleges from the *Barron's Profiles* editions in note 28 above.

part to the shrinkage in resources. In the Pennsylvania State System of Higher Education, one campus was less competitive in 1983, and six in 2016. With one of the lowest levels of state funding, these mostly rural schools grew little in three decades and accepted nearly all applicants. At all regional universities, a shift in major fields was apparent: in 1983 one of the three most popular majors was often social science or a STEM (sciences, technology, engineering, mathematics) field, along with business and education; now, besides permutations of business studies (business-lite), the most popular majors were criminal justice, health fields, parks and recreation, liberal or general studies, and other undemanding subjects. Such fields had low average graduate earnings.[32]

More positive change occurred among higher-quality public institutions, especially research universities. At the University of Maryland, College Park, in 1983, 65 percent of incoming students tested below 500 on the verbal SAT and 9 percent over 600; at the main campus of Ohio State these figures were 64 percent below 500 and 10 percent above 600. In 2016, 5 percent of Maryland students were below 500 and 73 percent above 600; at Ohio State, 5 percent were below 500 and 65 percent above 600.[33] Similar, if less dramatic, improvements occurred across major public universities. This was not the result of a trickle-down of able students rejected by increasingly selective private institutions: the numbers were too large—more than 3,300 freshmen above 600 (top 21 percent of test-takers) at College Park, more than 4,500 at Columbus. Influenced by the selectivity sweepstakes, increasing numbers of high school graduates sought higher-quality education at selective colleges and universities. Flagship public universities, although often like Maryland and Ohio State not initially selective, had a great deal to offer: brand names (and football teams), prominent graduates, extensive learning resources in libraries, laboratories, and distinguished professors. But above all, their huge menu of programs and majors offered horizontal differentiation—practical fields for the professionally oriented, STEM fields for the scientifically inclined, and rigorous academic pathways for intellectuals. Despite shrinking state support and rising tuition, flagship universities offered the most abundant opportunities for the lowest price. They became the latest and largest beneficiaries of the surge in applications to selective institutions.

This phenomenon was analyzed by John Bound and associates through 2004.[34] From 1982 to 2004, the number of high school graduates varied little, but atten-

---

32   Ibid.; cf. Clotfelter, *Unequal Colleges*, 186–90; Bowen et al., *Crossing the Finish Line*, 58–65.

33   *Barron's Profiles*, 1985, 2018. Ohio State resolved to upgrade selectivity in 1990; the admissions director called the *U.S. News* rankings "the biggest wake-up call this university ever had": Malcolm S. Baroway, *The Gee Years, 1990–1997* (Columbus: Ohio State University, 2002), 41–47, quote p. 44.

34   John Bound, Brad Hershbein, and Bridget Terry Long, "Playing the Admissions Game: Student Reactions to Increasing College Competition," NBER Working Paper No. 15272 (August 2009).

dance at four-year colleges grew from 31 to 47 percent, an increase of 520,000. Of these, 23,000 more attended selective private colleges, and an additional 100,000 attended selective publics. Acceptance rates declined as student places expanded only slowly at both types of institutions, and applicants adapted to the need for higher qualifications. Whereas just 2 percent of eighteen-year-olds took Advance Placement courses and exams in 1977, 30 percent did so in 2007. More students took calculus in high school, which was identified as a factor in the rising achievement of women. Students took the SAT tests multiple times, and more of them used test preparation services. They also applied to more institutions. A national convergence was evident in these behaviors, perhaps an indication of the national market, but also a reflection of the growing selectivity of state universities.[35]

The qualifications of students increased at similar rates for selective institutions (1986–2004). Student scores at the top twenty private colleges and universities remained about fifty points above the top twenty public ones.[36] The latter tracked almost exactly with the top twenty-one–fifty private universities. These institutions were in fact market competitors, since out-of-state tuition at flagship publics approximated the discounted tuition of this group of privates. The top twenty-one–fifty liberal arts colleges were consistently about fifteen points below these two groups. The top twenty-one–fifty public universities did not experience increasing student SAT scores until after 2000, a lag that suggests spillover demand and perhaps their pricing advantage. Together, the institutions of this selective sector enrolled about 16 percent of undergraduates at four-year institutions. Public universities may be less exclusive than the top private ones, but because of their size they recruited similar numbers of top students. A comparison of students scoring above 700 on the verbal and math SATs showed equal numbers at the top thirty-five public and private universities, each with 30 percent of the national total (1998). In the next five years, the thirteen most selective public universities increased the number of these students by 38 percent.[37]

---

35   Excess demand within states can cause high selectivity at favored institutions. This has been evident in the SUNY System, and most likely in Wisconsin. Despite the nationalization of the higher education market, in-state markets continue to affect the distribution of students and the relative roles of institutions.

36   Bound et al., "Playing the Admissions Game," Figure 1: based on Math SAT 75th percentile.

37   Roger L. Geiger, "The Competition for High-Ability Students: Universities in a Key Marketplace," in Steven Brint, ed., *The Future of the City of Intellect* (Stanford, CA: Stanford University Press, 2002), 82–106; Geiger, *Knowledge and Money: Research Universities and the Paradox of the Marketplace* (Stanford, CA: Stanford University Press, 2004), 86–93; Geiger, "Expert and Elite: The Incongruous Missions of Public Research Universities," in Roger L. Geiger et al., eds. *The Future of the American Public Research University* (Rotterdam: Sense, 2007), 15–34.

At least some programs of the leading public universities were as elite as their private counterparts, while institutions as a whole were more inclusive.

When all the evidence is considered, bifurcation would appear too strong a term to describe the market structure of American higher education in the twenty-first century. Undoubtedly the most important developments were the increasing proportion of students attending four-year colleges and the corresponding rise in bachelor's degrees. However, in light of the lack of progress in educational preparedness, it would appear that less prepared students were increasingly concentrated in community colleges.[38] This sector juggled multiple missions and experienced public disinvestment. In the lower two-thirds of the public sector—*Barron's* competitive and less competitive categories—the curriculum became increasingly fragmented to accommodate options for diverse professional careers, and students struggled to graduate in six years. But there was little evidence of overall decline since 2000. The greatest disparities existed among the strongest institutions, and those were simply continuations of trends fully evident by the 1990s. Steady financial strengthening took place across the private sector, but truly outsized gains occurred in the top 10 percent of those institutions, and far more so in the top 1 percent. The advantages in selectivity mirrored this same pattern.

The great change since 1980 was the advancement of public research universities. In terms of per-student expenditures and selectivity, the top 10 percent of publics exceeded all but the top decile of private institutions.[39] For comparison, the most affluent/selective 10 percent of privates enrolled approximately 275,000 undergraduates, while the twenty-five most selective public universities enrolled 625,000. The latter had a mixed population of undergraduates but included a large number of students who were comparable to their private-sector counterparts. American higher education became more unequal, first, in the relative concentration of high-ability students in the top public research universities and perhaps the top 15 percent of private institutions; and second, in the burgeoning wealth of the most affluent 5 percent of private universities. However, the broad middle ranks of American higher education appeared to function as they traditionally have—educating and graduating a mixed, moderately selective body of students. The shifting distribution of undergraduates in American higher education reflected both expectations and realities about prospects for learning and careers.

38   NCES, *Digest of Education Statistics: 2017*, Table 305:40; Steven Brint, "Few Remaining Dreams: Community Colleges since 1945," *Annals, AAPSS* 586 (March 2003): 16–36.
39   Clotfelter, *Unequal Colleges*, esp. 141–44, 222–5.

RETURNS TO HIGHER EDUCATION

In the postwar era, graduation from college conferred a recognized status in American society. Accumulating 120 credits of course work was assumed to attest to a distinctive level of culture, literacy, and specialized knowledge. Certain courses may have qualified individuals for specific careers, such as engineer or teacher, but the actual content of college courses bore little relation to many workplaces. A bachelor's degree signified a basic competence to proceed to further professional training or to fill a broad range of middle-class jobs. It amounted to what economists call a step function, elevating the graduate to a higher occupational level, which appeared to be validated by the earnings premium of graduates.

The sociologist David Baker explained in *The Schooled Society* the complex ways that the modern expansion of higher education has produced a society in which educational credentials largely determine occupational and social possibilities: "The educational credential signifies not just the *capability* to apply knowledge in the everyday world of occupational roles; it has become mandatory ... for entry into specific occupational statuses with exclusionary *control and rights* to apply such knowledge." Further, "the educational revolution over the past century has thoroughly equated educational performance with socially just merit, and the intensification of educational credentialing reinforces this process."[40] Baker insists that knowledge itself has driven this process. Not paper credentials, but the nexus with the "university's knowledge conglomerate" confers qualifications for occupations and wage premiums. Nor has educational expansion created crises of overeducation, since burgeoning cohorts of college-educated employees tend to alter workplaces to make them more intellectually complex and productive. This is the template of American society on which higher education operates in the twenty-first century.

Economists have offered a standard interpretation of the relation of higher education and earnings in the current era.[41] As in so many other respects, 1980 marked an inflection point. After the baby-boom generation passed through higher education, the annual cohort of college graduates stabilized and then grew

40 David P. Baker, *The Schooled Society: The Educational Transformation of Global Culture* (Stanford, CA: Stanford University Press, 2014), 181, 182.

41 Claudia Goldin and Lawrence F. Katz, *The Race between Education and Technology* (Cambridge, MA: Harvard University Press, 2008); David Autor, "The Polarization of Job Opportunities in the U.S. Labor Market," Center for American Progress, The Hamilton Project (April 2010); David H. Autor, "Skills, Education, and the Rise of Earnings Inequality among the 'Other 99 Percent,'" *Science* 334, 6186 (May 23, 2014): 843–51.

moderately until the end of the 1990s. This moderate growth was the combined effect of smaller college-age cohorts and rising enrollment rates in four-year institutions. At the same time, the earnings gap between college and high school graduates began a sustained rise that continued to the end of the century. These increasing returns to higher education were explained by the relative shortage of college graduates. A technologically advancing economy required increasing numbers of college-trained workers; given an inadequate supply, wages were bid higher. The college/high school earnings gap nearly doubled by 2000 for men, women, and households. However, the surge in enrollments that began in the later 1990s soon increased the supply of graduates. Whereas bachelor's degrees had grown by just one-third in the two decades after 1980, they rose by 50 percent from 2001 to 2014. The real wages of bachelors leveled off as the supply increased, as did the wage gap. But the relative wage advantage of holders of graduate and professional degrees continued to climb. And more Americans sought specialized university knowledge by taking advanced degrees. Master's degrees, for example, predominately in applied fields, doubled from 1990 to 2010, to a level equivalent to 46 percent of bachelor's degrees. This suggested a continuing relative scarcity of advanced university capabilities. What this supply-demand thesis failed to reveal was the considerable variability in the value and distribution of higher education credentials.

One significant variable was that many students failed to complete a college education. Students changed institutions and studied intermittently, so there was a degree of uncertainty in this figure, but the aggregate picture was clear. The Department of Education reported that about 59 percent of students who started at a four-year institution graduated within six years. Students graduated sooner from private institutions, which were heavily residential and had a wealthier clientele, but after six years the rates were comparable (65.6 vs. 58.5 percent). Graduation rates in both sectors varied with selectivity—that is, academic preparation and ability.[42] At community colleges, three-year graduation rates were 22 percent, although this figure understated their diverse roles and productivity. However, 43 percent of first-year students failed to enroll the following year. At public universities in *Barron's* competitive range, 30 percent of first-year students were not retained. These figures from 2015 showed some improvement since 2000, but the dropouts constituted a substantial portion of those the Census

---

42   NCES, *Digest of Education Statistics: 2017*, 326.10. Selectivity, preparedness, and academic ability all reflect a combination of intelligence and noncognitive skills, such as motivation, task completion, sociability, interpretation of instructions, comprehending situations, and practical problem solving. This combination of qualities produces success in schooling and in selective admissions: Michael Hout, "Social and Economic Returns to College Education in the United States," *Annual Review of Sociology* 38 (2012): 379–400.

Bureau classified as "some college." The earnings of those with some (often, not very much) college contracted in the 1980s, like those of high school graduates and dropouts. Since then, earnings for these three educational categories have moved in parallel, "as if they were three 'sizes' of the same underlying bundle of skills."[43]

Earning a baccalaureate degree brings substantial rewards and should be the goal of all capable students. The advantages are threefold: greater earnings; improved chances of leading a longer, healthier, and happier life; and acquisition of knowledge, which is far preferable to ignorance. Looking just at the economic returns, the earnings premium of college over high school graduates measured about 60 percent since 2000 and also well exceeded those with some college or an associate's degree. The premium is greater for males, since female high school graduates earn more and female college graduates, for various reasons, less. Moreover, the effects of finishing college are far-reaching. Although socioeconomic background has an enormous effect on college attainment, it exerts little or no influence on careers and earnings after graduation.[44] The effects of college are transformative. However, earnings data report averages. Inequality of earnings outcomes increased as education levels rose. One-sixth of college graduates earned less than the high school average.[45] What people studied made a difference.

Variations in career patterns for different fields affected earnings data. Some courses led to immediate, well-defined careers, like teaching and nursing, so that earnings for young adults bore some relation to their schooling. Humanities and social science graduates took longer to establish themselves in a greater variety of middle-class careers, so that their earnings more likely reflected personal qualities as much as college studies. In fields where graduate degrees were prevalent, individuals with only a bachelor's represented a negatively selected population. In 2012 the modal recent college graduates earned less than an experienced high school graduate ($36,000, although the median was slightly above $37,000).[46] Experienced college graduates averaged earnings of $67,000, but the dispersion remained large, with high-paying fields averaging about two-thirds more than low-paying ones. What stands out is the earnings advantage of quantitative fields. Engineering was the most highly rewarded, followed by computer science. A

43   NCES, *Digest of Education Statistics: 2017*, 326.10. 326.20; *National Collegiate Retention and Persistence-to-Degree Rates, 2016* (ACT, 2017); Autor, "Polarization," 26.

44   Hout, "Social and Economic Returns"; Baker, *Schooled Society*, 53–54.

45   Sandy Baum, *Higher Education Earnings Premium: Value, Variation, and Trends* (Washington, DC: Urban Institute, February 2014); Dennis A. Ahlburg, "Is Higher Education a Good Investment for All?" (Department of Economics, Trinity University, 2016).

46   Anthony P. Carnevale and Ban Cheah, *From Hard Times to Better Times: College Majors, Unemployment, and Earnings* (Washington, DC: Georgetown University, Center on Education and the Workforce, 2015). The following data are from this report.

premium was also apparent for quantitative business degrees (finance, business economics, information systems) as well as economics. In some fields, subject knowledge needed to be supplemented with experience: chemistry and biology had below-average starting salaries but were above average for experienced workers. For beginning and experienced workers, earnings were lowest in administered fields (education, social work) and in fields with large numbers of graduates (psychology, the arts). Earnings were poor in vocational majors offered in nonselective colleges (parks and recreation, criminal justice). Clearly, graduate earnings were strongly affected by what was studied in college. It also mattered where students studied.

Extensive research of the effects of college quality on outcomes—generally measured by earnings—has reached divergent conclusions.[47] The general impression (not consensus) has been that graduates of top institutions earned appreciably more on average, but that such advantages decline quickly as selectivity falls off. A comprehensive study by Liang Zhang has addressed the complications inherent in such comparisons and found, on balance, earnings margins of from 10–40 percent, depending on how quality is measured.[48] In general, he found, the smaller the proportion of institutions labeled as high quality, the larger the estimated effects on earnings. Careers develop in complex ways, but the advantage of a prestigious degree seemed to widen in the early stages. The earnings boost for students from modest backgrounds was considerably greater than that experienced by wealthy, top-scoring students (who would have done well anywhere). Institutional quality had large effects in majors like business, but none in engineering. College quality had the largest impact at the top of the earnings pyramid and comparatively little effect at lower levels. Finally, graduates of high-quality institutions were more likely to undertake graduate education, more often at research universities. Obtaining a postbaccalaureate degree had a large and growing influence on earnings, which was not reflected in comparisons of only bachelor's degrees. Zhang's findings elucidate why no single number or generalization can capture the educational benefits of attending a highly selective institution, but they underline the logic of the selectivity sweepstakes.

However, theoretical and practical questions are embedded in that logic. In terms of economic efficiency, who should attend the high-priced, high-quality institutions? Caroline Hoxby has pursued a line of research to determine if the abundant resources invested in students at elite institutions were justified by their subsequent productivity. As reported by Clotfelter, her data indicated that

---

47 Clotfelter, *Unequal Colleges*; Hout, "Social and Economic Returns."
48 Liang Zhang, *Does Quality Pay? Benefits of Attending a High-Cost, Prestigious College* (New York: Routledge, 2005), 117–27.

"the value-added is higher for graduates of more selective colleges than for those of less selective ones. This is a powerful finding [he adds], for it implies that the most able, academically ready students are best able to take advantage of the rich resources available at the most selective colleges." Since the social return on investments in these top students is higher, these findings "offer an economic rationale for the inequality we see across American colleges."[49] However, Hoxby's conclusions seemingly contradicted research by Zhang and others that found higher social returns to somewhat less well-prepared students. Most famously, William Bowen and Derek Bok demonstrated in *The Shape of the River* that "minority students admitted to selective colleges under race-sensitive policies have, overall, performed very well"—better than comparable students at less selective institutions. To summarize this research: "Young people with the most abilities may learn and ultimately earn the most, but their education augments their success less than it augments less-able people's success (in the range, roughly, from the median to the top of the ability distribution)."[50] Thus, if social returns are higher for upgrading educational opportunities for somewhat less talented students, selectivity criteria ought to be made more inclusive.

In practice, the Hoxby argument provided a rationalization for the status quo—as if one were needed. The selectivity sweepstakes and the exaggerated inequality it fostered, as explained above, have been driven by powerful market forces. But the large social returns to upgrading the educational opportunities of less privileged students posed a strong argument for developing policies that lean against those market forces.[51] The study by William Bowen and associates, *Crossing the Finish Line*, advocated such policies, specifically encouraging less advantaged students to enroll in the most selective institution possible. Like *Shape of the River*, they argued that fears of "overmatching" were erroneous and that the inferior outcomes from "undermatching" were the real problem.

49   Clotfelter, *Unequal Colleges*, 333–34: summarizing Caroline M. Hoxby, "The Productivity of U.S. Postsecondary Institutions" (paper presented at the NBER conference "Productivity in Higher Education," May 31–June 1, 2016).

50   Zhang, *Does Quality Pay?*, 63–80; William G. Bowen and Derek Bok, *The Shape of the River: Long-Term Consequences of Considering Race in College and University Admissions* (Princeton: Princeton University Press, 2000 [1998]), xxxi; Hout, "Social and Economic Returns," 384–86, quote p. 386.

51   I addressed this issue by arguing that the wealthiest institutions could increase their social contribution by expanding enrollments: "The Ivies have basically pursued a strategy of concentrating increasing resources on each student. The marginal benefits of this approach long ago surpassed any reasonable rate of return, and must now have diminished to the vanishing point. A greater social return would be achieved by making their abundant assets available to a greater number of students." Roger L. Geiger, "The Ivy League," in David Palfreyman and Ted Tapper, eds., *Structuring Mass Higher Education: The Role of Elite Institutions* (New York: Routledge, 2009), 281–302, quote pp. 297, 299.

This argument is contradicted by Richard Sander and Stuart Taylor with data that showed minority students having optimal outcomes when matriculating with students of similar academic ability. The larger the discrepancy between specially recruited students and average students, the more harmful the effects. Such discrepancies were smallest at the most highly selective institutions (those studied in *The Shape of the River*) but increased as selectivity dropped and institutions had to reach further into the talent pool.[52] Such findings would seem to add a qualification to the long-standing efforts of selective institutions to recruit disadvantaged students. But to little effect.[53]

In 2017 the Bloomberg Philanthropies organized the American Talent Initiative to stimulate just such upgrading. It promoted the recruitment of high-ability, low-income students to selective institutions that graduated more than 70 percent of their matriculates. In a year, membership grew from the thirty founders to ninety-seven universities. The goal: add 50,000 such students to America's selective colleges by 2025—an increase of more than 10 percent.[54] The number of such high-ability, low-income students has been an issue. One study established that if ability was set at a moderate level, above 1220 combined SAT score, many such students would be available. However, another study using a higher bar found the population currently unrecruited—unknown to elite schools—to be dispersed and hard to find.[55] Strategies for recruiting such students have been ongoing in the quest to mitigate the social inequality inherent to Clotfelter's *Unequal Colleges*.

Whether the returns to higher education are a public or private good has been another contentious issue. Proponents of higher education have long accused policymakers of assuming that private returns—individual earnings—justified transferring the financial burden to students through higher tuition. It seems doubtful that legislators actually posed the issue in these terms, but given public disinvestment, they have acted like they did. Although economists have devised

---

52   Richard Sander and Stuart Taylor, Jr., *Mismatch: How Affirmative Action Hurts Students It's Intended to Help, and Why Universities Won't Admit It* (New York: Basic Books, 2012).

53   While the Sander-Taylor findings are by no means definitive, they would seem to call for additional research.

54   American Talent Initiative, https://americantalentinitiative.org/. The ATI is one of several efforts to increase the attendance and success of first-generation and low-income students at high-quality universities: the University Innovation Alliance (eleven research universities); programs of the Bill and Melinda Gates Foundation; and efforts by Princeton University, which organized the first FGLI (first-generation, low-income) conference in February 2018.

55   Bowen et al., *Crossing the Finish Line*, 227–29; Gordon Winston and Catharine Bond Hill, "Access to the Most Selective Colleges by High-Ability, Low-Income Students: Are They Out There?," Discussion Paper No. 69, Williams Project on the Economics of Higher Education (October 2005); Caroline M. Hoxby and Christopher Avery, "The Missing 'One-Offs': The Hidden Supply of High-Achieving, Low-income Students," NBER Working Paper No. 18586 (December 2012).

theories to this effect,[56] the issue is not theoretical, but practical—a failure to acknowledge and act upon the social value of higher education. The nonmonetary returns to higher education have been seldom acknowledged in public discussion. Educated persons were more likely to have stable marriages, to raise children in two-parent households, and to transmit positive behaviors to their children. They make better citizens in terms of civic participation and have far lower rates of deviant behavior. Education seems to delay the onset of health problems, and graduates more frequently report high levels of happiness. Rough attempts to quantify these effects on higher tax revenues and lower demand for social services have estimated a payback of $4 for every $1 invested in higher education.[57]

The economic returns to individuals have a social dimension as well. Individual earnings represent productivity in the national economy—human capital. The shortfall of college-trained workers during the 1980s and 1990s, according to Claudia Goldin and Lawrence Katz, retarded economic growth and increased inequality. For Robert Gordon, not only the slowdown in educational attainment but also the declining quality of U.S. education have been a "headwind" to economic growth.[58] Internationally, the U.S. had the highest wage returns to cognitive skills—an indication of scarcity and a source of inequality.[59] The role of higher education in forming human capital is paramount. If the higher education system could create more human capital, it would not only generate greater social returns, it might tend to mitigate inequality.

Compared with other advanced democratic nations, the U.S. had the highest earnings premium for college graduates and the highest level of income inequality. According to the supply-demand thesis, the relative scarcity of educated talent drove graduate earnings higher, making incomes more unequal. Public indignation over income inequality has focused on the infamous "one percent," but their wealth had little relation to education. Higher education played a predominant role in the upper-income quintile below the one percent—the 80th to 98th percentiles, where earnings are closely linked with BA or higher degrees. Here the concern has been less with excessive earnings than with the social skew in who acquired the credentials to attain those earnings.[60]

---

56   For a critique, see Marginson, *The Dream Is Over*, 126–31.

57   Hout, "Social and Economic Returns," 392–94. Such calculations ignore self-selection.

58   Goldin and Katz, *Race between Education and Technology*; Robert J. Gordon, *The Rise and Fall of American Growth: The U.S. Standard of Living Since the Civil War* (Princeton: Princeton University Press, 2016), 624–27.

59   Autor, "Skills, Education," 845. Returns to higher education are also attributed to signaling and social preferences, as discussed in Steven Brint and Charles T. Clotfelter, "Higher Education Effectiveness," *Russell Sage Research Journal* 2, 1 (2016): 2–37.

60   Autor, "Skills, Education"; Brint, *Two Cheers*, 160–66.

Participation in higher education has always been strongly affected by parental SES, but this relationship evolved as enrollments rose.[61] From the early 1980s to the late 1990s, college-going and college graduation rates rose roughly 50 percent in each income quartile, but such uniform "progress" increased inequality as families above the median income produced four times as many graduates as those below. The largest gains occurred in the third-highest income quartile, where they might be expected as the propensity for college-going spread downward from the highest incomes. However, the largest contributors to this expansion were women from the highest quartile.[62] The social forces underlying this "income-achievement gap" were probed by Sean Reardon in a synthesis of longitudinal studies over the last fifty years. He found parental education to be the strongest predictor of achievement and that this relationship had been stable since 1960 (although the growing proportion of college graduates would by itself increase inequality). His principal finding was that academic achievement since 1960 has been increasingly affected by family income: "A dollar of income ... appears to buy more academic achievement than it did several decades ago."[63] This effect has been exacerbated by a trend toward assortative mating—educated people marrying each other and achieving higher family incomes.[64]

Upper-middle-class parents have invested greater effort and resources in the cognitive development of their offspring, spurred no doubt by the selectivity sweepstakes.[65] The consequences were evident, for example, in the large proportion of upper-quartile women capitalizing on these advantages. Surprisingly, though, increasing income inequality has not affected intergenerational mobility. U.S. mobility is quite low compared with other advanced nations, but the economist David Autor writes: "As far as we can measure, rising U.S. income inequality has not reduced intergenerational mobility so far." Nonetheless, this

61   In the high school class of 1992, 77 percent of students from the highest income quartile continued to college—about the same proportion as students from the top income quintile in the 1960 class. But the lower half of incomes sent just 28 percent of graduates to college in 1960, compared with 47 percent in 1992. In 1960, high school was still a significant social filter; for example, more students dropped out than continued to college. Since 1992 the social filters have operated largely within higher education. There are significant social differentials in preparation for college, attending a four-year rather than a two-year institution, selectivity of four-year colleges, persistence, degree completion, and preparation for and enrollment in postgraduate education.

62   Bailey and Dynarski, "Inequality in Postsecondary Education," 119–21.

63   Sean F. Reardon, "The Widening Academic Achievement Gap between the Rich and the Poor: New Evidence and Possible Explanations," in Duncan and Murnane, *Whither Opportunity?*, 91–115, quote p. 104.

64   Jeremy Greenwood et al., "Marry Your Like: Assortative Mating and Income Inequality," NBER Working Paper No. 7895 (2014).

65   Mitchell L. Stevens, *Creating a Class: College Admissions and the Education of Elites* (Cambridge, MA: Harvard University Press, 2007), 247–50.

inequality "means that the lifetime relative disadvantage of children born to low-versus high-income families has increased substantially."[66] Not only are there more advantaged children, they have raised the achievement bar. Government policies and institutional efforts to counteract this disadvantage may have played some role in preventing the existing degree of mobility from worsening.

In the *Schooled Society*, educational credentials are the coin of the realm. The higher education system is thus a crucial *intermediary* in shaping contemporary society, including income inequality. Higher education may have the potential to exert some influence at the margins, but its capabilities are largely determined by American society. In the second decade of the twenty-first century, judging by the stable earnings premium, the quantity of college graduates appeared to be in rough balance with opportunities in the job market. The four of every ten aspirants who fail to graduate represented a pool of potential employees who may have been impeded by some combination of poor preparedness, high costs, and public disinvestment. If some portion of them were to overcome these impediments to graduate and find appropriate employment, the increased social returns would outweigh any negative pressure on the earnings premium. There would appear to be a relative scarcity, indicated by high and growing salary premiums, for graduates with quantitative skills and/or postgraduate degrees.[67] American higher education thus serves its economic function of supplying the human capital needed to sustain national productivity. This process, by providing differential preparation and different credentials, makes graduates more unequal, among themselves and compared with nongraduates.

Until the 1960s, college attendance was ascribed to "motivation," and social differentials were assumed to be natural. Beginning in 1965, a concerted effort was made to rectify the underenrollment of African Americans, and by the 1970s a national commitment was evident to extend opportunities for higher education to all underrepresented groups. Since 2000, concern to reduce educational inequality has focused on lower-income classes. In the 2016 presidential campaign, a call for free higher education energized progressives, although it ignored the other two impediments to college completion mentioned above (poor preparedness and disinvestment). The many public and private efforts to increase

---

66   Autor, "Skills, Education," 848, 849. Intergenerational mobility in fact declined from ca. 90 percent for cohorts coming of age (20) in 1960 to ca. 50 percent for 2000, but almost all of the decline took place from 1960 to 1985: Raj Chetty et al., "The Fading American Dream: Trends in Absolute Income Mobility since 1940," NBER Working Paper No. 22910 (December 2016).

67   The situation for BA+ degrees—actually multiple markets—has not been analyzed. There has been a glut of law school graduates since the Great Recession; MDs and the health professions generally benefited from the growing share of GDP devoted to health care; PhDs in STEM and quantitative fields are well rewarded, other fields less so; master's degrees have grown by two-thirds (2001–2016) and are heavily professional.

the enrollment of disadvantaged students undoubtedly had positive effects, but their overall impact on the existing unequal system of colleges and universities has been marginal. Rather, the dominant market forces just described have assured creeping inequality—in educational outcomes and in incomes. The selectivity sweepstakes, its dominance by private institutions, the paucity of investment in public colleges and universities—all seem unlikely to be altered or significantly nudged under prevailing conditions. Mitigation of income inequality would have to be found outside of higher education. According to David Autor, "policies that appear most effective over the long haul in raising prosperity and reducing inequality are those that cultivate the skills of successive generations: excellent preschool through high school education."[68] American colleges and universities create human capital with the resources available, including students. Relatively high graduate earnings signify real value in the educational credentials they award.

THE LEARNING CONUNDRUM

Concern for student learning was always part of the internal higher education dialogue. From the Harvard Redbook through the next two decades, the principal focus was the liberal arts foundation that distinguished a college education. The academic revolution undermined credence in the value of a general education core, and in the more critical 1970s curricula evolved to correspond more directly with subsequent careers. A different level of concern appeared in the 1980s with external criticisms of college teaching and learning and explicit efforts to effect improvements.

In 1983, *A Nation at Risk*, an alarmist report from the Department of Education, garnered extensive publicity by alleging deficiencies in K-12 education. During the next three years, four sponsored reports sought to do the same for weaknesses in collegiate education.[69] *Involvement in Learning*, also from the Department of Education, called for improvements in college teaching by introducing active forms of learning in place of passive lectures. It advocated small, interactive classes and student presentations and projects, as well as rigorous standards

---

68 Autor, "Skills, Education," 850. See also Erik A. Hanushek, Ludger Woessmann, and Paul E. Peterson, *Endangering Prosperity: A Global View of the American School* (Washington, DC: Brookings Institution Press, 2013).

69 National Institute of Education, *Involvement in Learning: Realizing the Potential of American Higher Education* (Washington, DC: NIE and US Dept. of Education, 1984); American Association of Colleges, *Integrity in the College Curriculum: A Report to the Academic Community* (Washington, DC: AAC, 1985); Southern Regional Education Board, *Access to Quality Undergraduate Education* (Atlanta: SREB, 1985); and National Governors' Association, *A Time for Results* (Washington, DC: NGA, 1991).

for evaluation and continual feedback on student performance. Reforms to improve college teaching found an enthusiastic constituency both within higher education and among its patrons. Ernest Boyer's *College* (1987) and especially *Scholarship Reconsidered* (1989) conferred greater recognition and status on college teaching. An emerging ideology melded student-centered learning with civic engagement, democracy, and diversity, a movement that Steven Brint has termed the "new progressivism."[70] This cause was embraced by major foundations, which made it the theme of the American Commitments initiative in the 1990s. Innovations and patronage all flowed in one direction—toward greater student involvement in learning activities with the expectation that "engagement" would foster intellectual skills. Syracuse University and the University of Arizona officially declared themselves to be "student-center research universities" and made major institutional investments to that end.[71] The new progressivism was implicitly dismissive toward traditional forms of collegiate learning. It offered scant support for rigorous standards, ostensibly favoring intellectual skills rather than cognitive learning.

A parallel movement arose in the 1980s among state and federal officials calling for tangible measures of the outcomes of higher education. The justification was at once simplistic and sanctimonious: the public deserved to know the effectiveness of its investment of tax monies in colleges and universities. Hence, an ongoing effort ensued to assess the outcomes of college instruction. More than half of the states established some form of performance-based budgeting. These schemes either provided bonuses or adjusted regular appropriations for enrolling, retaining, or graduating target numbers of students. In some cases, they established perverse incentives or punished institutions serving less-prepared students.[72] A few states employed standardized multiple-choice tests of learning outcomes. Higher-education policy institutes were eager to assist by aggregating various outcomes into "report cards" for the states. The chief weakness of these forms of assessment was that outputs of colleges and universities largely reflected inputs, namely, the academic abilities of their students. To account for this, attempts

70 Steven Brint, "The Academic Devolution? Movements to Reform Teaching and Learning in US Colleges and Universities, 1985–2010," Research and Occasional Paper Series, CSHE Paper No. 12.09, Center for Studies in Higher Education, University of California, Berkeley (December 2009). The following draws from this paper, which is published in Joseph C. Hermanowicz, *The American Academic Profession: Transformation in Contemporary Higher Education* (Baltimore: Johns Hopkins University Press, 2011).

71 Geiger, *Knowledge and Money*, 101–15.

72 Kevin Dougherty et al., *Performance Funding for Higher Education* (Baltimore: Johns Hopkins University Press, 2015). This study failed to find significant positive impacts on student outcomes and found some negative unintended consequences.

were made to measure the value added, which was an even more uncertain process. A further strategy was to measure intellectual skills like critical thinking, but these also reflected entering abilities. The underlying flaw of these approaches was that college students studied multiple subjects, learning different things in different ways that could not be meaningfully captured by feasible assessment of outcomes.

Nonetheless, the assessment movement gained momentum after 2000. The secretary of education Margaret Spellings convened the blue-ribbon Commission on the Future of Higher Education. Charged to examine how well colleges were training students for the twenty-first-century workforce, its critical 2006 report called for substantially greater accountability, including a national database on student progress with measures of learning.[73] In the ensuing reauthorization of the Higher Education Act, many of the commission's far-reaching recommendations were considered, particularly the notion of tying accreditation to mandatory assessments of learning, much as had been done to K-12 education with the No Child Left Behind Act. Although such draconian measures were resisted, the Voluntary System of Accountability that resulted still placed a considerable burden of assessment on mostly public universities.

These movements and the pervasive concern with teaching and accountability had notable impacts on colleges and universities. A commitment to strengthen teaching was evident in the widespread establishment of teaching centers and the practice of providing pedagogical training for graduate students wishing to become faculty. Most hiring of new faculty now requested some evidence of teaching effectiveness. In 2000, the National Survey of Student Engagement (NSSE) was launched to provide institutions with an instrument for enhancing quality assurance. The NSSE surveys probed student behaviors associated with positive learning outcomes, such as contacts with faculty, collaborative learning, and educational enrichment experiences. Additional questions about academic advising or engagement with cultural diversity were further options. Participants could compare their results confidentially with similar institutions. Engagement was clearly related to positive educational experiences, and it was embraced by far more than the 725 NSSE participants (2017). But engagement was not learning and was not statistically correlated with learning gains. For that, the Collegiate Learning Assessment (CLA) emerged as the most credible instrument. It attempted to gauge the general dimensions of college learning—critical thinking, analytical reasoning, problem solving, and writing—through a written essay analyzing and resolving a hypothetical situation. Administered at two points in

---

73　Commission on the Future of the University, *A Test of Leadership: Charting the Future of U.S. Higher Education* (Washington, DC: U.S. Dept. of Education, 2006).

a college career, it would register gains in those general forms of learning expected to result from collegiate education. Notably, this definition of college learning ignored the intellectual and cultural content of a liberal or general education that had dominated conceptions of a college education in the postwar era; and it omitted the cognitive content of major subjects, where the largest amount of student learning occurred.

The assessment movement operated at cross-purposes with the interests of colleges and universities in the twenty-first century. They naturally voiced full support for student learning, but their actions belied other expectations that emanated from society and from their clientele. Cognitive learning, produced in academic classes, receded to only one of many university missions. Institutions also promised to enhance civic and community engagement, leadership, communication, sustainability, cultural diversity, and career preparation—rhetorical goals often having little substantive content in the curriculum.[74] Engagement was touted for developing social and interpersonal skills, as well as promoting personal development. Such qualities and/or skills may have been more attractive to students and parents than cognitive, classroom learning. These pursuits were validated by American society, which might acknowledge the value of "learning" but had greater appreciation for the college's role in the personal, social, and financial maturation of young people.[75] And colleges put their money into these missions: the increase of regular faculty lagged enrollment growth, but the numbers of professional staff serving students exceeded it.[76] This set of values was reflected in the behaviors of students.

The decline in student effort applied to academic work has been extensively documented. For the last fifty years, college students reduced the time spent on academic studies, in and out of class. A comprehensive study found that "sources for 1961 and earlier all show 38 to 40 hrs/wk academic time invested by college students, whereas sources for the post-2000 era produce estimates of 24 to 28 hrs/wk."[77] This trend held true for all types of students and all major fields. The best-selling study by Richard Arum and Josipa Roksa, *Academically Adrift*, found that in the first three semesters students increased their general knowledge, as measured by the CLA, only by 7 percent. A follow-up with seniors found that

---

74   Derek Bok has emphasized the lack of connection between avowed learning goals and curriculum in *Higher Education in America* (Princeton: Princeton University Press, 2013), 180–81.

75   Clotfelter, *Unequal Colleges*, 179–85.

76   Ibid., 196–201. The largest increases in the percentage of educational expenditures devoted to student services occurred at less wealthy schools: 0–90th percentile private ones and 0–50th percentile public ones. Also, Geiger, *Knowledge and Money*, 119–21.

77   Philip Babcock and Mindy Marks, "The Falling Time Costs of College: Evidence from Half a Century of Time Use Data," Department of Economics Working Paper, University of California Santa Barbara, http://escholarship.org/uc/item/7rc9d7vz.

one-third registered no learning gains at all on these measures, and gains on average were modest.[78]

More alarming, the OECD Program for the International Assessment of Adult Competence (PIAAC), administered in 2012, revealed a substantial and growing American inferiority. Young adults (sixteen to thirty-four years of age) ranked sixteenth (of twenty-two nations) in literacy and tied for last place in both numeracy and "problem solving in a technologically rich environment." America's best were not very good: those at the 90th percentile ranked sixteenth; those with bachelor's degrees, twentieth and holders of postgraduate degrees, nineteenth.

The PIAAC results would seem to indicate that the decline in academic effort by students led to a decline in learning relative to college graduates of other advanced nations and most likely to previous generations of Americans. Apparently, the CLA scores really did reflect that students were not learning very much. Moreover, they cast suspicion on the major preoccupations of the last generation. For three decades, public policies fixated on assessment and accountability, while the learning they purportedly monitored deteriorated. Pedagogically, active-learning approaches may well have been counterproductive. Expanding college enrollments from the bottom, as the college-for-all movement promoted, may have done more to create credentials than capabilities. The relative ineffectiveness of all these movements raised the question of just what forces were shaping American higher education in the twenty-first century.

Grade inflation was a certain indicator that college had gotten easier, no doubt from bottom to top. There were several dimensions of this trend. One was the decline of demanding courses. In an age of student evaluations, faculty had little inclination to require high performance and substantial work—for students or themselves. Such evaluations were, or were felt to be, critically important for the growing ranks of non-tenure-track faculty. Arum and Roksa repeatedly pointed to the rarity of twenty-page papers or forty-page weekly reading assignments. And for institutions, no matter what their rhetoric, stiffer standards would have unacceptable consequences for their diversity and completion agendas. Pedagogy evolved from the late 1960s to accommodate laxity. What were once standard coercive practices—homework, pop quizzes, strict attendance policies, grading curves—became rare outside of STEM fields. Classes with no examinations were not unusual. Active-learning classrooms could tolerate superficial discussion, and group projects invited free riders. Students who disliked math could avoid

78   Richard Arum and Josipa Roksa, *Academically Adrift: Limited Learning on College Campuses* (Chicago: University of Chicago Press, 2009); Richard Arum, *Aspiring Adults Adrift: Tentative Transitions of College Graduates* (Chicago: University of Chicago Press, 2014), 38–39.

classes above rudimentary levels—in both high school and college. And an abundance of easy courses, like film studies or human sexuality, eased student workloads, especially when taken online. Such courses would scarcely bolster one's score on the PIAAC assessments.[79]

Socialization is an important part of a college experience, although perhaps more so for the half of full-time students who reside at their colleges. Adapting to a diverse set of associates and developing interpersonal relations are important for success in college and afterwards in careers. Social activities may foster "soft skills" that seem to be valued in the workplace. For many students, socialization and enjoying the collegiate life assumed foremost priority, despite implicit goals of career preparation and academic success. A time-use study at the University of California found students spending as many hours socializing with friends and attending student organizations as they spent in class. However, they also devoted nearly as much time to watching TV and using computers for fun. Students who spent more time on these last pursuits had lower GPAs, and students who devoted more time to academics had higher GPAs.[80] Students commonly engaged in strategic balancing of academic commitments—choosing electives and general education courses with reputations for easy grading and little work. Faculty were complicit in posting lectures, guided notes, and PowerPoint slides; attending class became optional. For Arum and Roksa, minimizing commitments in this way was a symptom of students "adrift."[81]

For Brint, "the triumph of student consumerism lies at the heart of these trends. Many students have effectively resisted professorial demands for higher levels of effort by simply refusing to engage their studies at a deep level." Students determined the college workload, not the faculty. Students learn so little, he concluded, because so little is asked of them.[82] But students apparently felt that it was enough. Richard Arum's sample of students was overwhelmingly satisfied with their college experience two years after graduation. Moreover, a large majority cited what they considered gains in critical thinking and writing. By and large they credited their college education with providing the kind of generic skills that their CLA results found so meager.[83] True, the highest CLA scorers

79 Arum and Roksa, *Academically Adrift*, 76–79; Brint, "Academic Devolution?"

80 Steven Brint and Allison M. Cantwell, "Undergraduate Time Use and Academic Outcomes: Results from UCUES 2006," Research and Occasional Paper Series, Center for Studies in Higher Education, University of California, Berkeley, 2008.

81 Arum and Roksa, *Academically Adrift*, 75–77. The Internet is an additional factor in making college easier: cheating has become more prevalent (ibid., 14), and plagiarism, borderline or blatant, is rampant.

82 Brint and Cantwell, "Undergraduate Time Use," 18; Brint, *Two Cheers*, chap. 5.

83 Derek Bok cites surveys in which graduates in first jobs regretted learning deficiencies: *The Struggle to Reform Our Colleges* (Princeton: Princeton University Press, 2017), 76.

were somewhat more successful in the labor market than the lowest, but the difference was not great. None apparently expressed a wish to have studied more or learned more in college.[84]

This gloomy scenario depicts only one facet of the state of learning in American higher education. Large numbers of students are committed to their studies and learn a great deal. They can be readily identified. Students in quantitative fields must master cumulative subjects of increasing difficulty. They include STEM fields, economics, and some business majors—often selective tracks in selective universities. STEM degrees have composed 15 percent of bachelor's degrees since 1990, but these graduates were only half of the students who started in these fields—attrition that testifies to meaningful standards and learning. These subjects involved demanding courses taught by faculty who were invested in the competence of their charges. Tellingly, the most highly regarded effort to link accreditation and outcomes assessment occurred in engineering.[85]

Another locus of ambitious, high-achieving students has been honors colleges in public universities. These programs are distinguished by small classes, carefully selected faculty instructors, and much more work.[86] These students far exceeded the reading and writing thresholds used in *Academically Adrift* and usually wrote a senior thesis as well. Honors programs/colleges have grown in popularity, and in resources, at public universities. A similar growing trend has been arrangements for undergraduates to engage in research. Summer internships have been a popular opportunity, which often lead to continuing association with research groups. A growing number of students now opt for double majors. Such options require more advanced work in a second field, which crowds out dubious electives. Students taking double majors are anything but "adrift"— seeking to master two specialties in their college education.

Most pervasive, the challenge of gaining admission to graduate or professional school is a continual goad not only to getting good grades but also to learning. One-half of college graduates now enroll in postgraduate work at some point; probably half of those do so immediately after college. Grades and standardized tests are the chief merit criteria for admission to competitive programs. Despite grade inflation, extensive research has established that "college grades may well be the single best predictor of student persistence, degree completion, and graduate school enrollment." Students who strive for high grades demonstrate motivation

---

84   Arum, *Aspiring Adults*, 39, 47, 76–80. Larger surveys also find high degrees of satisfaction among graduates.

85   Brint, *Two Cheers*, chap. 5; Brint and Cantwell, "Undergraduate Time Use," 16–17; Accreditation Board for Engineering Technology, *Criteria for Accrediting Engineering Programs* (Baltimore: ABET, 2000).

86   Bowen et al., *Crossing the Finish Line*, 205–4.

and learning goals. On the Graduate Record Examination, average scores on the verbal test have declined, possibly indicating declining general knowledge, but scores on the subject tests have improved since 2000.[87] Cognitive learning still motivated a substantial portion of undergraduates.

UNIVERSITY CULTURE IN A POLARIZED AMERICA

In the twenty-first century, reverberations from the culture wars continued to perturb American higher education. The concerns over political correctness waned after the early 1990s; then, renewed attacks on university politics featured prominently in the next decade. As explained in Chapter 7, the conservative critique of academic liberalism was institutionalized in external advocacy organizations. On campuses, political correctness was scarcely inhibited. Rather, it became more entrenched and dogmatic, especially after 2013. But criticism or defense of the academic Left jumbled together a number of different phenomena. In the second decade, progressive orientations, activism, and liberal academic culture, although thoroughly entangled, were manifested somewhat differently among faculty, students, and university administrations.

In the mid-2000s, the liberal bias of professors again became an object of media attention and ostensible public concern. A succession of notorious cases highlighted the extreme political views of individual professors, but these incidents were given a more portentous interpretation by conservative commentators. David Horowitz, in particular, was a prototypical "mid-level moral entrepreneur," with his own eponymous "freedom center" to advance his causes and himself. His Big Idea was that radical professors were intentionally indoctrinating college students in left-wing beliefs. He outed *The 101 Most Dangerous Academics in America* and conducted a prolonged campaign to persuade states to enact an "academic bill of rights" to shield college students from *Indoctrination U* (another book title). Several states investigated but found no evidence for these charges, and media attention soon waned. Public perceptions of politics in higher education were shaped by media coverage of notorious incidents and partisan interpreters.[88]

---

87 Ernest T. Pasqarella and Patrick T. Terenzini, *How College Affects Students: Vol. 2, A Third Decade of Research* (San Francisco: Jossey-Bass, 2005), 396–97; NCES, *Digest of Education Statistics: 2017*, Table 327.10.

88 A search by the sociologist Neil Gross for the combination of "liberal bias" and "higher education" in major publications found a sixfold increase from 2001 to 2005, followed by an equally steep decline: Neil Gross, *Why Are Professors Liberal and Why Do Conservatives Care?* (Cambridge, MA: Harvard University Press, 2013), 220–51, 243; David A. Horowitz, *The Professors: The 101 Most Dangerous Academics in America* (New York: Regnery, 2006); Horowitz, *Indoctrination U.: The Left's War against Academic Freedom* (New York: Encounter Books, 2006). Horowitz's premise was in fact wrong: student political

The liberal proclivities of higher education faculty were scarcely new news. Previous chapters have described this phenomenon in the 1960s and the 1980s. A survey of faculty in 2006 found a pattern similar to earlier studies: 44 percent identified as liberal, 46 percent as moderate with a liberal lean, and just 9 percent conservative. As before, faculty were most liberal in the humanities and social sciences, as well as at the top research universities and, even more so, liberal arts colleges. Feminism probably accounted for women being somewhat further to the left than men and overrepresented among radicals, especially in the social sciences. Extremists on the Left outnumbered counterparts on the Right nine to one, but only a minority of those radicals felt it appropriate to promulgate their views in the classroom.[89] In 2006 more radicals were found among older professors than among the younger cohorts, but those demographics changed with an influx of more liberal neophytes. Since that date, according to a different survey, "far-left/liberal" faculty grew by ten points to comprise 60 percent of faculty.[90] This no doubt reflected the growing polarization of American politics.

Social and psychological theories have been proposed since the 1950s to explain the liberal orientation of academics; however, the pervasive underlying factor is cultural. Universities are heir to the Enlightenment traditions of "reason, science, humanism, and progress," as Steven Pinker has eloquently argued. The historical advancement of knowledge has produced a nearly inexorable improvement of the human condition.[91] Hence, highly educated individuals tend to have an ingrained cultural framework averring that scientific explanations provide superior depictions of the natural world; that governments should endeavor to improve the lives of the governed; and that education can enrich the lives of all. John Meyer and his associates have analyzed how these cultural frames spread worldwide in the last third of the twentieth century, in part through the proliferation of higher education. Universities embodied and implanted liberal individualism, which was in itself a manifestation of a pervasive "expansion of human agency"—the institutional empowerment of individuals to make choices that affect their life course and a rejection of the social constraints typical of traditional societies. Globally, this fostered child-centered education and promotion

---

orientations were largely formed outside classrooms. See Jim Sidanius et al., *The Diversity Challenge: Social Identity and Intergroup Relations on the College Campus* (New York: Russell Sage Foundation, 2008).

89   Gross, *Why Are Professors Liberal?*, 25–33, 202–9; Neil Gross and Solon Simmons, "The Social and Political Views of American College and University Professors," in Gross and Simmons, eds., *Professors and Their Politics* (Baltimore: Johns Hopkins University Press, 2014), 19–52.

90   https://heterodoxacademy.org/the-problem/; Greg Lukianoff and Jonathan Haidt, *The Coddling of the American Mind: How Good Intentions and Bad Ideas Are Setting Up a Generation for Failure* (New York: Penguin, 2018), 111.

91   Steven Pinker, *Enlightenment Now: The Case for Reason, Science, Humanism, and Progress* (New York: Viking, 2018).

of equality for women.[92] In the United States, such cultural axioms were reflected in the prevalence of a consumerist orientation in higher education and, politically, in what Eric Posner called "the extraordinary proliferation of human rights." Given its "vast ideological appeal," human rights have "become the lingua franca for political action, and the always-present temptation for professors and students to use the university as a vehicle for political advocacy."[93]

The different dimensions of academic politics had different implications for universities. The liberal bias of academics stemmed chiefly from their affinity for liberal knowledge traditions. But academics long proved to be more Democratic than liberal.[94] When faced with an either-or voting choice, and a Republican alternative that favored social conservatism and limited government, moderates too opted for the Democratic Party. Political advocacy represented a third dimension, further left than merely Democrat or liberal. In interviews with left-leaning faculty, Gross found "virtually indistinguishable" support for "women's rights, the rights of ethnic and racial minorities, gay rights, and environmental conservation and in 2007 opposition to the war in Iraq"—as well as a belief "that class inequality is the most significant ill affecting American society."[95] These positions came in strong and weak flavors, although they all implied some disidentification with the United States, as described in Chapter 7. Although Gross found them on the far left, they encompassed the main tenets of political correctness. Hence human rights, as interpreted by identity groups, provided a rationale for student advocacy.

Student politics in general defy characterization. On the one hand, at any given juncture, the large majority of students have little or no interest or involvement in political issues. On the other hand, a commonality of interests and interest groups exist among factions of students across campuses, especially in the selective sector. Incidents on one campus, inflated by the news media and spread by social media, can mobilize students elsewhere. Such a situation occurred in the mid-2010s and elevated student activism once more into the national spotlight.

---

92 Evan Schofer and John W. Meyer, "The Worldwide Expansion of Higher Education in the Twentieth Century," *American Sociological Review* 70, 6 (2005): 898–920; John W. Meyer, "Human Rights: World Society, the Welfare State, and the Life Course: An Institutionalist Perspective," in Georg Krücken and Gili S. Drori, eds., *World Society: The Writings of John W. Meyer*, (New York: Oxford University Press, 2009), 280–95.

93 Eric A. Posner, "The Human-Rights Charade," *Chronicle of Higher Education* (November 17, 2014).

94 Daniel B. Klein and Charlotta Stern, "By the Numbers: The Ideological Profile of Professors," in Robert Maranto, Richard E. Redding, and Frederick M. Hess, eds., *The Politically Correct University: Problems, Scope, and Reforms* (Washington, DC: AEI Press, 2009), 15–37.

95 This interviewee also sought "nothing short of a radical reconfiguration of the economic order": Gross, *Why Are Professors Liberal?*, 43.

Oddly, *Generation on a Tightrope: A Portrait of Today's College Student*, researched at the beginning of the decade, found students largely disengaged from traditional politics and possessing "little concrete knowledge about the world." They expressed a desire for change but were losing faith in the promises of President Obama and the Democrats to bring it about. Instead, they were moved by issues that had personal meaning. The Occupy Colleges Movement in 2011 was the only connected national movement. Emotionally charged by disapproval of class inequality, it was intellectually vacuous. One percent of students participated in a national walkout to protest the nefarious "one percent."[96] The book found evidence that racial relations on campus were improving, but an apparent deterioration soon followed.[97] Around 2013 a new generation of students began arriving on campus who had grown up immersed in social media. Dubbed the "iGen," they were generally less mature and more prone to anxiety disorders. Above all concerned with safety, they particularly sought safety from ideas they disagreed with.[98]

At mid-decade, campuses witnessed some of the most serious and widely covered protests since the 1960s. Demonstrations by black students at the University of Missouri over allegations of racism began in September 2015. They persisted for two months, until the president of the university system and the chancellor of the campus, both unpopular for other reasons, felt compelled to resign. At Yale, a letter mocking an administrative warning about offensive Halloween costumes touched off a furious protest by black students against the writer and her husband, a highly distinguished professor, who together were heads of a residential college. They were forced to relinquish those positions when the university wholly sided with the decidedly uncivil protesters. Yale established the Presidential Task Force on Diversity and Inclusion and promised $50 million for diversity initiatives. President Peter Salovey kept his job. In March 2017, at Middlebury College, the social scientist Charles Murray, who was reviled on the Left for discussing hereditary intelligence more than two decades earlier (*The Bell Curve*,

96   Arthur Levine and Diane R. Dean, *Generation on a Tightrope: A Portrait of Today's College Students* (San Francisco: Jossey-Bass, 2012), quote p. 117; Jonathan Zimmerman, *Campus Politics: What Everyone Needs to Know* (New York: Oxford University Press, 2016), 16–22.

97   Increased incidents of racial offenses, spread by social media and publicized nationally, have no doubt caused insecurity among minorities and pressured universities to strengthen hitherto ineffective diversity policies. Such random acts by miscreant individuals, often nonstudents, represented aberrations rather than conditions of higher education. They reflected the extreme polarities in American society and a growing coarseness in social relations: cf. Zimmerman, *Campus Politics*, 50–55.

98   Jean M. Twenge, *iGen: Why Today's Super-Connected Kids Are Growing Up Less Rebellious, More Tolerant, Less Happy—and Completely Unprepared for Adulthood—and What That Means for the Rest of Us* (New York: Atria Books, 2017); Lukianoff and Haidt, *Coddling the American Mind*, 146–61.

1994), was prevented by student protesters from delivering an invited lecture on an entirely different topic. He and his faculty escort were then attacked by a mob as they departed. The Middlebury fiasco crystalized what had been a growing controversy over free speech or its absence on campuses.[99]

The brazen, premeditated suppression of speech at Middlebury alarmed civil libertarians across the country, and it alerted the public to the existence of an extremist psychology among the student Left. But for these students, Middlebury was a model for preventing the expression of what they labeled hateful ideas.[100] The majority of college students had little regard for free speech, agreeing when polled that "colleges should prohibit [what they considered] racist/sexist speech on campus." On the Right, would-be provocateurs clamored for opportunities to speak at major universities, precisely in order to provoke confrontations. They too wished to pose as victims.[101] Students refused to disavow the heckler's veto, and polarization grew. Universities, not wishing to risk inflaming issues of race or gender, tended to side with students and political correctness. In contrast, the University of Chicago in 2015 produced the "Report of the Committee on Freedom of Expression" that stated an explicit commitment to protect ideas "thought by some or even by most members of the University community to be offensive, unwise, immoral, or wrong-headed." In three years, just twenty-two other institutions endorsed these principles.[102] In fact, most colleges and universities maintained restrictive speech codes, even though they had been ruled unconstitutional by the Supreme Court.[103]

Students in the 1960s had protested conditions in the world, American society, and universities; students in the twenty-first century were primarily concerned

99   Previous incidents of students threatening the heckler's veto had produced numbers of disinvitations. Students' objections to speakers they disapproved of and the implicit threat of disruption caused universities to withdraw invitations to speakers or speakers to withdraw from engagements they had accepted: the Foundation for Individual Rights in Education (FIRE) maintains a database of disinvitations: https://www.thefire.org/.

100   Stephen J. Ceci and Wendy M. Williams, "Who Decides What Is Acceptable Speech on Campus? Why Restricted Speech Is Not the Answer," *Perspectives on Psychological Science* (published online May 2, 2018).

101   Especially after the election of Donald Trump, external right-wing attacks on university leftists tended to validate their assumed victim status and was used to justify suppression of non-left speakers, creating a spiral of reciprocal extremism.

102   University of Chicago, "Report of the Committee on Freedom of Expression" (2015), https://provost.uchicago.edu/sites/default/files/documents/reports/FOECommitteeReport.pdf; https://heterodoxacademy.org/the-problem/.

103   A survey by FIRE of major colleges and universities found one-third to have highly restrictive speech codes and almost 60 percent to have moderately restrictive codes. The number of highly restrictive codes had been declining: *Spotlight on Speech Codes 2018: The State of Free Speech on Our Nation's Campuses* (Philadelphia: Foundation for Individual Rights in Education, 2018).

with themselves.[104] The college students of this era were "more likely to invoke the language of psychological health and illness, which has entered their political rhetoric as never before."[105] Enforcement of the canons of political correctness was justified by the psychological reactions of students. "Microaggressions" made them feel "uncomfortable" or "unsafe"; "trigger warnings" were needed for the same reason. Incorrect notions pertaining to race, class, or gender were "offensive," causing "harm" and "pain." By these broad definitions, any nonconforming material could be considered "racist, sexist, heterosexist, classist, or ableist" and labeled "hate speech," another source of psychological trauma. The sacrosanct sensitivities of identity groups were protected with a special vocabulary. "Campus climate" served as a barometer of discrimination. Condemnation of "cultural appropriation" affirmed exclusive identities. "Intersectionality"—having more than one identity—raised perplexing issues that fine-tuned the dimensions of victimhood. Outside academe, these concepts and corresponding mentalities were often regarded with some wonderment, the fragile student psyches referred to as "snowflakes"; but they were taken seriously by colleges and universities.

Since the 1970s, universities have responded to pressures from identity groups with administrative accommodations. Women's centers and African American centers were followed by centers or offices for other identity groups, including gay and lesbian students. Research units were often added as well, institutionalizing identity ideologies.[106] Every university established a central office for diversity and usually separate offices in academic colleges. Periodic campus protests were often resolved by promising additional resources to these units (e.g., Yale). The substantial numbers of diversity administrators and staff, together with cultural studies programs, upheld and validated the canons of political correctness for the identity groups they represented. University subsidies allowed them to sponsor speakers and conferences on these themes. Compulsory diversity training became a staple of student orientations. These programs typically included exercises intended to instill guilt over alleged white privilege. The identity communities were supported by student affairs professionals, who fully shared the diversity ideology. The fastest growing sectors of college and university person-

104   Student protests in the 1990s were campus-focused over diversity issues: Robert A. Rhoads, *Freedom's Web: Student Activism in an Age of Cultural Diversity* (Baltimore: Johns Hopkins University Press, 1998).

105   Zimmerman, *Campus Politics*, 90–108, quote p. 104; Jean M. Twenge, "The Rise of the Self and the Decline of Intellectual and Civic Interest," in Mark Bauerlein and Adam Bellow, eds., *The State of the American Mind* (West Conshohocken, PA: Templeton Press, 2015), 123–36.

106   For Mark Lilla the consequence of the obsession with personal identity is "self-Righteous narcissism": [A student now] "engages with the world and particularly politics for the limited aim of understanding and affirming what one already is": *The Once and Future Liberal: After Identity Politics* (New York: Harper Collins, 2017), 90, 102, 84.

nel were student affairs and institutional support, where diversity offices were located.[107] The institutionalization of diversity bureaucracies made the identity factions—who claimed to be victims of hate crimes, oppression, hostile climate, and microaggressions—in fact the most powerful groups on campus.

The overall effect was to balkanize campuses. Centers for identity groups provided a "safe space" for the committed to cultivate the psychology of oppression, and they kept these groups permanently mobilized to press their interests. They also reduced contact with students not belonging to those groups. For senior administrators, the diversity bureaucracy served as a kind of buffer. The chief diversity officer—a senior administrator—was expected to mediate between identity groups and the officers responsible for running the institution. Deans, provosts, and presidents were sincere academic liberals (a job requirement) who wholeheartedly supported diversity and multiculturalism.[108] In these political positions an incorrect word or deed could mean not only a forced resignation (e.g., Missouri), but potential blackballing of future career opportunities for those deemed "racist" or "sexist," no matter how unfairly. The hegemony of identity groups was ultimately due to the uncritical backing of administrators, whether out of fear or faith. Typical behavior was the rapid adoption of "bias response teams" on 100 campuses by 2016, 200 by 2018. These teams were intended to investigate and punish accusations of bias based on "identity characteristics," and thus they provided another weapon to enforce political correctness—and inhibit speech. At Michigan, and no doubt elsewhere, this mission justified additional administrators, who were expected to partner with cultural appropriation and social justice initiatives. Administrators created large bureaucracies to placate the identity partisans—and to protect themselves.[109]

A multiyear study at UCLA of the effects of diversity initiatives found little to encourage proponents. Students entered the university with well-formed and stable political and racial attitudes and changed little over four years. Students were predominately liberal on entrance and drifted toward somewhat greater liberalism and tolerance, but this seemed a result of immersion in pervasive campus

107   Zimmerman, *Campus Politics*, 50–3. Ronald G. Ehrenberg, "American Higher Education in Transition," *Journal of Economic Perspectives* 26 (2012): 193–216; Donna M. Desrochers and Rita Kirshstein, *Labor Intensive or Labor Expensive: Changing Staffing Patterns in Higher Education* (Washington, DC: Delta Cost Project, American Institutes for Research, 2014): Student services, the fastest growing category of staffing and spending, includes diverse services, such as admissions, financial aid, advising, and student affairs.

108   Benjamin Ginsberg, *The Fall of the Faculty: The Rise of the All-Administrative University and Why It Matters* (New York: Oxford University Press, 2013), 97–130.

109   Jeffrey Aaron Snyder and Amna Khalid, "The Rise of 'Bias Response Teams' on Campus," *New Republic* (March 30, 2016); Jillian Kay Melchior, "The Bias Response Team Is Watching," *Wall Street Journal* (May 9, 2018), A15.

norms. Diversity initiatives and required multicultural courses had no discernible effect. The most negative finding was that participation in ethnically based organizations promoted politicized ethnic identification—greater perceptions of ethnic conflict, victimization, and discrimination. This was true not only for the identity centers mentioned above but also in somewhat different forms for fraternities. Positively, the study found that interethnic contact reduced prejudice, but this occurred through individual interactions, which balkanization inhibited.[110]

Most students seemed able to ignore an institution's official diversity ideology in their college careers. Fraternity members, when asked, tended not to support the diversity agenda, and for good reason—it demonized masculinity and white males. Condemnation of "white privilege" was a standard idiom in this discourse. Extreme expressions—which were not rare—held that "racist ... applies to all white people (i.e., people of European descent) living in the United States, regardless of class, gender, religion, culture, or sexuality. By this definition, people of color cannot be racists."[111] One could scarcely argue against such self-serving dogma. White students consequently tended to remain silent when racial or gender issues were raised.[112] The intellectual space between diversity zealotry and (alleged) racism was ambiguous and perilous territory. Feminists and LGBT advocates—the most active identity group on most campuses—embraced a commitment to their cause, but the situation was more difficult for some African Americans. The prevailing obsession with race could be an inescapable burden. Participation in collegiate life with nonminorities could mean ostracism from the organized black campus community. Diversity policies in practice made campus life less diverse for most students.

The liberal stance of the professoriate affected the production of knowledge in several fields. When political homogeneity prevailed, disciplines tended to form "cohesive moral communities" that ceased to consider discordant ideas or people. A study of social psychology documented detrimental consequences: liberal values and assumptions became embedded into theory and methods; researchers selected topics that validated liberal narratives and avoided those that contradicted them; and negative attitudes toward conservatives caused mischaracterization of traits and attributes. Homogeneity promoted confirmation bias and groupthink, which research had shown to produce negative consequences,

---

110   Sidanius et al., *Diversity Challenge*, 301–24.

111   The quote continues: "A racist is one who is both privileged and socialized on the basis of race by a white supremacist (racial) system"—from a diversity trainer manual, University of Delaware: Maranto et al., *Politically Correct University*, 113, 197.

112   Arthur Levine and Jeanette S. Cureton, *When Hope and Fear Collide: A Portrait of Today's College Students* (San Francisco: Jossey-Bass, 1998), 72–74.

in contrast to the positive effects of viewpoint diversity. The predominance of liberal orientations in the academic profession was natural, as argued above, and reinforced by self-selection. However, the prejudicial mentality of a cohesive moral community caused outright discrimination and hostility to alternative views.[113]

Disciplinary communities contain a multitude of competing doctrines, theories, or orientations internally; yet they can become morally cohesive, and hence exclusionary, in other respects. Neil Gross, for example, described sociologists as employing diverse theoretical approaches and varying commitments to activism in research. However, sociologists also formed a cohesive moral community in associating their discipline with progress toward a more equal social order. For an individual who did not share this outlook, becoming a sociologist would be like "bashing his head against the wall."[114] Academic historians have cohered around disidentification with America and its past. Topics of wide general interest—the Founding Fathers, the Civil War, and political history generally—have been ceded to nonacademic writers (to their profit). Disidentification is perhaps most extreme in American Studies. A review of mainstream works observed that recent scholars had "developed a hatred for America so visceral that it makes one wonder why they bother studying America at all."[115]

The situation in literary studies further demonstrated the pitfalls of moral cohesion. A committee of Harvard faculty charged with addressing the "crisis in the humanities" approvingly described the prevailing consensus in literary studies as transcending the study of texts in order to focus "scholarly skepticism and distrust" on "operations of power." It embraced "liberating, transformative social movements," namely gender and race, and endorsed the "tribalist exclusion of those not regarded as part of the transhistorical identity." Students might feel "that some ideas are unspeakable in our classrooms"; but they were probably bad ideas, acquired from "parents … houses of worship … or from the media."[116] Embedded values, leftist narratives, mischaracterization, groupthink were blatant in

113   José L. Duarte et al., "Political Diversity Will Improve Social Psychological Science," *Behavioral and Brain Sciences* (2015: 38e130). A psychological study documented the negative effects of groupthink and the superiority of viewpoint diversity: Charlan Nemeth, *In Defense of Troublemakers: The Powers of Dissent in Life and Business* (New York: Basic, 2018), Similar points are made by Ceci and Williams, "Who Decides?"

114   Gross, *Why Are Professors Liberal?*, 149.

115   Maranto et al., *Politically Correct University*, 192–208; Alan Wolfe, "Anti-American Studies," *New Republic* 228, 5 (February 10, 2003): 25–33, quote p. 26.

116   [Harvard Faculty Working Group], *The Teaching of the Arts and Humanities at Harvard College: Mapping the Future*, (Cambridge, MA: Harvard University, 2013), 18–20, 42; Roger L. Geiger, "From the Land-Grant Tradition to the Current Crisis in the Humanities," in Gordon Hutner and Feisal G. Mohamed, eds., *A New Deal for the Humanities: Liberal Arts and the Future of Public Higher Education* (New Brunswick, NJ: Rutgers University Press, 2016), 18–30.

all these fields. As in social psychology, moral cohesion precluded disinterested study of much of the putative subject matter of their respective fields of knowledge. Much like McCarthyism in the 1950s, academics in these fields avoided broaching controversial topics that would challenge the political orthodoxy.

The social and political polarization occurring in the United States inevitably impinged on higher education. Universities as institutions sometimes abandoned the neutrality that should accompany their normative role in the disinterested pursuit of knowledge. The effects of national polarization were exacerbated by the Black Lives Matter movement beginning in 2014 and the "resistance" following the election of Donald Trump in 2016. The legitimate partisanship of students, faculty, and staff placed enormous pressure on university administrations, as in the past, to commit their institutions through word or deed to invariably polarized positions. But endorsing progressive groupthink had negative consequences in a country that leaned decidedly Republican in the 2016 elections. Public confidence in higher education was damaged by the Middlebury incident and ensuing controversies over the lack of free expression on campuses. According to the Pew Research Center, the proportion of Republicans believing that colleges have a positive influence on American society dropped from 58 to 38 percent (2015–2017).[117] In the 2017 Tax Cuts and Jobs Act, Congress imposed a 1.4 percent tax on net endowment earnings only for institutions having endowments of more than $500,000 per student. This levy was an unprecedented and purely vindictive gesture (it would raise insignificant revenue) aimed at a small number of the most prestigious, and notoriously liberal, colleges and universities. Beyond these mainstream developments, organizations of the Far Right were emboldened to publicize and attack examples (in their view) of egregious political bias. Most activities of colleges and universities were quite independent of the political biases described above and in fact depended in crucial ways on widespread public trust and support. This was particularly true for the advancement of knowledge.

RESEARCH UNIVERSITIES AND THE KNOWLEDGE SOCIETY

Clark Kerr and Daniel Bell foresaw in the 1960s not just the central role that universities had assumed, but that its prominence would be magnified in the future (Chapter 3). They were overly optimistic about the capacity of the social

---

117   Hannah Fingerhut, "Republicans Skeptical of Colleges Impact on the U.S.," FactTank: News in the Numbers, Pew Research Center, July 20, 2017. Other polls registered a similar fall in confidence in higher education.

sciences to shape society, but they were generally correct on much else. Kerr envisioned an economy increasingly drawing on university knowledge for problem-solving, innovation, and growth. Bell presciently emphasized the university's capacity to supply theoretical knowledge as the wellspring of new industries and progress. Kerr envisaged a knowledge economy; Bell's postindustrial society became known as the knowledge society. These basic insights have been expanded, refined, or questioned by innumerable writers since they wrote.[118] A pertinent alternative was offered in the early 1990s by Michael Gibbons with other higher education scholars. They viewed knowledge production as being increasingly distributed broadly across society (Mode 2) and saw this process superseding the predominance of hidebound universities (Mode 1), dominated as they were by academic disciplines and theory. These scholars correctly perceived the burgeoning role of knowledge throughout society and the multiplying nodes of knowledge creation, but they were wrong about universities.[119] They failed to realize that as society relied more heavily on knowledge creation, the most advanced forms of knowledge, which universities were best suited to cultivate, became more valuable and more influential. And they failed to acknowledge the pathways developing, foremost in the United States, for universities to make useful knowledge more readily available to society (Chapter 7). A half-century after Kerr's and Bell's insights, these last two developments were increasingly prominent features of American research universities.

Research activity in American universities continued to expand in the twenty-first century. Research spending grew 300 percent in constant dollars from 1980 to 2016. From 2000, it increased by 71 percent, but that growth was greater in constant dollars than the rise from 1980 to 2000 ($30 billion vs. $24 billion [2016 dollars]). Research universities extended the trend of growing research intensity, with research dollars per faculty member growing by 41 percent. Publications and citations also grew at impressive rates. By 2011, 60 percent of American scientific publications were authored by university scientists, and 80 percent of publications had at least one university author. The steady rise of this last figure is the best indication of the growing centrality of academic research to the total knowledge enterprise.[120]

118   Steven Brint, "Professionals and the 'Knowledge Economy': Rethinking the Theory of Postindustrial Society," *Current Sociology* 49, 4 (July 2001): 101–32.

119   Michael Gibbons et al., *The New Production of Knowledge: The Dynamics of Science and Research in Contemporary Societies* (London: Sage, 1994); Baker, *Schooled Society*, 77–81.

120   Publications grew by 190 percent (1979–2010) and citations by 146 percent (1979–2005): Steven Brint and Cynthia E. Carr, "The Scientific Research Output of U.S. Research Universities, 1980–2010," *Minerva* 55, 4 (2017): 435–57; Frank Fernandez and David P. Baker, "Science Production in the United States: An Unexpected Synergy between Mass Higher Education and the Super Research University," in Justin J. W. Powell, David P. Baker, and Frank Fernandez, eds., *The Century of Science: The Global*

The university research economy was affected by the Great Recession that struck in 2008. Federal funds for academic research were first boosted as part of the economic stimulus. More than $7 billion extra were allocated by 2011, accounting for virtually all the 2009–2011 growth. But federal funding was then reduced and in 2016 was still $1.5 billion less than 2011.[121] Funding from business and nonprofits rose during those years, but the largest additions to the research economy came from the universities themselves—$5.5 billion of a total increase of $7 billion. This acceleration of a long-term trend signified the growing reliance of universities on the research enterprise, the funding limitations of hard-pressed federal agencies, and the corresponding stress on university budgets. In the golden age of the 1960s, universities bolstered their research funding with 10 percent of their own funds. After 1970, when federal generosity ebbed, that figure rose gradually to near 20 percent in 1990, where it remained until 2010. By 2016, institutional support climbed to 25 percent. These funds were not diverted from student tuition. Substantial amounts were recycled from the clinical revenues of health centers. Some institutions in which medical research dominated used their own funds for 40 percent of separately budgeted research. The other principal source of institutional funds was indirect-cost reimbursements. Expenditure of these funds remained close to their sources: less than 20 percent were devoted to social science and nonscience departments.[122]

At the dawn of the postwar research economy, the sixteen prewar research universities had been best situated to benefit from the new federal support (Chapter 2). Fifty years later, in the last comprehensive rating of academic fields, they remained the most highly rated institutions. In 2016, twelve of those universities were among the top twenty research performers, but Chicago (no. 53), Caltech (no. 60) and Princeton (no. 76), while no less eminent, had expanded little in the high-dollar fields. The weakest of the prewar institutions, Johns Hopkins, Penn, and Stanford, were first, third, and ninth in research expenditures. The principal change in the research economy was the relative expansion of medical research—from 23 percent in 1980 to 31 percent in 2016. When biomedical research is added, these fields accounted for one-half of the total and federally funded academic research. Data on academic research is affected by the prodi-

Triumph of the Research University (Bingley, UK: Emerald Publishing, 2017), 85–112. This centrality is cogently argued by Jason Owen-Smith in *Research Universities and the Public Good: Discovery for an Uncertain Future* (Stanford, CA: Stanford University Press, 2018).

121   For apprehension over future federal support for academic science, see Gwilym Croucher, "Can the Research Model Move beyond Its Dominant Patron? The Future of Support for Fundamental Research in US Universities," Research and Occasional Papers, CSHE Paper No. 6.18 (2018), Center for Studies in Higher Education, University of California, Berkeley.

122   National Science Foundation, *Higher Education Research and Development Survey, Fiscal Year 2016*, Data Tables 1, 12, 21.

gious amounts of research and publication produced in the massive health centers of regular and medical universities. For example, nineteen of the twenty largest producers of scientific publications had such medical complexes, with Harvard's multiple medical units far in the lead. UC Berkeley was the lone exception without a medical school.[123]

The stability of the research university hierarchy, noted in Chapter 7, persisted in the twenty-first century. A study by Steven Brint and Cynthia Carr determined that the degree of inequality in R&D spending, publications, and citations remained constant at least through 2010. At the top of the hierarchy was an unchanging group of about thirty universities. Besides the prewar sixteen, five of the campuses of the University of California now qualified, and additional public high performers included Penn State, Ohio State, Washington-Seattle, and Colorado; among the private ones were Northwestern and Washington Universities. Despite the prosperity of the private sector, public universities predominated in research.[124] The authors found considerable short-term movement in the middle ranks, but more so in research volume than in qualitative measures of publications and citations. They concluded that "administrators who ... invest heavily in novel strategies for moving up in the rankings are likely to be disappointed."[125] However, they identified four institutions that did advance in quality measures—Emory, Arizona State, Georgia Tech, and Southern Florida. All not only aspired to larger research roles but also implemented deliberate strategies.

The Commission on Research at Emory was formed in 2001 for just that purpose. In two years of intensive work, it produced a state-of-the-art depiction of the foundations of the research mission and steps to advance it at Emory. The focus was purely on elevating the level and stature of basic academic research. It recommended using Emory's rising income to hire additional faculty in strategic areas and provide better infrastructure for research and scholarship. Eschewing the usual caveats, it unabashedly embraced excellence in research and mobilized the university community around this aspiration.[126]

When Michael M. Crow became president of Arizona State University in 2002, he announced an intention to create a model for the New American University. Its distinctive features were rejection of selectivity (exclusion) in favor of inclusion of all qualified students, hence unbounded expansion; advancement of ASU as a research university through a transdisciplinary reorganization (replacing

123   Ibid.; Fernandez and Baker, "Science Production in the United States," 104.

124   The ninety-nine principle research universities analyzed in *Knowledge and Money* were 2:1 public.

125   Brint and Carr, "Scientific Research Output."

126   Emory University, *Research at Emory: The Report of the Commission on Research* (Atlanta: October 2003).

disciplinary departments) with particular emphasis on innovation and application; engagement with local and regional communities through educational services and economic development; and extensive use of technology to accomplish all the above. Remarkably, the New American University charged ahead on all fronts. ASU succeeded in educating more students, of more kinds, in more subjects, in more settings. It also advanced as a research university, nearly doubling its share of research since 2000, and raising its rankings for publications and citations.[127]

Since the 1990s, Georgia Tech advanced from a regional technical university to one of the nation's top engineering schools. The impetus came from technology transfer. A succession of state policies promoted technology-based economic development, and assistance from the Atlanta business community provided strategic impetus. But the institute's leadership was instrumental in transforming its previous focus on applied research into leadership in science-based technologies.[128]

Finally, Southern Florida illustrated another facet of the twenty-first-century research economy—local embeddedness. It is seldom noted that a portion of what the NSF tabulates as R&D expenditures, or what universities record as sponsored research, is not in fact research. Awards classified as separately budgeted research include myriad activities other than investigations at the laboratory bench. And universities are not averse to padding their reported research totals. South Florida, for internal purposes, classified 65 percent of "sponsored research" as actual research, 8 percent as training, and 27 percent as "other." The "other," at USF and elsewhere, defied description. It consisted of hundreds of mostly small transactions in which external organizations purchased access to university expertise.[129] To recognize this in no way diminishes the research mission at USF—quite the opposite. It illustrates how university expertise was tapped by state and local governments (20 percent of funds), nonprofit organizations (19 percent), corporations (9 percent), and foundations (7 percent). The social uses of university knowledge extended well beyond technology transfer. Universities in large urban areas like Tampa—and Phoenix for ASU or Atlanta for Georgia Tech—had particularly rich opportunities to engage with their communities through the kinds of entities just listed. However, this was a general phe-

---

127   Michael M. Crow and William B. Dabars, *Designing the New American University* (Baltimore: Johns Hopkins University Press, 2015); Roger L. Geiger, "Prospects for a New American University: Implications for Research," (Pennsylvania State University, 2016).

128   Roger L. Geiger and Creso M. Sá, *Tapping the Riches of Science: Universities and the Promise of Economic Growth* (Cambridge, MA: Harvard University Press, 2008), 98–104.

129   University of South Florida, USF Research and Innovation, *Report of Research Activities: Fiscal Year 2016*, p. 30. The author has analyzed all corporate awards to Penn State for certain years and found multiple purposes: Roger L. Geiger, "Corporate-Sponsored Research at Penn State: A Report to the Vice President for Research," Pennsylvania State University (March 2008).

nomenon. Research universities have increasingly developed and disseminated expertise locally, nationally, and globally.

While the utilization of academic knowledge continued to expand, the demand for the individuals to create that knowledge became more problematic. The concern that American universities were producing too many PhDs had often been alleged, but an imbalance became evident in the twenty-first century. Doctoral students are both an input to research and an output of the research process. Inputs are largely determined by the volume of research funding, including traineeships.[130] Outputs should ideally bear some relationship to opportunities for employment in research—as faculty or as full-time researchers. But no connection existed between inputs and outputs. Science and engineering PhDs in the U.S. were employed roughly two-fifths in academic appointments, two-fifths in industry, and one-fifth in government or other. Most students entered graduate programs envisioning an academic career. If this were modeled as a natural system, it would be one that depended on growth. Research university professors reproduce themselves at rates that require growing numbers of additional positions for their clones. This condition was largely met during the Golden Age of the 1960s; afterward, there was little growth in higher education, or in PhDs. Doctorates were level from 1972 to 1988. In the humanities, PhDs far exceeded faculty openings during these years—and ever since. Total doctorates increased 31 percent from 1987 to 1996, plateaued for eight years, and then rose 32 percent from 2004 to 2014. These growth spurts were largely due to changes in immigration regulations that allowed more international students to study. Among citizens, science PhDs for white males were level since the 1970s; the entire increase in native-born science PhDs came from women and minorities.[131] Symptoms of overproduction were most evident in this last period (2004–2014). These included relatively modest economic returns to science and engineering PhDs; increasing proportions of degree recipients without definite job commitments; and more postdocs spending more time in those positions.[132]

Various commissions either warned of a looming shortage of researchers and a consequent decline in America's scientific preeminence or, alternatively,

---

130   "In 2008 ... 95,000 graduate students worked as research assistants in science and engineering departments in the United States. An additional 22,500 ... were supported on a fellowship ... another 7,615 were supported on a traineeship grant": Paula Stephan, *How Economics Shapes Science* (Cambridge, MA: Harvard University Press, 2012), 70.

131   Frank Fernandez et al., "A Culture of Access and Science Capacity: A Symbiosis of Mass Higher Education, STEM PhD Training, and Science in the U.S. over the 20th Century" [tentative title] (Pennsylvania State University 2018).

132   Stephan, *How Economics Shapes Science*, 152–61. These results are *relative*: labor market outcomes for science PhDs are substantial, even if delayed, and those employed in industry have the consolation of higher salaries.

recommended compensatory measures, like voluntary reductions by departments in the number of PhD candidates or training for alternative careers.[133] The market for PhD programs became truly global. Potential students for English-language PhD programs considered Australia, England, Hong Kong, and Canada, as well as universities in the United States. International students composed about one-half of American science and engineering doctorates, and most remained to enter the scientific workforce. Without these graduates, a shortfall of citizen PhDs would produce a real crisis.[134] In the liberal arts and social sciences, where most PhDs are native born, the contraction of faculty positions exacerbated a structural oversupply of doctorates.

Since 2000, increasing numbers of faculty were appointed to full-time positions outside of the tenure system.[135] Such positions always existed—for instructors in introductory English or math classes or for practitioner-lecturers in professional subjects.[136] Now, fully credentialed fixed-term teachers were appointed to teach undergraduate courses. Such teachers were hired to be generalists, to teach basic lower-division courses, precisely the role that specialized regular faculty often disdained. Essentially, research universities hired fixed-term faculty in part to teach the least attractive courses so that (more valuable) regular faculty could devote themselves to (more valuable) research and publication.[137]

For both public and private universities, what had been a minor trend in the 1990s accelerated after 2000. From 1999 to 2007, twice as many additional full-time positions were off the tenure track as were on it.[138] This trend accentuated between 2012 and 2014, when nearly three additional professorial positions were non-tenure-track for each additional tenure-track position. In all, at the top 108

133   Michael S. Teitelbaum, "The Myth of the Science and Engineering Shortage," *Atlantic* (March 2014); Stephan, *How Economics Shapes Science*, 162–81.

134   Stephan, *How Economics Shapes Science*, 183–202.

135   Roger L. Geiger, "Optimizing Research and Teaching: The Bifurcation of Faculty Roles at Research Universities," in Hermanowicz, *American Academic Profession*, 21–43.

136   Increasing numbers of part- and full-time contingent faculty have been a pronounced feature of all sectors of higher education: Steven Hurlburt and Michael McGarrah, *The Shifting Academic Workforce: Where Are the Contingent Faculty?* (Washington, DC: Delta Cost Project, American Institutes for Research, 2016). This trend has reduced expenditures for instructional salaries and benefits for faculty: Hurlburt and McGarrah, *Cost Savings or Cost Shifting? The Relationship between Part-Time Contingent Faculty and Institutional Spending* (Washington, DC: Delta Cost Project, American Institutes for Research, 2016).

137   Geiger ("Optimizing Research and Teaching") notes different roles for adjunct faculty in different fields. In business, they lecture large undergraduate courses, and MBA programs are key to rank and status; in sciences, the adjuncts lecture introductory classes and teach labs. Both practices arguably can improve instruction.

138   6,000 vs. 11,000 at public universities; 2,000 vs. 5,000 at privates: Liang Zhang, Ronald G. Ehrenberg, and Xiangmin Liu, "Changing Faculty Employment at Four Year Colleges and Universities in the United States" (Pennsylvania State University, 2016).

research universities, one-third of full-time faculty were not on tenure-track appointments in 2014 and hence not contributing to the research capacity of those institutions.[139]

Utilization of fixed-term faculty was encouraged by the growing role of online instruction. Most major universities sponsored online programs for degrees or certificates or blended courses. However, scholar-teachers were not necessary for iterated online courses, which could be taught by non-tenure-track faculty. Such appointments drew on the faculty salary pool, so that at least some of those positions substituted for regular faculty appointments.

The overproduction of PhDs and the increasing use of adjunct faculty were perturbations in an otherwise immense social system. The research economy and the academic labor market are the most tangible organizational fields of modern research universities in modern knowledge societies. Universities play an indispensable role in generating and processing knowledge itself. David Baker in *The Schooled Society*, following John Meyer, illustrated how universities create bodies of knowledge that are incorporated into society. Universities, for example, "not only create 'economic knowledge' which must be taken into account by rational actors. [They] also ... create the role of economist, justify economists' authority claims in society, and define precisely who is an economist."[140] This is just one of innumerable fields—management, demography, psychology, etc.—in which universities construct legitimate bodies of knowledge and legitimate the personnel authorized to practice them. But universities do not create all knowledge—substantial knowledge emanates from other social organizations and practitioners. The role of universities here has been to evaluate such knowledge according to cognitive standards prevailing in higher education: namely, employing highly organized, rational frameworks; complex and sophisticated perspectives; abstract, universal concepts; and rigorous empirical analytical tools.[141] Practitioners operate under various constraints and have neither the resources nor incentives to undertake such thorough and structured evaluation. Academic expertise thus supplies a "meta-cognitive orientation," in Steven Brint's term, such that universities provide "the ultimate cultural authority (and the privileged work space) that permits knowledge generated, whether in universities or elsewhere, to be examined, proven, deepened, revised, or rejected based on evidence."[142]

---

139   Data from IPEDs.

140   Baker, *Schooled Society*, 99–121, quote p. 121, quoting John W. Meyer, "The Effects of Education as an Institution," *American Journal of Sociology* 83, 1 (1977): 55–77, quote p. 68.

141   Brint, "Professionals" 114.

142   Steven Brint, "An Institutional Geography of Knowledge Exchange: Producers, Exports, Imports, Trade Routes, and Metacognitive Metropoles," in Jal Mehta and R. Scott Davies, eds., *Education in a New Society* (Chicago: University of Chicago Press, 2018), 115–43.

AMERICAN HIGHER EDUCATION IN
THE TWENTY-FIRST CENTURY

In the seventy years following World War II, three overriding developments defined the relationship of higher education and American society. The emergence of the American research university elevated and expanded the venerable university model and its traditional roles of preserving, advancing, and disseminating knowledge. The United States pioneered the first system of mass higher education and further extended access beyond 50 percent of age cohorts to attain universal higher education. Partly as a consequence, high-cost, high-quality institutions that restricted admission to high-ability students emerged as a distinctive sector of higher education. These developments were clearly foreshadowed historically, but the magnitude of these transformations and their impact on the lives of Americans have shaped the social, cultural, and economic world of the twenty-first century.

The American research university emerged as a distinctive institution after World War II. The pattern of locating wartime research at universities was institutionalized after 1945 by federal agencies. Their funds created an autonomous research mission in a select group of universities. Federally funded research might be carried out in huge, federally supported laboratories, in academic departments with relatively small grants, or in medical schools, but it was funded by and responsible to organizations external to universities. The Sputnik crisis ignited a massive expansion of this system, primarily through civilian agencies (NIH, NSF, NASA). It was accompanied by a coeval scientization of other academic fields. The academic revolution advanced the generation of knowledge as a primary mission of universities. The 1980s brought another organizational dimension—the explicit harnessing of university discoveries to technology-based economic development. But university knowledge interpenetrated society in myriad ways. Both social demand and scientific patronage fueled the continuing expansion of research at these universities.

The United States initially led the world in access to higher education, in part because it led the world in secondary education—high school graduates who qualified for college. Still, three principal features accelerated this trend after 1945—changing social attitudes, relatively open admission, and abundant supply. Most Americans circa 1945 had a restrictive view: college was mainly for offspring of professional families, some from the middle class, and a few from the working class—and all should have an IQ of at least 115. This view was challenged in theory by the radical growth projections of the President's Commission on Higher Education, but it was challenged in practice by the multitude of students from all backgrounds who took advantage of the GI Bill. Afterward, few argued that higher education should not expand. By the 1950s, as more American families became able to afford college for their children, institutions of higher education were widely accessible. As had always been the case, anyone who completed high school could find a path to college. But local availability was also a factor. Well-prepared students tended to be somewhat mobile, but for the marginal, first-generation student, a local institution often determined if attendance was feasible—hence, the strategic role played by teachers colleges, which ballooned in the 1950s and then assumed the university model. The next decade brought urban service universities, the boom in community colleges, and branch campuses of state universities. All brought convenient, low-cost higher education to just about anyone who sought it, and all were made possible by an enormous public investment in the provision of higher education.

Universal higher education also required two demographic transformations. The civil rights movement ended de jure segregation in the South and de facto segregation in the North. Practices of exclusion were replaced by policies promoting social inclusion for African Americans and other formerly underrepresented groups. For women, aspirations for higher education expanded after 1960, and career opportunities for graduates did the same, mostly after 1970. Women soon exceeded men in attending and graduating from institutions of higher education.

In the United States, preoccupations with higher education focused predominately on the undergraduate college, the institution and stage of life in which adolescents were expected to evolve into responsible adults. The American system accomplished this through a gamut of institutions extending from the peak of the selective sector to the humblest community college. In most advanced countries, governments used national examinations to distribute students across stratified educational places. In the United States, individuals chose the institutions they wished to attend, and institutions selected from applicants the individuals they wished to admit. Students were sorted in the admissions market into slots that affected lifetime possibilities.

American colleges and universities were always grossly unequal, but they were unequal in different ways. Before the war, Harvard and Yale were hugely wealthy, but few others came close. A handful of colleges had a predominantly affluent clientele, but postwar institutions all suffered from years of austerity. Harvard, Yale, and others were socially elite, although most admitted some unwealthy local students. From 1945 to 1965, the Ivy League gradually and haltingly diluted the social elite with a meritocratic elite, and after that date they recruited minority students in a commitment to social inclusion. Through the 1970s, the social and academic composition of classes at the leading colleges and universities was in flux. After 1980, the dynamics of the selectivity sweepstakes took hold.

For private colleges and universities, higher spending and greater selectivity resulted in greater prestige and still higher income. These dynamics were irresistible for institutions and persisted into the twenty-first century. They shaped a market-driven selective sector that became a defining feature of American higher education.

These three historical dimensions of American higher education developed further in the twenty-first century. The first decade saw widespread endorsement of the college-for-all doctrine and policies to encourage lower-income and first-generation youth to attend. Enrollment growth included the pathological expansion of corporate universities. But after 2010, expansion confronted two limitations. Although secondary school students received strong encouragement to go to college, many lacked the academic preparation needed to succeed there. And the cost of college surpassed affordability, a decades-long trend exacerbated by large tuition increases following the Great Recession. Funds for higher education came predominantly from government and students. States essentially capped their appropriations for public colleges and universities, and student charges exceeded the financial capacity of more than 60 percent of attendees and their families. The difference was provided by federal student loans—a conveniently elastic source. Borrowing became necessary for most students to go to college, and it affected where students went and whether they went.

The prominence of the selectivity sweepstakes heightened in the twenty-first century. Accomplished students from families sufficiently affluent to afford the high costs were sought by and attracted to the academically strongest institutions. The competition for the best students and their preferences for the best colleges and universities exaggerated the highly stratified selective sector with extreme stratification at the very top. The hierarchy was accentuated by the skew in donative resources, and wealth increased geometrically at the pinnacle. Further down the status ladder, institutions were pressed to uphold student quality, competitive spending levels, and rankings. The growth in tuition discounting was a barometer of rising competition, evidence of the recruitment pressures facing most private colleges and universities. For the top 15 percent, discounting reflected the ineluctable dynamics of the selectivity sweepstakes.

Public research universities became increasingly competitive in the selectivity sweepstakes. Stratification grew there as well, but these universities formed a relatively flat hierarchy in which differences in academic reputation, instructional spending, and student selectivity were incremental. Academic distinction served to attract ever more applications and increased the quality of undergraduate classes. Student demand allowed these universities to compensate for anemic state support by boosting tuition revenues. These universities too resorted to tuition discounts, evidence of rising tuitions and heightened competition. As noted, internal differentiation permitted these universities to make ample resources available to their most able students, while also accommodating large enrollments across numerous colleges of varying rigor. A handful of smaller, distinctive public colleges also qualified for the selective sector. But elsewhere, public regional colleges experienced an erosion of able students and of state support.

The supply-demand interpretation of labor markets held that the shortfall of college-educated workers after 1980 caused the earnings premium to escalate and wage inequality to rise. The increase of college graduates after 2000 stabilized the earnings premium for bachelor's degrees, but still growing returns to graduate and professional degrees indicated a robust social demand for advanced skills—and the persistence of inequality. Concerns for economic inequality in American society had difficulty reconciling the two principal ways in which higher education affected life chances—sorting and training. Students were pre-sorted by their entry points into higher education. Given unequal academic abilities and preparation, social and cultural capital, and financial resources, large social differentials in all these traits were reflected in how and where students attended, what they studied, and their odds of graduation. Hence, college graduates were even more skewed in terms of socioeconomic status than entering students. But the economic function of college is cognitive upgrading—forming human capital, or competence, to contribute productively to society. College graduates were differentiated by their major fields of study, the academic rigor of their schools, and their relative performance. They emerged with different kinds and degrees of competence, which were rewarded differentially in labor markets. For given educational credentials, the social backgrounds of graduates largely ceased to affect labor market outcomes. In essence, opportunities for higher education were strongly influenced by socioeconomic status, but what students learned guided their careers. Accordingly, an abundance of public and private programs rightly focused on expanding opportunities for higher education, and no doubt mitigated social inequality to some degree. But in the economy, differential returns to diverse competencies were largely unaffected by public policies.

Student learning showed no sign of strengthening in the current era, but not from want of trying. Higher education associations and foundations proposed ameliorative strategies employing assessment, accountability, and testing, which were enthusiastically implemented by universities. But consumerism swamped the best of intentions. Universities, through their rhetoric and deployment of resources, deemphasized cognitive learning in favor of objectives more attractive to their customers—engagement, leadership, citizenship, community involvement, and creative expression. Institutions developed "supply-side" curricular innovations to stimulate student interest in liberal arts topics, with few tangible results. Students, for their part, decreased the time and effort applied to academic work. Studies documented a paucity of learning, but also a high degree of consumer satisfaction. Colleges had always comingled slackers and scholars, but grade inflation insulated modern slackers from academic sanctions. Scholars, on the other hand, continued to make the most of the academic opportunities offered by honors programs, undergraduate research, and demanding quantitative majors. Competitive admission to graduate and professional schools served as constant goad to achievement. Internationally, however, the weaknesses of education in the United States became increasingly apparent. Other developed countries surpassed the U.S. in the proportion of young people earning postsecondary credentials and on international knowledge tests for reading, mathematics, and problem solving.

The politicization of American universities in the 2010s was the most extreme since the 1960s. As in that decade, partisan advocacy was led by relatively small numbers of activist students and faculty, but now they were institutionalized, chiefly as identity groups, inside departments, centers, and administrative staff. Like affirmative admissions had at the University of California, commitment to social inclusion made universities lose their bearings on issues of race and gender. Universities have long been, and should be, liberal institutions. They are dedicated, above all, to the free and unfettered search for knowledge and respect for diverse modes of thought. However, the ideologies of identity groups and the academic Left were fundamentally illiberal. They rejected reason as merely a pretext for power, objectivity as the basis for science, humanism in favor of rivalrous identities, and progress stemming from the foundations of Western civilization. University administrations acquiesced in these manifestations out of expediency, appeasement, and uncritical adherence to political correctness. At times, dissident students exhibited a naïve psychological vulnerability—fear of being oppressed by supposedly hateful speech. But underlying such postures was deep-seated anti-intellectualism—a void of rational understanding of complex social issues and an inability to comprehend the perspectives of others. Such deficiencies may affect a minority of students, but their tacit endorsement by universities represented a failure to nurture precisely the qualities that are promised in a liberal education.

But for universities, reason and science remained ascendant, and consequently, universities continued to play central and indispensable roles in the knowledge society. Everyday discourse is suffused with terms and concepts that originated in academic scholarship. Such concepts embody complex ideas that enhance the sophistication and content of understanding. Previous sections have detailed the multiple, growing pathways by which university expertise was accessed by American society. Given the inexorable growth of knowledge, universities have become more research intensive, focusing a greater portion of their efforts on knowledge creation and elaboration. More than other institutions, universities provide the settings and the culture for deep analysis of subjects based on abstract and universalized concepts, theoretical paradigms, and rigorous analytical methods. Moreover, as argued above, given the expanding role of knowledge throughout society and the world, the most advanced concentrations of knowledge and scholarship are the most valuable. American research universities give the United States that advantage. In the Annual Rating of World Universities, they occupied 13 of the top 15 positions, 48 of the top 100. And that last figure understated the number of universities engaged with scientific frontiers in a multitude of fields. The global preeminence of these universities is emblematic of their enormous contribution to the welfare and progress of American society, economy, and civilization.

INDEX